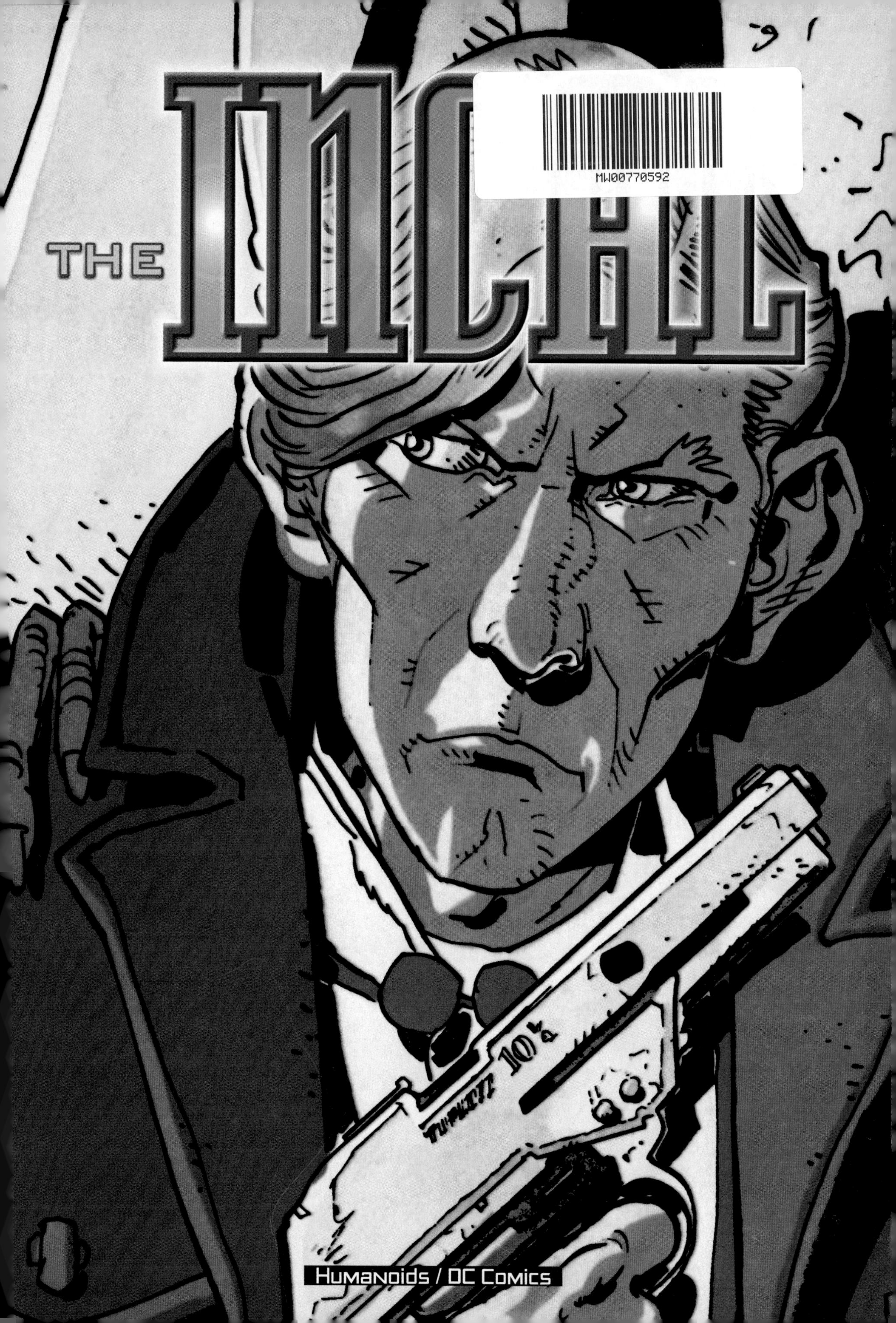
THE INCAL
Humanoids / DC Comics

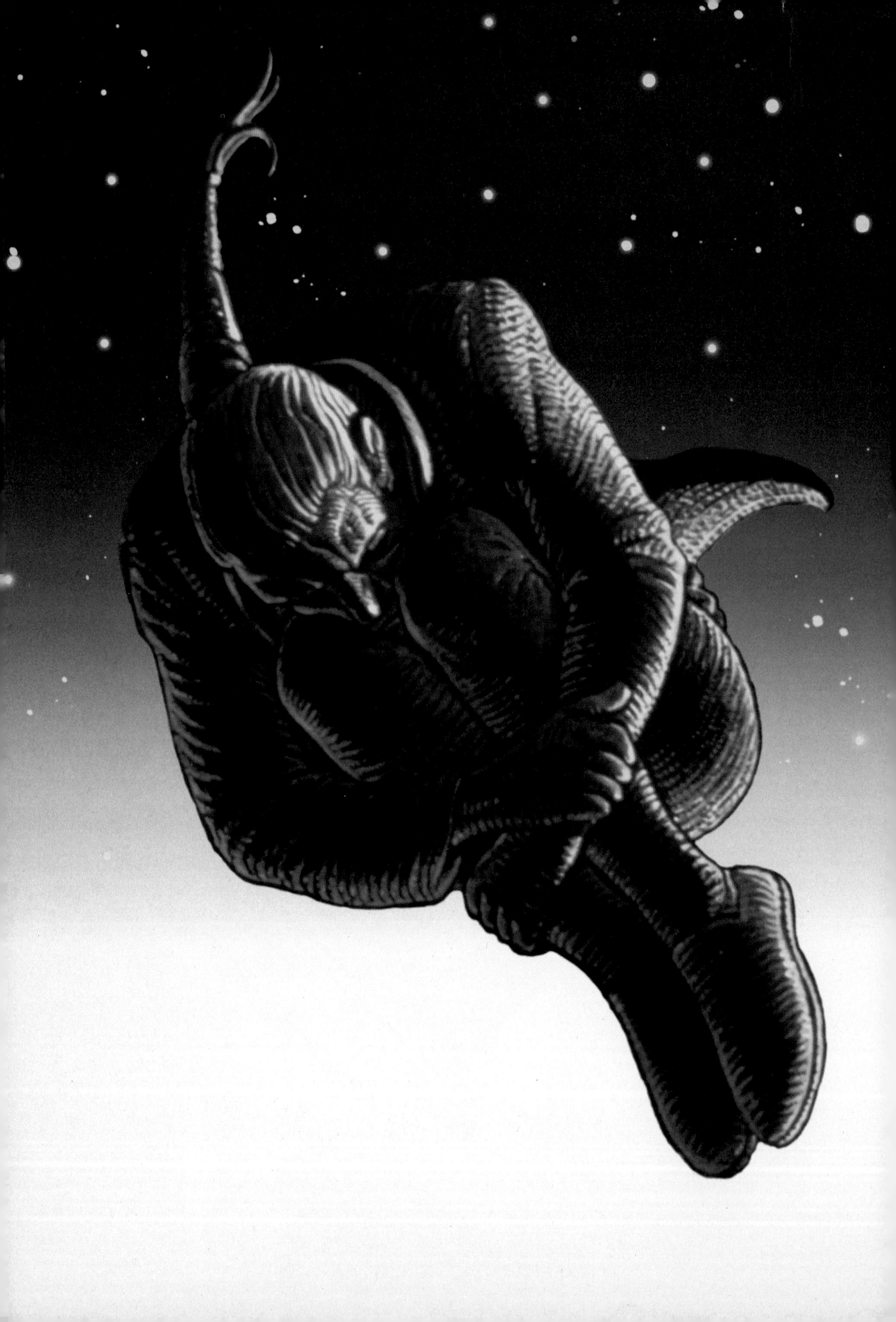

JODOROWSKY & MŒBIUS

THE INCAL

THE EPIC JOURNEY

Humanoids / DC Comics

ALEXANDRO JODOROWSKY, Writer
MŒBIUS, Artist
VALÉRIE BELTRAN, Colorist
SASHA WATSON & JUSTIN KELLY, Translators

THIERRY FRISSEN, Book Designer & Letterer
LADRONN, Back cover art
FRANCIS LOMBARD, Editor, Collected Edition
BRUNO LECIGNE & FABRICE GIGER, Editors, Original Edition

DC COMICS:
PAUL LEVITZ, President & Publisher
GEORG BREWER, VP-Design & Retail Product Development
RICHARD BRUNING, Senior VP-Creative Director
PATRICK CALDON, Senior VP-Finance & Operations
CHRIS CARAMALIS, VP-Finance
TERRI CUNNINGHAM, VP-Managing Editor
STEPHANIE FIERMAN, Senior VP-Sales & Marketing
ALISON GILL, VP-Manufacturing
RICH JOHNSON, VP-Book Trade Sales
HANK KANALZ, VP-General Manager, WildStorm
LILLIAN LASERSON, Senior VP & General Counsel
JIM LEE, Editorial Director-WildStorm
PAULA LOWITT, Senior VP-Business & Legal Affairs
DAVID MCKILLIPS, VP-Advertising & Custom Publishing
JOHN NEE, VP-Business Development
GREGORY NOVECK, Senior VP-Creative Affairs
CHERYL RUBIN, Senior VP-Brand Management
BOB WAYNE, VP-Sales

THE INCAL: THE EPIC JOURNEY, Humanoids Publishing. PO Box 931658, Hollywood, CA 90094. This is a publication of DC Comics, 1700 Broadway, New York, NY 10019.

VITAVIL H2O

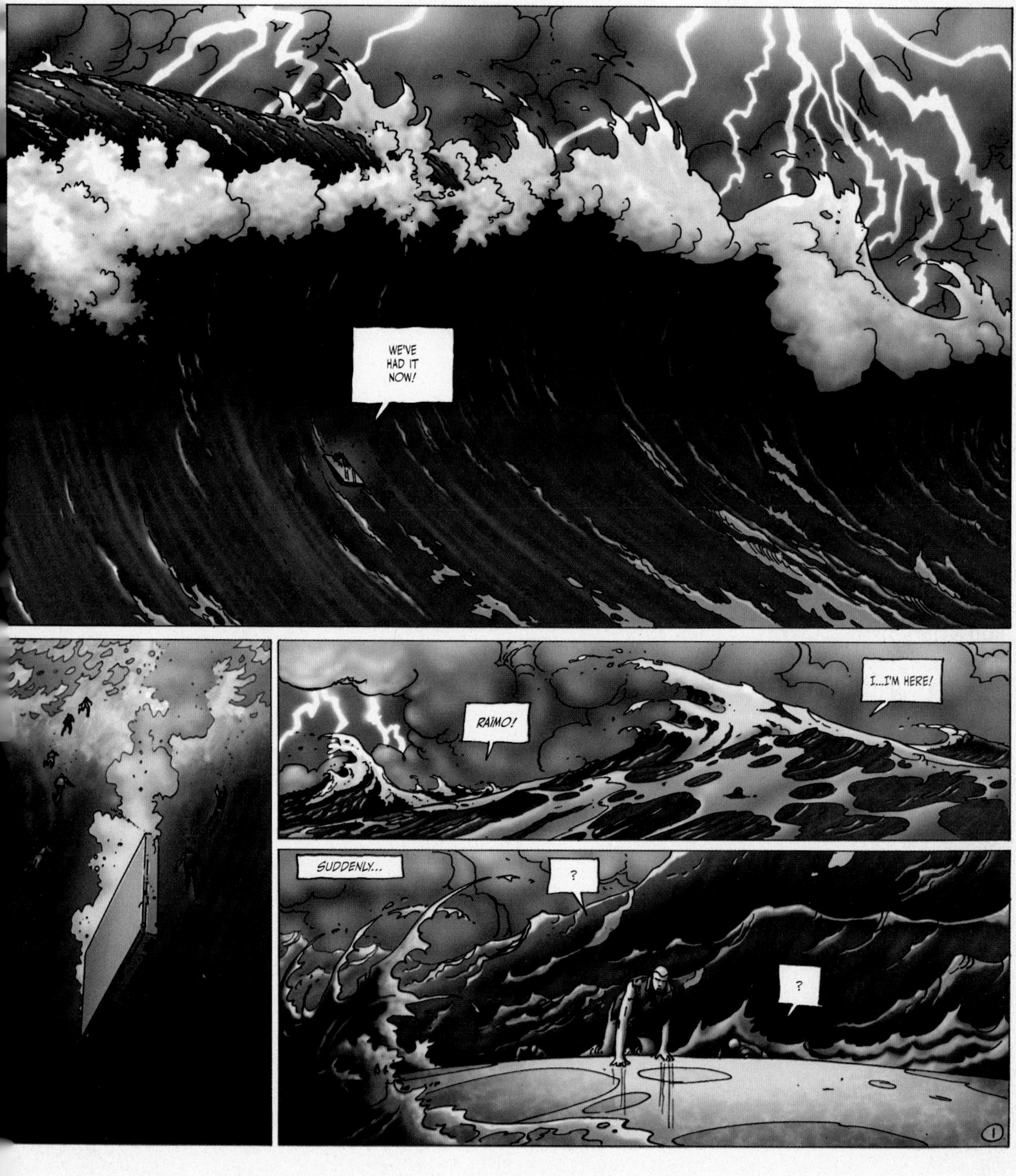
WE'VE HAD IT NOW!
RAIMO!
I...I'M HERE!
SUDDENLY...
?
?
1

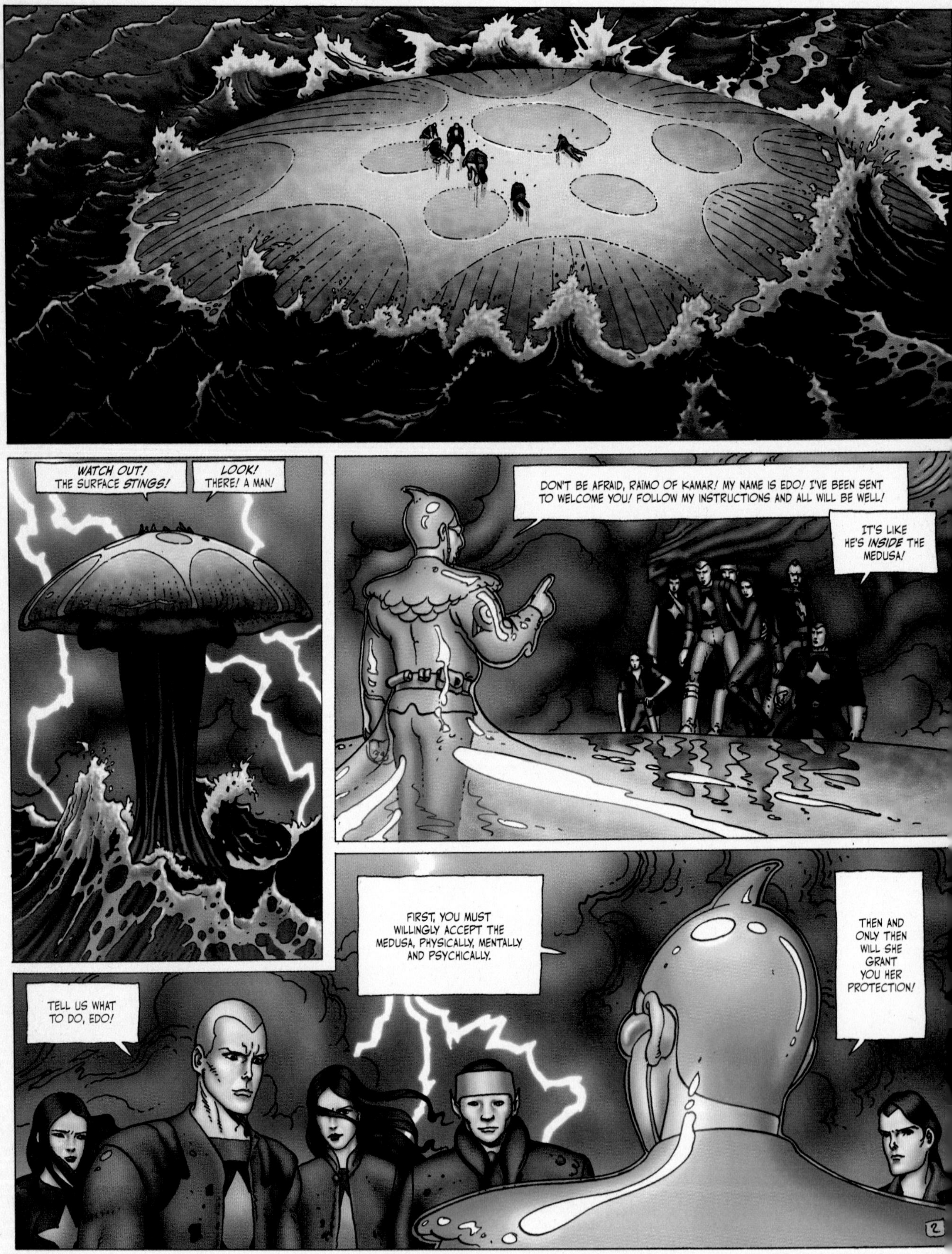

WATCH OUT! THE SURFACE STINGS!
LOOK! THERE! A MAN!
DON'T BE AFRAID, RAÏMO OF KAMAR! MY NAME IS EDO! I'VE BEEN SENT TO WELCOME YOU! FOLLOW MY INSTRUCTIONS AND ALL WILL BE WELL!
IT'S LIKE HE'S INSIDE THE MEDUSA!
FIRST, YOU MUST WILLINGLY ACCEPT THE MEDUSA, PHYSICALLY, MENTALLY AND PSYCHICALLY.
THEN AND ONLY THEN WILL SHE GRANT YOU HER PROTECTION!
TELL US WHAT TO DO, EDO!
2

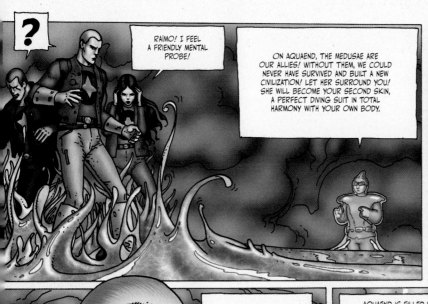

? RAÏMO! I FEEL A FRIENDLY MENTAL PROBE!

ON AQUAEND, THE MEDUSAE ARE OUR ALLIES! WITHOUT THEM, WE COULD NEVER HAVE SURVIVED AND BUILT A NEW CIVILIZATION! LET HER SURROUND YOU! SHE WILL BECOME YOUR SECOND SKIN, A PERFECT DIVING SUIT IN TOTAL HARMONY WITH YOUR OWN BODY.

SHE WILL ENABLE YOU TO BREATHE FREELY UNDERWATER. SHE WILL INSULATE YOU FROM THE PRESSURE OF THE DEPTHS.

BUT, WHERE ARE YOU TAKING US? EVERYONE KNOWS THAT AQUAEND IS A WATER WORLD, WITHOUT LAND OR EVEN A SOLID PLANETARY CORE! THAT'S WHY IT WAS TURNED INTO A PRISON!

AQUAEND IS FILLED WITH MANY SURPRISES! YOU'LL SEE.

FIRST, LET THE MEDUSA RECEIVE YOU INTO HER HEART!

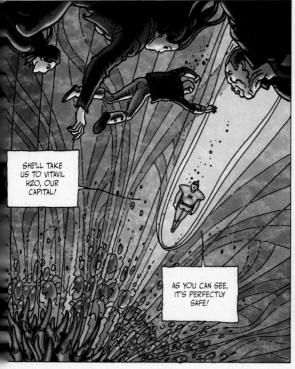

SHE'LL TAKE US TO VITAVIL H2O, OUR CAPITAL!

AS YOU CAN SEE, IT'S PERFECTLY SAFE!

FOLLOW ME!

SOMEONE WAITS FOR YOU BELOW!

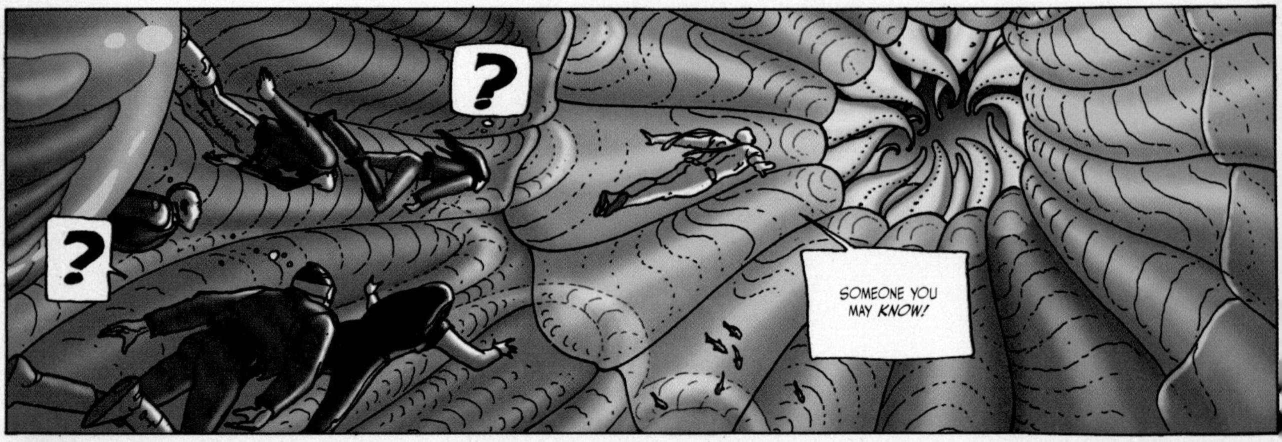
?
?
SOMEONE YOU MAY KNOW!

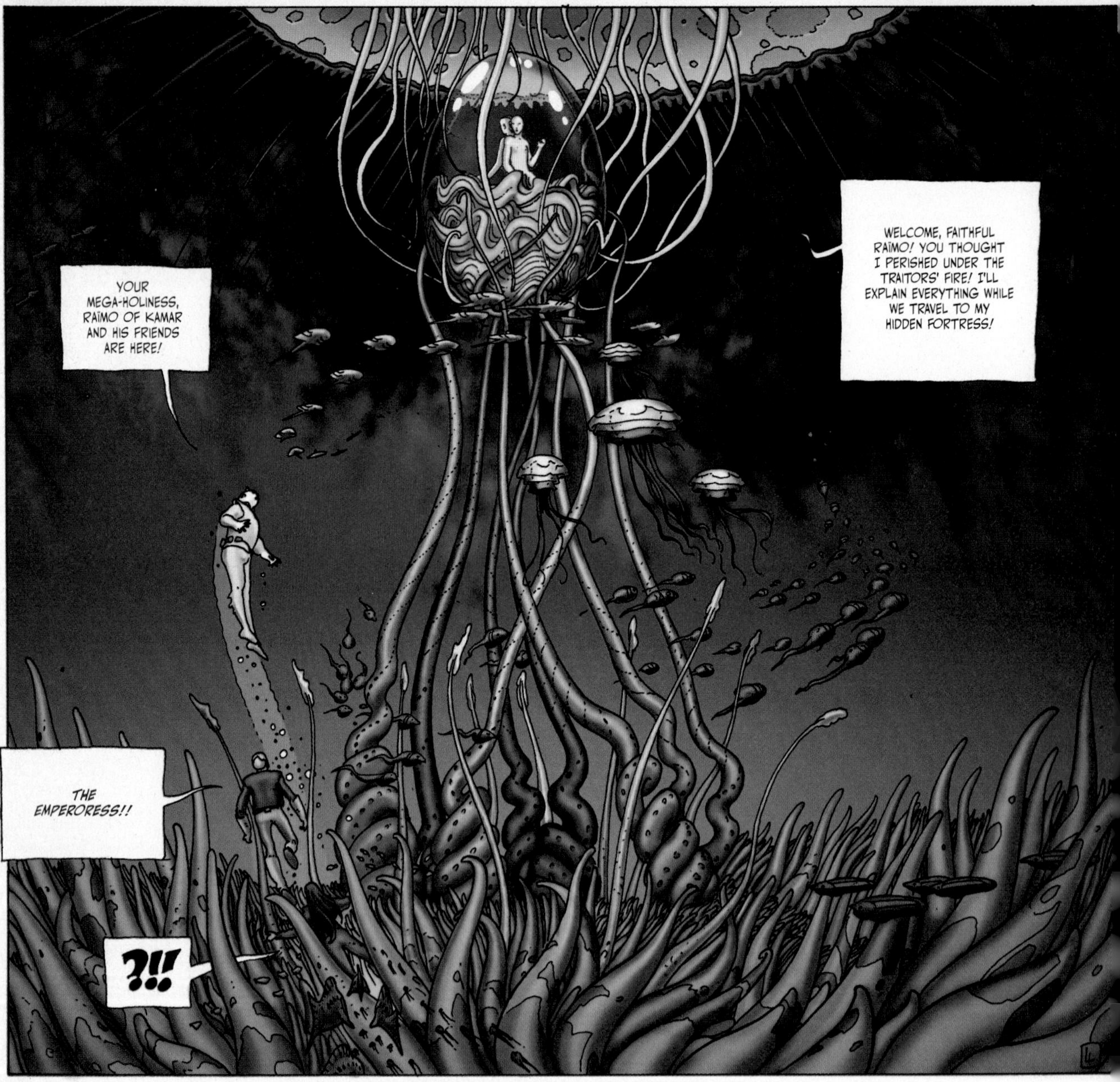
YOUR MEGA-HOLINESS, RAÏMO OF KAMAR AND HIS FRIENDS ARE HERE!
WELCOME, FAITHFUL RAÏMO! YOU THOUGHT I PERISHED UNDER THE TRAITORS' FIRE! I'LL EXPLAIN EVERYTHING WHILE WE TRAVEL TO MY HIDDEN FORTRESS!
THE EMPERORESS!!
?!!

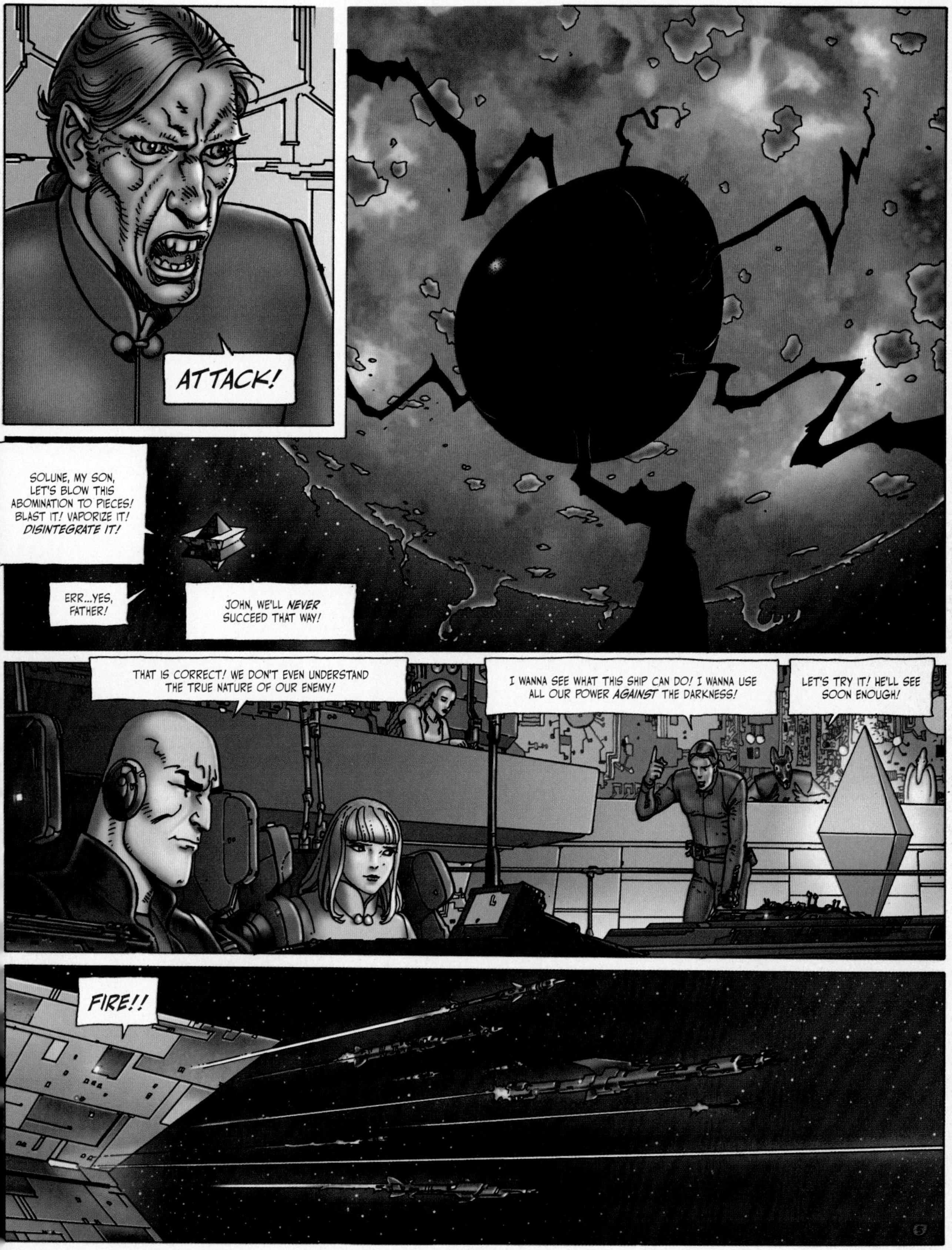
ATTACK!
SOLUNE, MY SON, LET'S BLOW THIS ABOMINATION TO PIECES! BLAST IT! VAPORIZE IT! *DISINTEGRATE IT!*
ERR...YES, FATHER!
JOHN, WE'LL *NEVER* SUCCEED THAT WAY!
THAT IS CORRECT! WE DON'T EVEN UNDERSTAND THE TRUE NATURE OF OUR ENEMY!
I WANNA SEE WHAT THIS SHIP CAN DO! I WANNA USE ALL OUR POWER *AGAINST* THE DARKNESS!
LET'S TRY IT! HE'LL SEE SOON ENOUGH!
FIRE!!

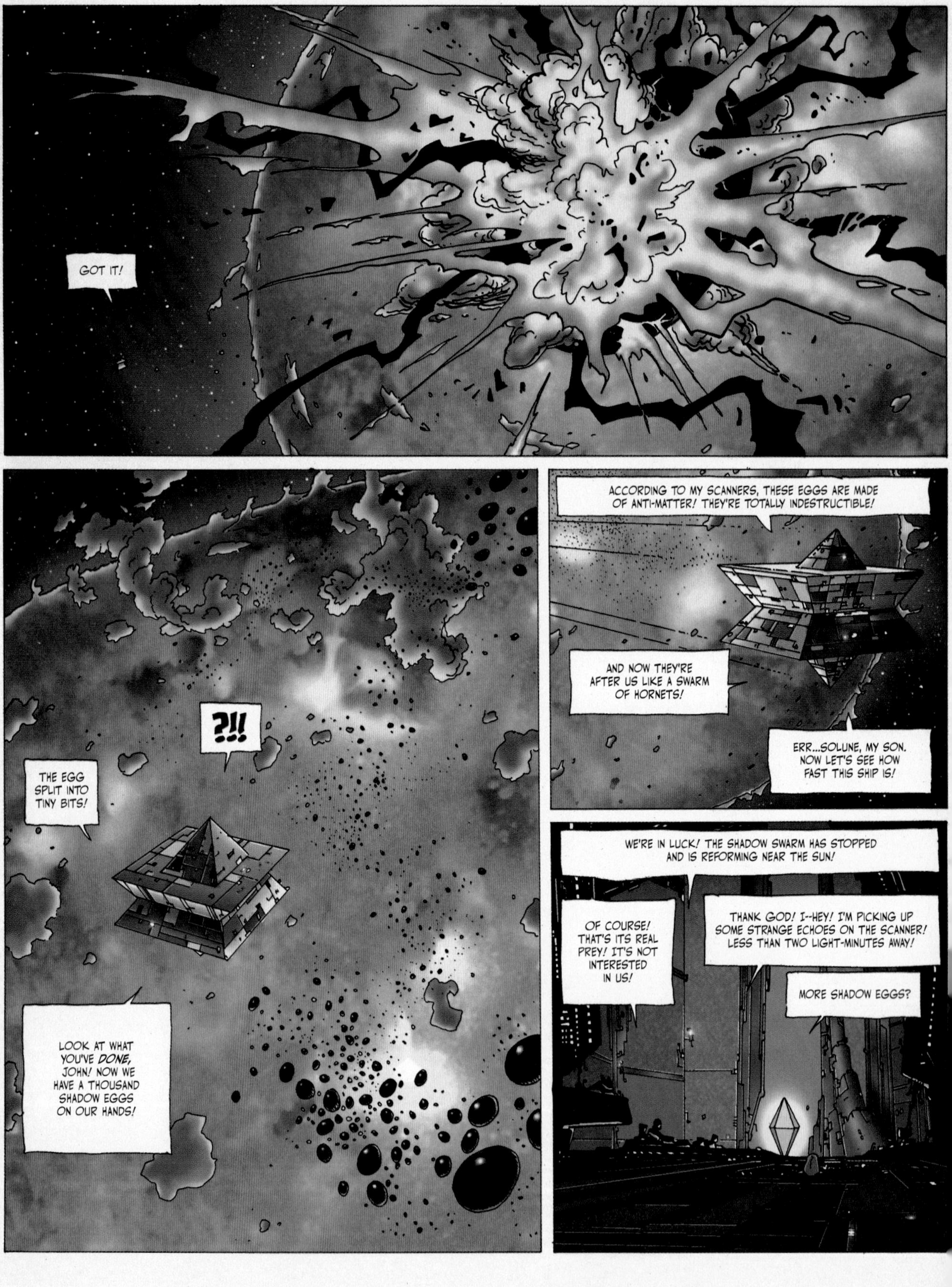
GOT IT!
?!!
THE EGG SPLIT INTO TINY BITS!
LOOK AT WHAT YOU'VE *DONE,* JOHN! NOW WE HAVE A THOUSAND SHADOW EGGS ON OUR HANDS!
ACCORDING TO MY SCANNERS, THESE EGGS ARE MADE OF ANTI-MATTER! THEY'RE TOTALLY INDESTRUCTIBLE!
AND NOW THEY'RE AFTER US LIKE A SWARM OF HORNETS!
ERR...SOLUNE, MY SON. NOW LET'S SEE HOW FAST THIS SHIP IS!
WE'RE IN LUCK! THE SHADOW SWARM HAS STOPPED AND IS REFORMING NEAR THE SUN!
OF COURSE! THAT'S ITS REAL PREY! IT'S NOT INTERESTED IN US!
THANK GOD! I--HEY! I'M PICKING UP SOME STRANGE ECHOES ON THE SCANNER! LESS THAN TWO LIGHT-MINUTES AWAY!
MORE SHADOW EGGS?

THE BERG FLEET!

THEIR ARMADA HAS INVADED THIS GALAXY! *THEY SEE US!*

RIGHT! AT LEAST THOSE DAMNED PARAKEETS AREN'T MADE OF ANTI-MATTER! SOLUNE, THIS TIME WE'RE GOING TO HAVE OURSELVES SOME FUN! LET'S *BLAST* THE SUCKERS!

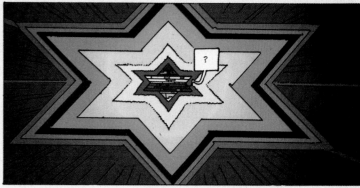

?

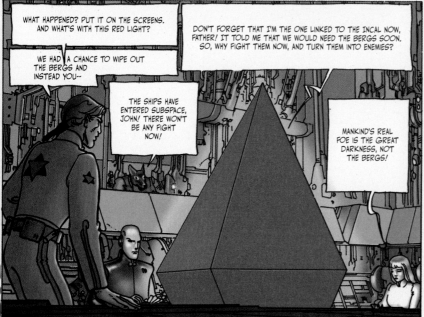

WHAT HAPPENED? PUT IT ON THE SCREENS. AND WHAT'S WITH THIS RED LIGHT?

WE HAD A CHANCE TO WIPE OUT THE BERGS AND INSTEAD YOU--

THE SHIPS HAVE ENTERED SUBSPACE, JOHN! THERE WON'T BE ANY FIGHT NOW!

DON'T FORGET THAT I'M THE ONE LINKED TO THE INCAL NOW, FATHER! IT TOLD ME THAT WE WOULD NEED THE BERGS SOON. SO, WHY FIGHT THEM NOW, AND TURN THEM INTO ENEMIES?

MANKIND'S REAL FOE IS THE GREAT DARKNESS, NOT THE BERGS!

BESIDES, YOU SAW HOW POWERLESS WE WERE AGAINST THE SHADOW EGGS! WHAT WE NEED TO DO IS INHIBIT THEIR FORMIDABLY INDESTRUCTIBLE DEFENSES!

INHIBIT THEIR WHAT? OKAY, GREAT, BUT, HOW? YEAH... TELL ME HOW WE DO THIS?

THE INCAL SAYS THAT THERE EXISTS SOMETHING THAT CAN CONTROL ANTI-MATTER.

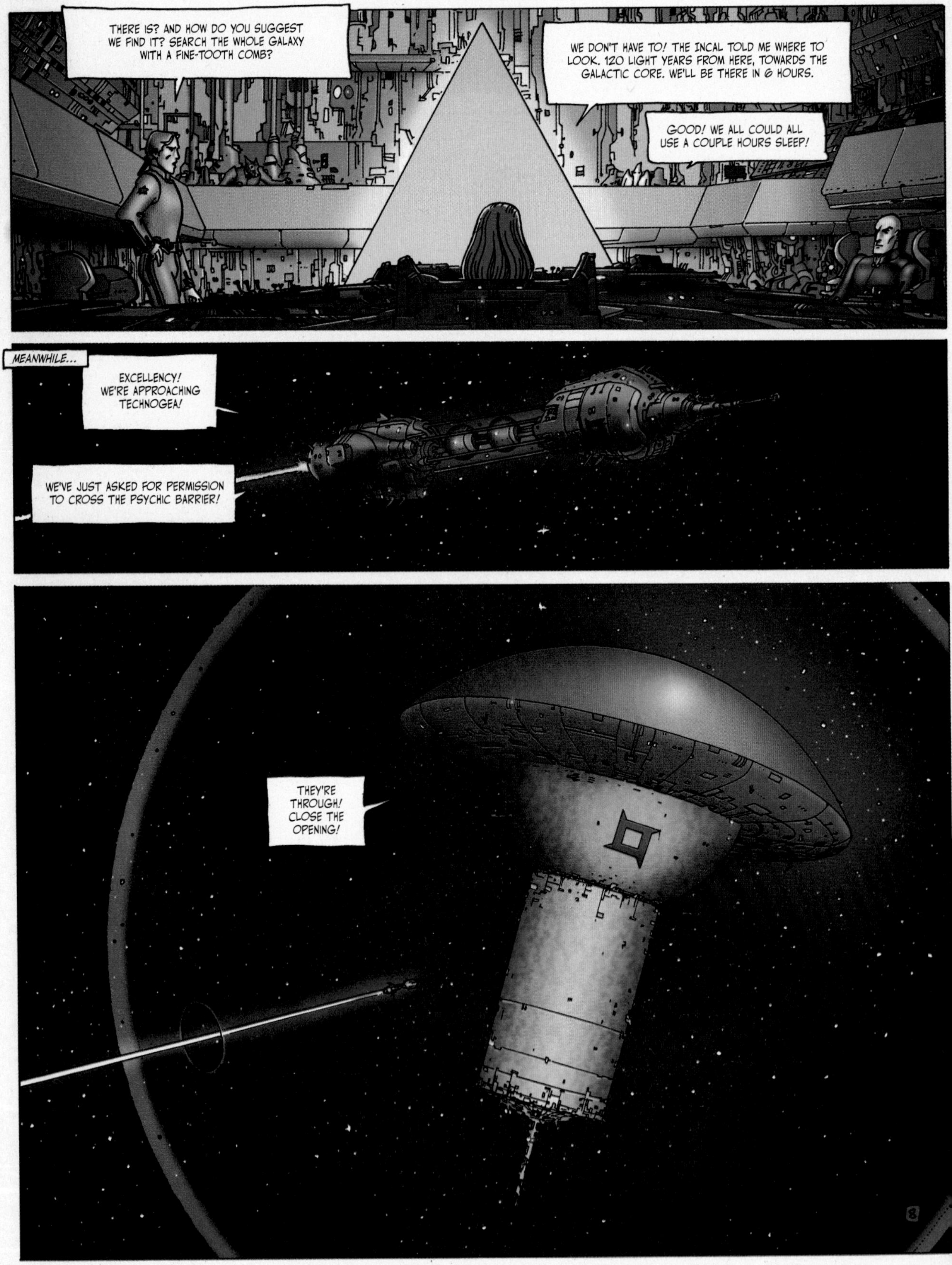
THERE IS? AND HOW DO YOU SUGGEST WE FIND IT? SEARCH THE WHOLE GALAXY WITH A FINE-TOOTH COMB?
WE DON'T HAVE TO! THE INCAL TOLD ME WHERE TO LOOK. 120 LIGHT YEARS FROM HERE, TOWARDS THE GALACTIC CORE. WE'LL BE THERE IN 6 HOURS.
GOOD! WE ALL COULD ALL USE A COUPLE HOURS SLEEP!
MEANWHILE...
EXCELLENCY! WE'RE APPROACHING TECHNOGEA!
WE'VE JUST ASKED FOR PERMISSION TO CROSS THE PSYCHIC BARRIER!
THEY'RE THROUGH! CLOSE THE OPENING!

THE TECHNO-CENTREUR AND THE CYCLIC COUNCIL ARE EXPECTING YOU!

I'M RECORDING, MASTER S'12! *SPEAK!*

ALL PROCEEDED ACCORDING TO PLAN, TECHNO-CENTREUR! THE EMPEROESS IS DEAD!

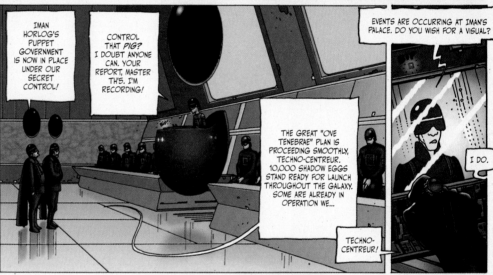

IMAN HORLOG'S PUPPET GOVERNMENT IS NOW IN PLACE UNDER OUR SECRET CONTROL!

CONTROL THAT *PIG?* I DOUBT ANYONE CAN. YOUR REPORT, MASTER TH'5. I'M RECORDING!

THE GREAT "OVE TENEBRAE" PLAN IS PROCEEDING SMOOTHLY, TECHNO-CENTREUR. 10,000 SHADOW EGGS STAND READY FOR LAUNCH THROUGHOUT THE GALAXY. SOME ARE ALREADY IN OPERATION WE...

EVENTS ARE OCCURRING AT IMAN'S PALACE. DO YOU WISH FOR A VISUAL?

I DO.

TECHNO-CENTREUR!

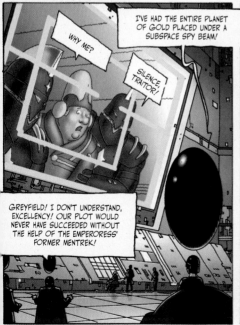

WHY ME?

SILENCE TRAITOR!

I'VE HAD THE ENTIRE PLANET OF GOLD PLACED UNDER A SUBSPACE SPY BEAM!

GREYFIELD! I DON'T UNDERSTAND, EXCELLENCY! OUR PLOT WOULD NEVER HAVE SUCCEEDED WITHOUT THE HELP OF THE EMPEROESS' FORMER MENTREK!

YOUR INFORMATION WAS INCOMPLETE, MASTER S'12! GREYFIELD WAS A DOUBLE AGENT FROM THE BEGINNING! THE IMAN HAS ALMOST CERTAINLY DISCOVERED THE TRUTH!

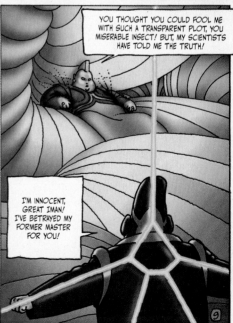

YOU THOUGHT YOU COULD FOOL ME WITH SUCH A TRANSPARENT PLOT, YOU MISERABLE INSECT! BUT, MY SCIENTISTS HAVE TOLD ME THE TRUTH!

I'M INNOCENT, GREAT IMAN! I'VE BETRAYED MY FORMER MASTER FOR YOU!

THAT THING KILLED IN THE PARLIAMENT WAS NOT THE REAL EMPERORESS, IT WAS A CLONE! A CLEVER TRICK, BUT DID YOU *REALLY* BELIEVE YOU COULD FOOL ME?

WHAT DO YOU ASK OF ME?

WHERE IS HE, GREYFIELD? AS LONG AS THE DAMNED, TWO-HEADED FETUS IS STILL ALIVE, MY POWER WILL NEVER BE SECURE!

YOU'RE WASTING YOUR TIME! *I WON'T TALK!*

THAT'S WHAT YOU THINK!

I'VE HAD INTEGRATED CONDITIONING THAT PREVENTS ME FROM TALKING! NO AMOUNT OF *TORTURE* CAN BREAK IT!

MAYBE NOT, BUT DO YOU THINK I'M A FOOL? A MENTREK OF YOUR CALIBER CAN OVERCOME ANY CONDITIONING! YOU JUST NEED A STRONG MOTIVATION! HA! HA!

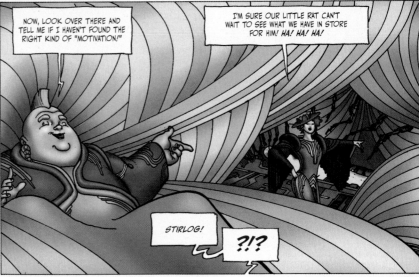

NOW, LOOK OVER THERE AND TELL ME IF I HAVEN'T FOUND THE RIGHT KIND OF "MOTIVATION!"

I'M SURE OUR LITTLE RAT CAN'T WAIT TO SEE WHAT WE HAVE IN STORE FOR HIM! HA! HA! HA!

STIRLOG!

?!?

SO? I'M WAITING FOR *APPLAUSE* FROM THE AUDIENCE!

AH! AT LAST!

NO!!!

CRYSTAL! MY GRANDDAUGHTER!

MONSTERS!

DON'T *DARE* HARM HER!

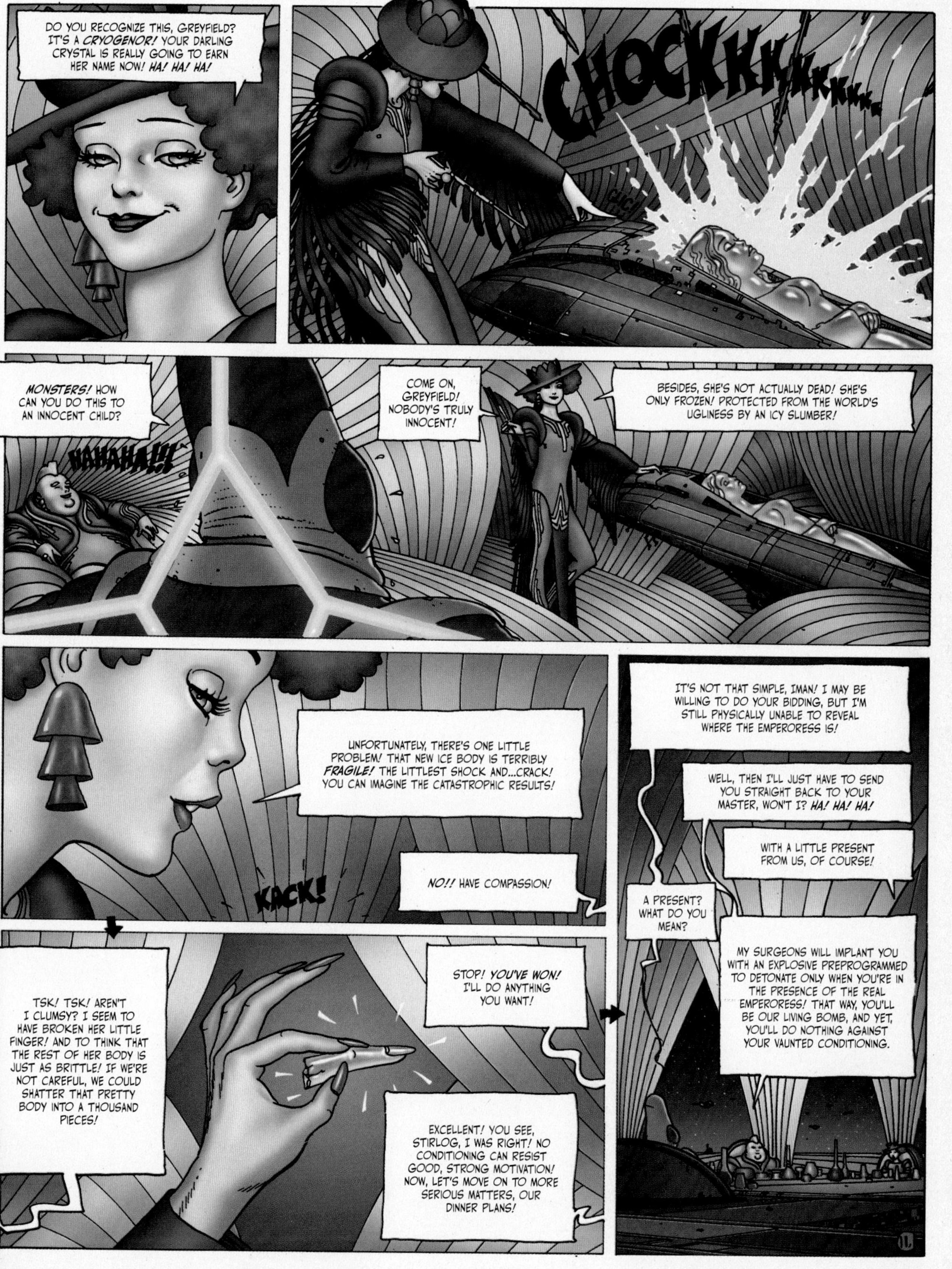

DO YOU RECOGNIZE THIS, GREYFIELD? IT'S A CRYOGENOR! YOUR DARLING CRYSTAL IS REALLY GOING TO EARN HER NAME NOW! HA! HA! HA!
CHOCKKKKKKKK
MONSTERS! HOW CAN YOU DO THIS TO AN INNOCENT CHILD?
HAHAHA!!!
COME ON, GREYFIELD! NOBODY'S TRULY INNOCENT!
BESIDES, SHE'S NOT ACTUALLY DEAD! SHE'S ONLY FROZEN! PROTECTED FROM THE WORLD'S UGLINESS BY AN ICY SLUMBER!
UNFORTUNATELY, THERE'S ONE LITTLE PROBLEM! THAT NEW ICE BODY IS TERRIBLY FRAGILE! THE LITTLEST SHOCK AND...CRACK! YOU CAN IMAGINE THE CATASTROPHIC RESULTS!
NO!! HAVE COMPASSION!
KACK!
TSK! TSK! AREN'T I CLUMSY? I SEEM TO HAVE BROKEN HER LITTLE FINGER! AND TO THINK THAT THE REST OF HER BODY IS JUST AS BRITTLE! IF WE'RE NOT CAREFUL, WE COULD SHATTER THAT PRETTY BODY INTO A THOUSAND PIECES!
STOP! YOU'VE WON! I'LL DO ANYTHING YOU WANT!
EXCELLENT! YOU SEE, STIRLOG, I WAS RIGHT! NO CONDITIONING CAN RESIST GOOD, STRONG MOTIVATION! NOW, LET'S MOVE ON TO MORE SERIOUS MATTERS, OUR DINNER PLANS!
IT'S NOT THAT SIMPLE, IMAN! I MAY BE WILLING TO DO YOUR BIDDING, BUT I'M STILL PHYSICALLY UNABLE TO REVEAL WHERE THE EMPERORESS IS!
WELL, THEN I'LL JUST HAVE TO SEND YOU STRAIGHT BACK TO YOUR MASTER, WON'T I? HA! HA! HA!
WITH A LITTLE PRESENT FROM US, OF COURSE!
A PRESENT? WHAT DO YOU MEAN?
MY SURGEONS WILL IMPLANT YOU WITH AN EXPLOSIVE PREPROGRAMMED TO DETONATE ONLY WHEN YOU'RE IN THE PRESENCE OF THE REAL EMPERORESS! THAT WAY, YOU'LL BE OUR LIVING BOMB, AND YET, YOU'LL DO NOTHING AGAINST YOUR VAUNTED CONDITIONING.
11.

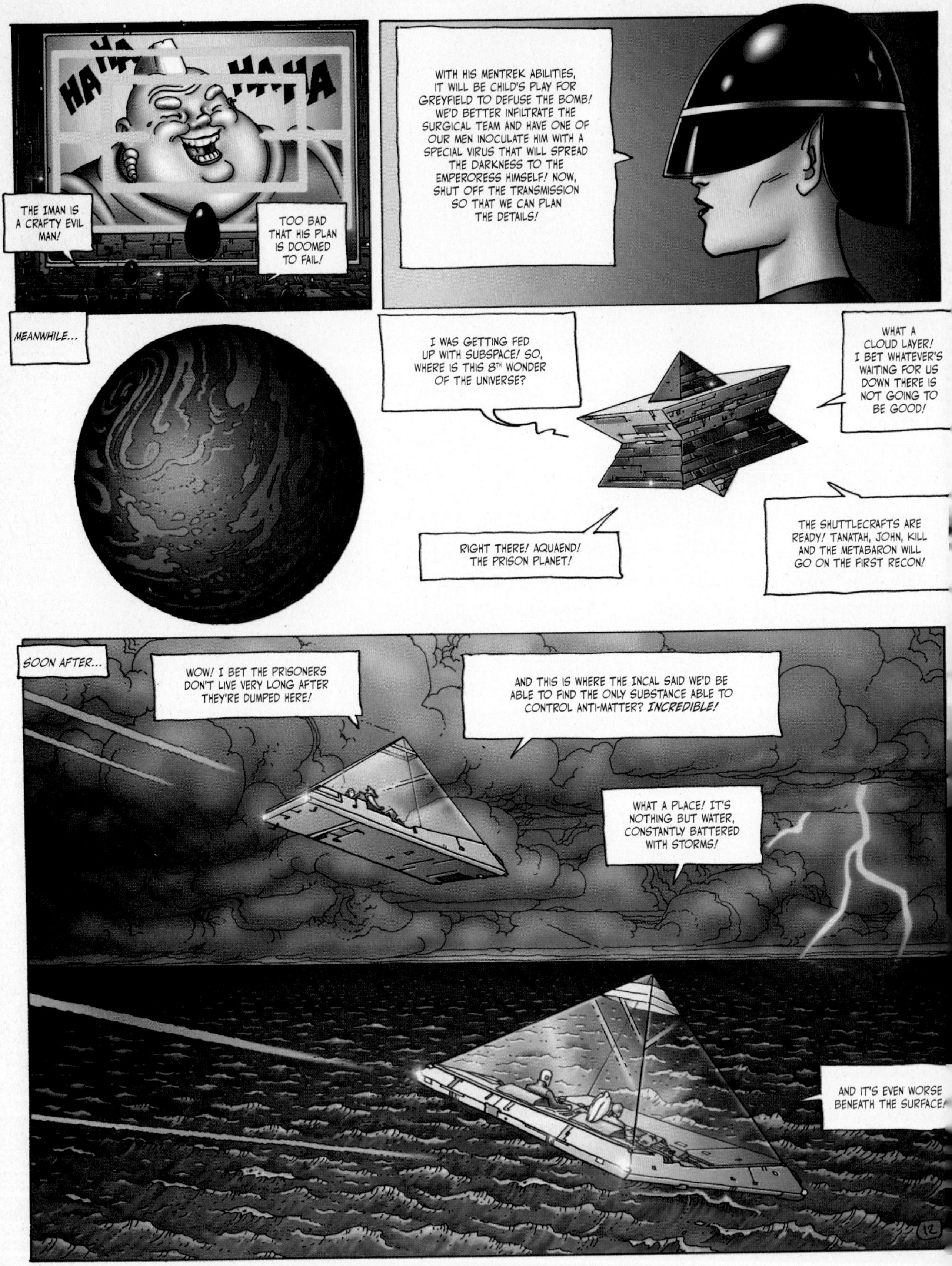
HA HA HA HA
THE IMAN IS A CRAFTY EVIL MAN!
TOO BAD THAT HIS PLAN IS DOOMED TO FAIL!
WITH HIS MENTREK ABILITIES, IT WILL BE CHILD'S PLAY FOR GREYFIELD TO DEFUSE THE BOMB! WE'D BETTER INFILTRATE THE SURGICAL TEAM AND HAVE ONE OF OUR MEN INOCULATE HIM WITH A SPECIAL VIRUS THAT WILL SPREAD THE DARKNESS TO THE EMPERORESS HIMSELF! NOW, SHUT OFF THE TRANSMISSION SO THAT WE CAN PLAN THE DETAILS!
MEANWHILE...
I WAS GETTING FED UP WITH SUBSPACE! SO, WHERE IS THIS 8TH WONDER OF THE UNIVERSE?
WHAT A CLOUD LAYER! I BET WHATEVER'S WAITING FOR US DOWN THERE IS NOT GOING TO BE GOOD!
RIGHT THERE! AQUAEND! THE PRISON PLANET!
THE SHUTTLECRAFTS ARE READY! TANATAH, JOHN, KILL AND THE METABARON WILL GO ON THE FIRST RECON!
SOON AFTER...
WOW! I BET THE PRISONERS DON'T LIVE VERY LONG AFTER THEY'RE DUMPED HERE!
AND THIS IS WHERE THE INCAL SAID WE'D BE ABLE TO FIND THE ONLY SUBSTANCE ABLE TO CONTROL ANTI-MATTER? INCREDIBLE!
WHAT A PLACE! IT'S NOTHING BUT WATER, CONSTANTLY BATTERED WITH STORMS!
AND IT'S EVEN WORSE BENEATH THE SURFACE!
12

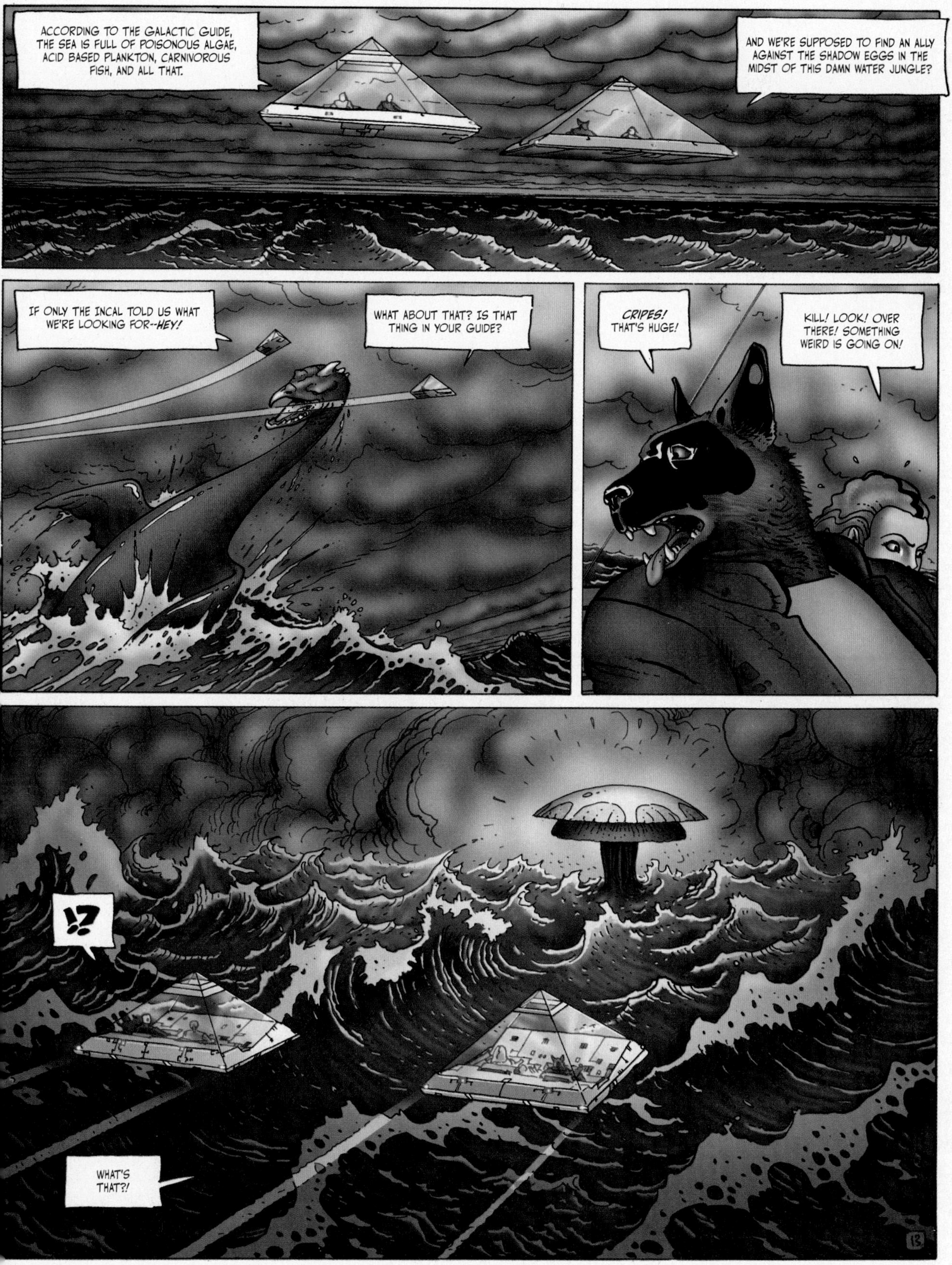
ACCORDING TO THE GALACTIC GUIDE, THE SEA IS FULL OF POISONOUS ALGAE, ACID BASED PLANKTON, CARNIVOROUS FISH, AND ALL THAT.
AND WE'RE SUPPOSED TO FIND AN ALLY AGAINST THE SHADOW EGGS IN THE MIDST OF THIS DAMN WATER JUNGLE?
IF ONLY THE INCAL TOLD US WHAT WE'RE LOOKING FOR--*HEY!*
WHAT ABOUT THAT? IS THAT THING IN YOUR GUIDE?
CRIPES! THAT'S HUGE!
KILL! LOOK! OVER THERE! SOMETHING WEIRD IS GOING ON!
!?
WHAT'S THAT?!
13

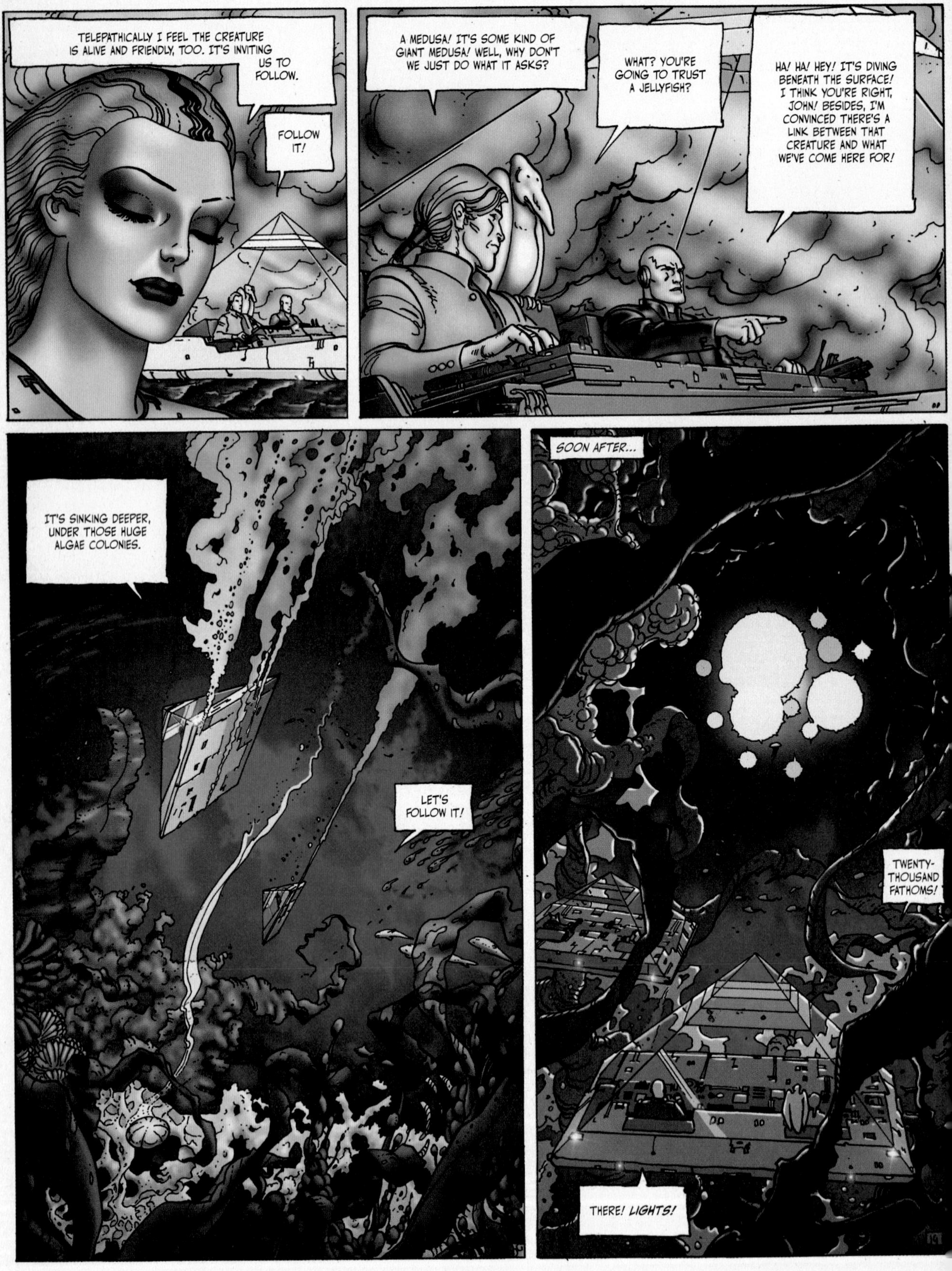
TELEPATHICALLY I FEEL THE CREATURE IS ALIVE AND FRIENDLY, TOO. IT'S INVITING US TO FOLLOW.
FOLLOW IT!
A MEDUSA! IT'S SOME KIND OF GIANT MEDUSA! WELL, WHY DON'T WE JUST DO WHAT IT ASKS?
WHAT? YOU'RE GOING TO TRUST A JELLYFISH?
HA! HA! HEY! IT'S DIVING BENEATH THE SURFACE! I THINK YOU'RE RIGHT, JOHN! BESIDES, I'M CONVINCED THERE'S A LINK BETWEEN THAT CREATURE AND WHAT WE'VE COME HERE FOR!
IT'S SINKING DEEPER, UNDER THOSE HUGE ALGAE COLONIES.
LET'S FOLLOW IT!
SOON AFTER...
TWENTY-THOUSAND FATHOMS!
THERE! LIGHTS!

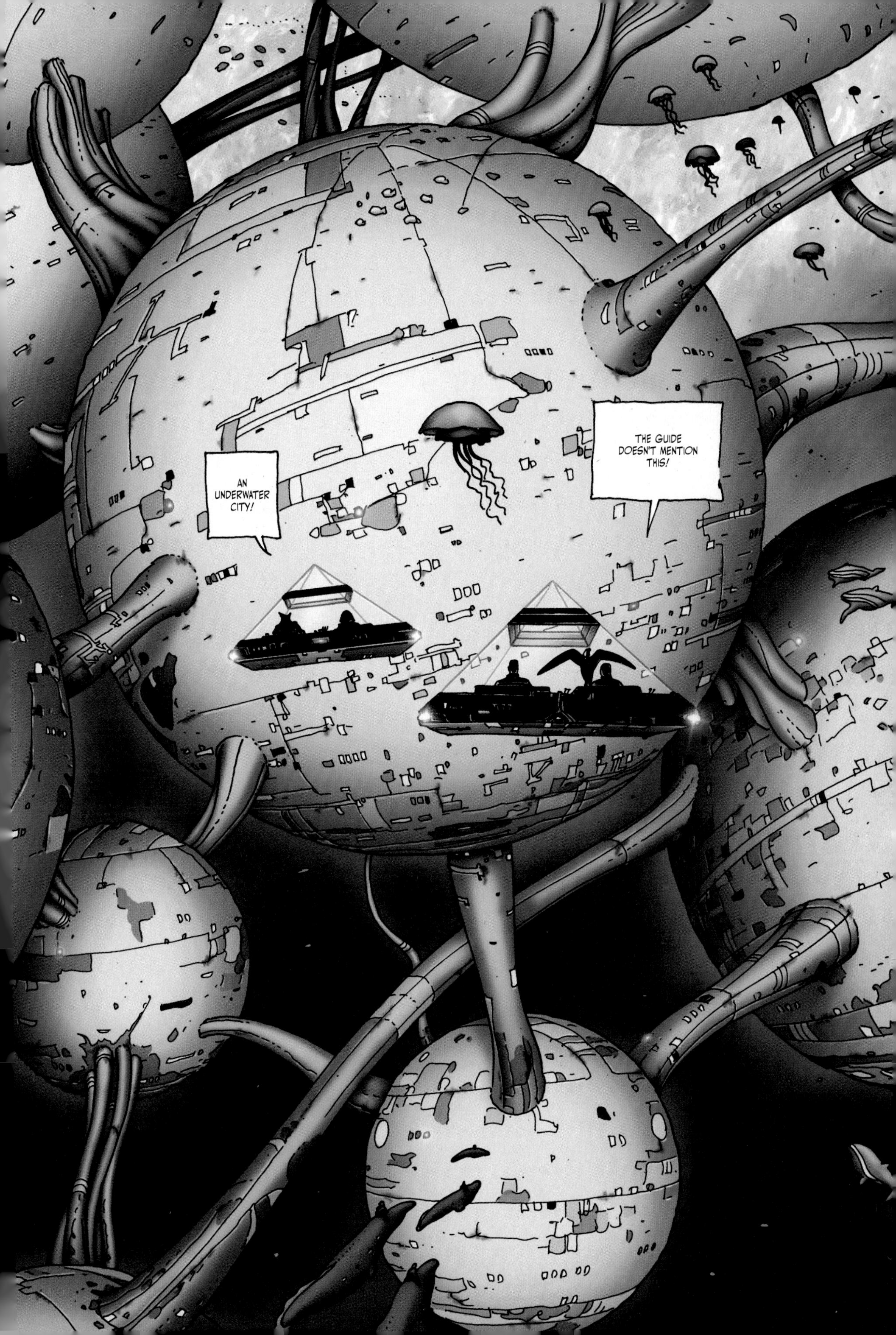
AN UNDERWATER CITY!
THE GUIDE DOESN'T MENTION THIS!

THE MEDUSA STRATEGY

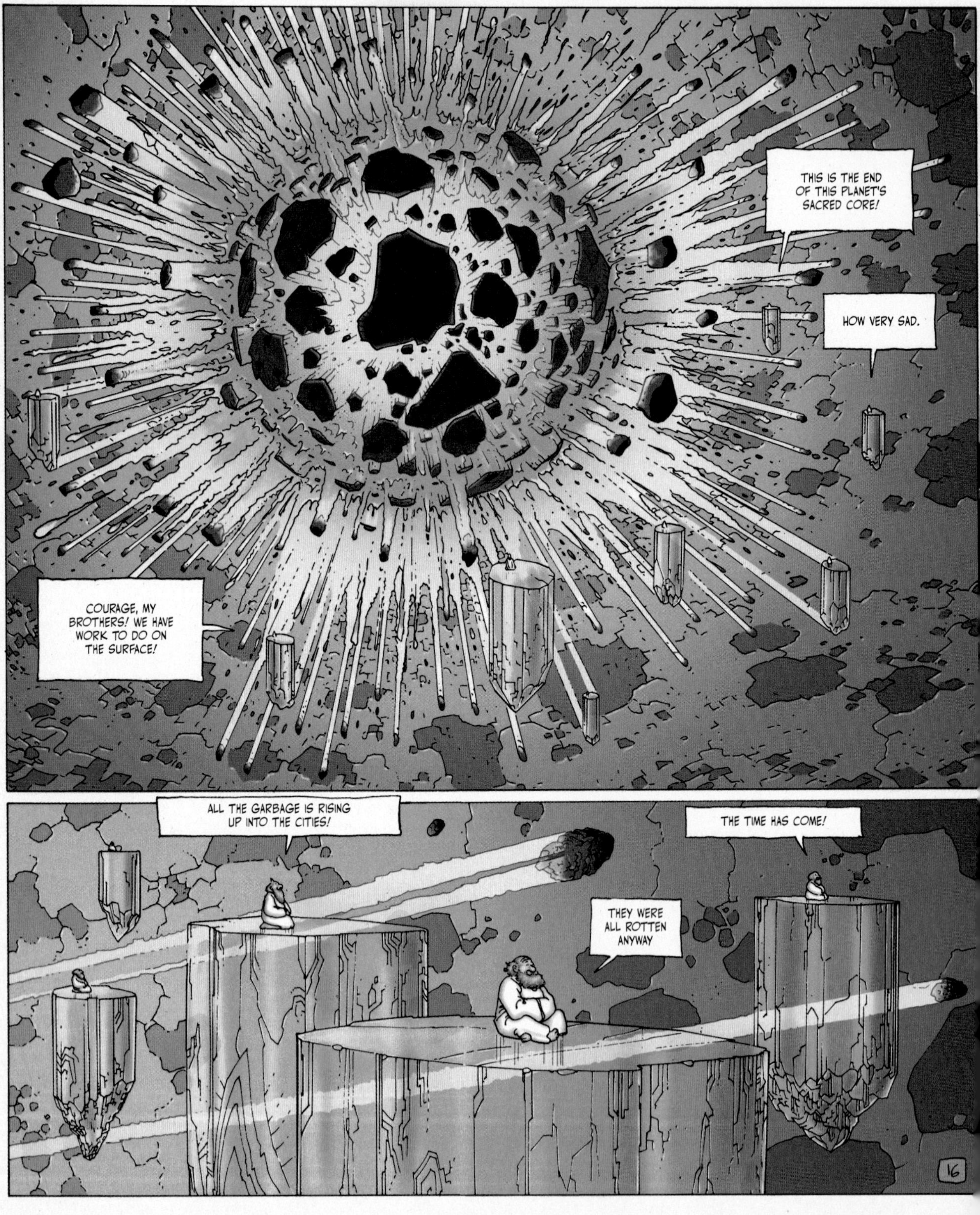
THIS IS THE END OF THIS PLANET'S SACRED CORE!
HOW VERY SAD.
COURAGE, MY BROTHERS! WE HAVE WORK TO DO ON THE SURFACE!
ALL THE GARBAGE IS RISING UP INTO THE CITIES!
THE TIME HAS COME!
THEY WERE ALL ROTTEN ANYWAY
16

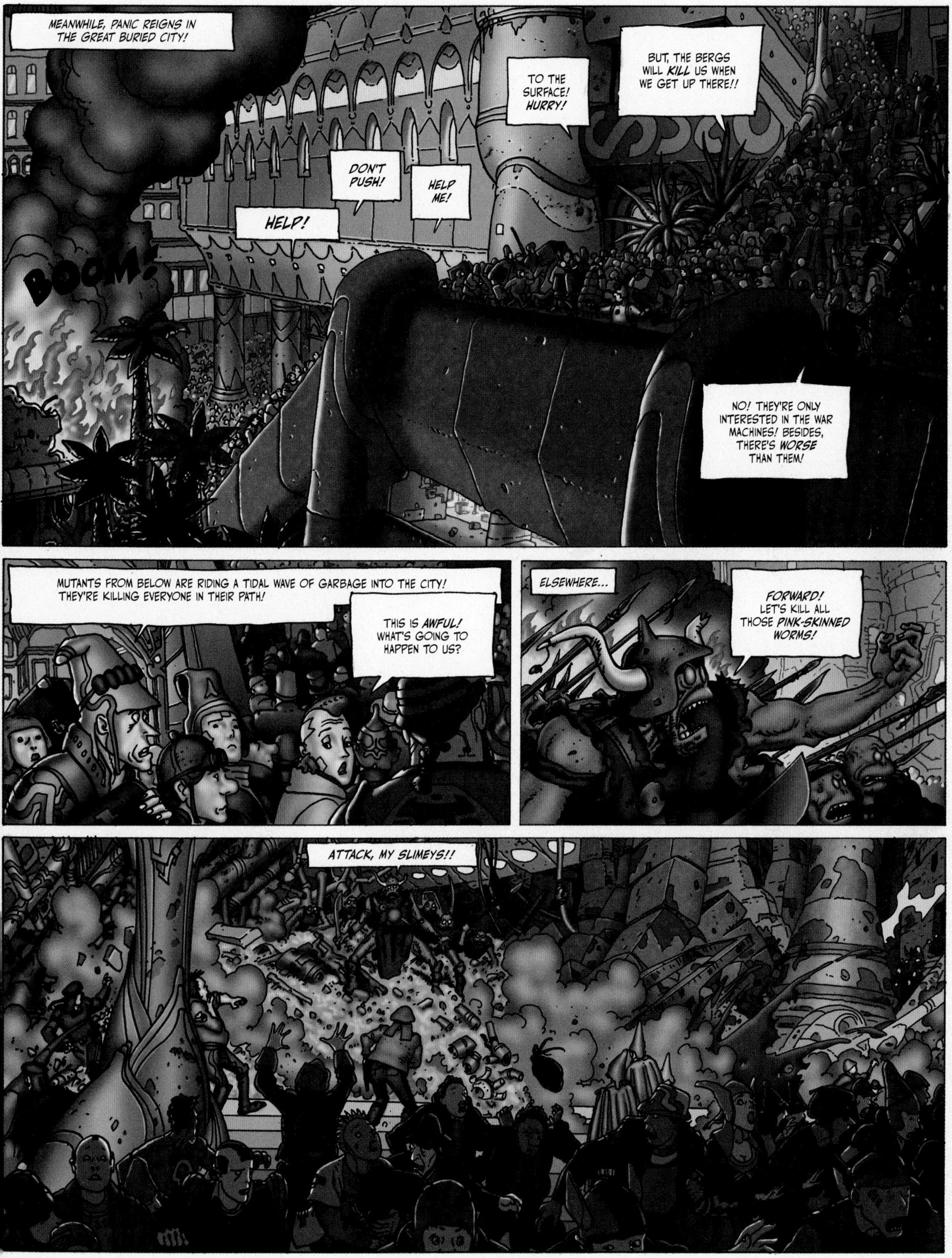
MEANWHILE, PANIC REIGNS IN THE GREAT BURIED CITY!
BOOM!
HELP!
DON'T PUSH!
HELP ME!
TO THE SURFACE! HURRY!
BUT, THE BERGS WILL KILL US WHEN WE GET UP THERE!!
NO! THEY'RE ONLY INTERESTED IN THE WAR MACHINES! BESIDES, THERE'S WORSE THAN THEM!
MUTANTS FROM BELOW ARE RIDING A TIDAL WAVE OF GARBAGE INTO THE CITY! THEY'RE KILLING EVERYONE IN THEIR PATH!
THIS IS AWFUL! WHAT'S GOING TO HAPPEN TO US?
ELSEWHERE...
FORWARD! LET'S KILL ALL THOSE PINK-SKINNED WORMS!
ATTACK, MY SLIMEYS!!

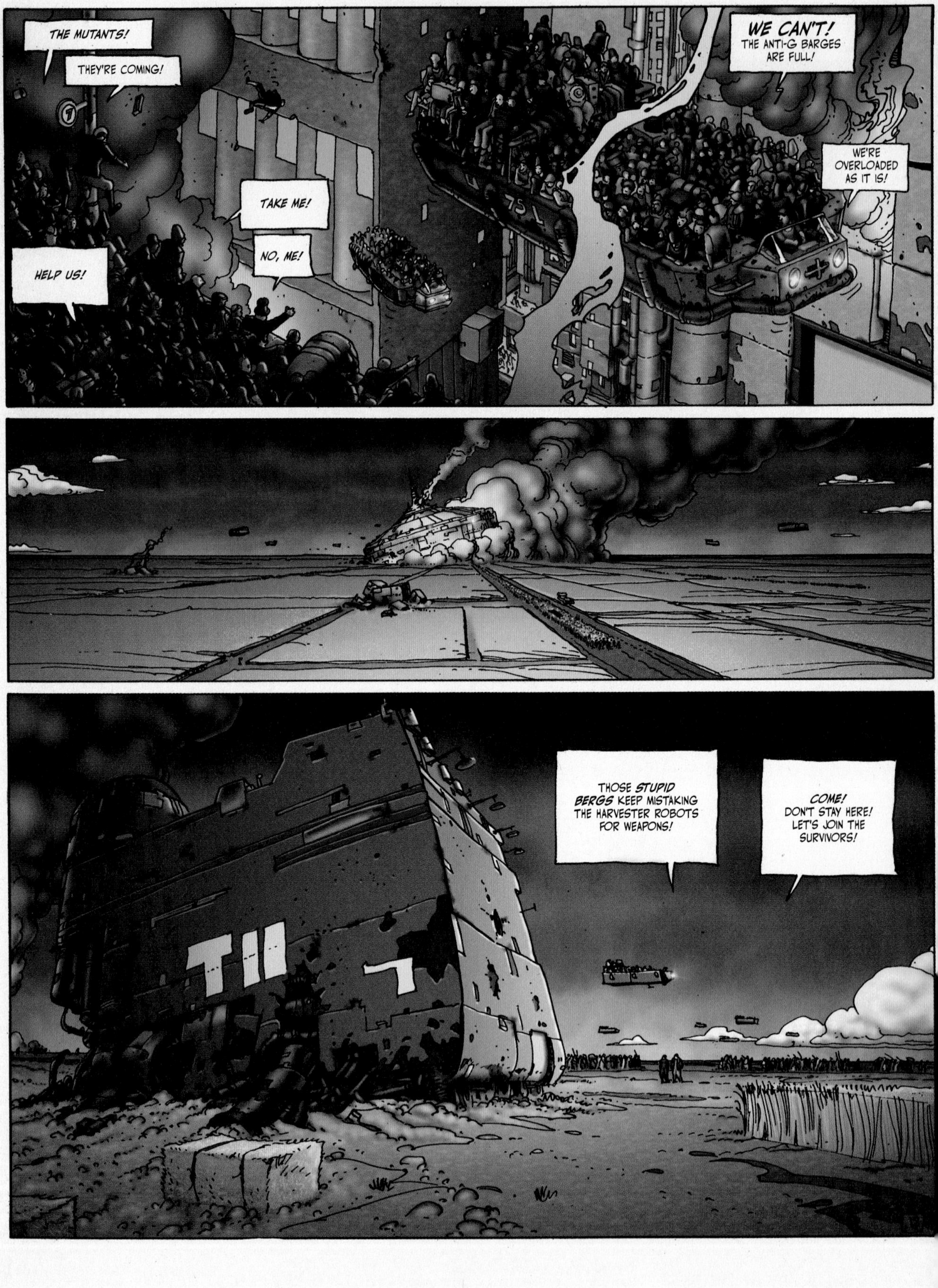
THE MUTANTS!
THEY'RE COMING!
TAKE ME!
NO, ME!
HELP US!
WE CAN'T! THE ANTI-G BARGES ARE FULL!
WE'RE OVERLOADED AS IT IS!
THOSE STUPID BERGS KEEP MISTAKING THE HARVESTER ROBOTS FOR WEAPONS!
COME! DON'T STAY HERE! LET'S JOIN THE SURVIVORS!

ALL RESISTANCE HAS BEEN PUT DOWN! THE PLANET IS OURS!
GOOD! SOON, WE CAN BEGIN SELECTING THE MOST AGGRESSIVE HUMANS!
WHAT ABOUT ALL THOSE REFUGEES, CHIEF?
THEY'RE NOTHING BUT OLD MEN AND CHILDREN! THEY'LL NEVER BE ABLE TO COPE ON THE SURFACE! THEY'LL DIE SOON!
BUT, OTHER EYES ARE ALSO OBSERVING...
LOOK AT THOSE POOR UNHAPPY HUMANS!
MY EYES AREN'T AS GOOD AS THEY USED TO BE, BUT I SEE THEM!
THEY'RE ORPHANS NOW!
ORPHANS LIKE US WHO HAVE LOST OUR SACRED SUN-CORE!
BROTHERS, THE SUN-CORE WAS LIKE A RIPENED FRUIT! WE ARE ITS PRECIOUS SEEDS ENTRUSTED TO THE WINDS!
TRUE! WE SHALL TEACH THESE MEN TO CULTIVATE THE VIRTUES OF THEIR EARTH MOTHER!
YES! LET US SHOW THEM THE WAY!
FORM A NEW ALLIANCE!
SOON, THESE CHILDREN WILL LEARN HOW TO SOW, TO REAP...TO LIVE!
19

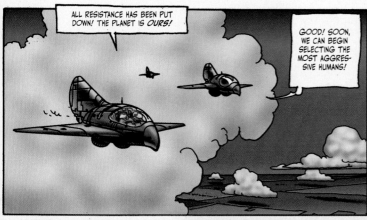

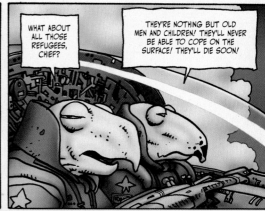

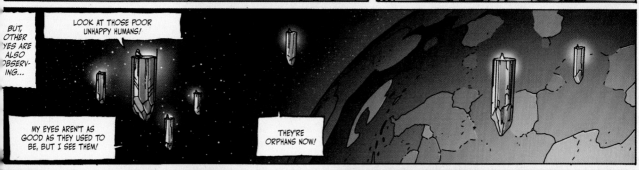

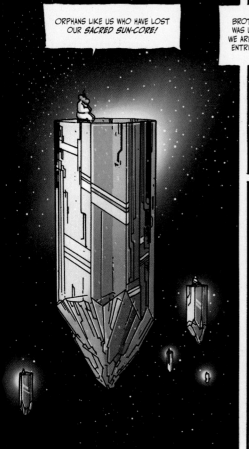

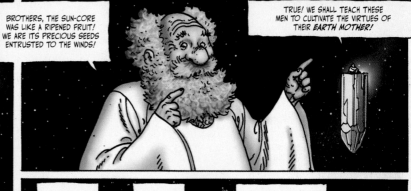

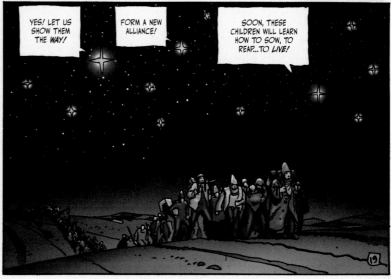

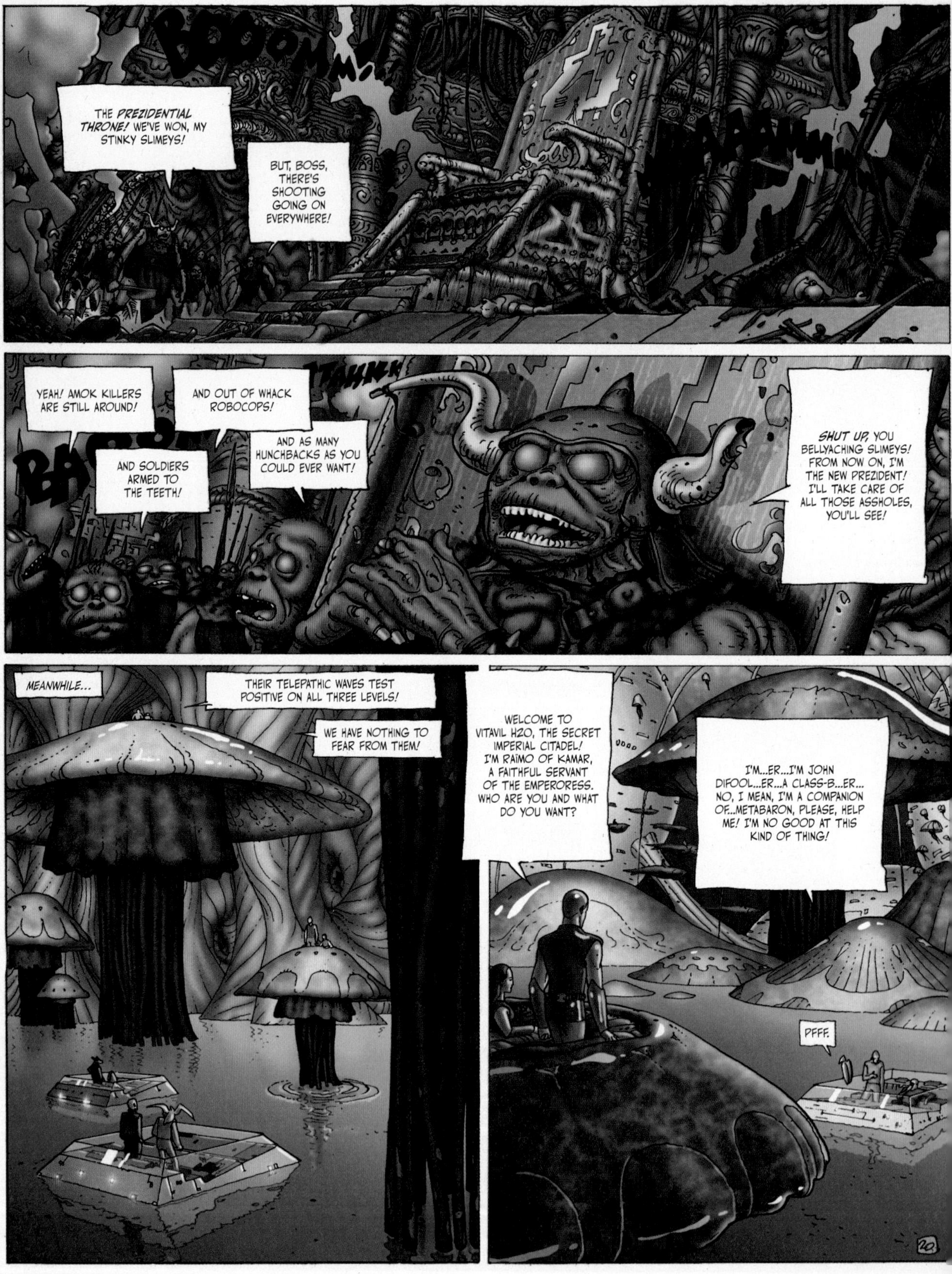
BOOOOMM...!
THE PREZIDENTIAL THRONE! WE'VE WON, MY STINKY SLIMEYS!
BUT, BOSS, THERE'S SHOOTING GOING ON EVERYWHERE!
YEAH! AMOK KILLERS ARE STILL AROUND!
AND OUT OF WHACK ROBOCOPS!
AND SOLDIERS ARMED TO THE TEETH!
AND AS MANY HUNCHBACKS AS YOU COULD EVER WANT!
SHUT UP, YOU BELLYACHING SLIMEYS! FROM NOW ON, I'M THE NEW PREZIDENT! I'LL TAKE CARE OF ALL THOSE ASSHOLES, YOU'LL SEE!
MEANWHILE...
THEIR TELEPATHIC WAVES TEST POSITIVE ON ALL THREE LEVELS!
WE HAVE NOTHING TO FEAR FROM THEM!
WELCOME TO VITAVIL H2O, THE SECRET IMPERIAL CITADEL! I'M RAIMO OF KAMAR, A FAITHFUL SERVANT OF THE EMPERORESS. WHO ARE YOU AND WHAT DO YOU WANT?
I'M...ER...I'M JOHN DIFOOL...ER...A CLASS-B...ER... NO, I MEAN, I'M A COMPANION OF...METABARON, PLEASE, HELP ME! I'M NO GOOD AT THIS KIND OF THING!
PFFF.
20

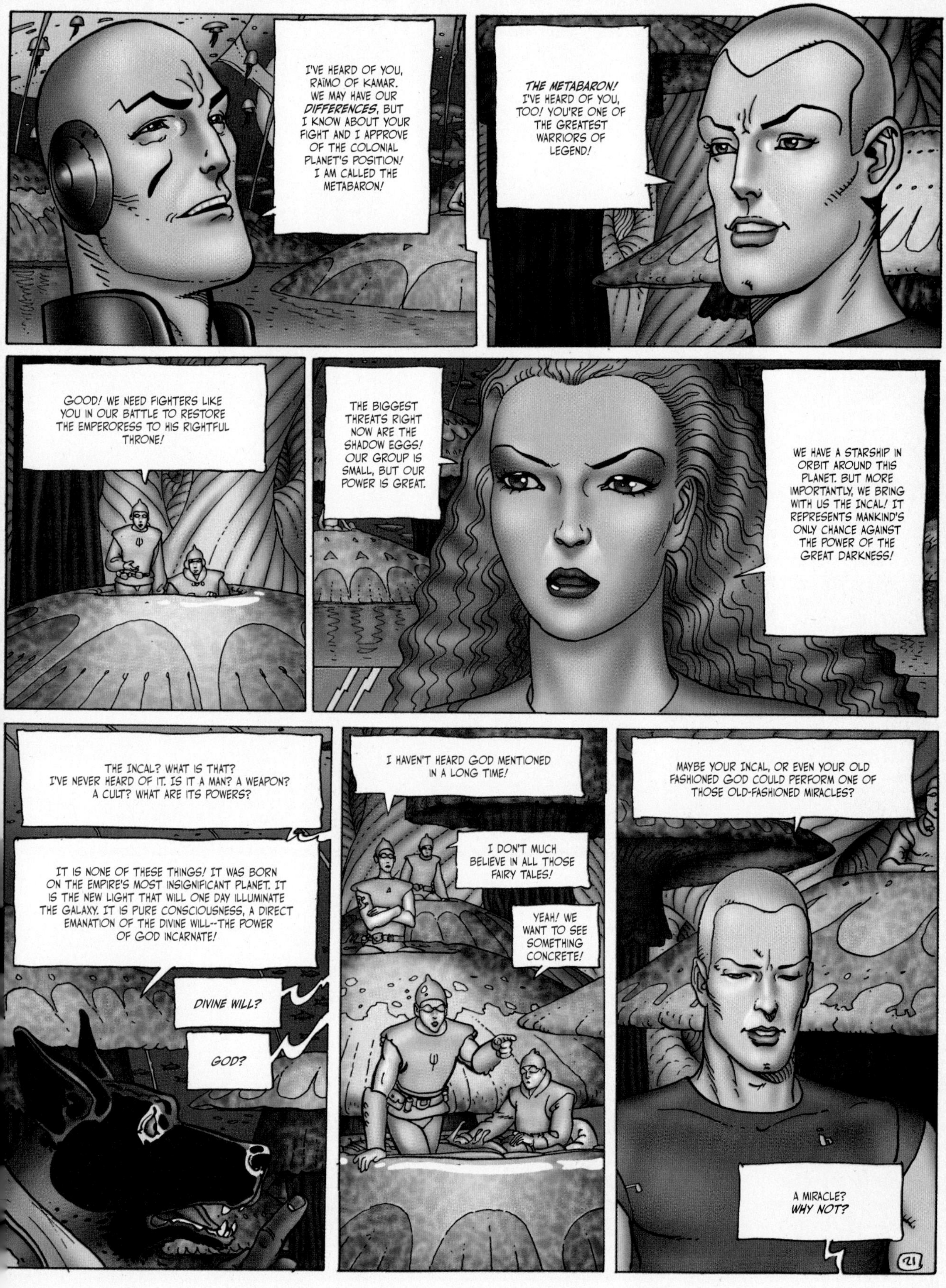
I'VE HEARD OF YOU, RAÏMO OF KAMAR. WE MAY HAVE OUR DIFFERENCES, BUT I KNOW ABOUT YOUR FIGHT AND I APPROVE OF THE COLONIAL PLANET'S POSITION! I AM CALLED THE METABARON!
THE METABARON! I'VE HEARD OF YOU, TOO! YOU'RE ONE OF THE GREATEST WARRIORS OF LEGEND!
GOOD! WE NEED FIGHTERS LIKE YOU IN OUR BATTLE TO RESTORE THE EMPERORESS TO HIS RIGHTFUL THRONE!
THE BIGGEST THREATS RIGHT NOW ARE THE SHADOW EGGS! OUR GROUP IS SMALL, BUT OUR POWER IS GREAT.
WE HAVE A STARSHIP IN ORBIT AROUND THIS PLANET. BUT MORE IMPORTANTLY, WE BRING WITH US THE INCAL! IT REPRESENTS MANKIND'S ONLY CHANCE AGAINST THE POWER OF THE GREAT DARKNESS!
THE INCAL? WHAT IS THAT? I'VE NEVER HEARD OF IT. IS IT A MAN? A WEAPON? A CULT? WHAT ARE ITS POWERS?
IT IS NONE OF THESE THINGS! IT WAS BORN ON THE EMPIRE'S MOST INSIGNIFICANT PLANET. IT IS THE NEW LIGHT THAT WILL ONE DAY ILLUMINATE THE GALAXY. IT IS PURE CONSCIOUSNESS, A DIRECT EMANATION OF THE DIVINE WILL--THE POWER OF GOD INCARNATE!
DIVINE WILL?
GOD?
I HAVEN'T HEARD GOD MENTIONED IN A LONG TIME!
I DON'T MUCH BELIEVE IN ALL THOSE FAIRY TALES!
YEAH! WE WANT TO SEE SOMETHING CONCRETE!
MAYBE YOUR INCAL, OR EVEN YOUR OLD FASHIONED GOD COULD PERFORM ONE OF THOSE OLD-FASHIONED MIRACLES?
A MIRACLE? WHY NOT?
21

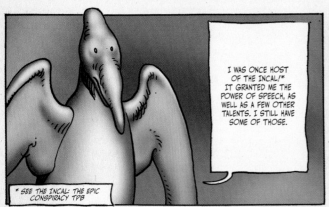

I WAS ONCE HOST OF THE INCAL!* IT GRANTED ME THE POWER OF SPEECH, AS WELL AS A FEW OTHER TALENTS. I STILL HAVE SOME OF THOSE.

* SEE THE INCAL: THE EPIC CONSPIRACY TPB

OH, INCAL! HELP ME CONVINCE THIS MIGHTY WARRIOR!

HOLD YOUR HAND OUT TO ME, RAIMO!

?

WELL, I DON'T MIND PLAYING YOUR LITTLE GAME, BIRD, BUT...

BUT...

!!?

INCREDIBLE! IT LOOKS JUST LIKE A ROSE!

BUT, THAT'S IMPOSSIBLE!

A ROSE?!

IT'S A LEGENDARY FLOWER THAT HAS BEEN EXTINCT FOR GENERATIONS!

IT'S A MIRACLE!!

HA! HA! CONGRATULATIONS, LITTLE CONCRETE SEAGULL! YOU'VE WON! NOW WE'LL TAKE YOU TO SEE HIS MEGA-HOLINESS, THE EMPERORESS!

WAIT! I'LL CALL THE OTHERS!

AND SOON...

I AM CONVINCED THAT YOUR HELP IS ESSENTIAL! WHAT IS YOUR PLAN?

YOUR MEGA-HOLINESS, OUR PLAN IS SIMPLE, YET MAY SEEM CRAZY. THE INCAL HAS THE POWER TO MUTATE THIS PLANET'S GIANT MEDUSA INTO A LIVING WEAPON CAPABLE OF DEFEATING THE THREAT OF THE SHADOW EGGS!

BUT, OUR VICTORY WILL DEPEND ON PERFECT COORDINATION--ON SEVERAL LEVELS! LET US EXPLAIN OUR STRATEGY--

HEY! DEEPO FELL ASLEEP!

HIS MIRACLE MUST HAVE WORN HIM OUT!

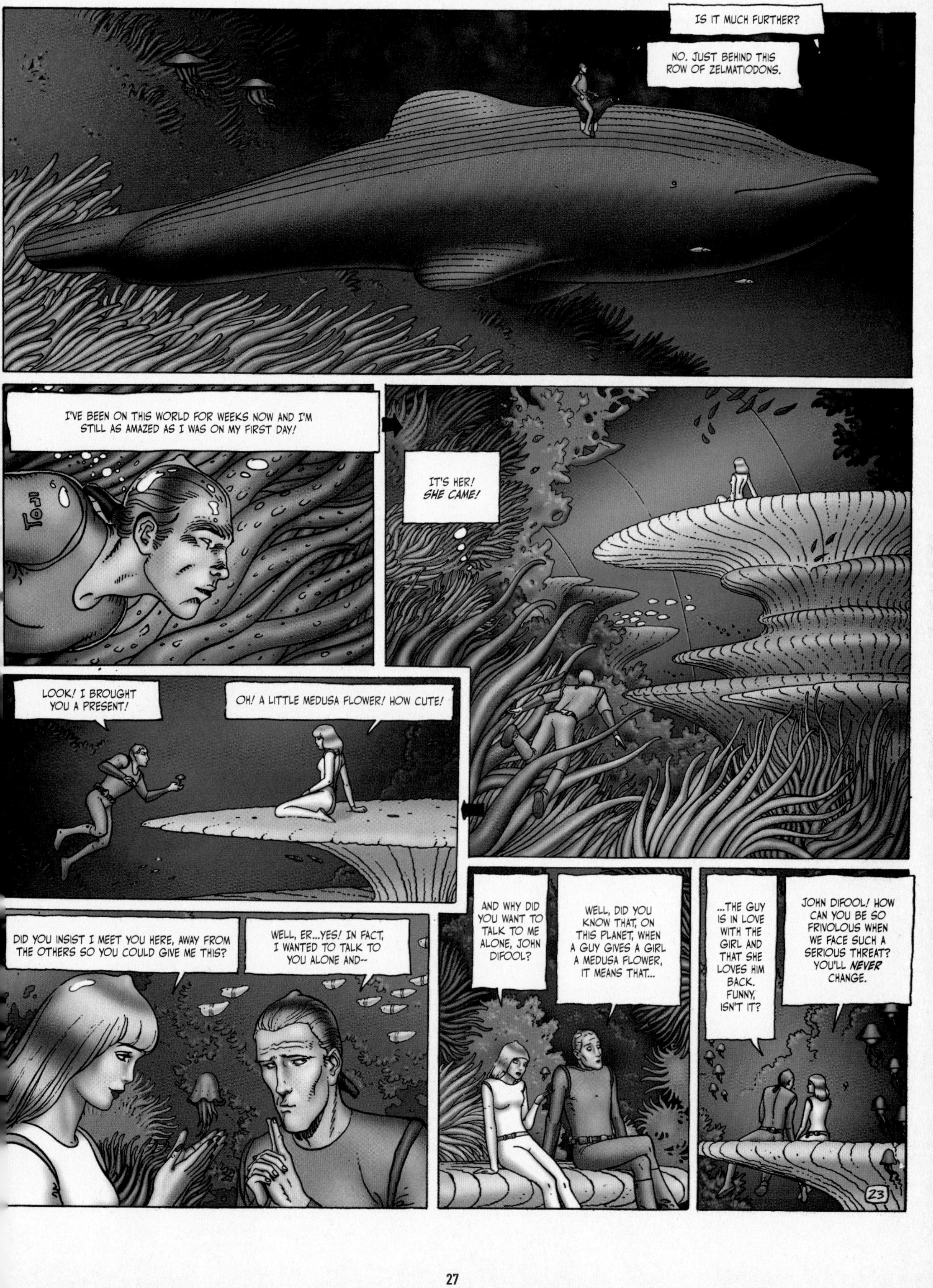
IS IT MUCH FURTHER?
NO. JUST BEHIND THIS ROW OF ZELMATIODONS.
I'VE BEEN ON THIS WORLD FOR WEEKS NOW AND I'M STILL AS AMAZED AS I WAS ON MY FIRST DAY!
IT'S HER! SHE CAME!
LOOK! I BROUGHT YOU A PRESENT!
OH! A LITTLE MEDUSA FLOWER! HOW CUTE!
DID YOU INSIST I MEET YOU HERE, AWAY FROM THE OTHERS SO YOU COULD GIVE ME THIS?
WELL, ER...YES! IN FACT, I WANTED TO TALK TO YOU ALONE AND--
AND WHY DID YOU WANT TO TALK TO ME ALONE, JOHN DIFOOL?
WELL, DID YOU KNOW THAT, ON THIS PLANET, WHEN A GUY GIVES A GIRL A MEDUSA FLOWER, IT MEANS THAT...
...THE GUY IS IN LOVE WITH THE GIRL AND THAT SHE LOVES HIM BACK. FUNNY, ISN'T IT?
JOHN DIFOOL! HOW CAN YOU BE SO FRIVOLOUS WHEN WE FACE SUCH A SERIOUS THREAT? YOU'LL NEVER CHANGE.
23

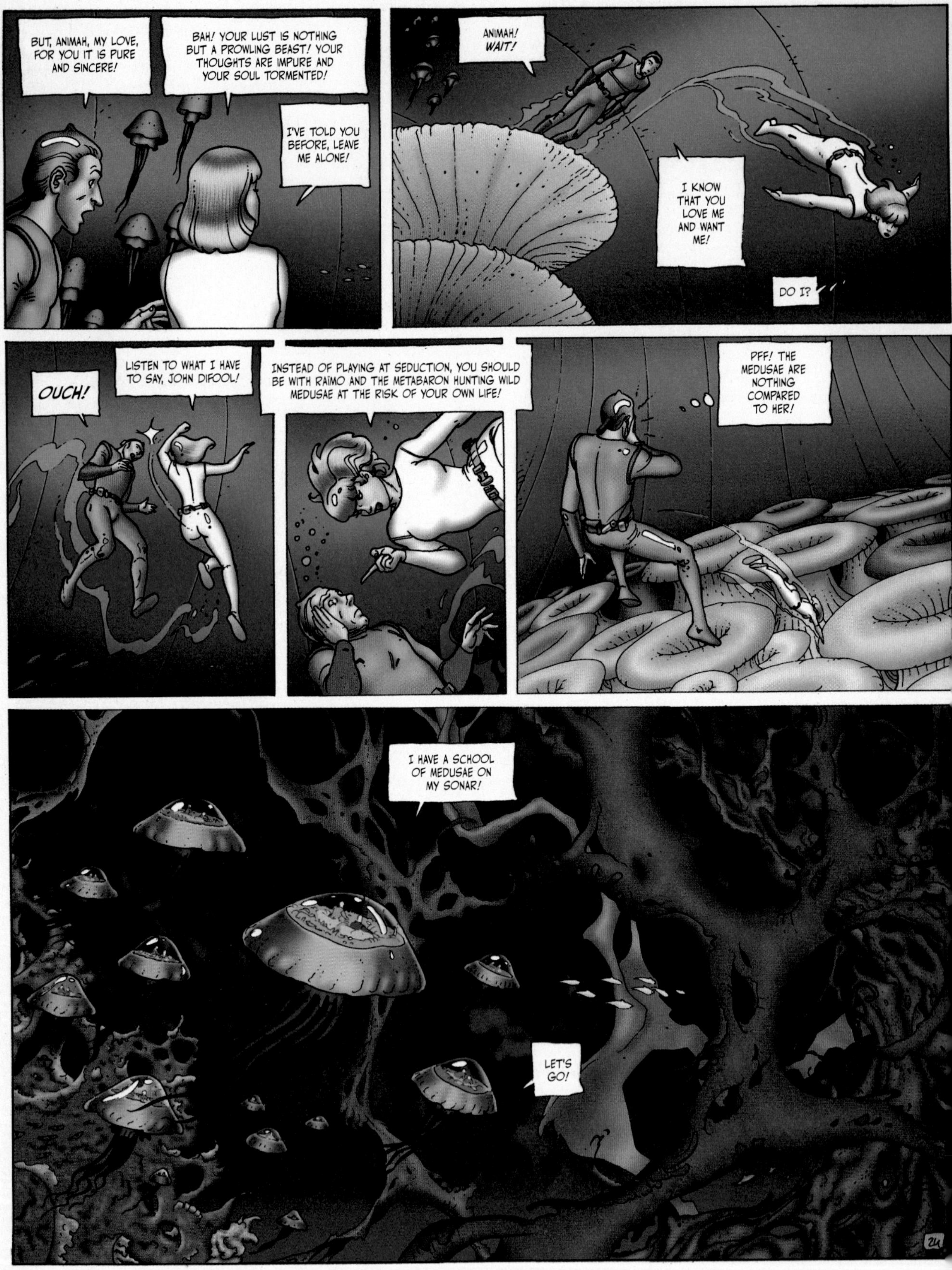
BUT, ANIMAH, MY LOVE, FOR YOU IT IS PURE AND SINCERE!
BAH! YOUR LUST IS NOTHING BUT A PROWLING BEAST! YOUR THOUGHTS ARE IMPURE AND YOUR SOUL TORMENTED!
I'VE TOLD YOU BEFORE, LEAVE ME ALONE!
ANIMAH! WAIT!
I KNOW THAT YOU LOVE ME AND WANT ME!
DO I?
OUCH!
LISTEN TO WHAT I HAVE TO SAY, JOHN DIFOOL!
INSTEAD OF PLAYING AT SEDUCTION, YOU SHOULD BE WITH RAÏMO AND THE METABARON HUNTING WILD MEDUSAE AT THE RISK OF YOUR OWN LIFE!
PFF! THE MEDUSAE ARE NOTHING COMPARED TO HER!
I HAVE A SCHOOL OF MEDUSAE ON MY SONAR!
LET'S GO!
24

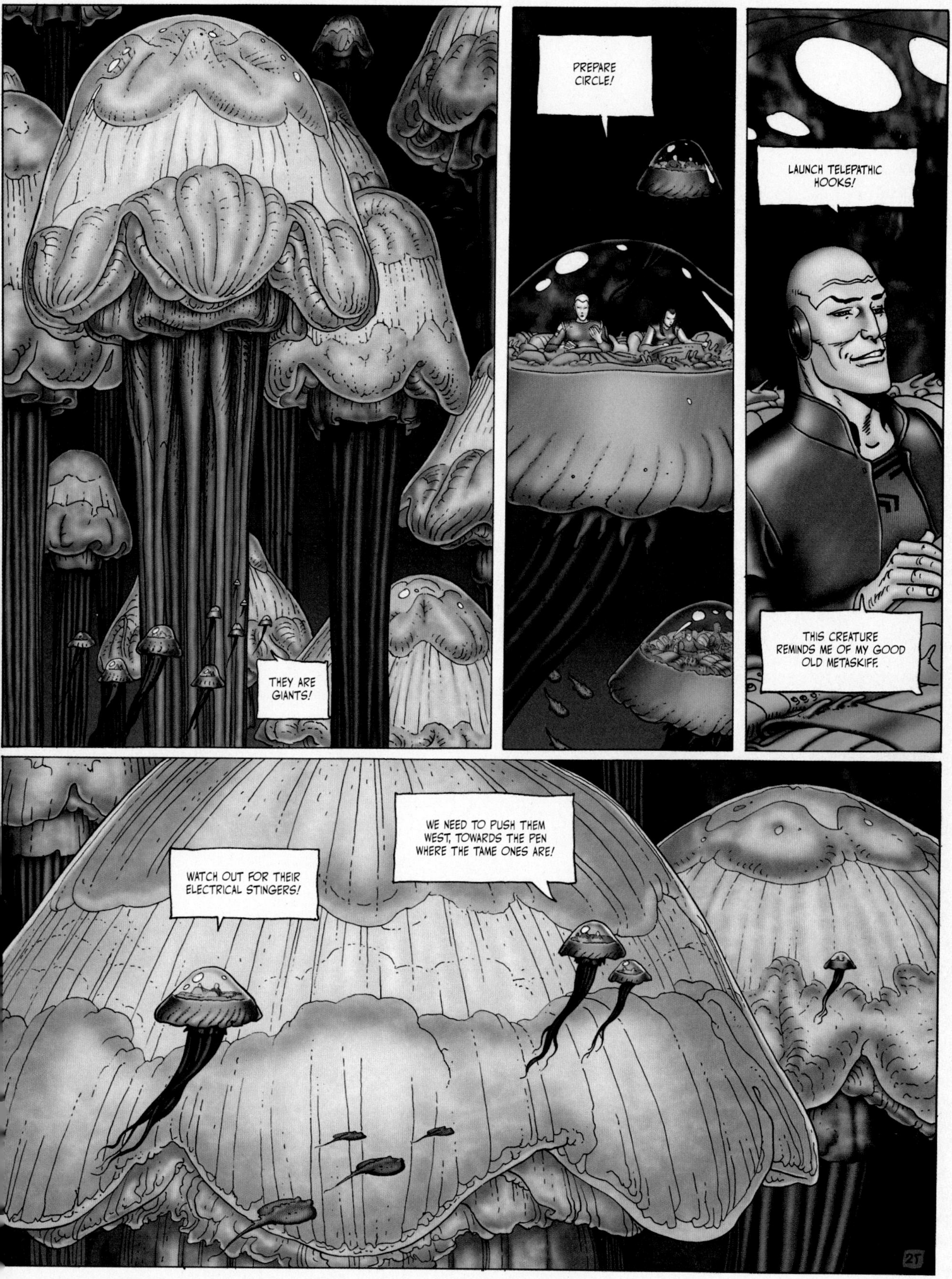
THEY ARE GIANTS!
PREPARE CIRCLE!
LAUNCH TELEPATHIC HOOKS!
THIS CREATURE REMINDS ME OF MY GOOD OLD METASKIFF.
WATCH OUT FOR THEIR ELECTRICAL STINGERS!
WE NEED TO PUSH THEM WEST, TOWARDS THE PEN WHERE THE TAME ONES ARE!

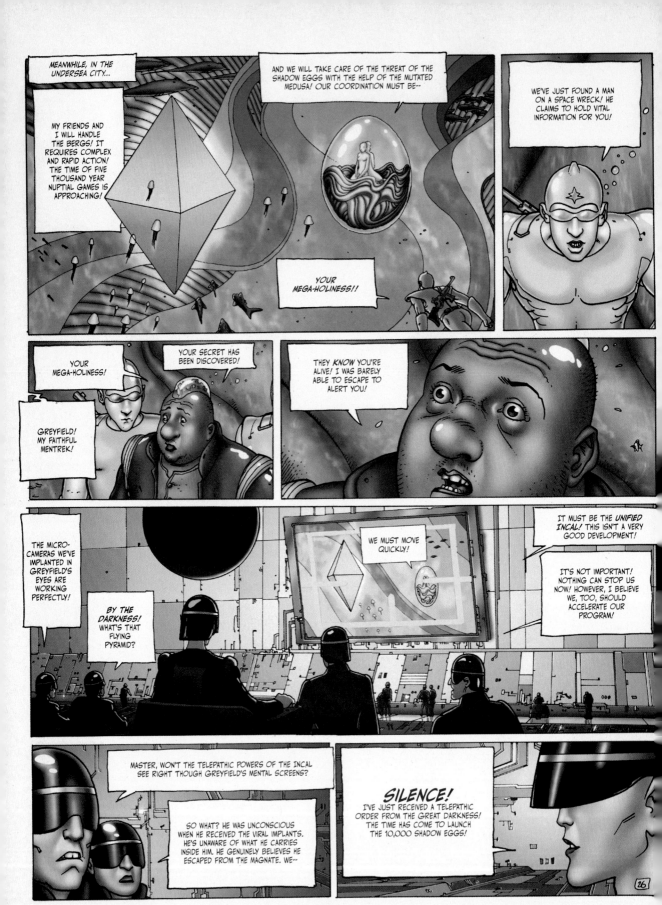

MEANWHILE, IN THE UNDERSEA CITY...

MY FRIENDS AND I WILL HANDLE THE BERGS! IT REQUIRES COMPLEX AND RAPID ACTION! THE TIME OF FIVE THOUSAND YEAR NUPTIAL GAMES IS APPROACHING!

AND WE WILL TAKE CARE OF THE THREAT OF THE SHADOW EGGS WITH THE HELP OF THE MUTATED MEDUSA! OUR COORDINATION MUST BE--

YOUR MEGA-HOLINESS!!

WE'VE JUST FOUND A MAN ON A SPACE WRECK! HE CLAIMS TO HOLD VITAL INFORMATION FOR YOU!

YOUR MEGA-HOLINESS!

YOUR SECRET HAS BEEN DISCOVERED!

THEY *KNOW* YOU'RE ALIVE! I WAS BARELY ABLE TO ESCAPE TO ALERT YOU!

GREYFIELD! MY FAITHFUL MENTREK!

THE MICRO-CAMERAS WE'VE IMPLANTED IN GREYFIELD'S EYES ARE WORKING PERFECTLY!

BY THE DARKNESS! WHAT'S THAT FLYING PYRAMID?

WE MUST MOVE QUICKLY!

IT MUST BE THE *UNIFIED INCAL!* THIS ISN'T A VERY GOOD DEVELOPMENT!

IT'S NOT IMPORTANT! NOTHING CAN STOP US NOW! HOWEVER, I BELIEVE WE, TOO, SHOULD ACCELERATE OUR PROGRAM!

MASTER, WON'T THE TELEPATHIC POWERS OF THE INCAL SEE RIGHT THROUGH GREYFIELD'S MENTAL SCREENS?

SO WHAT? HE WAS UNCONSCIOUS WHEN HE RECEIVED THE VIRAL IMPLANTS. HE'S UNAWARE OF WHAT HE CARRIES INSIDE HIM. HE GENUINELY BELIEVES HE ESCAPED FROM THE MAGNATE. WE--

SILENCE! I'VE JUST RECEIVED A TELEPATHIC ORDER FROM THE GREAT DARKNESS! THE TIME HAS COME TO LAUNCH THE 10,000 SHADOW EGGS!

26

APPROACH!

YOU'RE CRAZY!

I WON'T DO IT!

YOU WANT TO DROP ME ALONE ON THE BERGS' HOME WORLD? FACE TO...ER...BEAK WITH THOSE GODDAMN PARAKEETS! AND YOU WANT ME TO IMPREGNATE SOME KIND OF QUEEN, TOO? NO WAY! A THOUSAND TIMES *NO!*

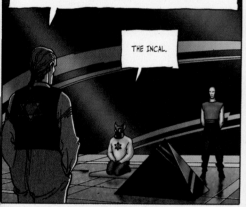

WHY DON'T YOU SEND THE METABARON? HE'S THE MIGHTY WARRIOR, NOT ME! REMEMBER, I DON'T HAVE THE INCAL INSIDE ME ANYMORE! SO, WHO'S THE GENIUS THAT THOUGHT UP THIS CRAZY IDEA ANYWAY.

THE INCAL.

THE INCAL? ERR... WELL...I GUESS IT'S OKAY THEN! WHAT'S THAT PYRAMID THERE?

IT'S YOUR ROBOTRAINER. I'VE PROGRAMMED IT ESPECIALLY FOR YOU. IT'LL MAKE YOU INTO A *CHAMPION!*

ME? A CHAMPION? HA!

FIRST, IT WILL EVALUATE, THEN DEVELOP YOUR STRENGTH, SPEED, ENDURANCE AND SKILL.

"JUNK," YOU SAY? HA! HA! HA! I TOLD YOU, JOHN, I PROGRAMMED IT MYSELF!

I *HATE* IT ALREADY!

WE'LL START ON THE SLOWEST SPEED.

WHY? DO YOU THINK I'M AFRAID OF THAT HUNK O' JUNK?

BIG DEAL! I'VE WORKED WITH ROBOTS BEFORE IN DETECTIVE SCHOOL!

MAYBE YOU DID, BUT THIS ONE IS A LITTLE MORE ADVANCED. THERE ARE TEN LEVELS. I'LL START YOU ON LEVEL ONE.

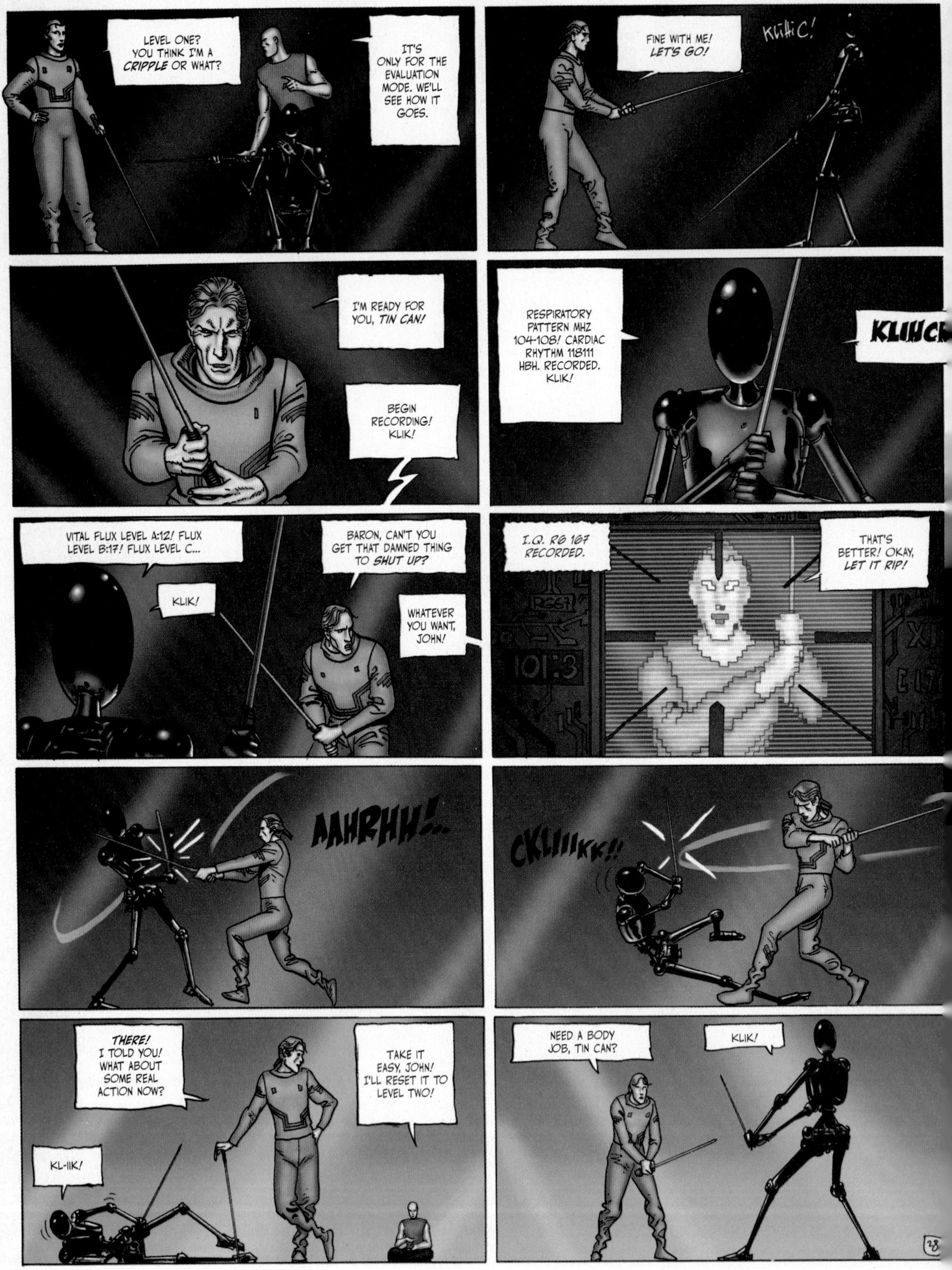
LEVEL ONE? YOU THINK I'M A CRIPPLE OR WHAT?
IT'S ONLY FOR THE EVALUATION MODE. WE'LL SEE HOW IT GOES.
FINE WITH ME! LET'S GO!
KLIHIC!
I'M READY FOR YOU, TIN CAN!
BEGIN RECORDING! KLIK!
RESPIRATORY PATTERN MHZ 104-108! CARDIAC RHYTHM 118111 HBH. RECORDED. KLIK!
KLIHC
VITAL FLUX LEVEL A:12! FLUX LEVEL B:17! FLUX LEVEL C...
KLIK!
BARON, CAN'T YOU GET THAT DAMNED THING TO SHUT UP?
WHATEVER YOU WANT, JOHN!
I.Q. RG 167 RECORDED.
THAT'S BETTER! OKAY, LET IT RIP!
AAHRHH!..
CKLIIIKK!!
THERE! I TOLD YOU! WHAT ABOUT SOME REAL ACTION NOW?
TAKE IT EASY, JOHN! I'LL RESET IT TO LEVEL TWO!
KL-IIK!
NEED A BODY JOB, TIN CAN?
KLIK!

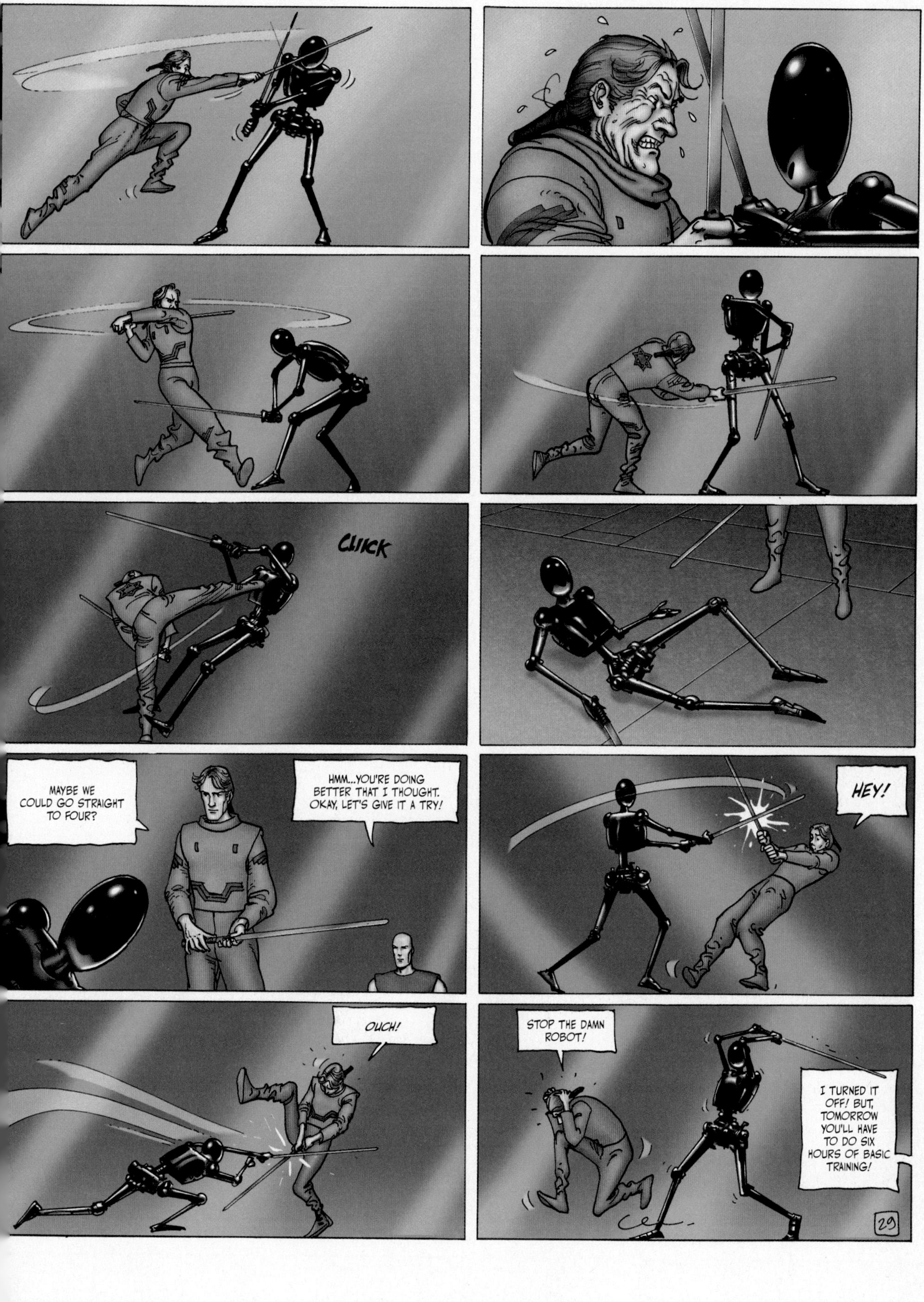
CLICK
MAYBE WE COULD GO STRAIGHT TO FOUR?
HMM...YOU'RE DOING BETTER THAT I THOUGHT. OKAY, LET'S GIVE IT A TRY!
HEY!
OUCH!
STOP THE DAMN ROBOT!
I TURNED IT OFF! BUT, TOMORROW YOU'LL HAVE TO DO SIX HOURS OF BASIC TRAINING!
29

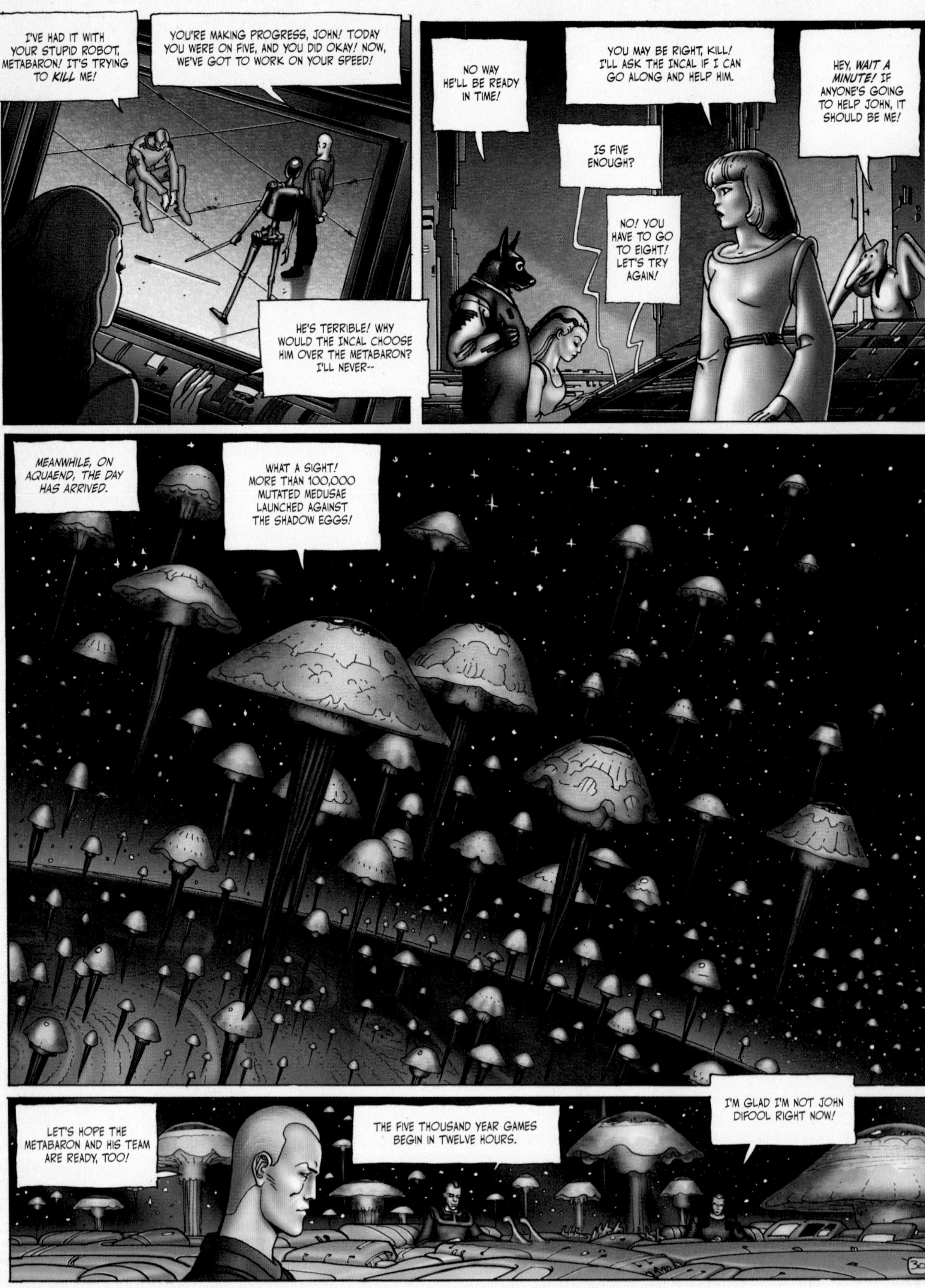

I'VE HAD IT WITH YOUR STUPID ROBOT, METABARON! IT'S TRYING TO *KILL* ME!
YOU'RE MAKING PROGRESS, JOHN! TODAY YOU WERE ON FIVE, AND YOU DID OKAY! NOW, WE'VE GOT TO WORK ON YOUR SPEED!
HE'S TERRIBLE! WHY WOULD THE INCAL CHOOSE HIM OVER THE METABARON? I'LL NEVER--
NO WAY HE'LL BE READY IN TIME!
IS FIVE ENOUGH?
NO! YOU HAVE TO GO TO EIGHT! LET'S TRY AGAIN!
YOU MAY BE RIGHT, KILL! I'LL ASK THE INCAL IF I CAN GO ALONG AND HELP HIM.
HEY, *WAIT A MINUTE!* IF ANYONE'S GOING TO HELP JOHN, IT SHOULD BE ME!
MEANWHILE, ON AQUAEND, THE DAY HAS ARRIVED.
WHAT A SIGHT! MORE THAN 100,000 MUTATED MEDUSAE LAUNCHED AGAINST THE SHADOW EGGS!
LET'S HOPE THE METABARON AND HIS TEAM ARE READY, TOO!
THE FIVE THOUSAND YEAR GAMES BEGIN IN TWELVE HOURS.
I'M GLAD I'M NOT JOHN DIFOOL RIGHT NOW!
30

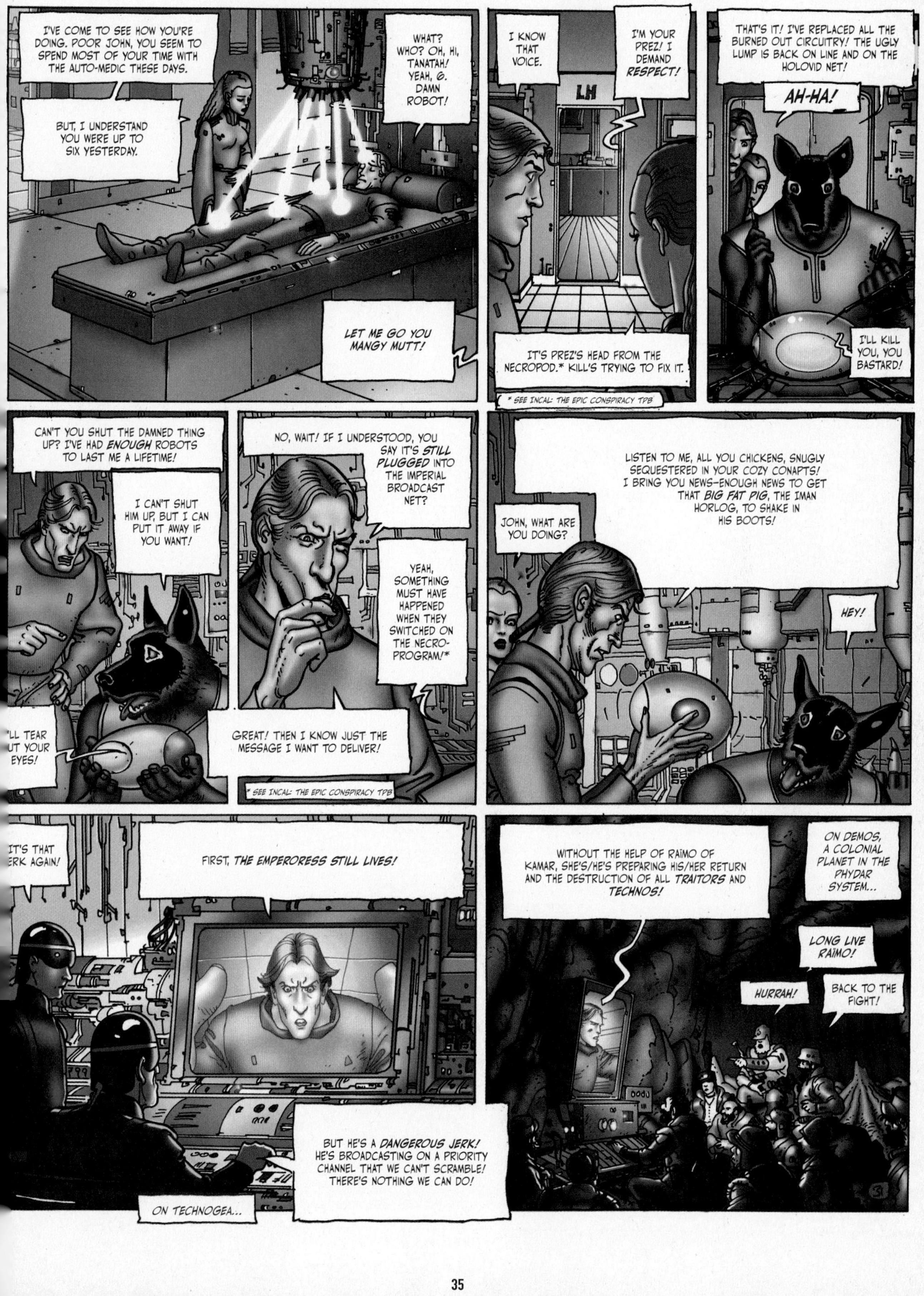
I'VE COME TO SEE HOW YOU'RE DOING. POOR JOHN, YOU SEEM TO SPEND MOST OF YOUR TIME WITH THE AUTO-MEDIC THESE DAYS.
BUT, I UNDERSTAND YOU WERE UP TO SIX YESTERDAY.
WHAT? WHO? OH, HI, TANATAH! YEAH, 6. DAMN ROBOT!
LET ME GO YOU MANGY MUTT!
I KNOW THAT VOICE.
I'M YOUR PREZ! I DEMAND RESPECT!
LH
IT'S PREZ'S HEAD FROM THE NECROPOD.* KILL'S TRYING TO FIX IT.
* SEE INCAL: THE EPIC CONSPIRACY TPB
THAT'S IT! I'VE REPLACED ALL THE BURNED OUT CIRCUITRY! THE UGLY LUMP IS BACK ON LINE AND ON THE HOLOVID NET!
AH-HA!
I'LL KILL YOU, YOU BASTARD!
CAN'T YOU SHUT THE DAMNED THING UP? I'VE HAD ENOUGH ROBOTS TO LAST ME A LIFETIME!
I CAN'T SHUT HIM UP, BUT I CAN PUT IT AWAY IF YOU WANT!
'LL TEAR UT YOUR EYES!
NO, WAIT! IF I UNDERSTOOD, YOU SAY IT'S STILL PLUGGED INTO THE IMPERIAL BROADCAST NET?
YEAH, SOMETHING MUST HAVE HAPPENED WHEN THEY SWITCHED ON THE NECRO-PROGRAM!*
GREAT! THEN I KNOW JUST THE MESSAGE I WANT TO DELIVER!
* SEE INCAL: THE EPIC CONSPIRACY TPB
LISTEN TO ME, ALL YOU CHICKENS, SNUGLY SEQUESTERED IN YOUR COZY CONAPTS! I BRING YOU NEWS—ENOUGH NEWS TO GET THAT BIG FAT PIG, THE IMAN HORLOG, TO SHAKE IN HIS BOOTS!
JOHN, WHAT ARE YOU DOING?
HEY!
IT'S THAT ERK AGAIN!
FIRST, THE EMPERORESS STILL LIVES!
BUT HE'S A DANGEROUS JERK! HE'S BROADCASTING ON A PRIORITY CHANNEL THAT WE CAN'T SCRAMBLE! THERE'S NOTHING WE CAN DO!
ON TECHNOGEA...
WITHOUT THE HELP OF RAÏMO OF KAMAR, SHE'S/HE'S PREPARING HIS/HER RETURN AND THE DESTRUCTION OF ALL TRAITORS AND TECHNOS!
ON DEMOS, A COLONIAL PLANET IN THE PHYDAR SYSTEM...
LONG LIVE RAÏMO!
HURRAH!
BACK TO THE FIGHT!

BUT, THE WORST IS THAT BECAUSE OF THE TRAITORS, *10,000 SHADOW EGGS* ARE GOING TO ATTACK AND DEVOUR OUR SUNS!

ON ALYX III...

WHAT!?

HUH!?

CURSES!

ON BADMEK...

YOUR MAJESTY, THE REBELS NOW CONTROL THE HIGH TERMITARIUM! THE SITUATION IS BECOMING MORE CRITICAL!

DAMN! IT'S BECAUSE OF THAT MADMAN ON THE HOLOVID!

AND ON THE PLANET OF GOLD...

WHAT?! THIS IS INTOLERABLE! 300 RIM WORLDS HAVE JOINED THE REBELLION! A THOUSAND MORE ARE RIOTING! EVEN THIS PLANET IS BEING TORN APART! I'LL USE THE PURPLE ENDOGUARD TO BRING THE REBELS TO THEIR KNEES! I'LL ORDER A *BLOODBATH!*

PREPARE A SHIP FOR TECHNOGEA! I WANT TO HAVE A WORD OR TWO WITH THAT TECHNO-CENTREUR!

RIGHT-O BIG BOY! CAN'T LET THOSE *PEASANTS* WALK ALL OVER US!

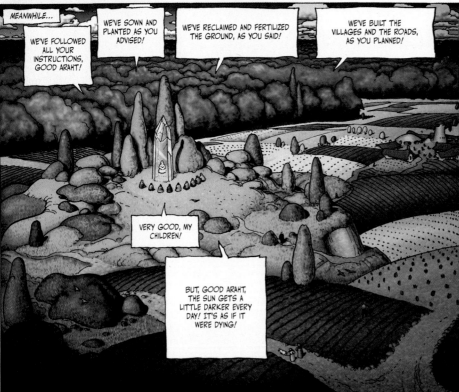

MEANWHILE...

WE'VE FOLLOWED ALL YOUR INSTRUCTIONS, GOOD ARAHT!

WE'VE SOWN AND PLANTED AS YOU ADVISED!

WE'VE RECLAIMED AND FERTILIZED THE GROUND, AS YOU SAID!

WE'VE BUILT THE VILLAGES AND THE ROADS, AS YOU PLANNED!

VERY GOOD, MY CHILDREN!

BUT, GOOD ARAHT, THE SUN GETS A LITTLE DARKER EVERY DAY! IT'S AS IF IT WERE DYING!

IT IS NOTHING! DO NOT CONCERN YOURSELVES! CONCENTRATE ON MAKING PROGRESS IN YOUR TASKS!

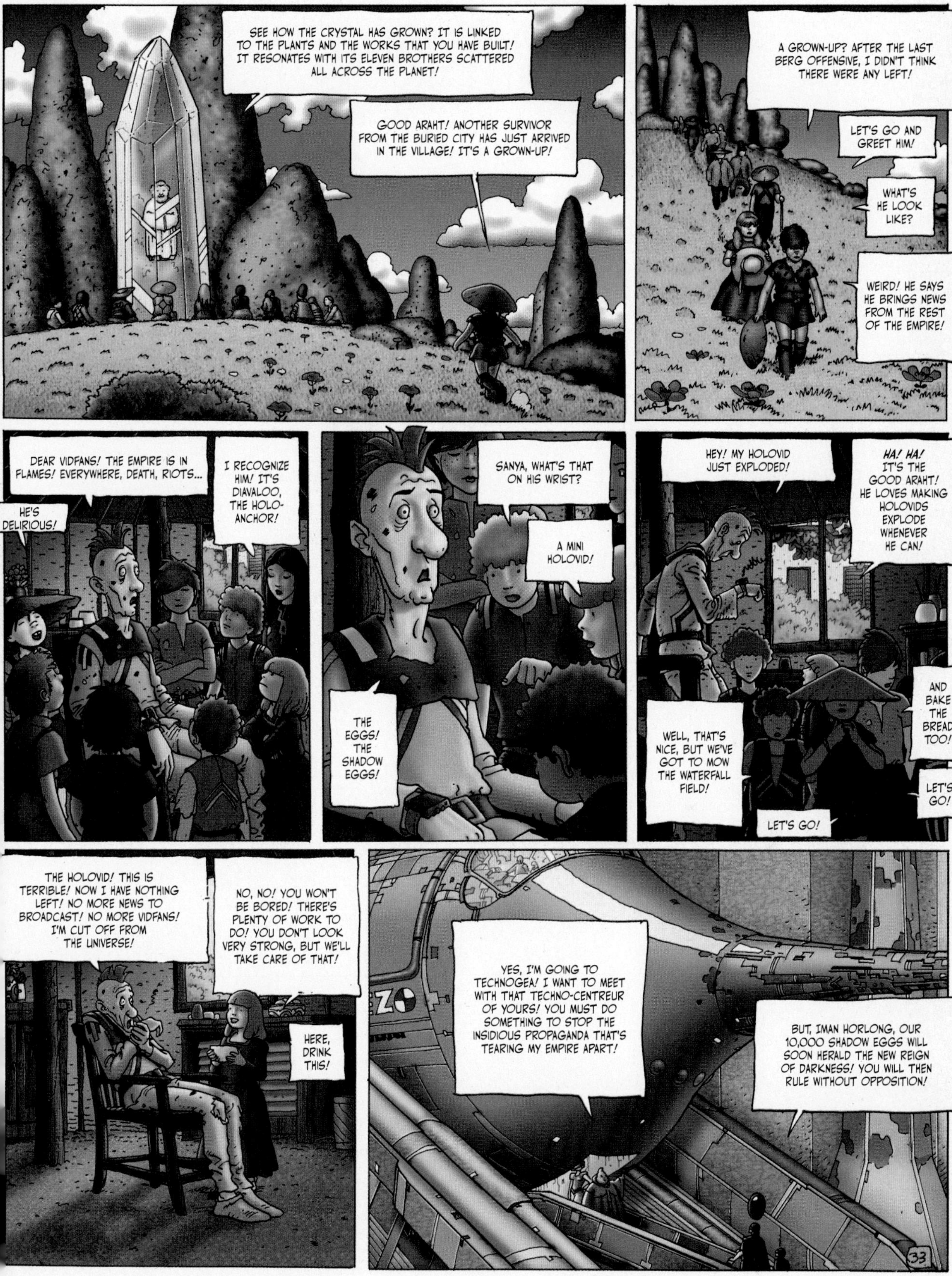
SEE HOW THE CRYSTAL HAS GROWN? IT IS LINKED TO THE PLANTS AND THE WORKS THAT YOU HAVE BUILT! IT RESONATES WITH ITS ELEVEN BROTHERS SCATTERED ALL ACROSS THE PLANET!
GOOD ARAHT! ANOTHER SURVIVOR FROM THE BURIED CITY HAS JUST ARRIVED IN THE VILLAGE! IT'S A GROWN-UP!
A GROWN-UP? AFTER THE LAST BERG OFFENSIVE, I DIDN'T THINK THERE WERE ANY LEFT!
LET'S GO AND GREET HIM!
WHAT'S HE LOOK LIKE?
WEIRD! HE SAYS HE BRINGS NEWS FROM THE REST OF THE EMPIRE!
DEAR VIDFANS! THE EMPIRE IS IN FLAMES! EVERYWHERE, DEATH, RIOTS...
HE'S DELIRIOUS!
I RECOGNIZE HIM! IT'S DIAVALOO, THE HOLO-ANCHOR!
SANYA, WHAT'S THAT ON HIS WRIST?
A MINI HOLOVID!
THE EGGS! THE SHADOW EGGS!
HEY! MY HOLOVID JUST EXPLODED!
HA! HA! IT'S THE GOOD ARAHT! HE LOVES MAKING HOLOVIDS EXPLODE WHENEVER HE CAN!
WELL, THAT'S NICE, BUT WE'VE GOT TO MOW THE WATERFALL FIELD!
AND BAKE THE BREAD TOO!
LET'S GO!
LET'S GO!
THE HOLOVID! THIS IS TERRIBLE! NOW I HAVE NOTHING LEFT! NO MORE NEWS TO BROADCAST! NO MORE VIDFANS! I'M CUT OFF FROM THE UNIVERSE!
NO, NO! YOU WON'T BE BORED! THERE'S PLENTY OF WORK TO DO! YOU DON'T LOOK VERY STRONG, BUT WE'LL TAKE CARE OF THAT!
HERE, DRINK THIS!
YES, I'M GOING TO TECHNOGEA! I WANT TO MEET WITH THAT TECHNO-CENTREUR OF YOURS! YOU MUST DO SOMETHING TO STOP THE INSIDIOUS PROPAGANDA THAT'S TEARING MY EMPIRE APART!
BUT, IMAN HORLONG, OUR 10,000 SHADOW EGGS WILL SOON HERALD THE NEW REIGN OF DARKNESS! YOU WILL THEN RULE WITHOUT OPPOSITION!
33

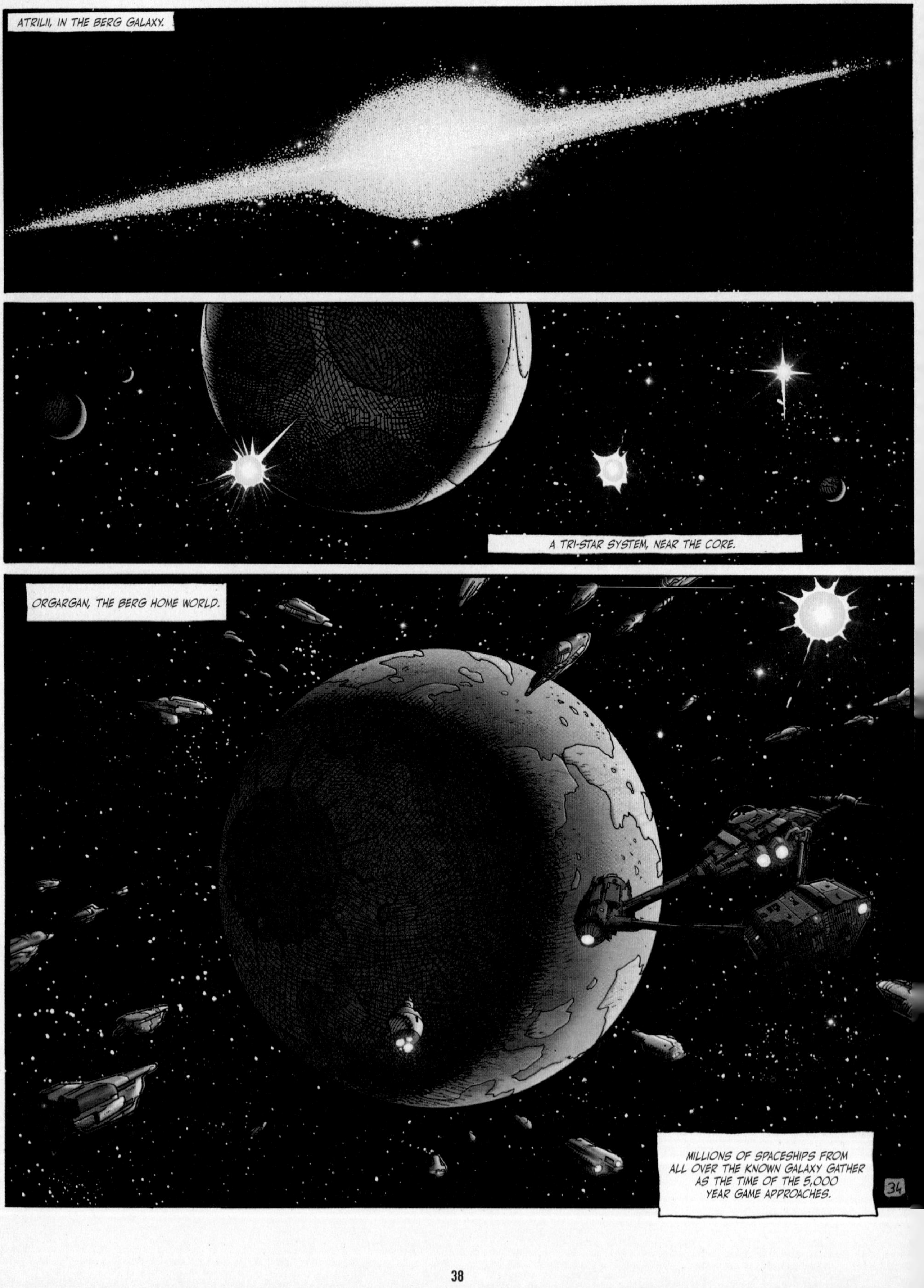
ATRILII, IN THE BERG GALAXY.
A TRI-STAR SYSTEM, NEAR THE CORE.
ORGARGAN, THE BERG HOME WORLD.
MILLIONS OF SPACESHIPS FROM ALL OVER THE KNOWN GALAXY GATHER AS THE TIME OF THE 5,000 YEAR GAME APPROACHES.
34

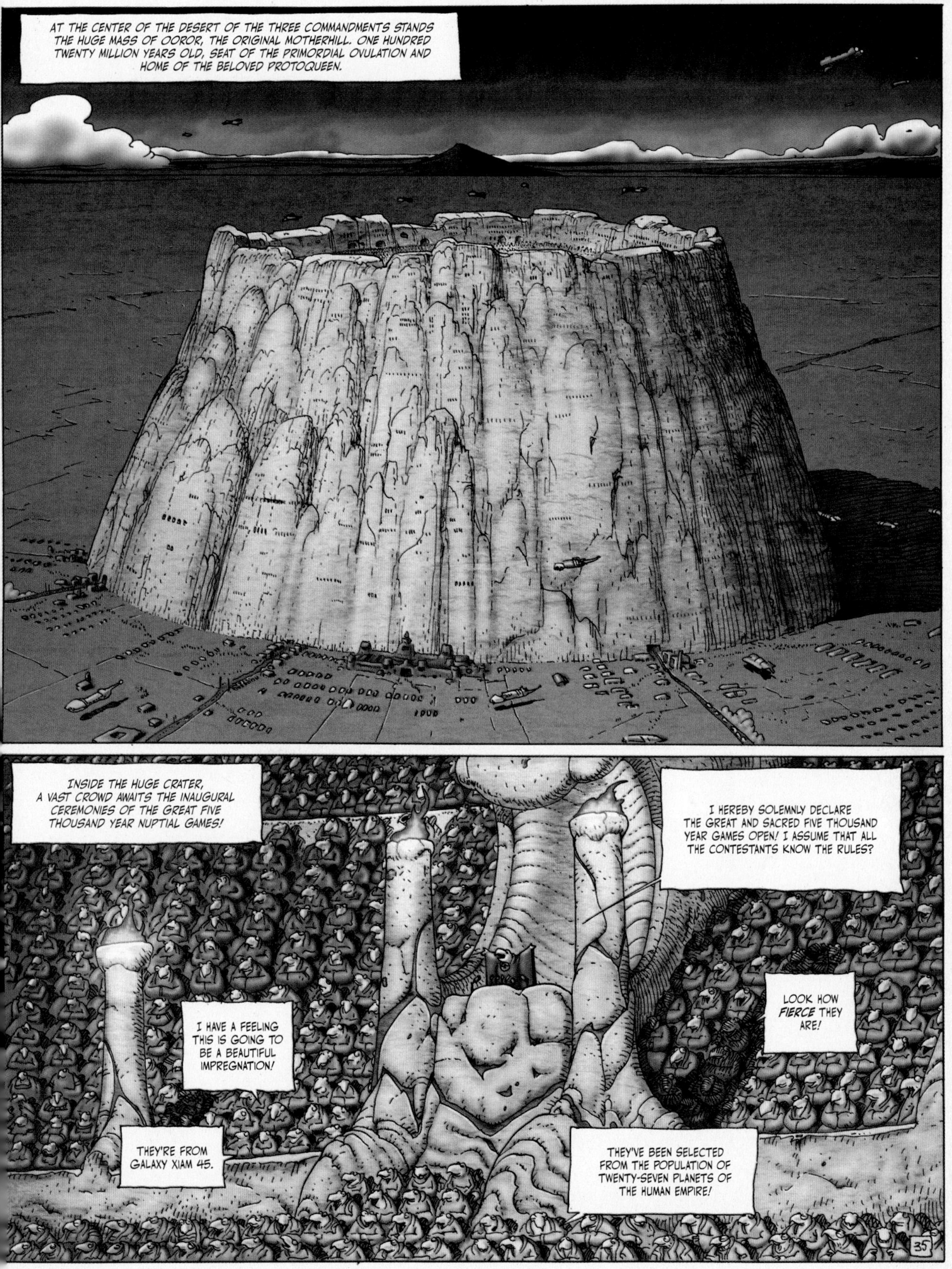
AT THE CENTER OF THE DESERT OF THE THREE COMMANDMENTS STANDS THE HUGE MASS OF OOROR, THE ORIGINAL MOTHERHILL. ONE HUNDRED TWENTY MILLION YEARS OLD, SEAT OF THE PRIMORDIAL OVULATION AND HOME OF THE BELOVED PROTOQUEEN.
INSIDE THE HUGE CRATER, A VAST CROWD AWAITS THE INAUGURAL CEREMONIES OF THE GREAT FIVE THOUSAND YEAR NUPTIAL GAMES!
I HEREBY SOLEMNLY DECLARE THE GREAT AND SACRED FIVE THOUSAND YEAR GAMES OPEN! I ASSUME THAT ALL THE CONTESTANTS KNOW THE RULES?
I HAVE A FEELING THIS IS GOING TO BE A BEAUTIFUL IMPREGNATION!
LOOK HOW *FIERCE* THEY ARE!
THEY'RE FROM GALAXY XIAM 45.
THEY'VE BEEN SELECTED FROM THE POPULATION OF TWENTY-SEVEN PLANETS OF THE HUMAN EMPIRE!
35

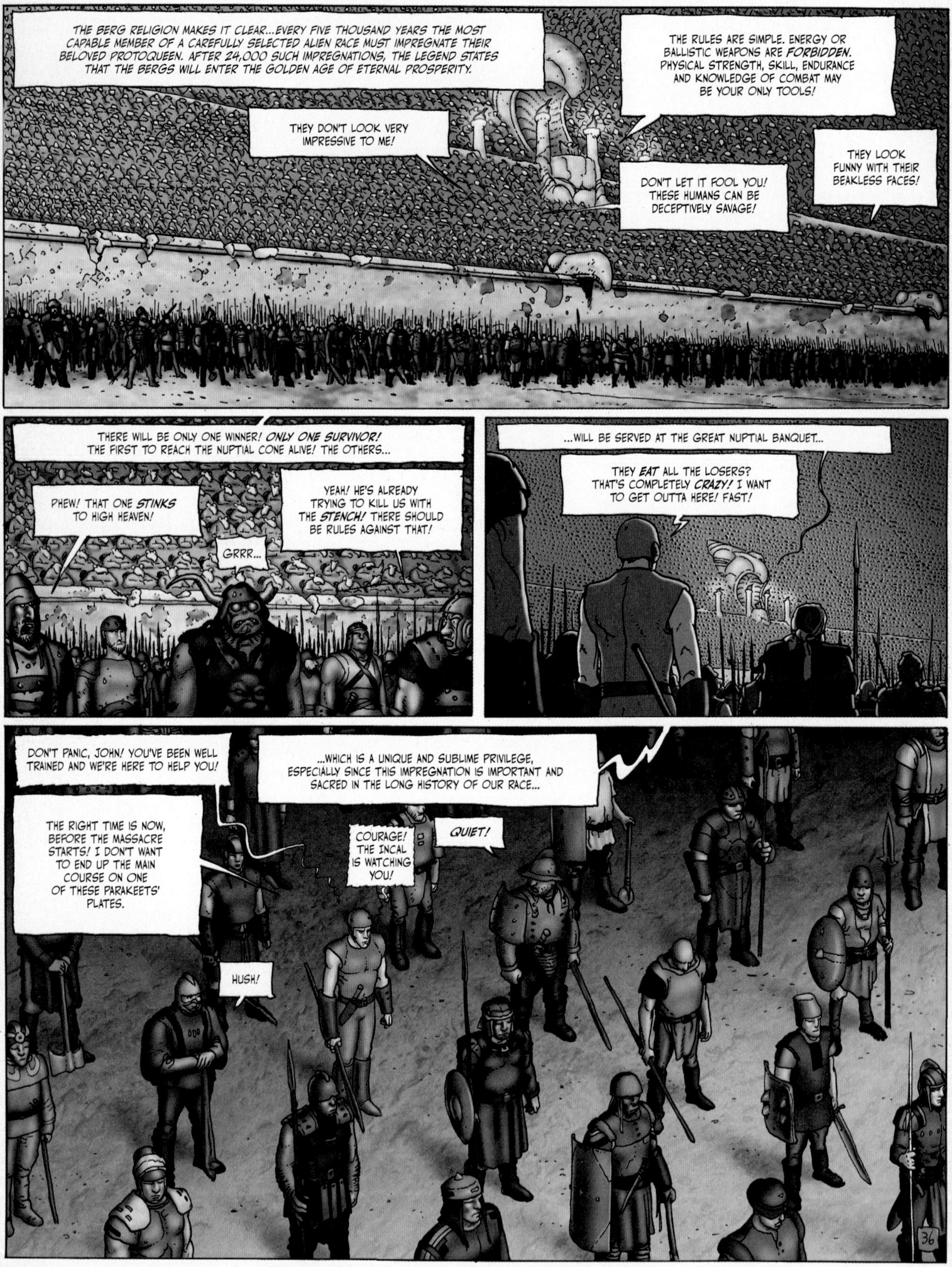
THE BERG RELIGION MAKES IT CLEAR...EVERY FIVE THOUSAND YEARS THE MOST CAPABLE MEMBER OF A CAREFULLY SELECTED ALIEN RACE MUST IMPREGNATE THEIR BELOVED PROTOQUEEN. AFTER 24,000 SUCH IMPREGNATIONS, THE LEGEND STATES THAT THE BERGS WILL ENTER THE GOLDEN AGE OF ETERNAL PROSPERITY.
THE RULES ARE SIMPLE. ENERGY OR BALLISTIC WEAPONS ARE FORBIDDEN. PHYSICAL STRENGTH, SKILL, ENDURANCE AND KNOWLEDGE OF COMBAT MAY BE YOUR ONLY TOOLS!
THEY DON'T LOOK VERY IMPRESSIVE TO ME!
DON'T LET IT FOOL YOU! THESE HUMANS CAN BE DECEPTIVELY SAVAGE!
THEY LOOK FUNNY WITH THEIR BEAKLESS FACES!
THERE WILL BE ONLY ONE WINNER! ONLY ONE SURVIVOR! THE FIRST TO REACH THE NUPTIAL CONE ALIVE! THE OTHERS...
PHEW! THAT ONE STINKS TO HIGH HEAVEN!
YEAH! HE'S ALREADY TRYING TO KILL US WITH THE STENCH! THERE SHOULD BE RULES AGAINST THAT!
GRRR...
...WILL BE SERVED AT THE GREAT NUPTIAL BANQUET...
THEY EAT ALL THE LOSERS? THAT'S COMPLETELY CRAZY! I WANT TO GET OUTTA HERE! FAST!
DON'T PANIC, JOHN! YOU'VE BEEN WELL TRAINED AND WE'RE HERE TO HELP YOU!
...WHICH IS A UNIQUE AND SUBLIME PRIVILEGE, ESPECIALLY SINCE THIS IMPREGNATION IS IMPORTANT AND SACRED IN THE LONG HISTORY OF OUR RACE...
THE RIGHT TIME IS NOW, BEFORE THE MASSACRE STARTS! I DON'T WANT TO END UP THE MAIN COURSE ON ONE OF THESE PARAKEETS' PLATES.
COURAGE! THE INCAL IS WATCHING YOU!
QUIET!
HUSH!
36

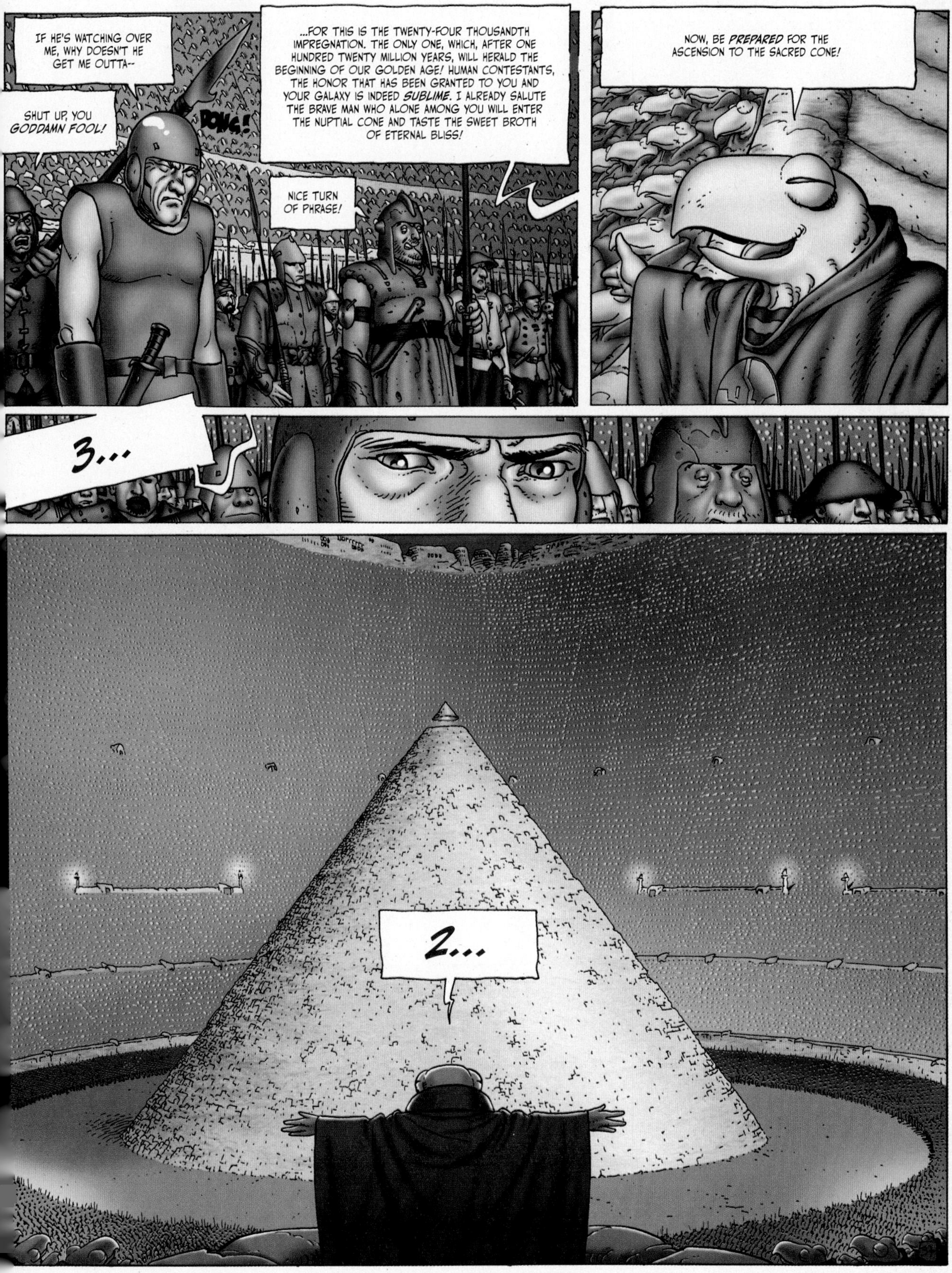
IF HE'S WATCHING OVER ME, WHY DOESN'T HE GET ME OUTTA--
SHUT UP, YOU GODDAMN FOOL!
BONG!
...FOR THIS IS THE TWENTY-FOUR THOUSANDTH IMPREGNATION. THE ONLY ONE, WHICH, AFTER ONE HUNDRED TWENTY MILLION YEARS, WILL HERALD THE BEGINNING OF OUR GOLDEN AGE! HUMAN CONTESTANTS, THE HONOR THAT HAS BEEN GRANTED TO YOU AND YOUR GALAXY IS INDEED SUBLIME. I ALREADY SALUTE THE BRAVE MAN WHO ALONE AMONG YOU WILL ENTER THE NUPTIAL CONE AND TASTE THE SWEET BROTH OF ETERNAL BLISS!
NICE TURN OF PHRASE!
NOW, BE PREPARED FOR THE ASCENSION TO THE SACRED CONE!
3...
2...

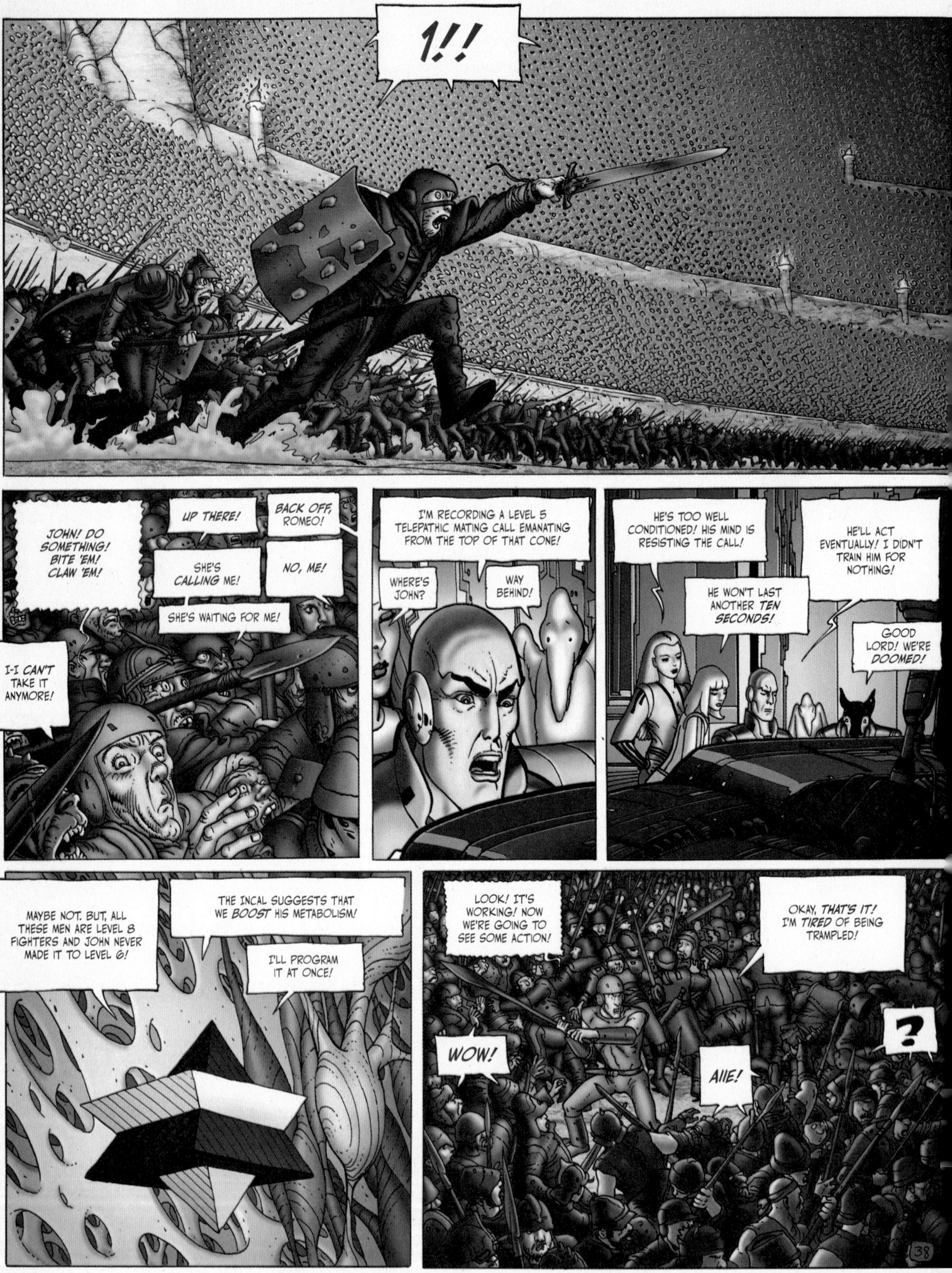

1!!
JOHN! DO SOMETHING! BITE 'EM! CLAW 'EM!
UP THERE!
BACK OFF, ROMEO!
SHE'S CALLING ME!
NO, ME!
SHE'S WAITING FOR ME!
I-I CAN'T TAKE IT ANYMORE!
I'M RECORDING A LEVEL 5 TELEPATHIC MATING CALL EMANATING FROM THE TOP OF THAT CONE!
WHERE'S JOHN?
WAY BEHIND!
HE'S TOO WELL CONDITIONED! HIS MIND IS RESISTING THE CALL!
HE WON'T LAST ANOTHER TEN SECONDS!
HE'LL ACT EVENTUALLY! I DIDN'T TRAIN HIM FOR NOTHING!
GOOD LORD! WE'RE DOOMED!
MAYBE NOT. BUT, ALL THESE MEN ARE LEVEL 8 FIGHTERS AND JOHN NEVER MADE IT TO LEVEL 6!
THE INCAL SUGGESTS THAT WE BOOST HIS METABOLISM!
I'LL PROGRAM IT AT ONCE!
LOOK! IT'S WORKING! NOW WE'RE GOING TO SEE SOME ACTION!
OKAY, THAT'S IT! I'M TIRED OF BEING TRAMPLED!
WOW!
AIIE!
?
38

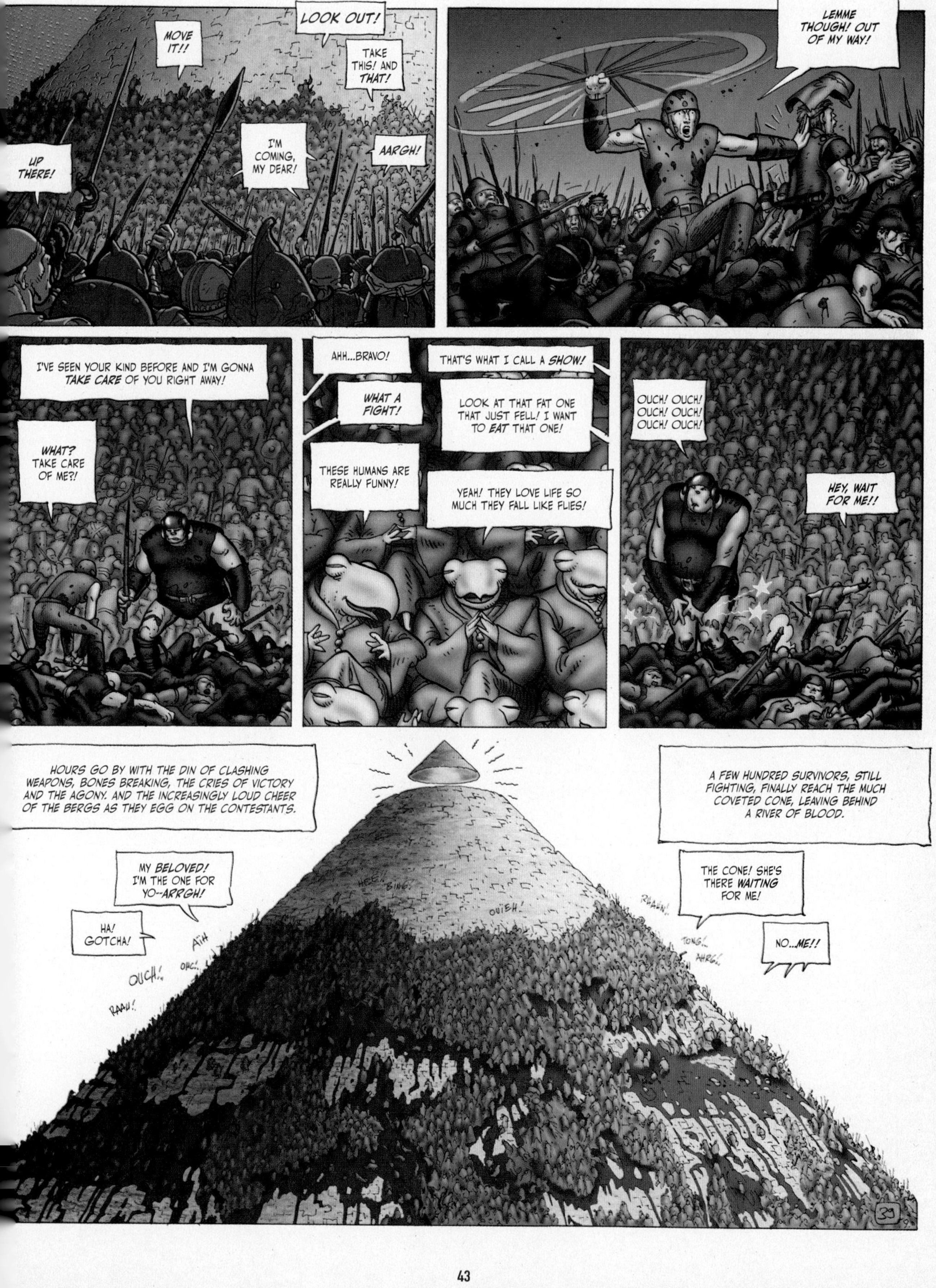

LOOK OUT!
MOVE IT!!
TAKE THIS! AND THAT!
UP THERE!
I'M COMING, MY DEAR!
AARGH!
LEMME THOUGH! OUT OF MY WAY!
I'VE SEEN YOUR KIND BEFORE AND I'M GONNA TAKE CARE OF YOU RIGHT AWAY!
WHAT? TAKE CARE OF ME?!
AHH...BRAVO!
THAT'S WHAT I CALL A SHOW!
WHAT A FIGHT!
LOOK AT THAT FAT ONE THAT JUST FELL! I WANT TO EAT THAT ONE!
THESE HUMANS ARE REALLY FUNNY!
YEAH! THEY LOVE LIFE SO MUCH THEY FALL LIKE FLIES!
OUCH! OUCH! OUCH! OUCH! OUCH! OUCH!
HEY, WAIT FOR ME!!
HOURS GO BY WITH THE DIN OF CLASHING WEAPONS, BONES BREAKING, THE CRIES OF VICTORY AND THE AGONY. AND THE INCREASINGLY LOUD CHEER OF THE BERGS AS THEY EGG ON THE CONTESTANTS.
A FEW HUNDRED SURVIVORS, STILL FIGHTING, FINALLY REACH THE MUCH COVETED CONE, LEAVING BEHIND A RIVER OF BLOOD.
MY BELOVED! I'M THE ONE FOR YO--ARRGH!
HA! GOTCHA!
AÏH
OHC!
OUCH!
RAAH!
BING!
OUÏEH!
RAAAH!
TONG!
AHRG!
THE CONE! SHE'S THERE WAITING FOR ME!
NO...ME!!
39

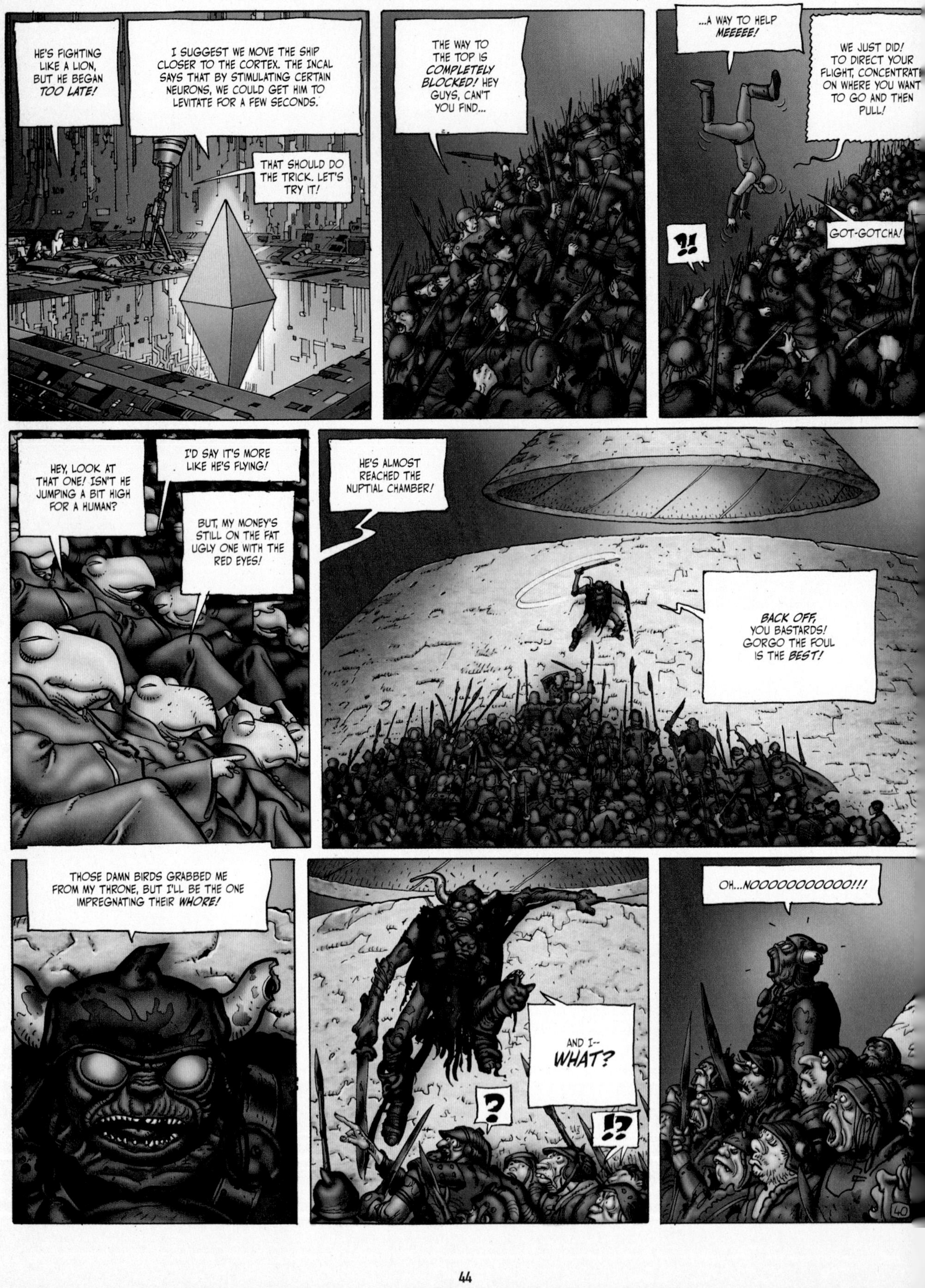

HE'S FIGHTING LIKE A LION, BUT HE BEGAN *TOO LATE!*
I SUGGEST WE MOVE THE SHIP CLOSER TO THE CORTEX. THE INCAL SAYS THAT BY STIMULATING CERTAIN NEURONS, WE COULD GET HIM TO LEVITATE FOR A FEW SECONDS.
THAT SHOULD DO THE TRICK. LET'S TRY IT!
THE WAY TO THE TOP IS *COMPLETELY BLOCKED!* HEY GUYS, CAN'T YOU FIND...
...A WAY TO HELP *MEEEEE!*
WE JUST DID! TO DIRECT YOUR FLIGHT, CONCENTRATE ON WHERE YOU WANT TO GO AND THEN PULL!
?!
GOT-GOTCHA!
HEY, LOOK AT THAT ONE! ISN'T HE JUMPING A BIT HIGH FOR A HUMAN?
I'D SAY IT'S MORE LIKE HE'S FLYING!
BUT, MY MONEY'S STILL ON THE FAT UGLY ONE WITH THE RED EYES!
HE'S ALMOST REACHED THE NUPTIAL CHAMBER!
BACK OFF, YOU BASTARDS! GORGO THE FOUL IS THE *BEST!*
THOSE DAMN BIRDS GRABBED ME FROM MY THRONE, BUT I'LL BE THE ONE IMPREGNATING THEIR *WHORE!*
AND I-- *WHAT?*
?
!?
OH...*NOOOOOOOOOOO!!!*
40

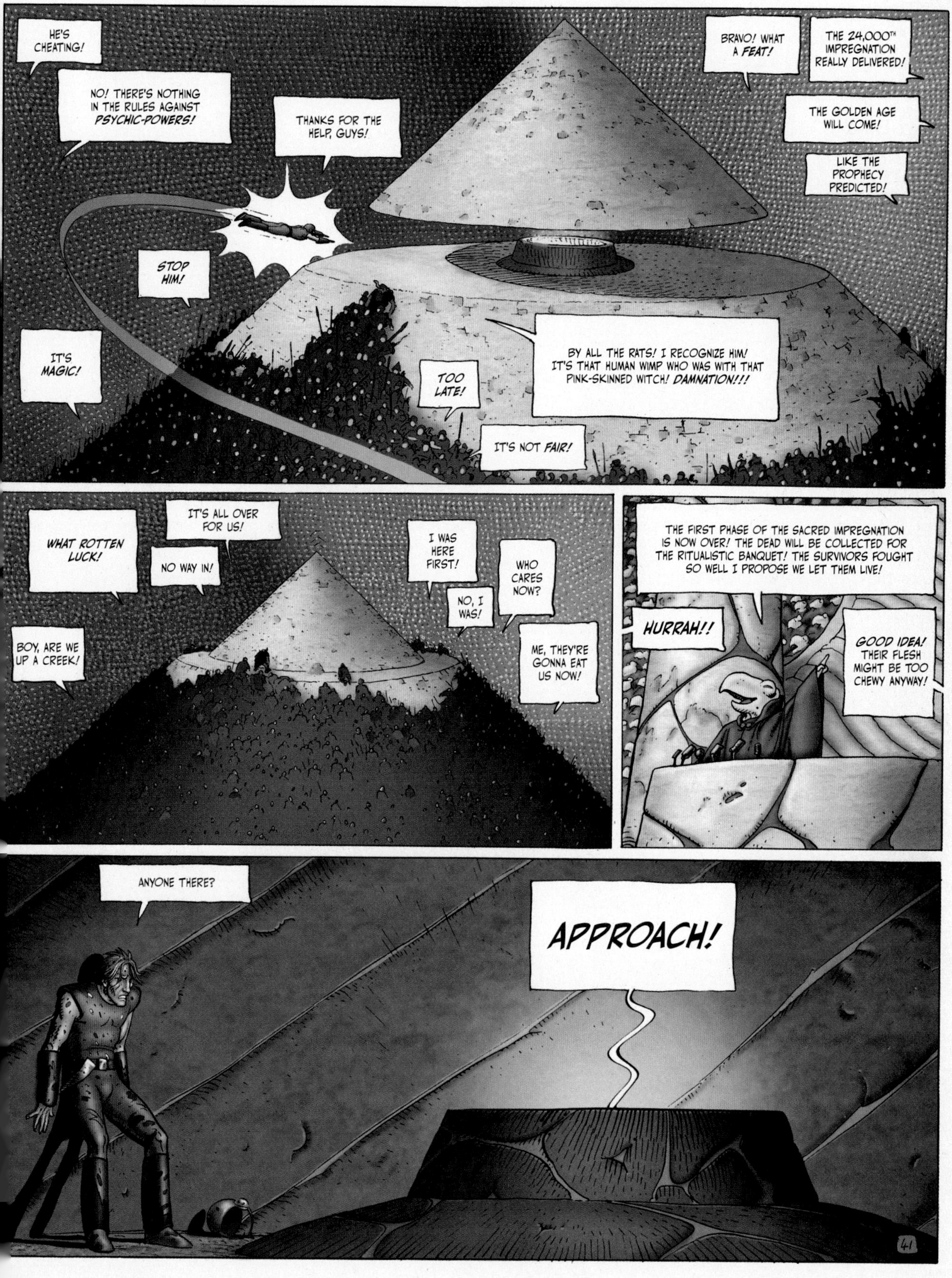
HE'S CHEATING!
NO! THERE'S NOTHING IN THE RULES AGAINST PSYCHIC-POWERS!
THANKS FOR THE HELP, GUYS!
BRAVO! WHAT A FEAT!
THE 24,000TH IMPREGNATION REALLY DELIVERED!
THE GOLDEN AGE WILL COME!
LIKE THE PROPHECY PREDICTED!
STOP HIM!
IT'S MAGIC!
TOO LATE!
BY ALL THE RATS! I RECOGNIZE HIM! IT'S THAT HUMAN WIMP WHO WAS WITH THAT PINK-SKINNED WITCH! DAMNATION!!!
IT'S NOT FAIR!
WHAT ROTTEN LUCK!
IT'S ALL OVER FOR US!
NO WAY IN!
BOY, ARE WE UP A CREEK!
I WAS HERE FIRST!
NO, I WAS!
WHO CARES NOW?
ME, THEY'RE GONNA EAT US NOW!
THE FIRST PHASE OF THE SACRED IMPREGNATION IS NOW OVER! THE DEAD WILL BE COLLECTED FOR THE RITUALISTIC BANQUET! THE SURVIVORS FOUGHT SO WELL I PROPOSE WE LET THEM LIVE!
HURRAH!!
GOOD IDEA! THEIR FLESH MIGHT BE TOO CHEWY ANYWAY!
ANYONE THERE?
APPROACH!
41

THE ROYAL WEDDING

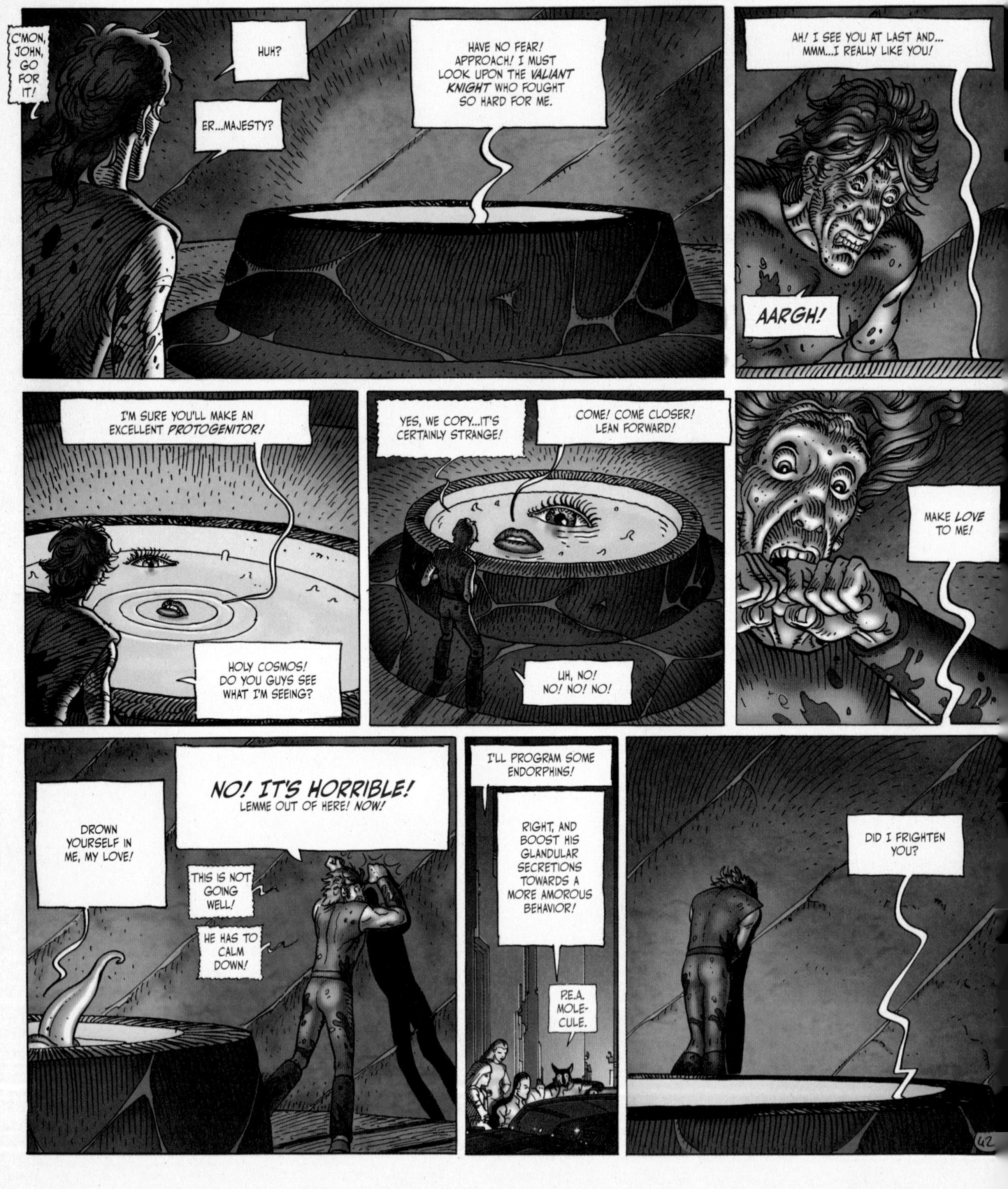
C'MON, JOHN, GO FOR IT!
HUH?
ER...MAJESTY?
HAVE NO FEAR! APPROACH! I MUST LOOK UPON THE VALIANT KNIGHT WHO FOUGHT SO HARD FOR ME.
AH! I SEE YOU AT LAST AND... MMM...I REALLY LIKE YOU!
AARGH!
I'M SURE YOU'LL MAKE AN EXCELLENT PROTOGENITOR!
HOLY COSMOS! DO YOU GUYS SEE WHAT I'M SEEING?
YES, WE COPY...IT'S CERTAINLY STRANGE!
COME! COME CLOSER! LEAN FORWARD!
UH, NO! NO! NO! NO!
MAKE LOVE TO ME!
DROWN YOURSELF IN ME, MY LOVE!
NO! IT'S HORRIBLE! LEMME OUT OF HERE! NOW!
THIS IS NOT GOING WELL!
HE HAS TO CALM DOWN!
I'LL PROGRAM SOME ENDORPHINS!
RIGHT, AND BOOST HIS GLANDULAR SECRETIONS TOWARDS A MORE AMOROUS BEHAVIOR!
P.E.A. MOLE-CULE.
DID I FRIGHTEN YOU?
42

IT'S...IT'S A **NIGHTMARE.**

SOB!

FORGIVE ME! I SHOULD HAVE REMEMBERED!

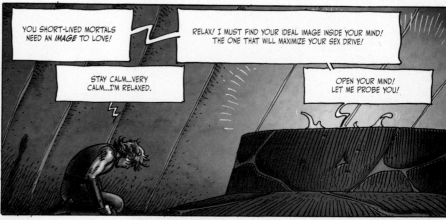

YOU SHORT-LIVED MORTALS NEED AN *IMAGE* TO LOVE!

STAY CALM...VERY CALM...I'M RELAXED.

RELAX! I MUST FIND YOUR IDEAL IMAGE INSIDE YOUR MIND! THE ONE THAT WILL MAXIMIZE YOUR SEX DRIVE!

OPEN YOUR MIND! LET ME PROBE YOU!

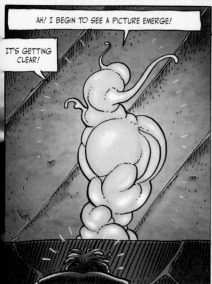

AH! I BEGIN TO SEE A PICTURE EMERGE!

IT'S GETTING CLEAR!

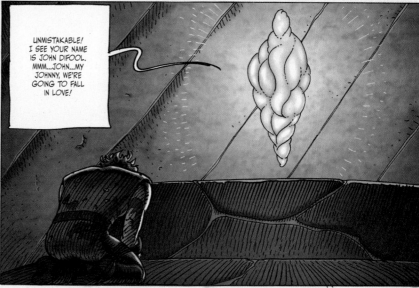

UNMISTAKABLE! I SEE YOUR NAME IS JOHN DIFOOL. MMM...JOHN...MY JOHNNY, WE'RE GOING TO FALL IN LOVE!

Madly IN LOVE!

I CAN'T, I WON'T!

?

JOHN DIFOOL, YOU *SPINELESS WIMP!* WHERE'S YOUR VAUNTED AGGRESSIVENESS? GO FOR IT! *DO IT!*

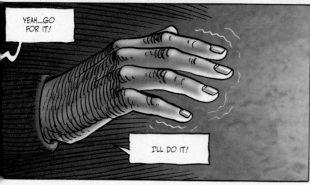

YEAH...GO FOR IT!

I'LL DO IT!

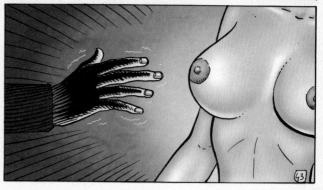

43

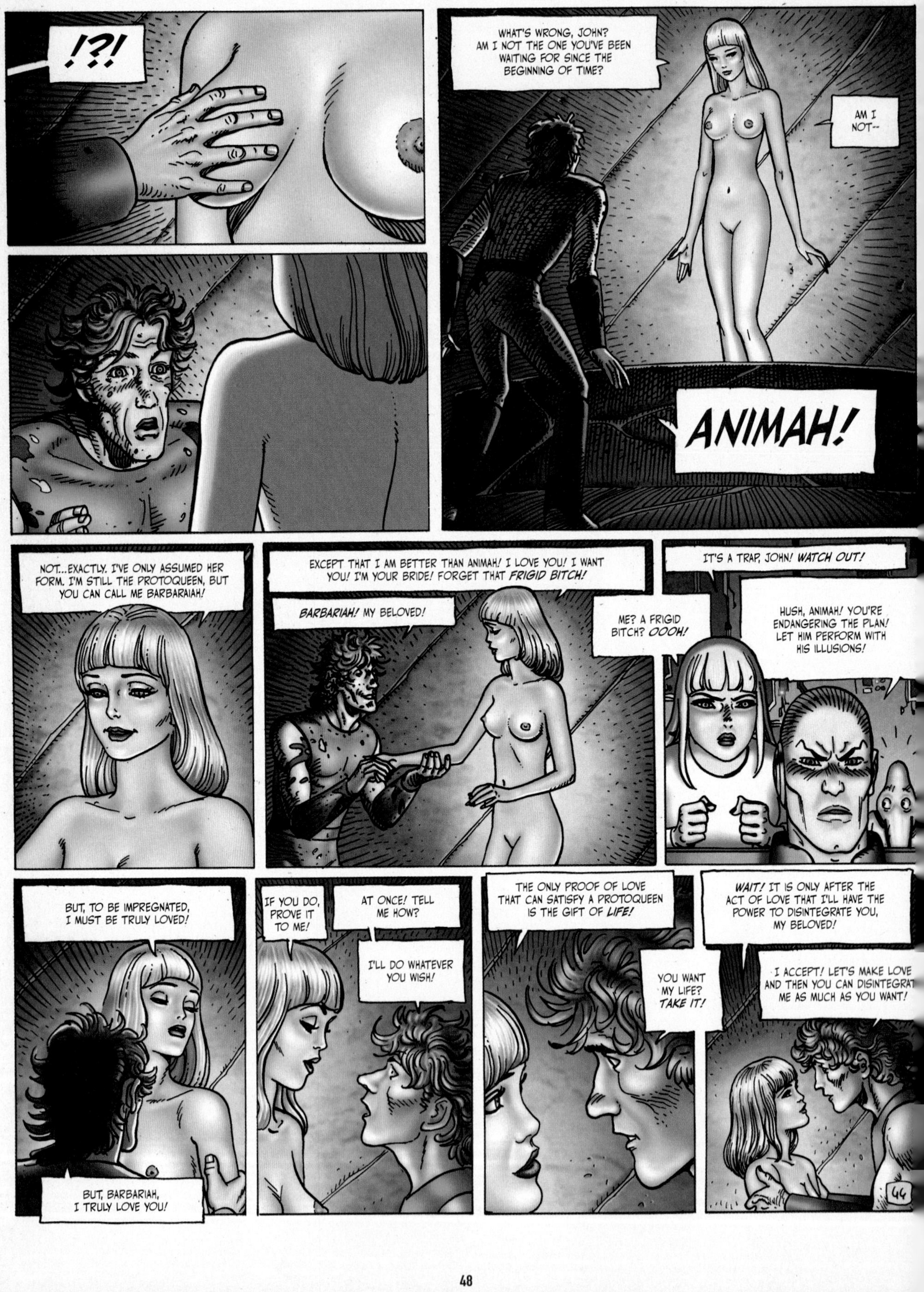
!?!
WHAT'S WRONG, JOHN? AM I NOT THE ONE YOU'VE BEEN WAITING FOR SINCE THE BEGINNING OF TIME?
AM I NOT--
ANIMAH!
NOT...EXACTLY. I'VE ONLY ASSUMED HER FORM. I'M STILL THE PROTOQUEEN, BUT YOU CAN CALL ME BARBARAIAH!
EXCEPT THAT I AM BETTER THAN ANIMAH! I LOVE YOU! I WANT YOU! I'M YOUR BRIDE! FORGET THAT FRIGID BITCH!
BARBARIAH! MY BELOVED!
ME? A FRIGID BITCH? OOOH!
IT'S A TRAP, JOHN! WATCH OUT!
HUSH, ANIMAH! YOU'RE ENDANGERING THE PLAN! LET HIM PERFORM WITH HIS ILLUSIONS!
BUT, TO BE IMPREGNATED, I MUST BE TRULY LOVED!
BUT, BARBARIAH, I TRULY LOVE YOU!
IF YOU DO, PROVE IT TO ME!
AT ONCE! TELL ME HOW?
I'LL DO WHATEVER YOU WISH!
THE ONLY PROOF OF LOVE THAT CAN SATISFY A PROTOQUEEN IS THE GIFT OF LIFE!
YOU WANT MY LIFE? TAKE IT!
WAIT! IT IS ONLY AFTER THE ACT OF LOVE THAT I'LL HAVE THE POWER TO DISINTEGRATE YOU, MY BELOVED!
I ACCEPT! LET'S MAKE LOVE AND THEN YOU CAN DISINTEGRAT ME AS MUCH AS YOU WANT!
44

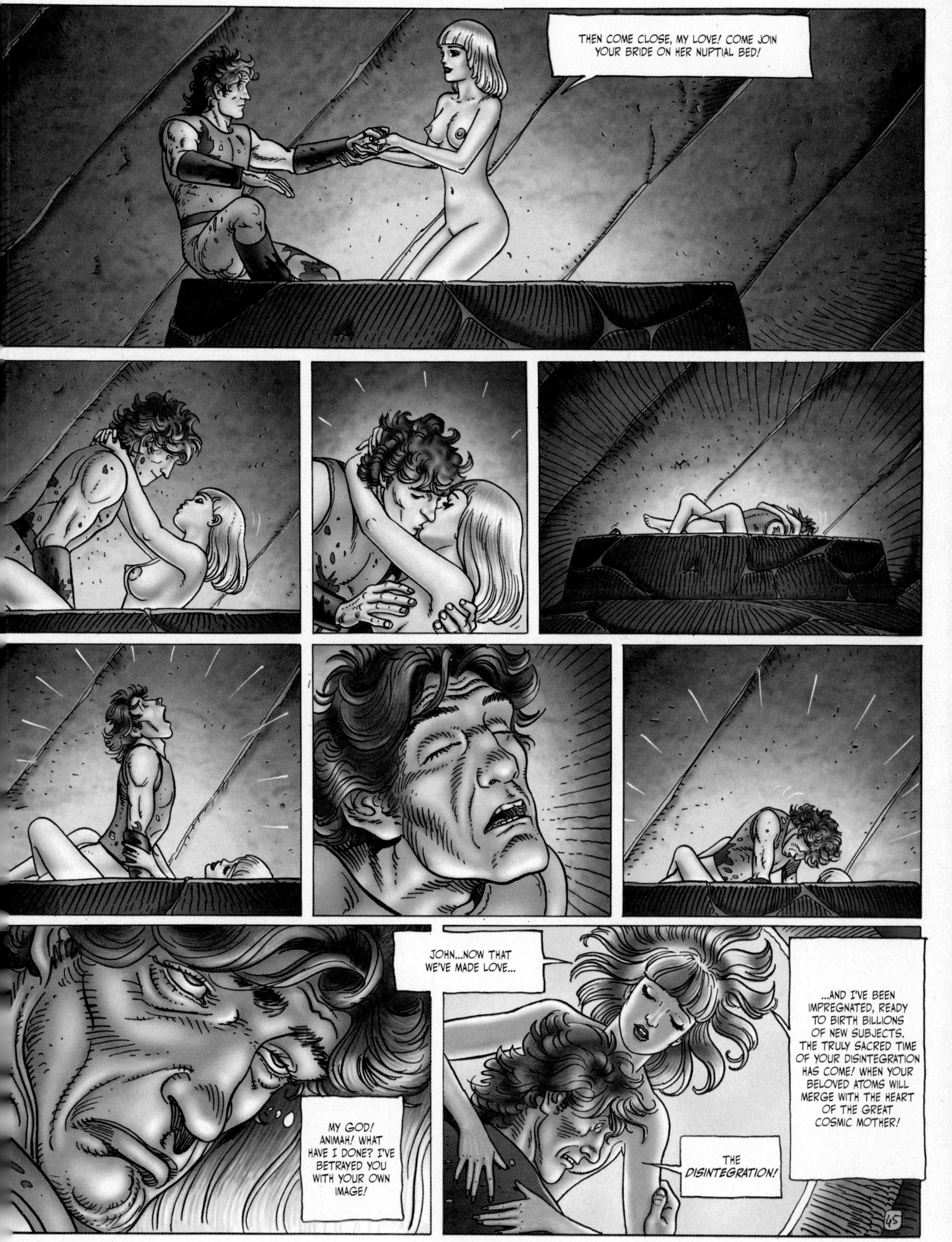
THEN COME CLOSE, MY LOVE! COME JOIN YOUR BRIDE ON HER NUPTIAL BED!
MY GOD! ANIMAH! WHAT HAVE I DONE? I'VE BETRAYED YOU WITH YOUR OWN IMAGE!
JOHN...NOW THAT WE'VE MADE LOVE...
...AND I'VE BEEN IMPREGNATED, READY TO BIRTH BILLIONS OF NEW SUBJECTS. THE TRULY SACRED TIME OF YOUR DISINTEGRATION HAS COME! WHEN YOUR BELOVED ATOMS WILL MERGE WITH THE HEART OF THE GREAT COSMIC MOTHER!
THE *DISINTEGRATION!*
45

NO, WAIT!

THE GREAT COSMIC MOTHER AWAITS YOU, JOHN DIFOOL!

STOP!

I'VE GOT A BETTER OFFER FOR YOU, BETTER THAN MY LIFE!

BETTER THAN YOUR LIFE?

DO SOMETHING! THAT *HORRIBLE CREATURE* IS TRYING TO DISINTEGRATE JOHN!

STOP WORRYING, ANIMAH! THE INCAL PLANNED FOR ALL THIS!

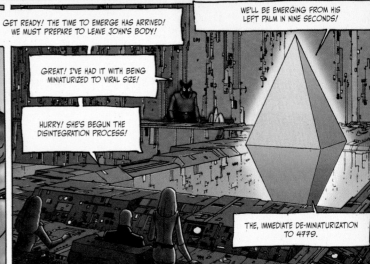

GET READY! THE TIME TO EMERGE HAS ARRIVED! WE MUST PREPARE TO LEAVE JOHN'S BODY!

GREAT! I'VE HAD IT WITH BEING MINIATURIZED TO VIRAL SIZE!

HURRY! SHE'S BEGUN THE DISINTEGRATION PROCESS!

WE'LL BE EMERGING FROM HIS LEFT PALM IN NINE SECONDS!

THE, IMMEDIATE DE-MINIATURIZATION TO 4779.

WHAT DARE YOU OFFER IN EXCHANGE FOR YOUR LIFE?

I HAVE SOMETHING IN MY HAND THAT THE ENTIRE BERG EMPIRE COVETS!

THE INCAL RIGHTFULLY BELONGS TO THE BERGS! THE HIDDEN PART OF THE PROPHECY REVEALS THAT IT IS THE KEY TO OUR GOLDEN AGE!

THEN, WATCH *THIS*!

THE *INCAL*!

THE *INCAL*!

THE INCAL! GIVE IT TO ME! NOW!

OKAY, BUT...

...YOU WON'T EVEN BE ABLE TO TOUCH IT UNLESS YOU GIVE ME WHAT I WANT FIRST!

OOOH!

A GIFT THAT I WILL CHOOSE FOR MYSELF!

ASK FOR WHAT YOU WANT AND YOU SHALL HAVE IT!

WELL...ER...I WANT...I WANT...

JOHN...

I WANT A SMALL PLANET OF PARADISE WITH LOTSA FLOWERS AND BANANAS, BEACHES AND HOMEO-WHORES OF ALL COLORS...

HE'S GONE MAD!

WHAT AN ASSHOLE! WHAT A JERK!

JOHN, STOP YOUR STUPID JOKE!

WE'VE WON. PREPARE TO EXPAND! WE'LL HAVE TO LEAD THE BERG FLEET TO TECHNOGEA!

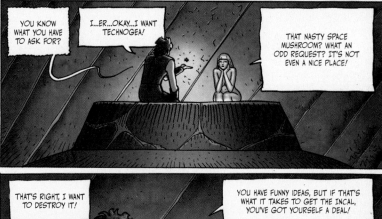

YOU KNOW WHAT YOU HAVE TO ASK FOR?

I...ER...OKAY...I WANT TECHNOGEA!

THAT NASTY SPACE MUSHROOM? WHAT AN ODD REQUEST? IT'S NOT EVEN A NICE PLACE!

THAT'S RIGHT, I WANT TO DESTROY IT!

YOU HAVE FUNNY IDEAS, BUT IF THAT'S WHAT IT TAKES TO GET THE INCAL, YOU'VE GOT YOURSELF A DEAL!

BUT, FIRST MY HUMAN FORM NEEDS MORE LOVE! COME, MY JOHNNY, LOVE ME WITH ALL YOUR PASSION!

MEANWHILE, LIGHT-YEARS AWAY IN THE HUMAN EMPIRE...
THIS SUN HAS A STRANGE SHAPE!
THAT'S BECAUSE IT IS DYING!
WE'RE JUST IN TIME, THEN!
PREPARE THE MEDUSA FOR PLASMA BURSTS! THAT SHADOW EGG MUST NOT ESCAPE!
NOT MORE THAN THE OTHERS.
CRAAC
CRRAAACCC
CRAAAAC
AND AFTER HOURS OF EFFORT...
TO THE COMET CLOUD! WE'LL STORE IT WITH THE OTHERS!
WE'VE WON! YET ANOTHER SUN RESCUED FROM THE DARKNESS!
IT WAS THE LAST ACTIVE ONE IN THE QUADRANT. OU VICTORY IS NEAR!
THE SHADOW EGG IS FINALLY RENDERED HARMLESS, SURROUNDED BY A COCOON OF SOLID PLASMA!

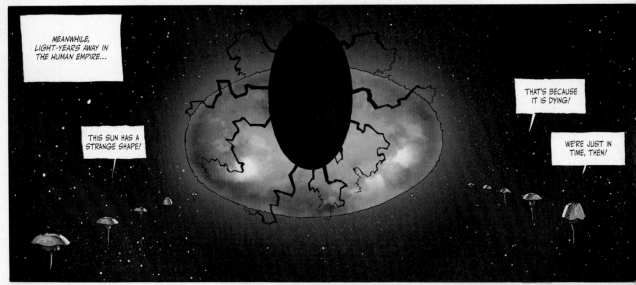

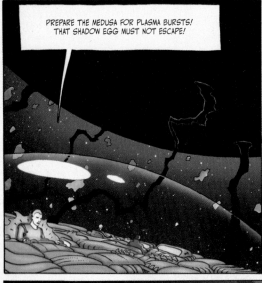

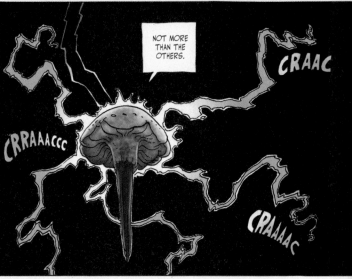

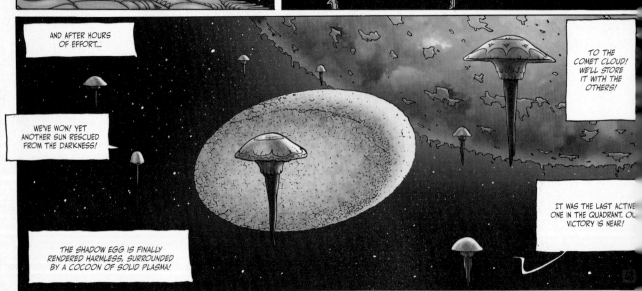

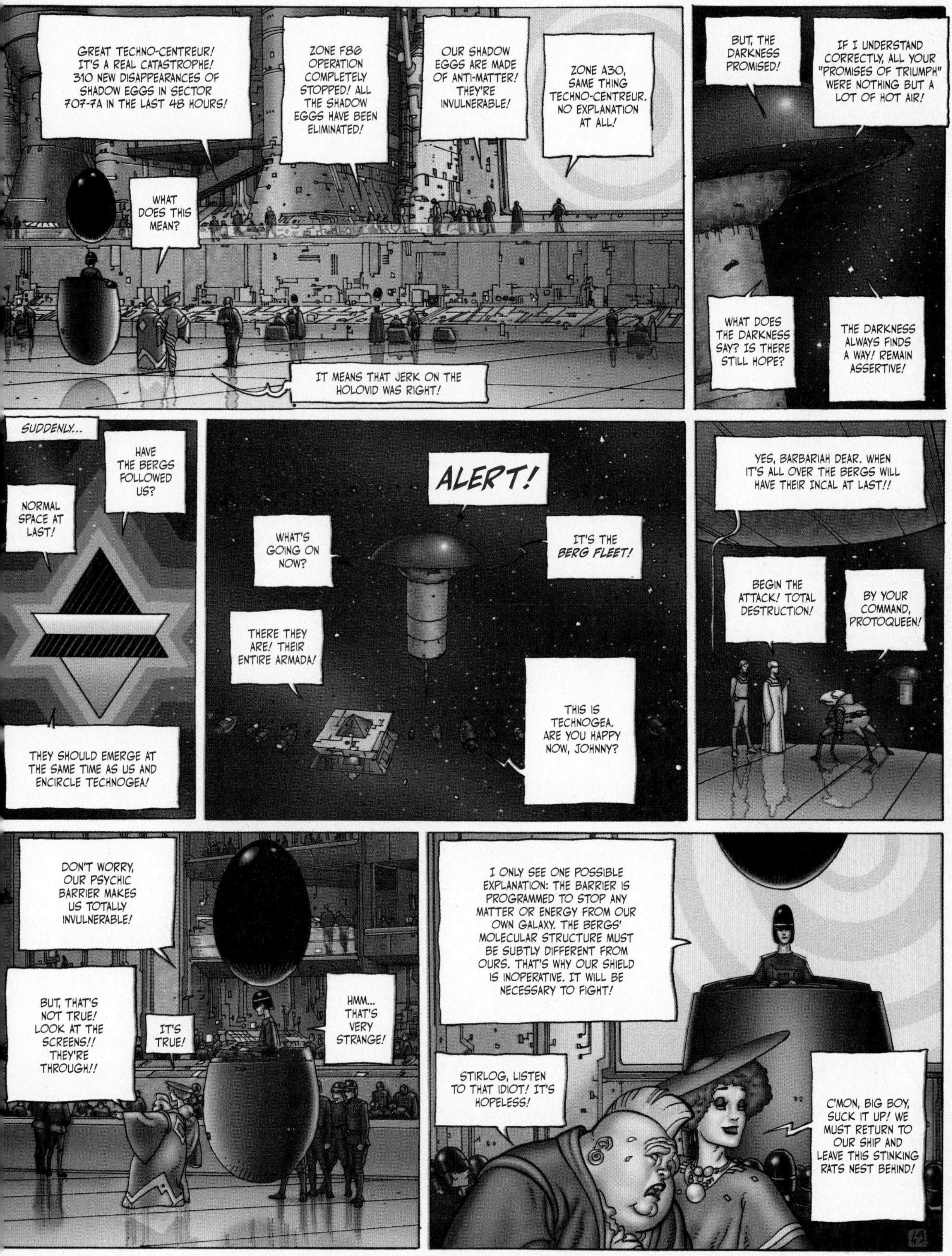
GREAT TECHNO-CENTREUR! IT'S A REAL CATASTROPHE! 310 NEW DISAPPEARANCES OF SHADOW EGGS IN SECTOR 707-7A IN THE LAST 48 HOURS!
WHAT DOES THIS MEAN?
ZONE F86 OPERATION COMPLETELY STOPPED! ALL THE SHADOW EGGS HAVE BEEN ELIMINATED!
OUR SHADOW EGGS ARE MADE OF ANTI-MATTER! THEY'RE INVULNERABLE!
ZONE A30, SAME THING TECHNO-CENTREUR. NO EXPLANATION AT ALL!
IT MEANS THAT JERK ON THE HOLOVID WAS RIGHT!
BUT, THE DARKNESS PROMISED!
IF I UNDERSTAND CORRECTLY, ALL YOUR "PROMISES OF TRIUMPH" WERE NOTHING BUT A LOT OF HOT AIR!
WHAT DOES THE DARKNESS SAY? IS THERE STILL HOPE?
THE DARKNESS ALWAYS FINDS A WAY! REMAIN ASSERTIVE!
SUDDENLY...
NORMAL SPACE AT LAST!
HAVE THE BERGS FOLLOWED US?
THEY SHOULD EMERGE AT THE SAME TIME AS US AND ENCIRCLE TECHNOGEA!
ALERT!
WHAT'S GOING ON NOW?
IT'S THE *BERG FLEET!*
THERE THEY ARE! THEIR ENTIRE ARMADA!
THIS IS TECHNOGEA. ARE YOU HAPPY NOW, JOHNNY?
YES, BARBARIAH DEAR. WHEN IT'S ALL OVER THE BERGS WILL HAVE THEIR INCAL AT LAST!!
BEGIN THE ATTACK! TOTAL DESTRUCTION!
BY YOUR COMMAND, PROTOQUEEN!
DON'T WORRY, OUR PSYCHIC BARRIER MAKES US TOTALLY INVULNERABLE!
BUT, THAT'S NOT TRUE! LOOK AT THE SCREENS!! THEY'RE THROUGH!!
IT'S TRUE!
HMM... THAT'S VERY STRANGE!
I ONLY SEE ONE POSSIBLE EXPLANATION: THE BARRIER IS PROGRAMMED TO STOP ANY MATTER OR ENERGY FROM OUR OWN GALAXY. THE BERGS' MOLECULAR STRUCTURE MUST BE SUBTLY DIFFERENT FROM OURS. THAT'S WHY OUR SHIELD IS INOPERATIVE. IT WILL BE NECESSARY TO FIGHT!
STIRLOG, LISTEN TO THAT IDIOT! IT'S HOPELESS!
C'MON, BIG BOY, SUCK IT UP! WE MUST RETURN TO OUR SHIP AND LEAVE THIS STINKING RATS NEST BEHIND!
49

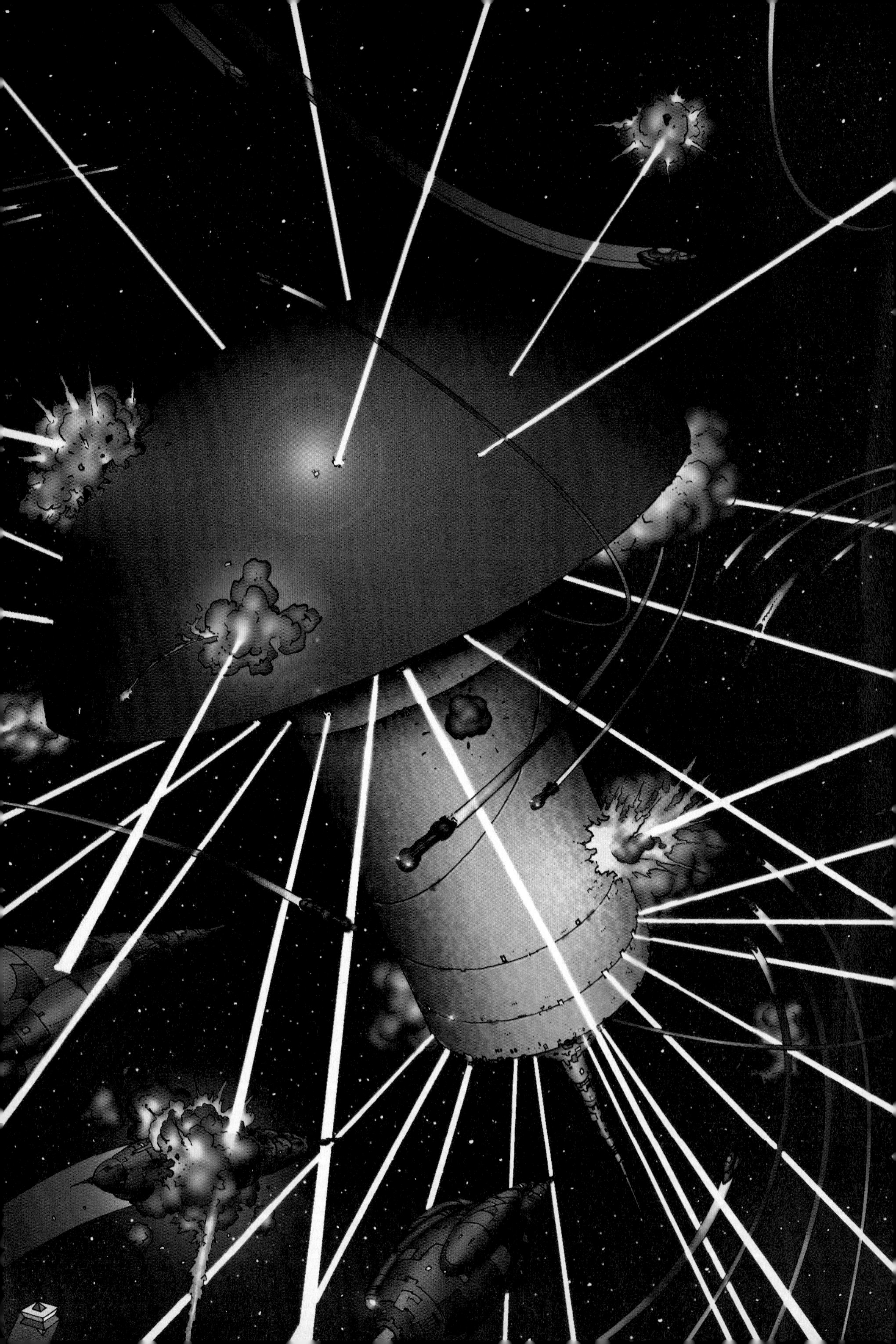

PSYCHO VIRUS

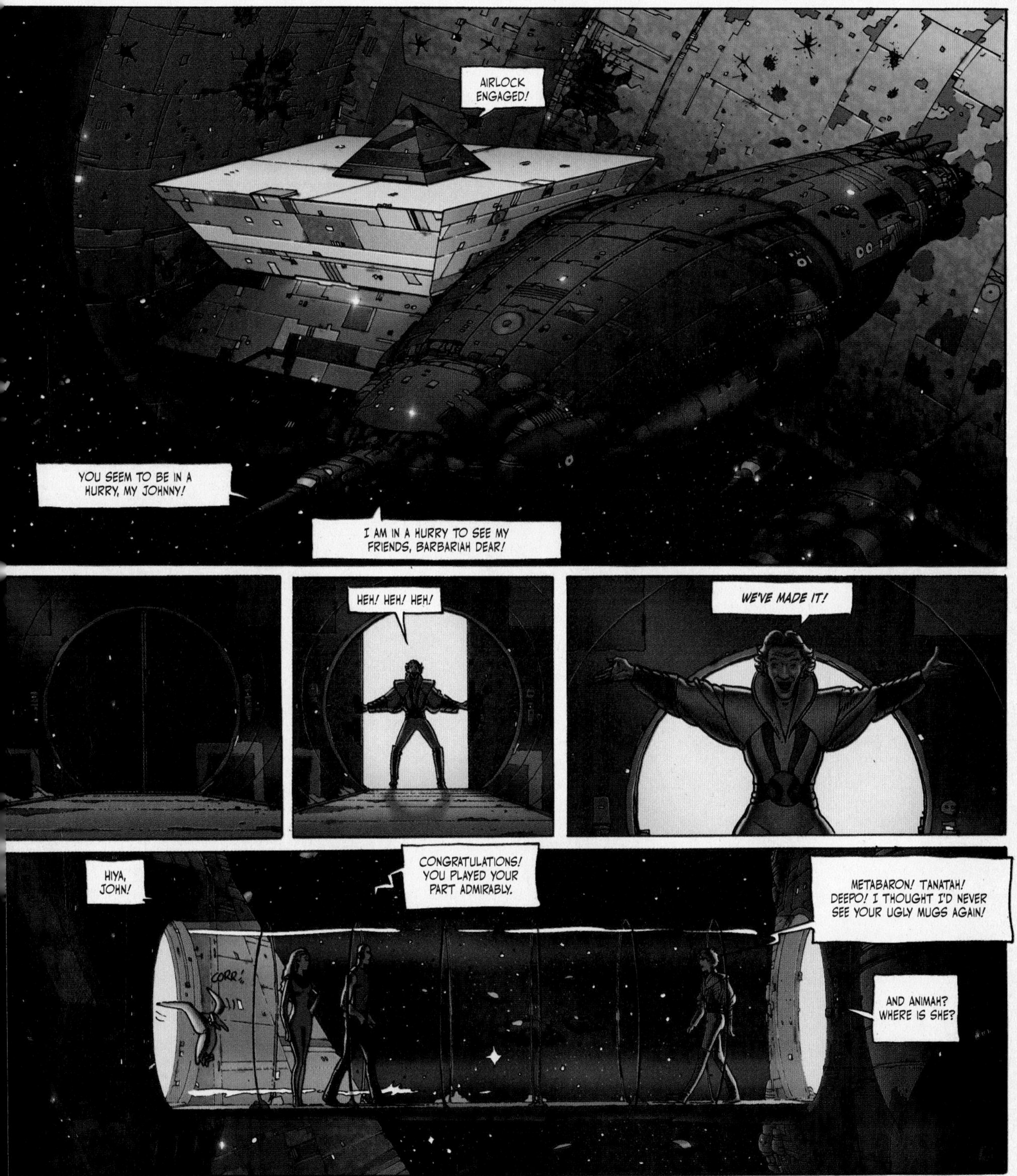
AIRLOCK ENGAGED!
YOU SEEM TO BE IN A HURRY, MY JOHNNY!
I AM IN A HURRY TO SEE MY FRIENDS, BARBARIAH DEAR!
HEH! HEH! HEH!
WE'VE MADE IT!
HIYA, JOHN!
CONGRATULATIONS! YOU PLAYED YOUR PART ADMIRABLY.
METABARON! TANATAH! DEEPO! I THOUGHT I'D NEVER SEE YOUR UGLY MUGS AGAIN!
CORR!
AND ANIMAH? WHERE IS SHE?

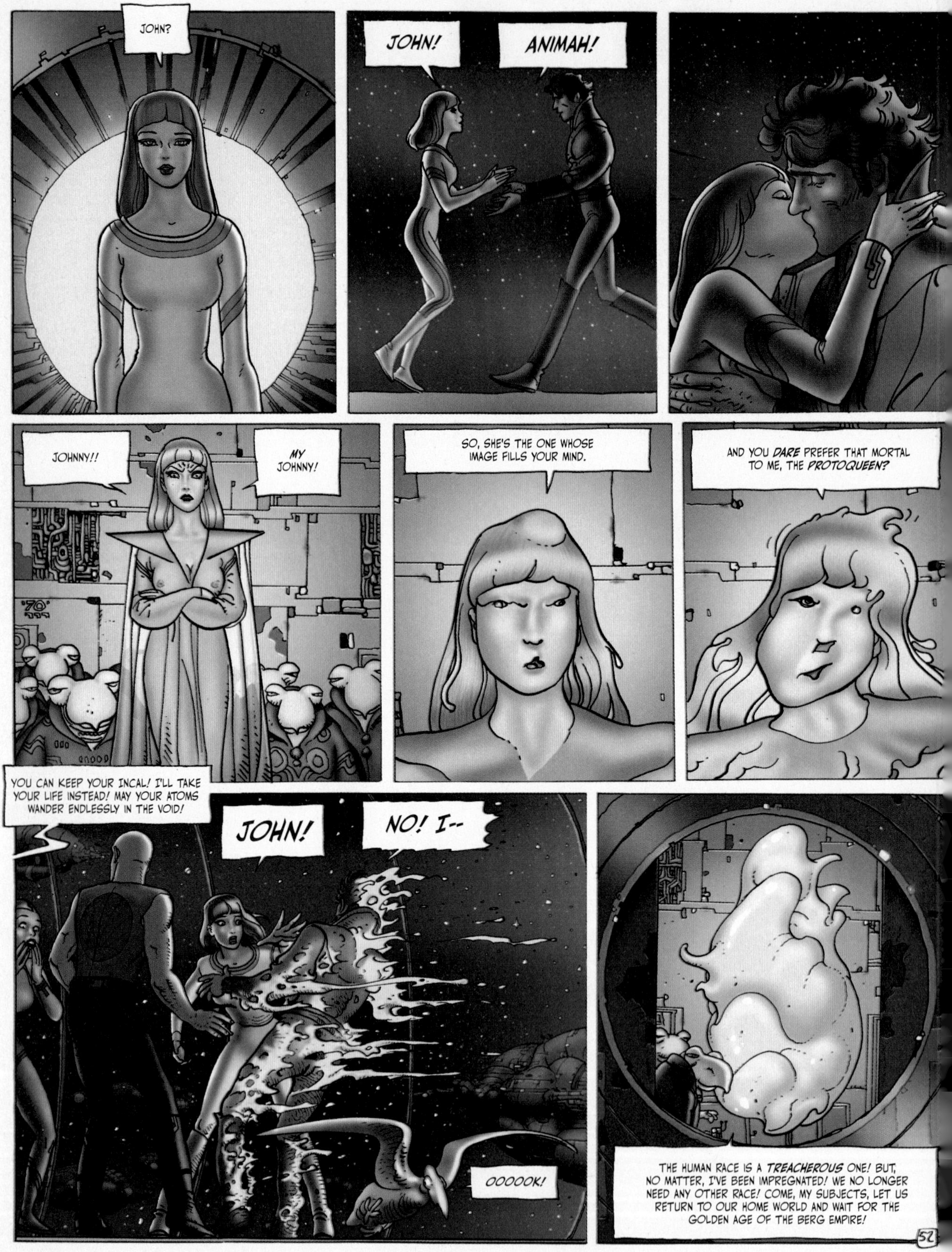

JOHN?
JOHN!
ANIMAH!
JOHNNY!!
MY JOHNNY!
SO, SHE'S THE ONE WHOSE IMAGE FILLS YOUR MIND.
AND YOU *DARE* PREFER THAT MORTAL TO ME, THE *PROTOQUEEN?*
YOU CAN KEEP YOUR INCAL! I'LL TAKE YOUR LIFE INSTEAD! MAY YOUR ATOMS WANDER ENDLESSLY IN THE VOID!
JOHN!
NO! I--
OOOOOK!
THE HUMAN RACE IS A *TREACHEROUS* ONE! BUT, NO MATTER, I'VE BEEN IMPREGNATED! WE NO LONGER NEED ANY OTHER RACE! COME, MY SUBJECTS, LET US RETURN TO OUR HOME WORLD AND WAIT FOR THE GOLDEN AGE OF THE BERG EMPIRE!
52

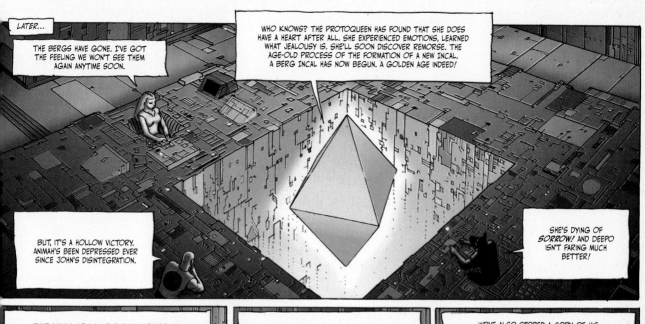

LATER...

THE BERGS HAVE GONE. I'VE GOT THE FEELING WE WON'T SEE THEM AGAIN ANYTIME SOON.

WHO KNOWS? THE PROTOQUEEN HAS FOUND THAT SHE DOES HAVE A HEART AFTER ALL. SHE EXPERIENCED EMOTIONS, LEARNED WHAT JEALOUSY IS. SHE'LL SOON DISCOVER REMORSE. THE AGE-OLD PROCESS OF THE FORMATION OF A NEW INCAL. A BERG INCAL HAS NOW BEGUN. A GOLDEN AGE INDEED!

BUT, IT'S A HOLLOW VICTORY. ANIMAH'S BEEN DEPRESSED EVER SINCE JOHN'S DISINTEGRATION.

SHE'S DYING OF *SORROW!* AND DEEPO ISN'T FARING MUCH BETTER!

THAT ANIMAH COULD LOVE THAT *WORTHLESS BUM* IS BEYOND ME! BUT, WHAT CAN WE DO NOW? HIS ATOMS MUST HAVE BEEN SCATTERED ALL OVER SPACE. IT'S HOPELESS.

NO! IT'S NOT HOPELESS! YES, ANIMAH LOVES JOHN DIFOOL, AND ONLY HIS REINCARNATION CAN SAVE HER!

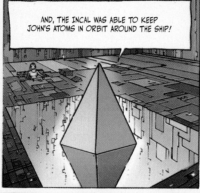

AND, THE INCAL WAS ABLE TO KEEP JOHN'S ATOMS IN ORBIT AROUND THE SHIP!

WE'VE ALSO STORED A COPY OF HIS BIO-PSYCHIC IMPRINT IN THE COMPUTER. IT ALL DEPENDS ON YOU NOW!

WHAT SHOULD WE DO?

SPEAK, SOLUNE! TELL US WHAT TO DO!

ONLY THE POWER OF LOVE CAN GATHER AND BIND A BILLION SCATTERED ATOMS!

TWO OF YOU MUST THEREFORE CREATE A MALE-FEMALE VORTEX!

I'LL DO IT!

WHY GO TO ALL THE EFFORT? WOULDN'T IT BE EASIER TO TRY TO HEAL ANIMAH? HELP CURE HER OF THAT FOOLISH LOVE!

?!

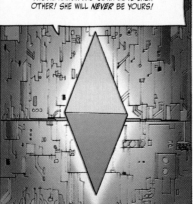

IT'S *USELESS*, METABARON! FACE THE TRUTH: ANIMAH AND JOHN LOVE EACH OTHER! SHE WILL *NEVER* BE YOURS!

STOP!

COME TO YOUR SENSES, METABARON! ACCEPT THE LOSS OF MY SISTER! I AM HERE IN HER PLACE!

YOU?

YES, ME! LET'S JOIN OUR ENERGIES AND BRING BACK THAT IDIOT, JOHN DIFOOL.

EH...I'LL GO SEE HOW DEEPO'S DOING! THE POOR THING WAS FEELING PRETTY LOW!

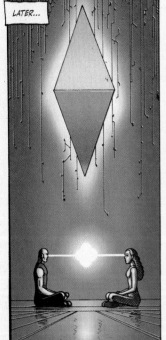

LATER...

SOON AFTER...

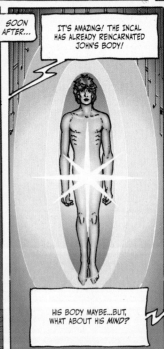

IT'S AMAZING! THE INCAL HAS ALREADY REINCARNATED JOHN'S BODY!

HIS BODY MAYBE...BUT, WHAT ABOUT HIS *MIND*?

ANIMAH! WHERE ARE YOU, ANIMAH?

IN MY OPINION HIS MIND IS FINE! WELCOME BACK, JOHN DIFOOL!

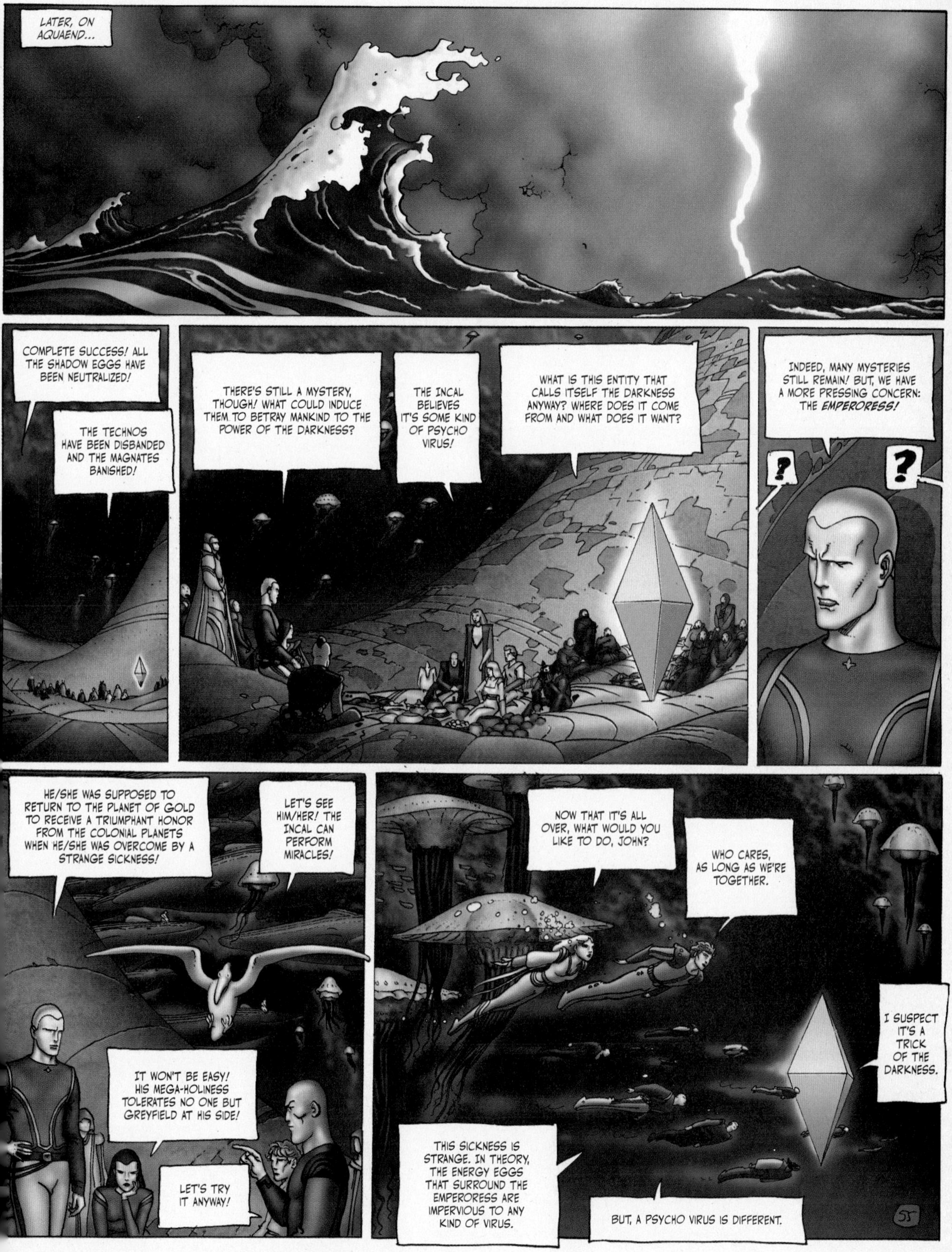
LATER, ON AQUAEND...
COMPLETE SUCCESS! ALL THE SHADOW EGGS HAVE BEEN NEUTRALIZED!
THE TECHNOS HAVE BEEN DISBANDED AND THE MAGNATES BANISHED!
THERE'S STILL A MYSTERY, THOUGH! WHAT COULD INDUCE THEM TO BETRAY MANKIND TO THE POWER OF THE DARKNESS?
THE INCAL BELIEVES IT'S SOME KIND OF PSYCHO VIRUS!
WHAT IS THIS ENTITY THAT CALLS ITSELF THE DARKNESS ANYWAY? WHERE DOES IT COME FROM AND WHAT DOES IT WANT?
INDEED, MANY MYSTERIES STILL REMAIN! BUT, WE HAVE A MORE PRESSING CONCERN: THE EMPERORESS!
?
?
HE/SHE WAS SUPPOSED TO RETURN TO THE PLANET OF GOLD TO RECEIVE A TRIUMPHANT HONOR FROM THE COLONIAL PLANETS WHEN HE/SHE WAS OVERCOME BY A STRANGE SICKNESS!
LET'S SEE HIM/HER! THE INCAL CAN PERFORM MIRACLES!
IT WON'T BE EASY! HIS MEGA-HOLINESS TOLERATES NO ONE BUT GREYFIELD AT HIS SIDE!
LET'S TRY IT ANYWAY!
NOW THAT IT'S ALL OVER, WHAT WOULD YOU LIKE TO DO, JOHN?
WHO CARES, AS LONG AS WE'RE TOGETHER.
I SUSPECT IT'S A TRICK OF THE DARKNESS.
THIS SICKNESS IS STRANGE. IN THEORY, THE ENERGY EGGS THAT SURROUND THE EMPERORESS ARE IMPERVIOUS TO ANY KIND OF VIRUS.
BUT, A PSYCHO VIRUS IS DIFFERENT.
55

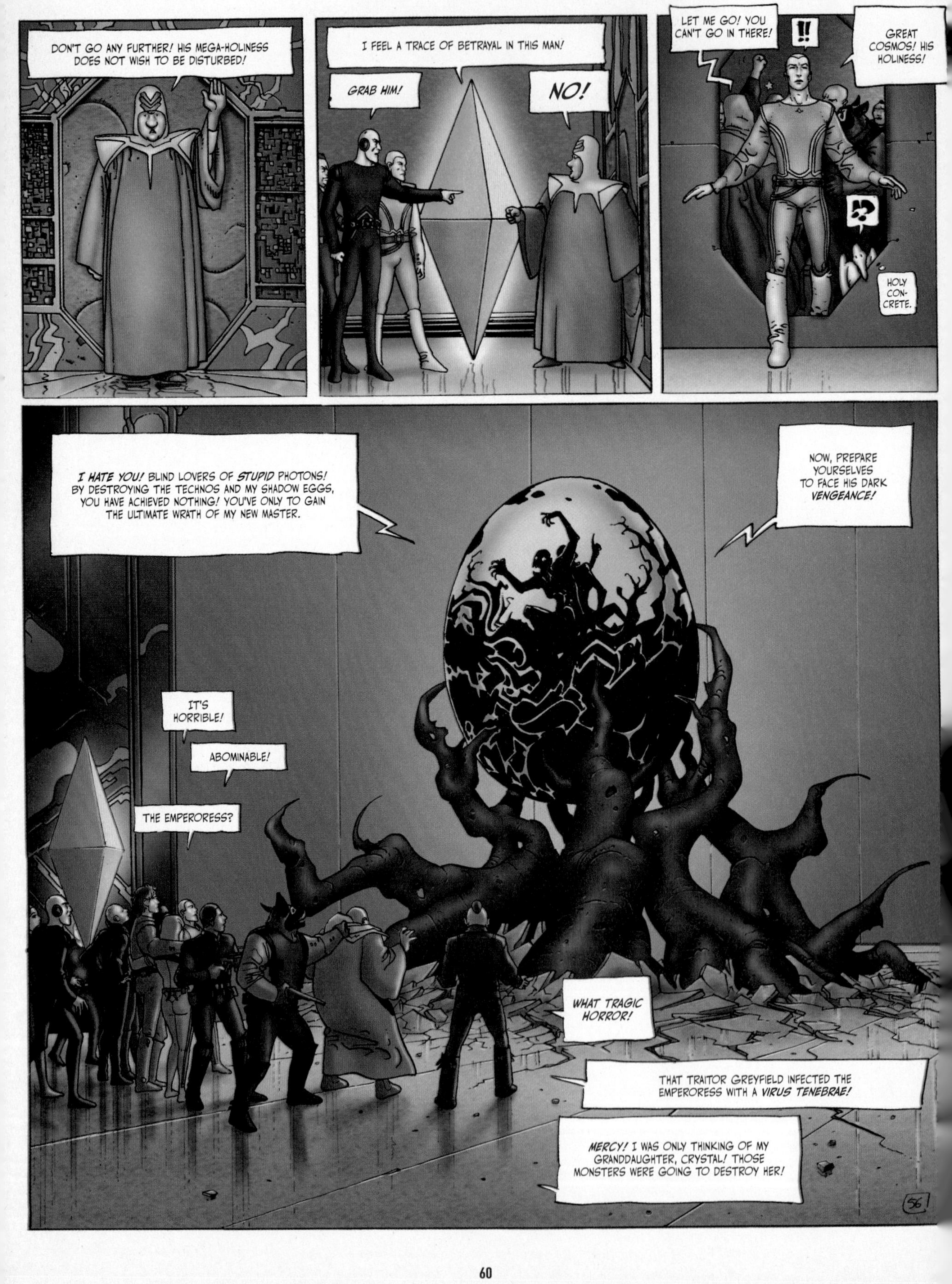
DON'T GO ANY FURTHER! HIS MEGA-HOLINESS DOES NOT WISH TO BE DISTURBED!
I FEEL A TRACE OF BETRAYAL IN THIS MAN!
GRAB HIM!
NO!
LET ME GO! YOU CAN'T GO IN THERE!
!!
GREAT COSMOS! HIS HOLINESS!
?
HOLY CON-CRETE.
I HATE YOU! BLIND LOVERS OF STUPID PHOTONS! BY DESTROYING THE TECHNOS AND MY SHADOW EGGS, YOU HAVE ACHIEVED NOTHING! YOU'VE ONLY TO GAIN THE ULTIMATE WRATH OF MY NEW MASTER.
NOW, PREPARE YOURSELVES TO FACE HIS DARK VENGEANCE!
IT'S HORRIBLE!
ABOMINABLE!
THE EMPERORESS?
WHAT TRAGIC HORROR!
THAT TRAITOR GREYFIELD INFECTED THE EMPERORESS WITH A VIRUS TENEBRAE!
MERCY! I WAS ONLY THINKING OF MY GRANDDAUGHTER, CRYSTAL! THOSE MONSTERS WERE GOING TO DESTROY HER!
56

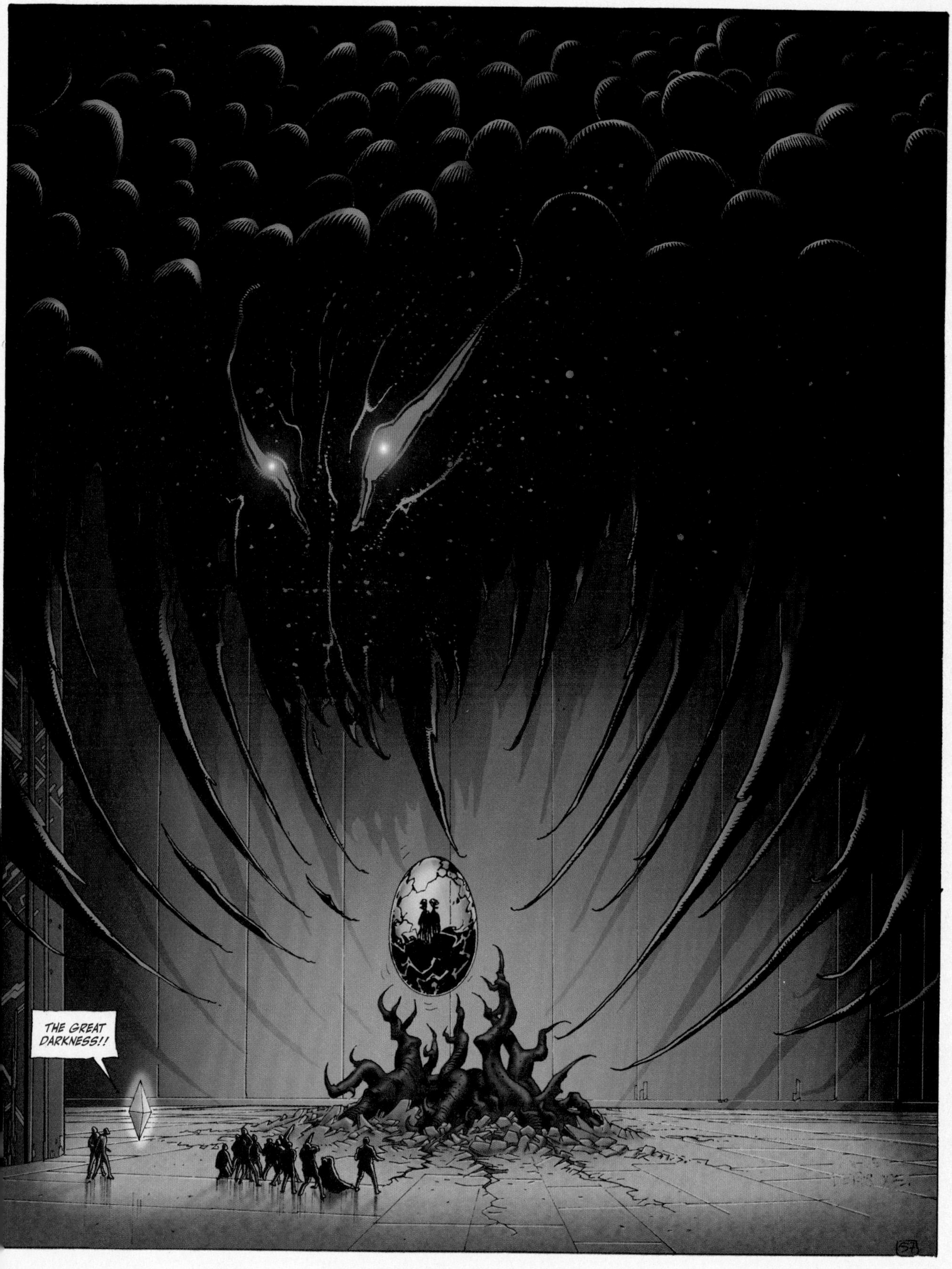
THE GREAT DARKNESS!!

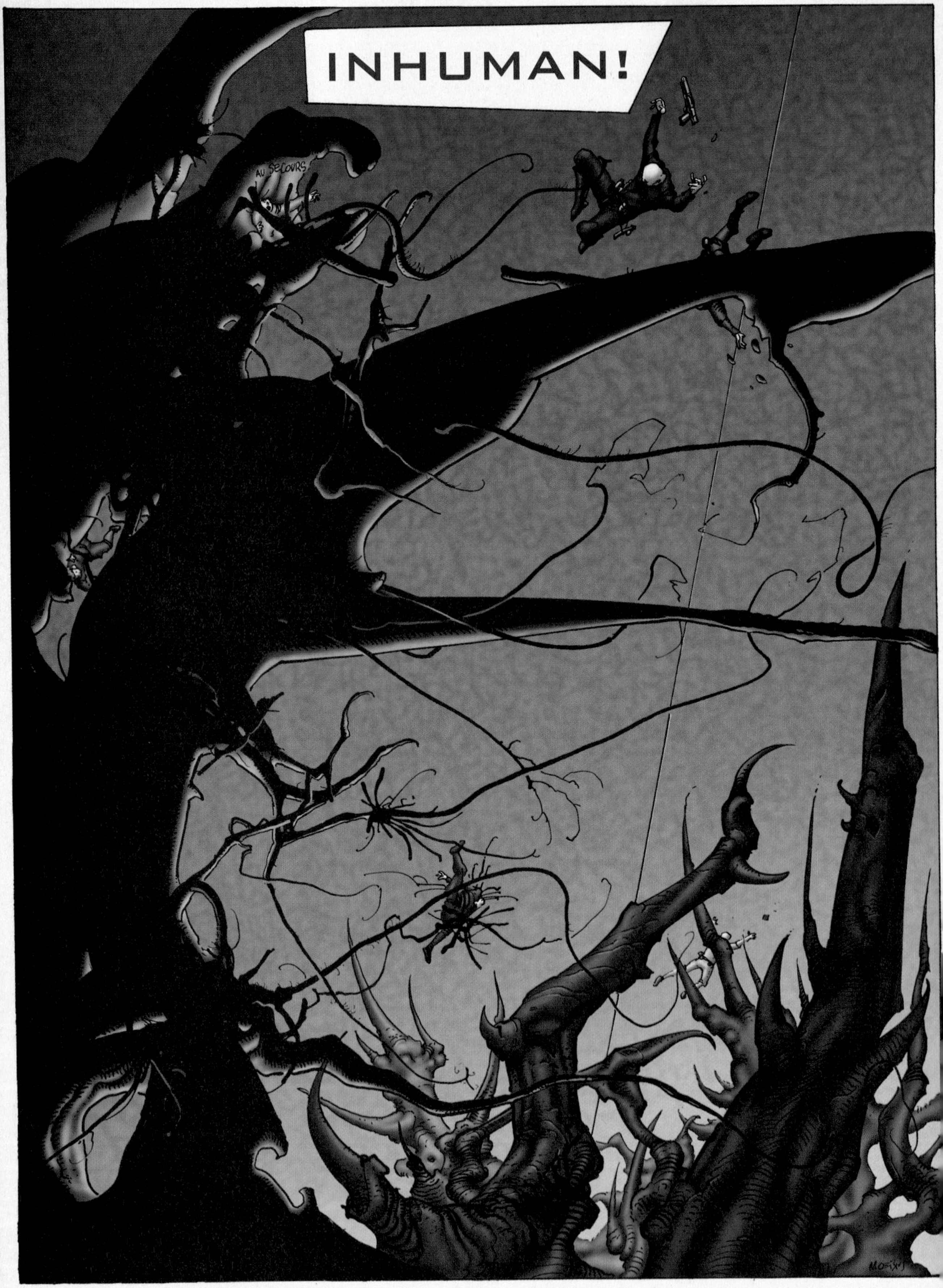
INHUMAN!
AU SECOURS

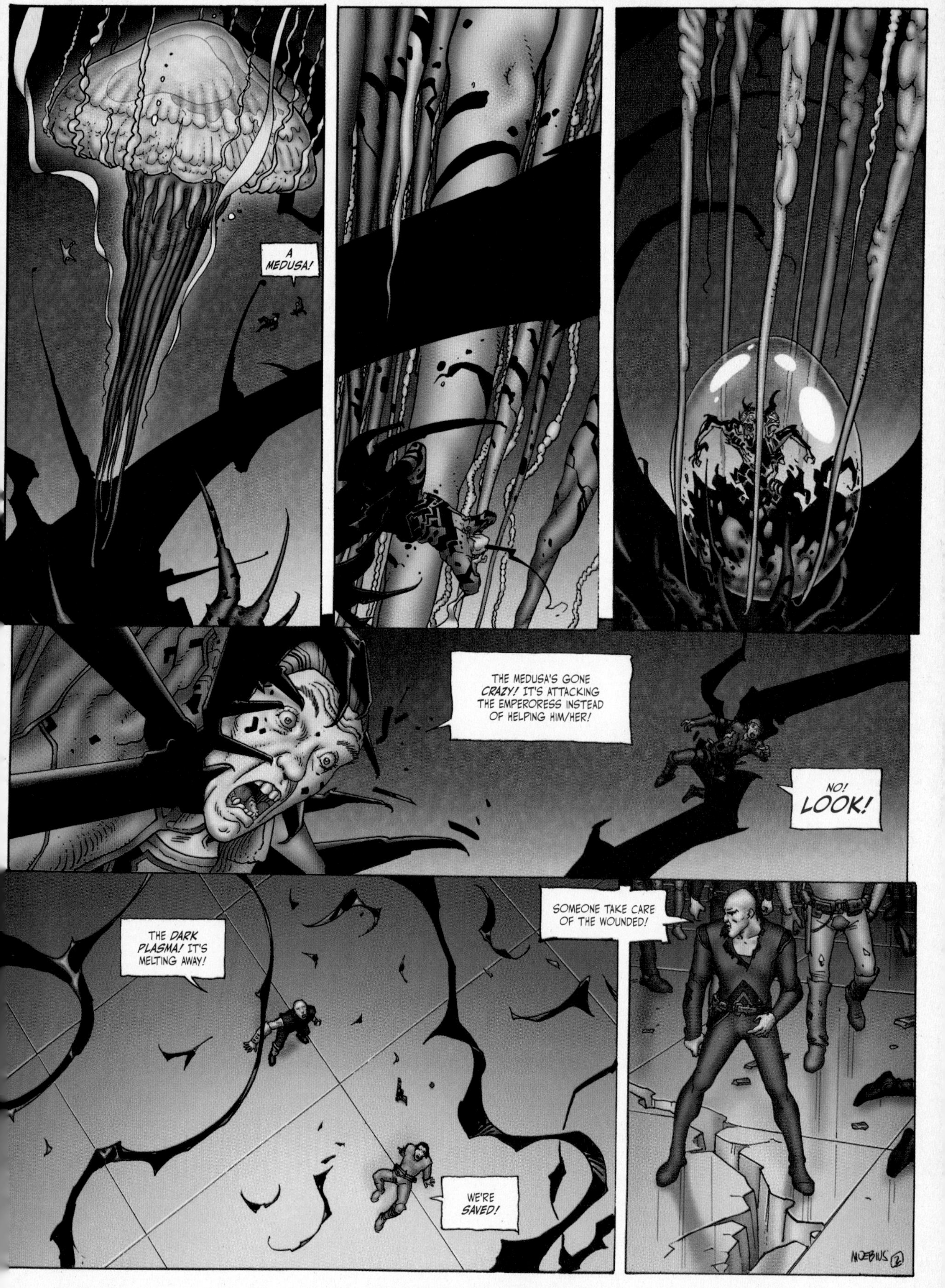

A MEDUSA!
THE MEDUSA'S GONE CRAZY! IT'S ATTACKING THE EMPERORESS INSTEAD OF HELPING HIM/HER!
NO! LOOK!
THE DARK PLASMA! IT'S MELTING AWAY!
WE'RE SAVED!
SOMEONE TAKE CARE OF THE WOUNDED!
MOEBIUS

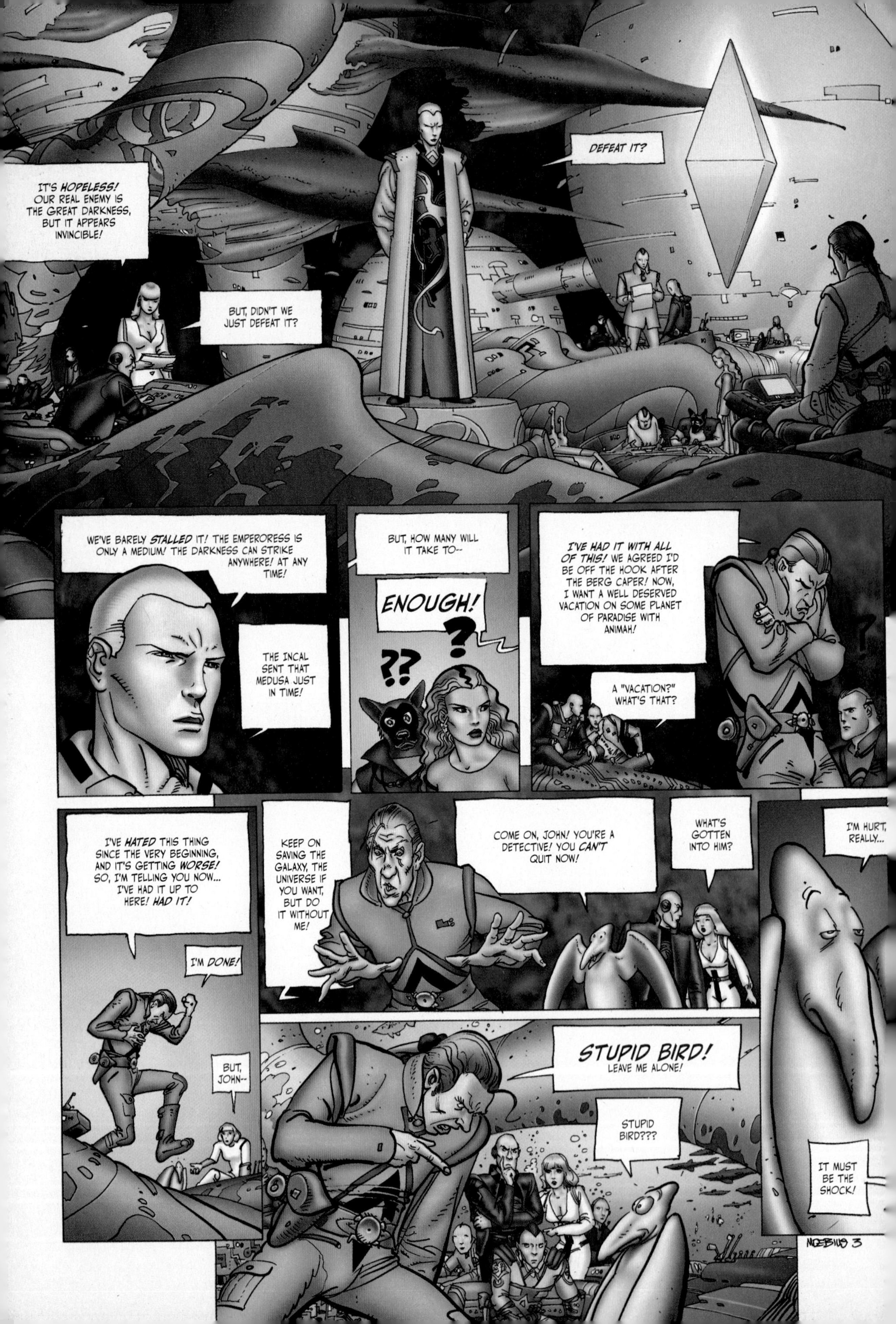
IT'S HOPELESS! OUR REAL ENEMY IS THE GREAT DARKNESS, BUT IT APPEARS INVINCIBLE!
BUT, DIDN'T WE JUST DEFEAT IT?
DEFEAT IT?
WE'VE BARELY STALLED IT! THE EMPERORESS IS ONLY A MEDIUM! THE DARKNESS CAN STRIKE ANYWHERE! AT ANY TIME!
THE INCAL SENT THAT MEDUSA JUST IN TIME!
BUT, HOW MANY WILL IT TAKE TO--
ENOUGH!
??
?
I'VE HAD IT WITH ALL OF THIS! WE AGREED I'D BE OFF THE HOOK AFTER THE BERG CAPER! NOW, I WANT A WELL DESERVED VACATION ON SOME PLANET OF PARADISE WITH ANIMAH!
A "VACATION?" WHAT'S THAT?
?
I'VE HATED THIS THING SINCE THE VERY BEGINNING, AND IT'S GETTING WORSE! SO, I'M TELLING YOU NOW... I'VE HAD IT UP TO HERE! HAD IT!
I'M DONE!
BUT, JOHN--
KEEP ON SAVING THE GALAXY, THE UNIVERSE IF YOU WANT, BUT DO IT WITHOUT ME!
COME ON, JOHN! YOU'RE A DETECTIVE! YOU CAN'T QUIT NOW!
WHAT'S GOTTEN INTO HIM?
I'M HURT, REALLY...
STUPID BIRD! LEAVE ME ALONE!
STUPID BIRD???
IT MUST BE THE SHOCK!
MOEBIUS 3

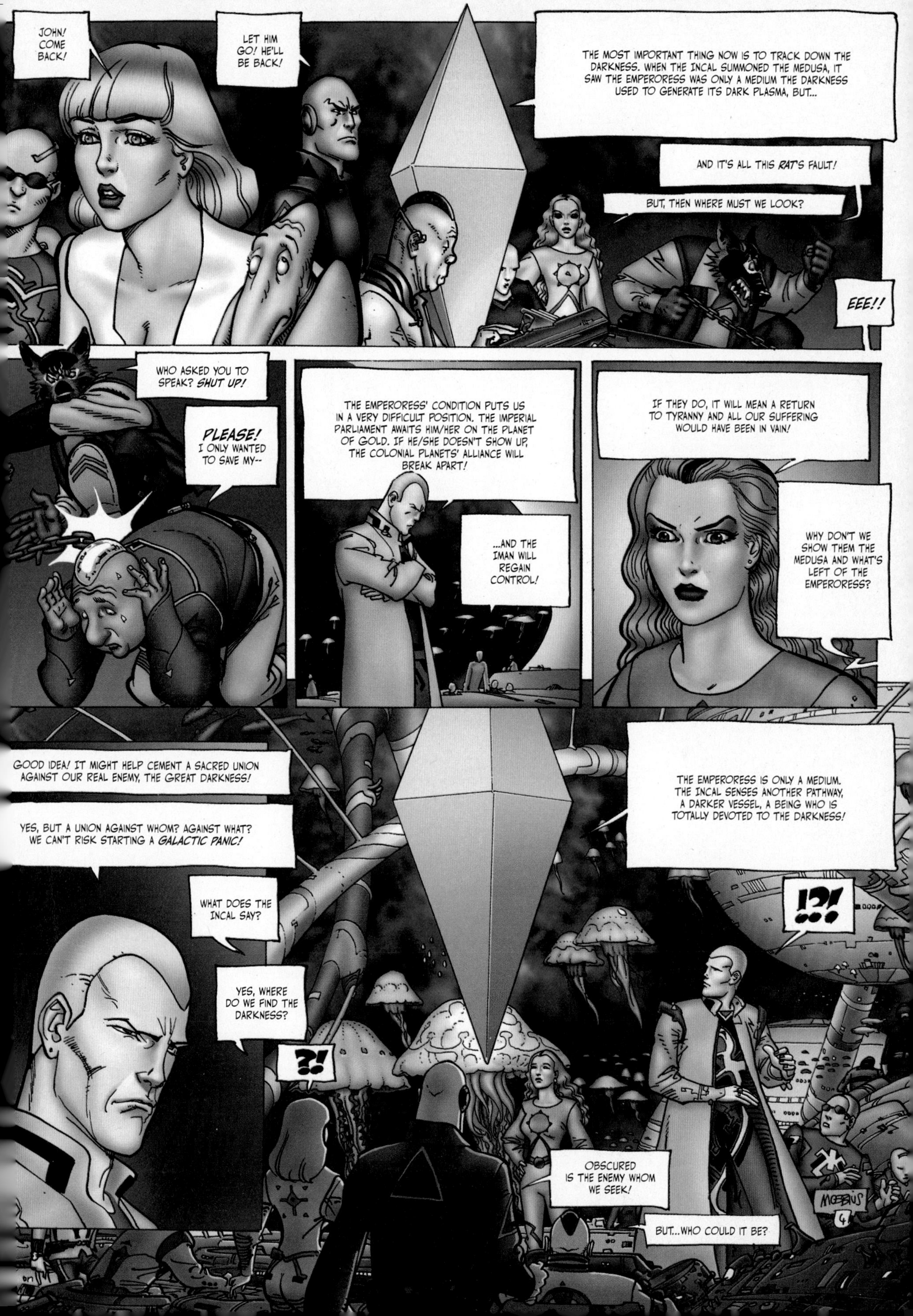
JOHN! COME BACK!
LET HIM GO! HE'LL BE BACK!
THE MOST IMPORTANT THING NOW IS TO TRACK DOWN THE DARKNESS. WHEN THE INCAL SUMMONED THE MEDUSA, IT SAW THE EMPERORESS WAS ONLY A MEDIUM THE DARKNESS USED TO GENERATE ITS DARK PLASMA, BUT...
AND IT'S ALL THIS RAT'S FAULT!
BUT, THEN WHERE MUST WE LOOK?
EEE!!
WHO ASKED YOU TO SPEAK? SHUT UP!
PLEASE! I ONLY WANTED TO SAVE MY--
THE EMPERORESS' CONDITION PUTS US IN A VERY DIFFICULT POSITION. THE IMPERIAL PARLIAMENT AWAITS HIM/HER ON THE PLANET OF GOLD. IF HE/SHE DOESN'T SHOW UP, THE COLONIAL PLANETS' ALLIANCE WILL BREAK APART!
...AND THE IMAN WILL REGAIN CONTROL!
IF THEY DO, IT WILL MEAN A RETURN TO TYRANNY AND ALL OUR SUFFERING WOULD HAVE BEEN IN VAIN!
WHY DON'T WE SHOW THEM THE MEDUSA AND WHAT'S LEFT OF THE EMPERORESS?
GOOD IDEA! IT MIGHT HELP CEMENT A SACRED UNION AGAINST OUR REAL ENEMY, THE GREAT DARKNESS!
YES, BUT A UNION AGAINST WHOM? AGAINST WHAT? WE CAN'T RISK STARTING A GALACTIC PANIC!
WHAT DOES THE INCAL SAY?
YES, WHERE DO WE FIND THE DARKNESS?
?!
THE EMPERORESS IS ONLY A MEDIUM. THE INCAL SENSES ANOTHER PATHWAY, A DARKER VESSEL, A BEING WHO IS TOTALLY DEVOTED TO THE DARKNESS!
!?!
OBSCURED IS THE ENEMY WHOM WE SEEK!
BUT...WHO COULD IT BE?
MOEBIUS 4

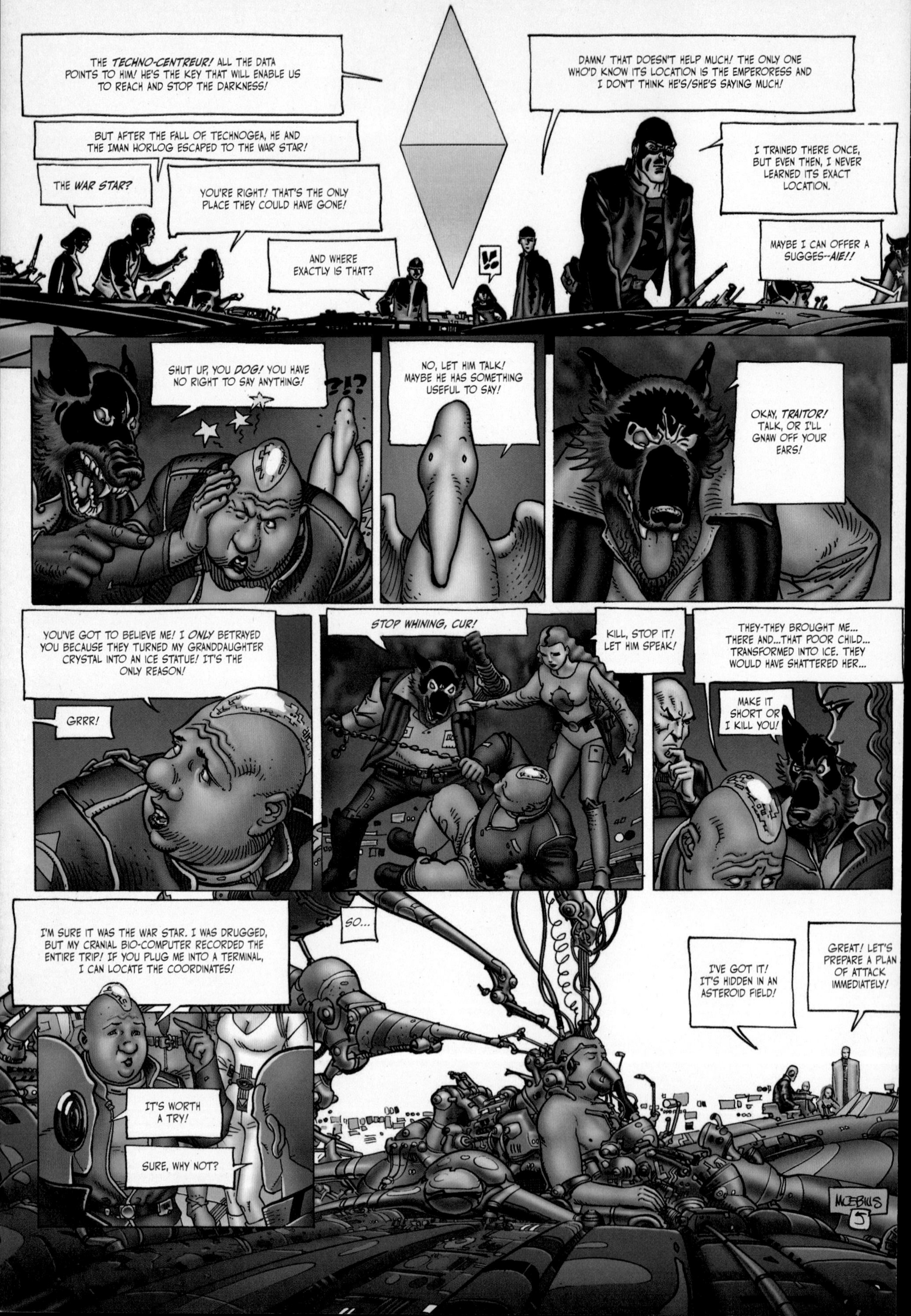
THE TECHNO-CENTREUR! ALL THE DATA POINTS TO HIM! HE'S THE KEY THAT WILL ENABLE US TO REACH AND STOP THE DARKNESS!
BUT AFTER THE FALL OF TECHNOGEA, HE AND THE IMAN HORLOG ESCAPED TO THE WAR STAR!
THE WAR STAR?
YOU'RE RIGHT! THAT'S THE ONLY PLACE THEY COULD HAVE GONE!
AND WHERE EXACTLY IS THAT?
DAMN! THAT DOESN'T HELP MUCH! THE ONLY ONE WHO'D KNOW ITS LOCATION IS THE EMPERORESS AND I DON'T THINK HE'S/SHE'S SAYING MUCH!
I TRAINED THERE ONCE, BUT EVEN THEN, I NEVER LEARNED ITS EXACT LOCATION.
MAYBE I CAN OFFER A SUGGES--AIE!!
SHUT UP, YOU DOG! YOU HAVE NO RIGHT TO SAY ANYTHING!
?!?
NO, LET HIM TALK! MAYBE HE HAS SOMETHING USEFUL TO SAY!
OKAY, TRAITOR! TALK, OR I'LL GNAW OFF YOUR EARS!
YOU'VE GOT TO BELIEVE ME! I ONLY BETRAYED YOU BECAUSE THEY TURNED MY GRANDDAUGHTER CRYSTAL INTO AN ICE STATUE! IT'S THE ONLY REASON!
GRRR!
STOP WHINING, CUR!
KILL, STOP IT! LET HIM SPEAK!
THEY-THEY BROUGHT ME... THERE AND...THAT POOR CHILD... TRANSFORMED INTO ICE. THEY WOULD HAVE SHATTERED HER...
MAKE IT SHORT OR I KILL YOU!
I'M SURE IT WAS THE WAR STAR. I WAS DRUGGED, BUT MY CRANIAL BIO-COMPUTER RECORDED THE ENTIRE TRIP! IF YOU PLUG ME INTO A TERMINAL, I CAN LOCATE THE COORDINATES!
IT'S WORTH A TRY!
SURE, WHY NOT?
SO...
I'VE GOT IT! IT'S HIDDEN IN AN ASTEROID FIELD!
GREAT! LET'S PREPARE A PLAN OF ATTACK IMMEDIATELY!
MOEBIUS
5

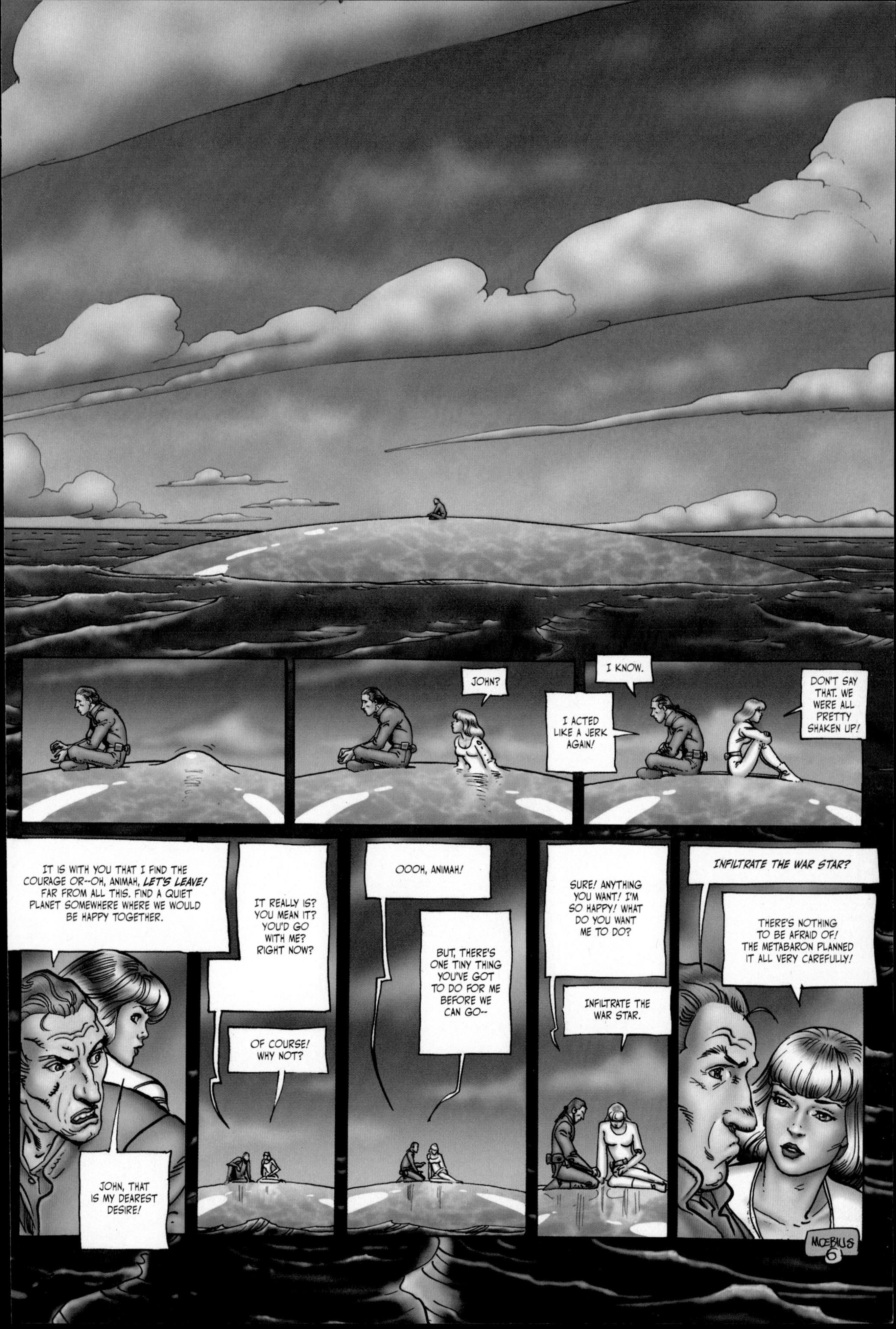
JOHN?
I KNOW.
I ACTED LIKE A JERK AGAIN!
DON'T SAY THAT. WE WERE ALL PRETTY SHAKEN UP!
IT IS WITH YOU THAT I FIND THE COURAGE OR--OH, ANIMAH, LET'S LEAVE! FAR FROM ALL THIS. FIND A QUIET PLANET SOMEWHERE WHERE WE WOULD BE HAPPY TOGETHER.
JOHN, THAT IS MY DEAREST DESIRE!
IT REALLY IS? YOU MEAN IT? YOU'D GO WITH ME? RIGHT NOW?
OF COURSE! WHY NOT?
OOOH, ANIMAH!
BUT, THERE'S ONE TINY THING YOU'VE GOT TO DO FOR ME BEFORE WE CAN GO--
SURE! ANYTHING YOU WANT! I'M SO HAPPY! WHAT DO YOU WANT ME TO DO?
INFILTRATE THE WAR STAR.
INFILTRATE THE WAR STAR?
THERE'S NOTHING TO BE AFRAID OF! THE METABARON PLANNED IT ALL VERY CAREFULLY!
MOEBIUS
6

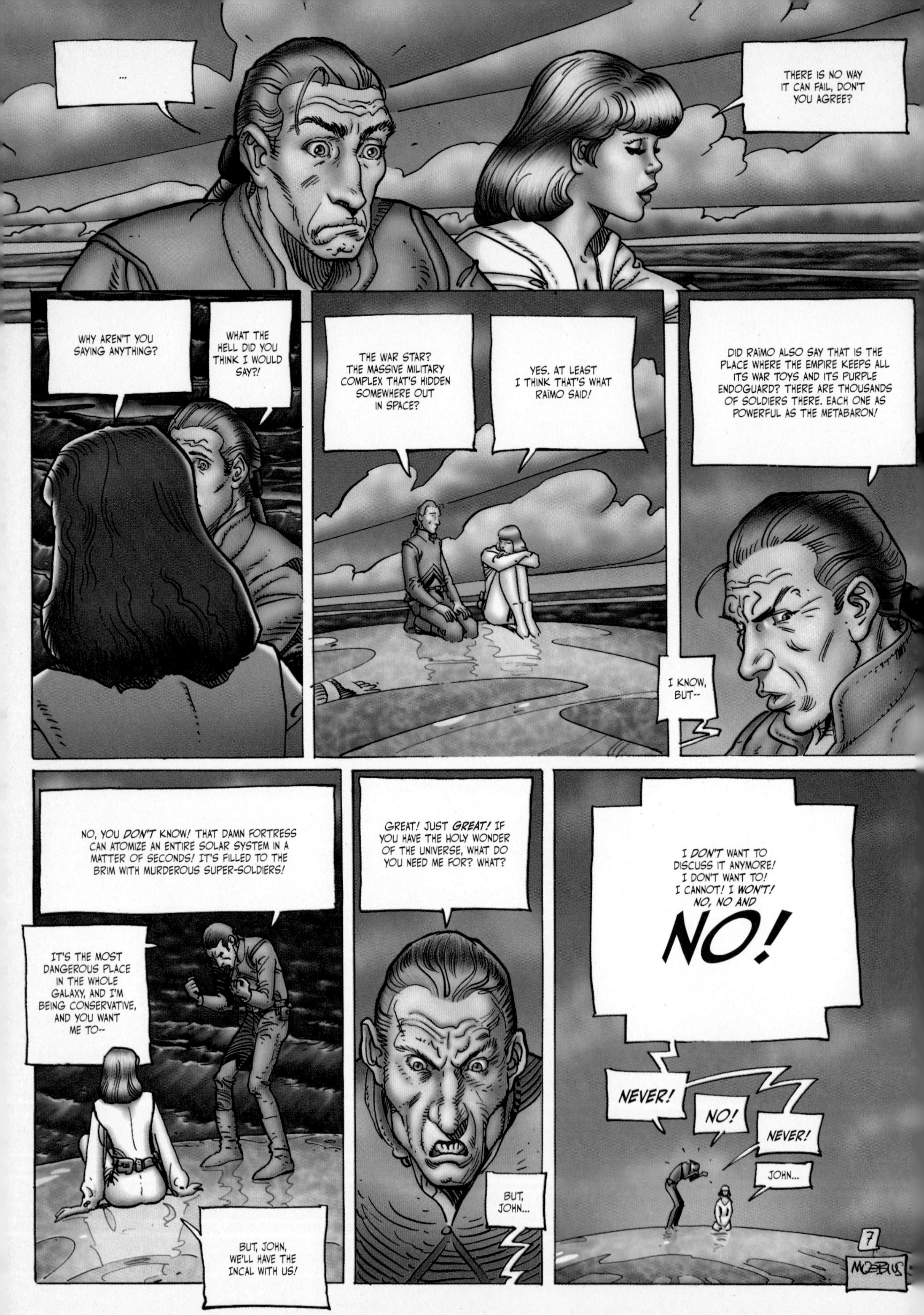
...
THERE IS NO WAY IT CAN FAIL, DON'T YOU AGREE?
WHY AREN'T YOU SAYING ANYTHING?
WHAT THE HELL DID YOU THINK I WOULD SAY?!
THE WAR STAR? THE MASSIVE MILITARY COMPLEX THAT'S HIDDEN SOMEWHERE OUT IN SPACE?
YES. AT LEAST I THINK THAT'S WHAT RAÏMO SAID!
DID RAÏMO ALSO SAY THAT IS THE PLACE WHERE THE EMPIRE KEEPS ALL ITS WAR TOYS AND ITS PURPLE ENDOGUARD? THERE ARE THOUSANDS OF SOLDIERS THERE. EACH ONE AS POWERFUL AS THE METABARON!
I KNOW, BUT--
NO, YOU *DON'T* KNOW! THAT DAMN FORTRESS CAN ATOMIZE AN ENTIRE SOLAR SYSTEM IN A MATTER OF SECONDS! IT'S FILLED TO THE BRIM WITH MURDEROUS SUPER-SOLDIERS!
IT'S THE MOST DANGEROUS PLACE IN THE WHOLE GALAXY, AND I'M BEING CONSERVATIVE, AND YOU WANT ME TO--
BUT, JOHN, WE'LL HAVE THE INCAL WITH US!
GREAT! JUST *GREAT!* IF YOU HAVE THE HOLY WONDER OF THE UNIVERSE, WHAT DO YOU NEED ME FOR? WHAT?
BUT, JOHN...
I *DON'T* WANT TO DISCUSS IT ANYMORE! I DON'T WANT TO! I CANNOT! I *WON'T!* NO, NO AND
NO!
NEVER!
NO!
NEVER!
JOHN...
7
MOEBIUS

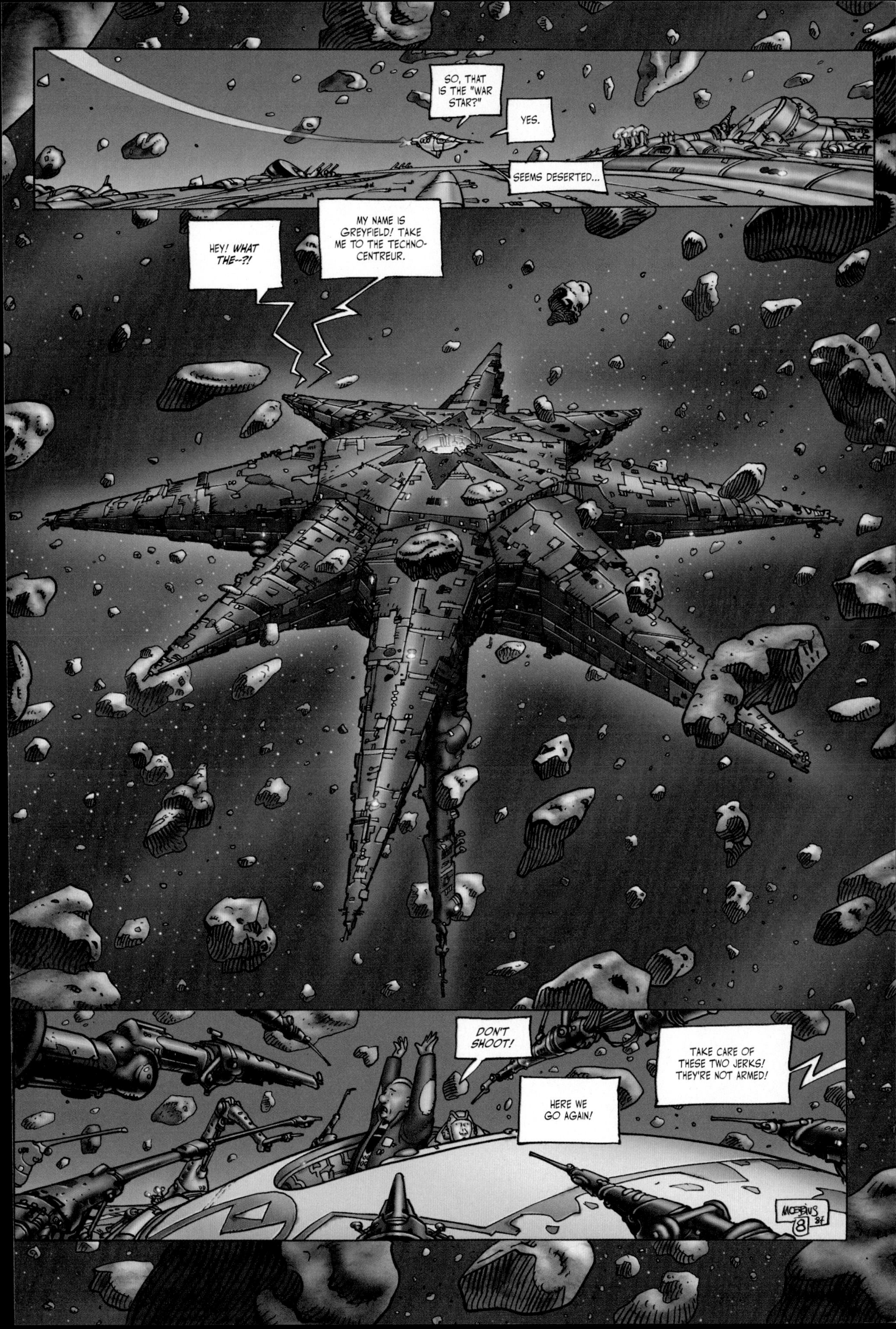
SO, THAT IS THE "WAR STAR?"
YES.
SEEMS DESERTED...
HEY! *WHAT THE--?!*
MY NAME IS GREYFIELD! TAKE ME TO THE TECHNO-CENTREUR.
DON'T SHOOT!
HERE WE GO AGAIN!
TAKE CARE OF THESE TWO JERKS! THEY'RE NOT ARMED!
MOEBIUS

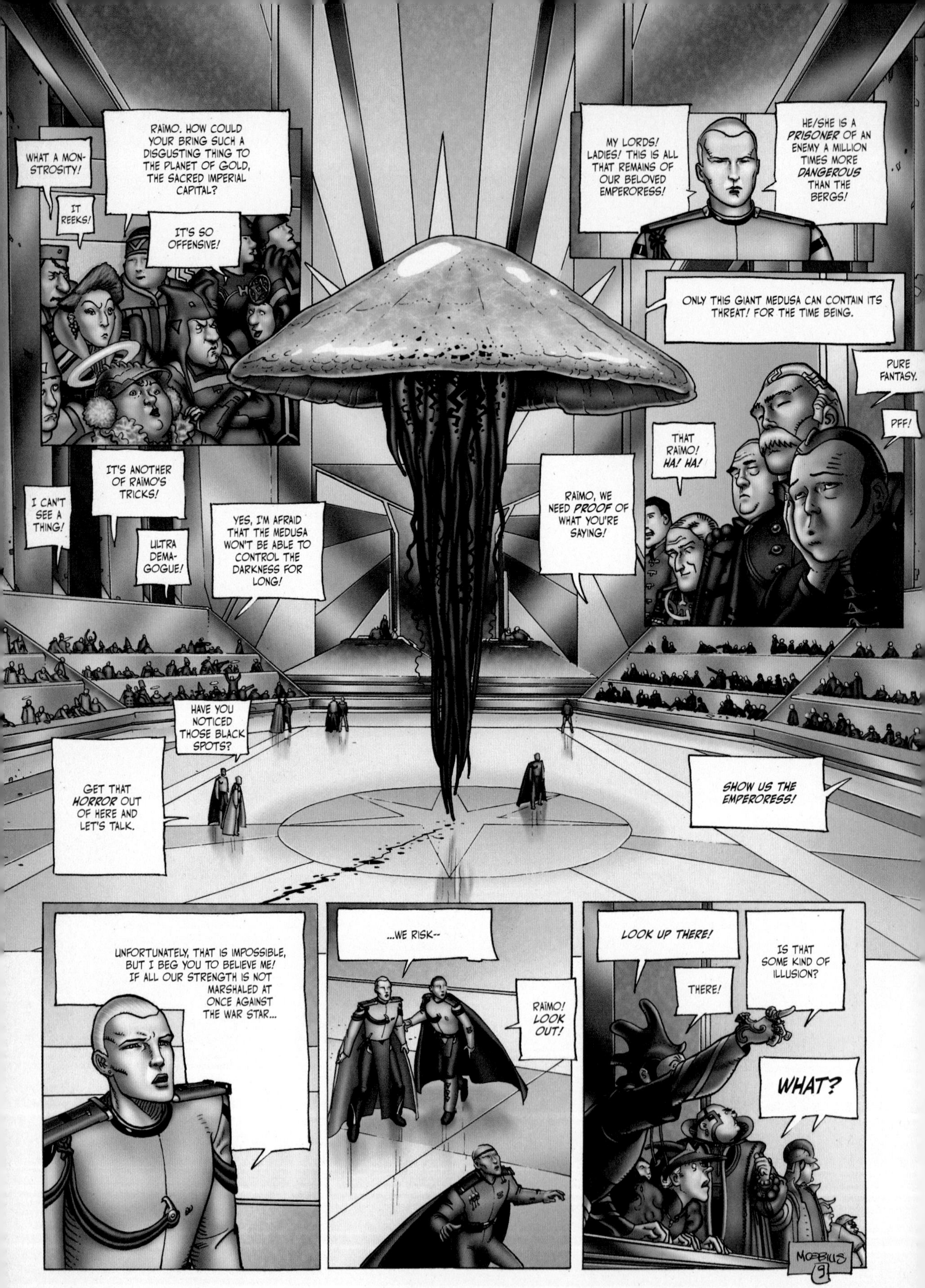
WHAT A MONSTROSITY!
RAÏMO. HOW COULD YOUR BRING SUCH A DISGUSTING THING TO THE PLANET OF GOLD, THE SACRED IMPERIAL CAPITAL?
IT REEKS!
IT'S SO OFFENSIVE!
MY LORDS! LADIES! THIS IS ALL THAT REMAINS OF OUR BELOVED EMPERORESS!
HE/SHE IS A PRISONER OF AN ENEMY A MILLION TIMES MORE DANGEROUS THAN THE BERGS!
ONLY THIS GIANT MEDUSA CAN CONTAIN ITS THREAT! FOR THE TIME BEING.
PURE FANTASY.
PFF!
THAT RAÏMO! HA! HA!
I CAN'T SEE A THING!
IT'S ANOTHER OF RAÏMO'S TRICKS!
ULTRA DEMAGOGUE!
YES, I'M AFRAID THAT THE MEDUSA WON'T BE ABLE TO CONTROL THE DARKNESS FOR LONG!
RAÏMO, WE NEED PROOF OF WHAT YOU'RE SAYING!
HAVE YOU NOTICED THOSE BLACK SPOTS?
GET THAT HORROR OUT OF HERE AND LET'S TALK.
SHOW US THE EMPERORESS!
UNFORTUNATELY, THAT IS IMPOSSIBLE, BUT I BEG YOU TO BELIEVE ME! IF ALL OUR STRENGTH IS NOT MARSHALED AT ONCE AGAINST THE WAR STAR...
...WE RISK--
RAÏMO! LOOK OUT!
LOOK UP THERE!
THERE!
IS THAT SOME KIND OF ILLUSION?
WHAT?
MOEBIUS

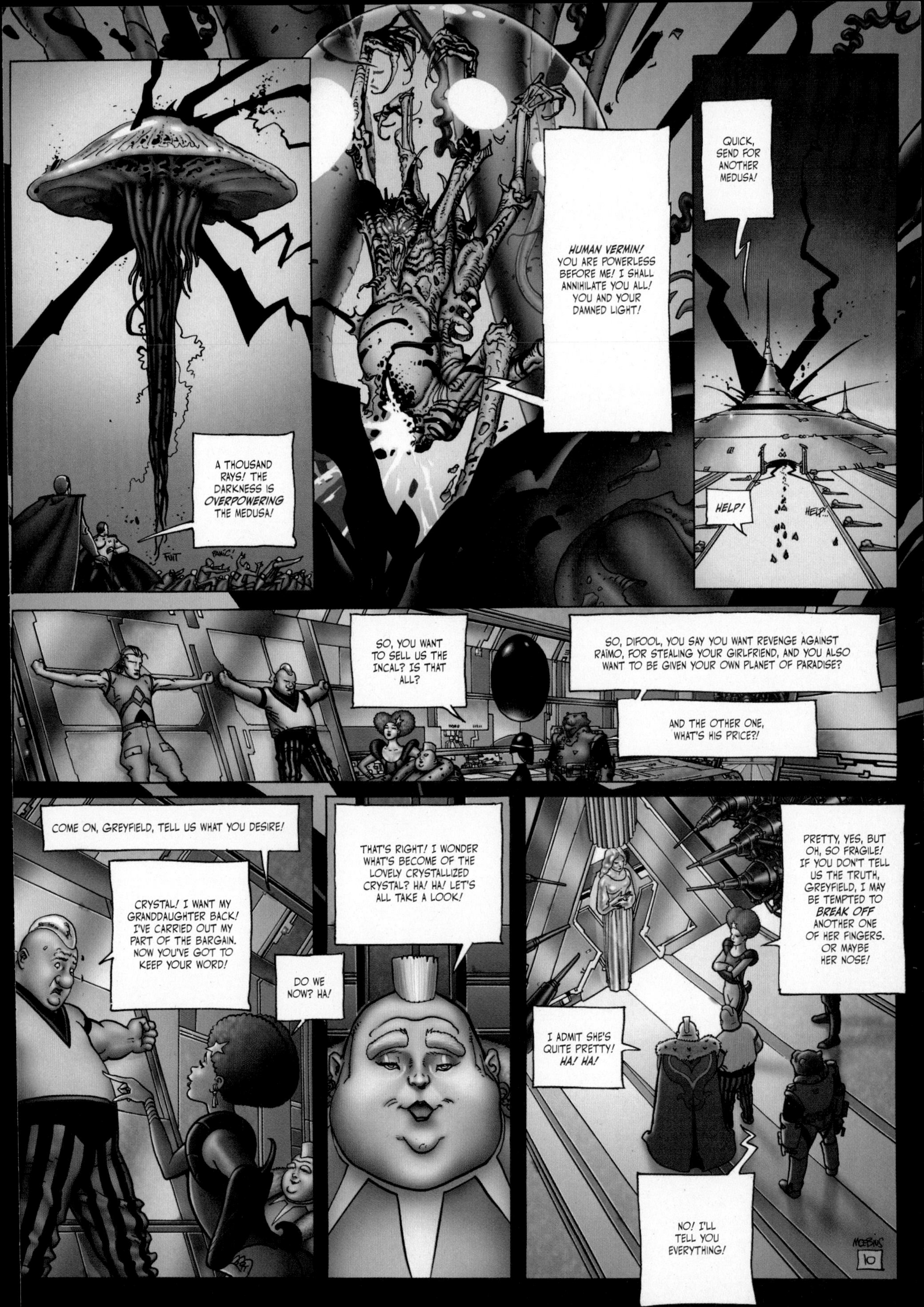

A THOUSAND RAYS! THE DARKNESS IS *OVERPOWERING* THE MEDUSA!
FUIT
PANIC!
HUMAN VERMIN! YOU ARE POWERLESS BEFORE ME! I SHALL ANNIHILATE YOU ALL! YOU AND YOUR DAMNED LIGHT!
QUICK, SEND FOR ANOTHER MEDUSA!
HELP!
HELP!...
SO, YOU WANT TO SELL US THE INCAL? IS THAT ALL?
SO, DIFOOL, YOU SAY YOU WANT REVENGE AGAINST RAÏMO, FOR STEALING YOUR GIRLFRIEND, AND YOU ALSO WANT TO BE GIVEN YOUR OWN PLANET OF PARADISE?
AND THE OTHER ONE, WHAT'S HIS PRICE?!
COME ON, GREYFIELD, TELL US WHAT YOU DESIRE!
CRYSTAL! I WANT MY GRANDDAUGHTER BACK! I'VE CARRIED OUT MY PART OF THE BARGAIN. NOW YOU'VE GOT TO KEEP YOUR WORD!
DO WE NOW? HA!
THAT'S RIGHT! I WONDER WHAT'S BECOME OF THE LOVELY CRYSTALLIZED CRYSTAL? HA! HA! LET'S ALL TAKE A LOOK!
I ADMIT SHE'S QUITE PRETTY! *HA! HA!*
PRETTY, YES, BUT OH, SO FRAGILE! IF YOU DON'T TELL US THE TRUTH, GREYFIELD, I MAY BE TEMPTED TO *BREAK OFF* ANOTHER ONE OF HER FINGERS. OR MAYBE HER NOSE!
NO! I'LL TELL YOU EVERYTHING!
MOEBIUS

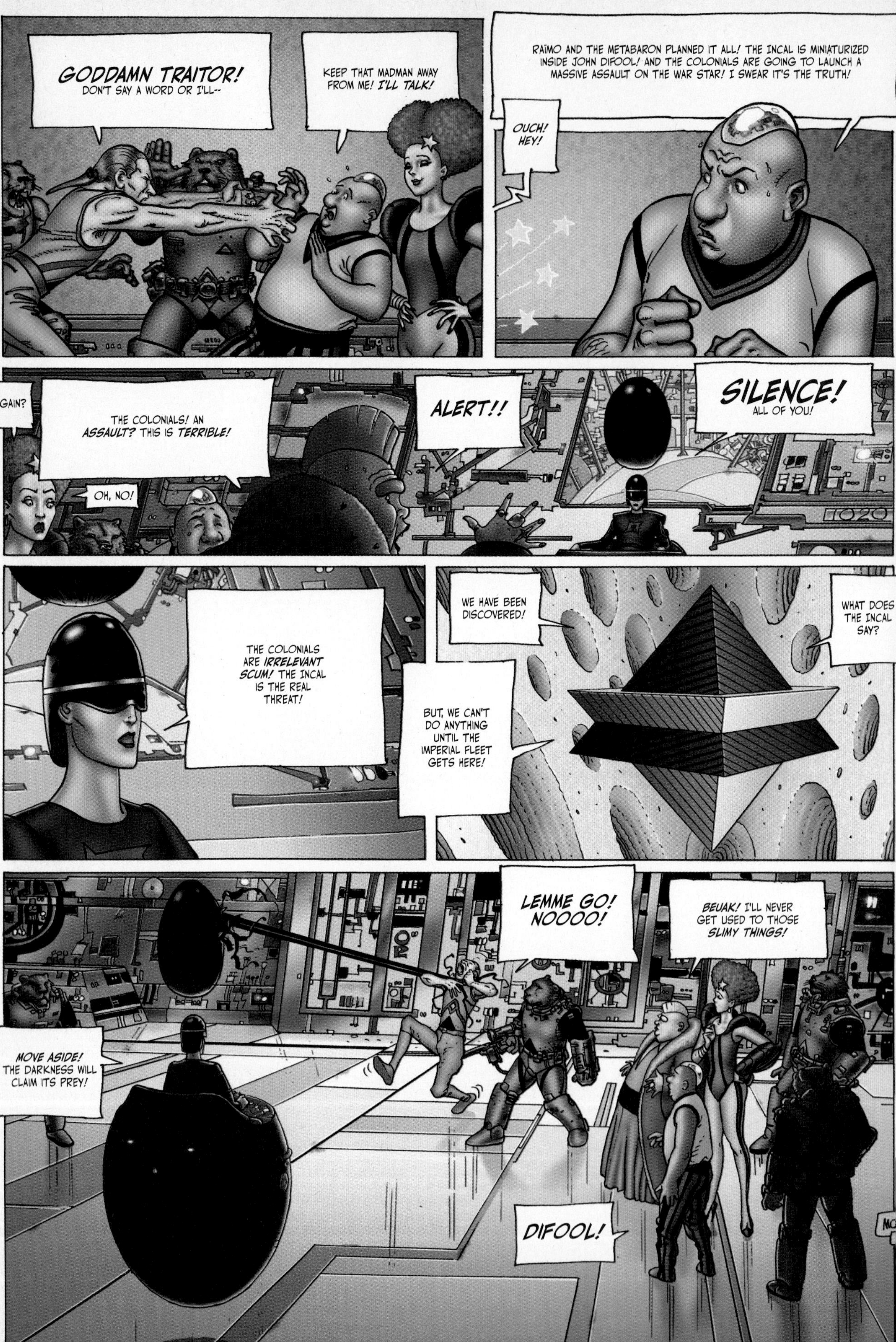

GODDAMN TRAITOR! DON'T SAY A WORD OR I'LL--
KEEP THAT MADMAN AWAY FROM ME! I'LL TALK!
OUCH! HEY!
RAÏMO AND THE METABARON PLANNED IT ALL! THE INCAL IS MINIATURIZED INSIDE JOHN DIFOOL! AND THE COLONIALS ARE GOING TO LAUNCH A MASSIVE ASSAULT ON THE WAR STAR! I SWEAR IT'S THE TRUTH!
AGAIN?
THE COLONIALS! AN ASSAULT? THIS IS TERRIBLE!
OH, NO!
ALERT!!
SILENCE! ALL OF YOU!
1020
THE COLONIALS ARE IRRELEVANT SCUM! THE INCAL IS THE REAL THREAT!
WE HAVE BEEN DISCOVERED!
BUT, WE CAN'T DO ANYTHING UNTIL THE IMPERIAL FLEET GETS HERE!
WHAT DOES THE INCAL SAY?
LEMME GO! NOOOO!
BEUAK! I'LL NEVER GET USED TO THOSE SLIMY THINGS!
MOVE ASIDE! THE DARKNESS WILL CLAIM ITS PREY!
DIFOOL!

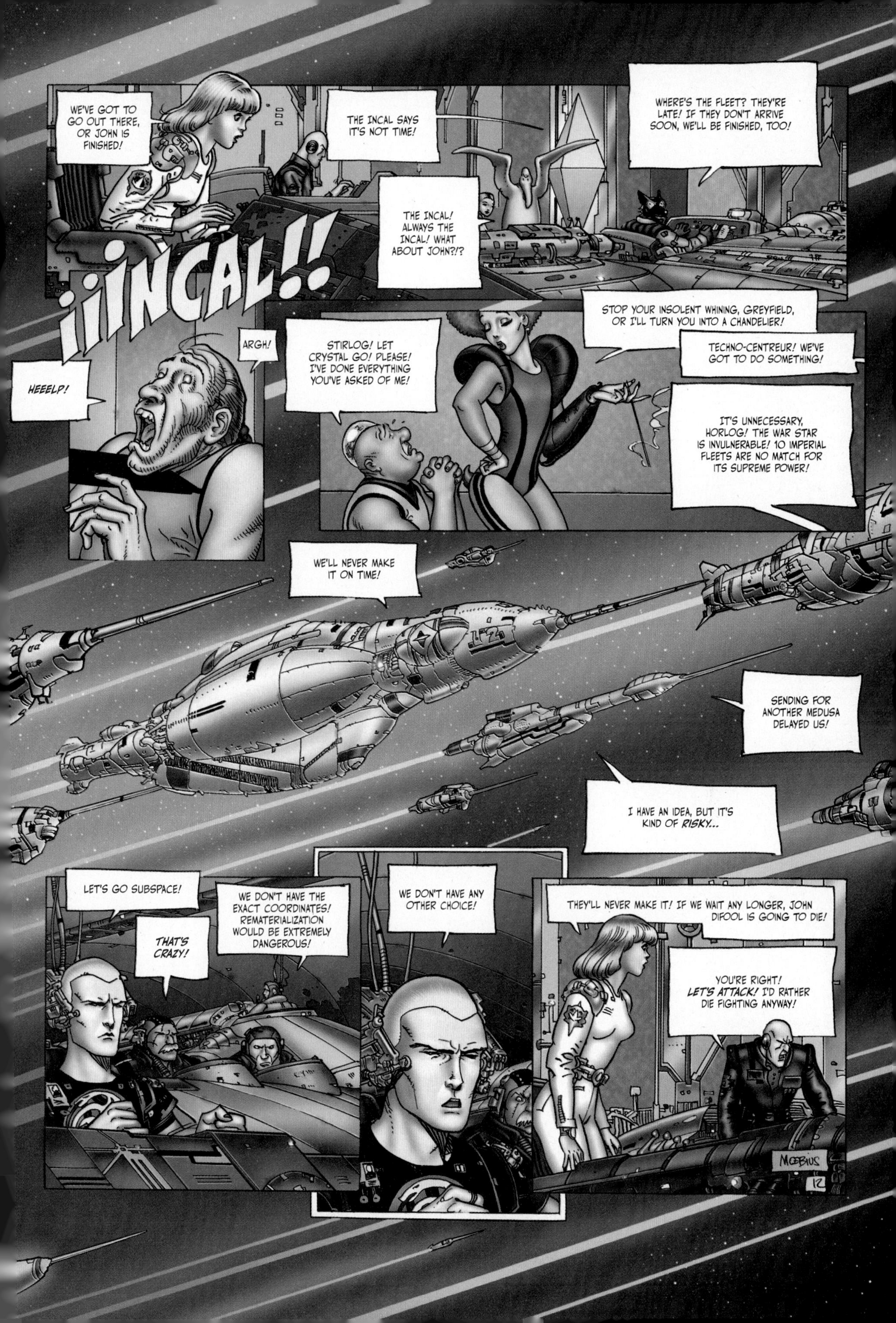

WE'VE GOT TO GO OUT THERE, OR JOHN IS FINISHED!
THE INCAL SAYS IT'S NOT TIME!
THE INCAL! ALWAYS THE INCAL! WHAT ABOUT JOHN?!?
WHERE'S THE FLEET? THEY'RE LATE! IF THEY DON'T ARRIVE SOON, WE'LL BE FINISHED, TOO!
¡¡INCAL!!
HEEELP!
ARGH!
STIRLOG! LET CRYSTAL GO! PLEASE! I'VE DONE EVERYTHING YOU'VE ASKED OF ME!
STOP YOUR INSOLENT WHINING, GREYFIELD, OR I'LL TURN YOU INTO A CHANDELIER!
TECHNO-CENTREUR! WE'VE GOT TO DO SOMETHING!
IT'S UNNECESSARY, HORLOG! THE WAR STAR IS INVULNERABLE! 10 IMPERIAL FLEETS ARE NO MATCH FOR ITS SUPREME POWER!
WE'LL NEVER MAKE IT ON TIME!
SENDING FOR ANOTHER MEDUSA DELAYED US!
I HAVE AN IDEA, BUT IT'S KIND OF RISKY...
LET'S GO SUBSPACE!
THAT'S CRAZY!
WE DON'T HAVE THE EXACT COORDINATES! REMATERIALIZATION WOULD BE EXTREMELY DANGEROUS!
WE DON'T HAVE ANY OTHER CHOICE!
THEY'LL NEVER MAKE IT! IF WE WAIT ANY LONGER, JOHN DIFOOL IS GOING TO DIE!
YOU'RE RIGHT! LET'S ATTACK! I'D RATHER DIE FIGHTING ANYWAY!
MOEBIUS
12

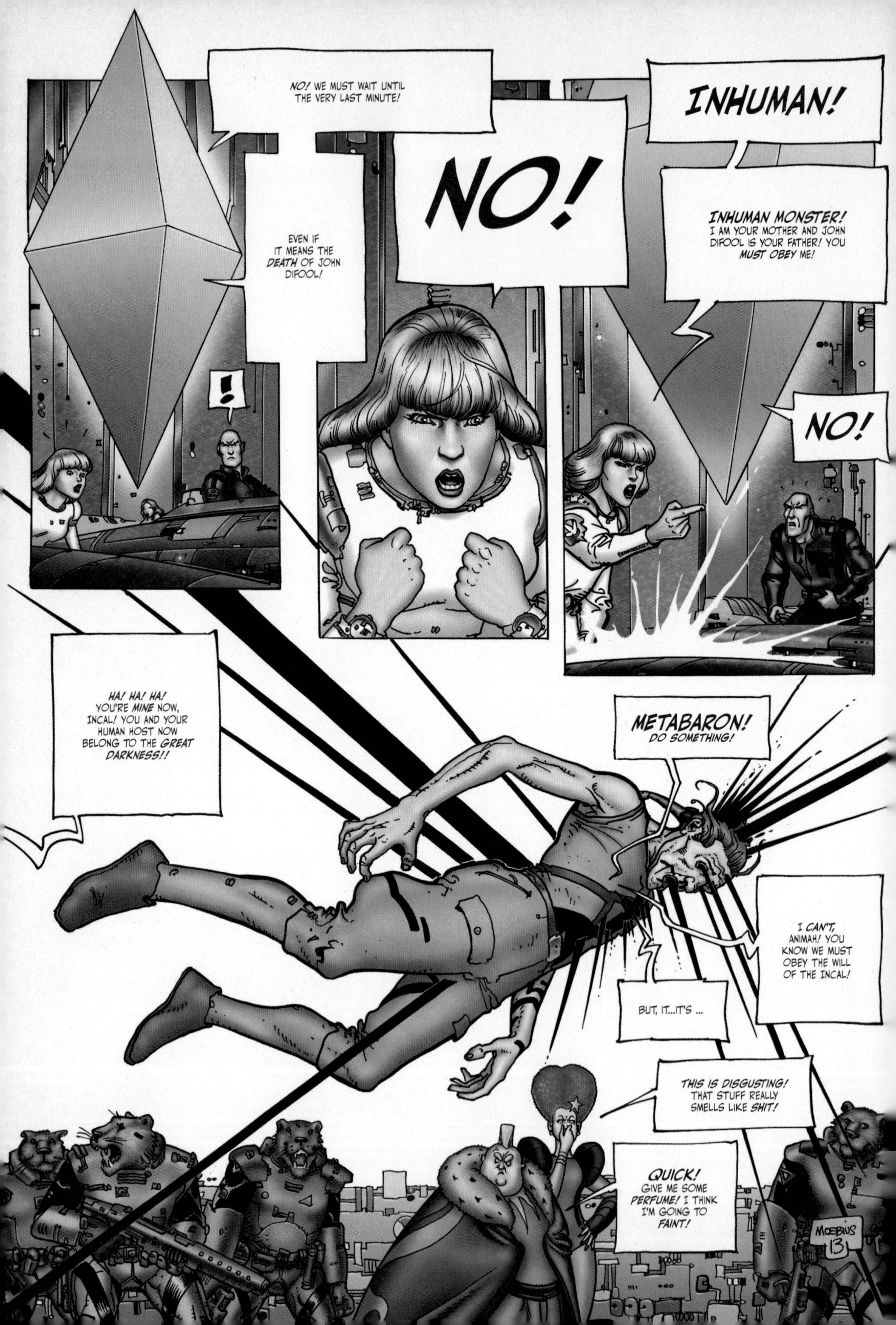
NO! WE MUST WAIT UNTIL THE VERY LAST MINUTE!
EVEN IF IT MEANS THE DEATH OF JOHN DIFOOL!
!
NO!
INHUMAN!
INHUMAN MONSTER! I AM YOUR MOTHER AND JOHN DIFOOL IS YOUR FATHER! YOU MUST OBEY ME!
NO!
HA! HA! HA! YOU'RE MINE NOW, INCAL! YOU AND YOUR HUMAN HOST NOW BELONG TO THE GREAT DARKNESS!!
METABARON! DO SOMETHING!
I CAN'T, ANIMAH! YOU KNOW WE MUST OBEY THE WILL OF THE INCAL!
BUT, IT...IT'S ...
THIS IS DISGUSTING! THAT STUFF REALLY SMELLS LIKE SHIT!
QUICK! GIVE ME SOME PERFUME! I THINK I'M GOING TO FAINT!
MOEBIUS 13

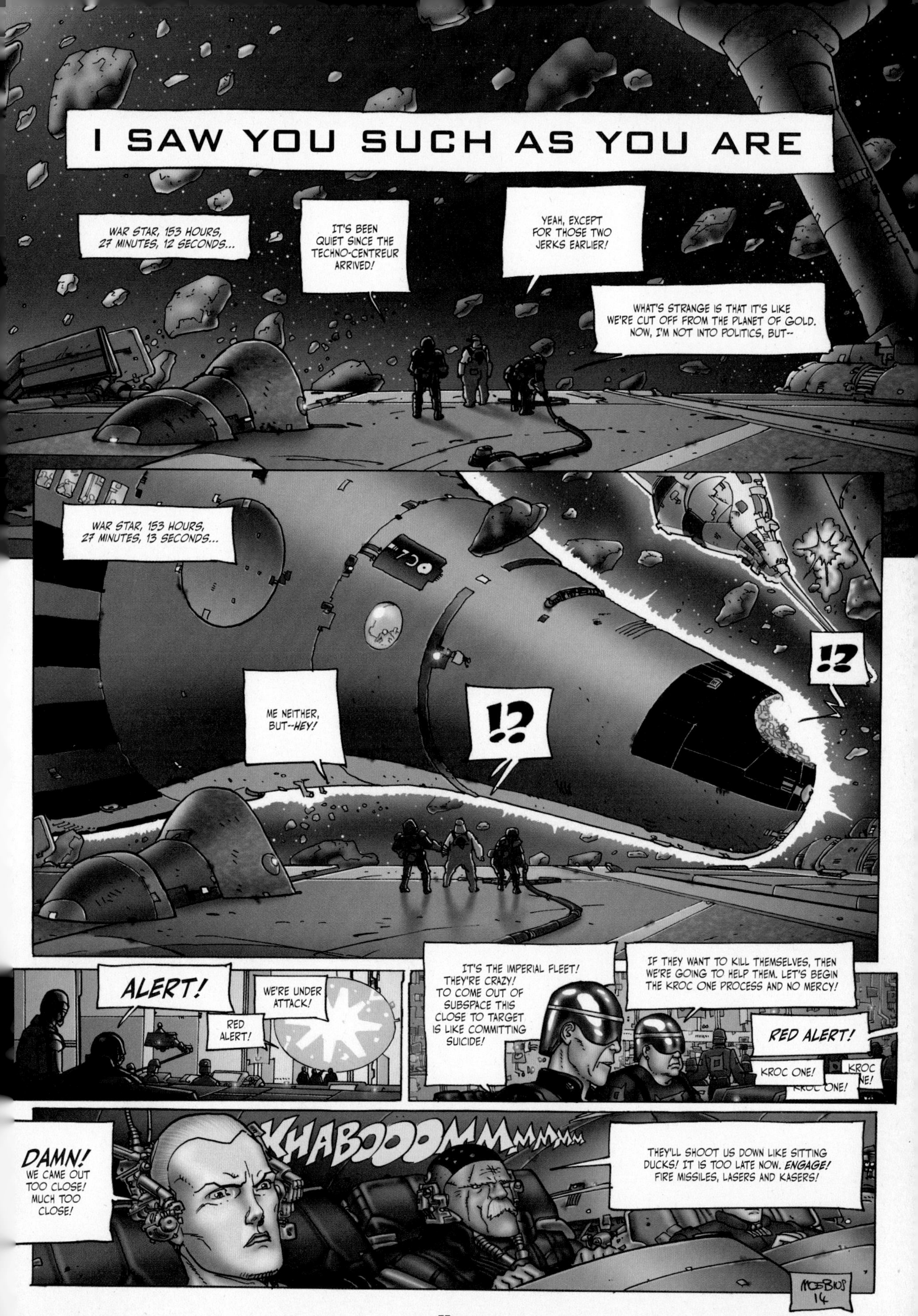

I SAW YOU SUCH AS YOU ARE
WAR STAR, 153 HOURS, 27 MINUTES, 12 SECONDS...
IT'S BEEN QUIET SINCE THE TECHNO-CENTREUR ARRIVED!
YEAH, EXCEPT FOR THOSE TWO JERKS EARLIER!
WHAT'S STRANGE IS THAT IT'S LIKE WE'RE CUT OFF FROM THE PLANET OF GOLD. NOW, I'M NOT INTO POLITICS, BUT--
WAR STAR, 153 HOURS, 27 MINUTES, 13 SECONDS...
ME NEITHER, BUT--HEY!
!?
!?
ALERT!
WE'RE UNDER ATTACK!
RED ALERT!
IT'S THE IMPERIAL FLEET! THEY'RE CRAZY! TO COME OUT OF SUBSPACE THIS CLOSE TO TARGET IS LIKE COMMITTING SUICIDE!
IF THEY WANT TO KILL THEMSELVES, THEN WE'RE GOING TO HELP THEM. LET'S BEGIN THE KROC ONE PROCESS AND NO MERCY!
RED ALERT!
KROC ONE!
KROC ONE!
DAMN! WE CAME OUT TOO CLOSE! MUCH TOO CLOSE!
KHABOOOMMMMMM
THEY'LL SHOOT US DOWN LIKE SITTING DUCKS! IT IS TOO LATE NOW. ENGAGE! FIRE MISSILES, LASERS AND KASERS!
MOEBIUS 14

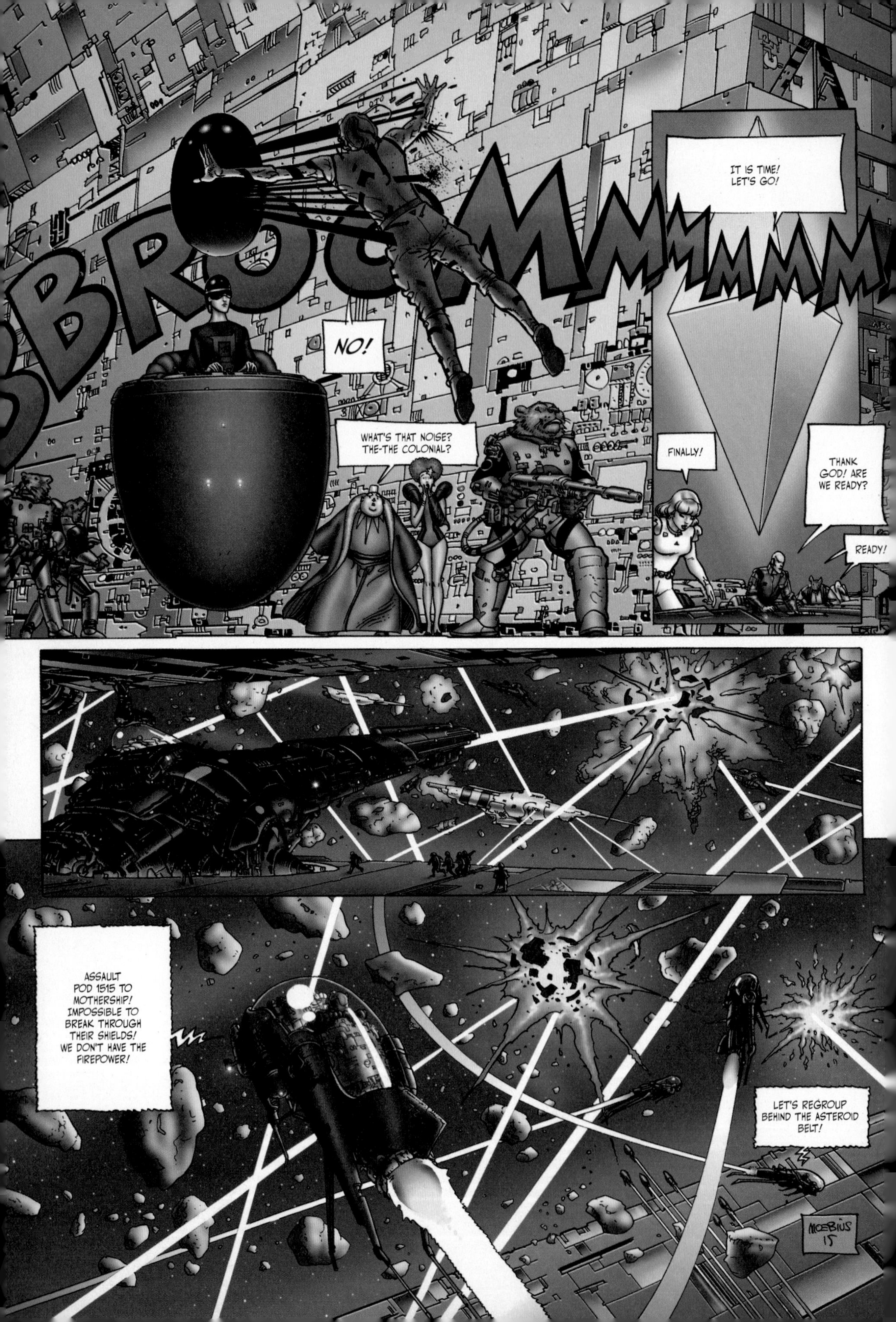

BBROOMMMMMMMMM
IT IS TIME! LET'S GO!
NO!
WHAT'S THAT NOISE? THE-THE COLONIAL?
FINALLY!
THANK GOD! ARE WE READY?
READY!
ASSAULT POD 1515 TO MOTHERSHIP! IMPOSSIBLE TO BREAK THROUGH THEIR SHIELDS! WE DON'T HAVE THE FIREPOWER!
LET'S REGROUP BEHIND THE ASTEROID BELT!
MOEBIUS
15

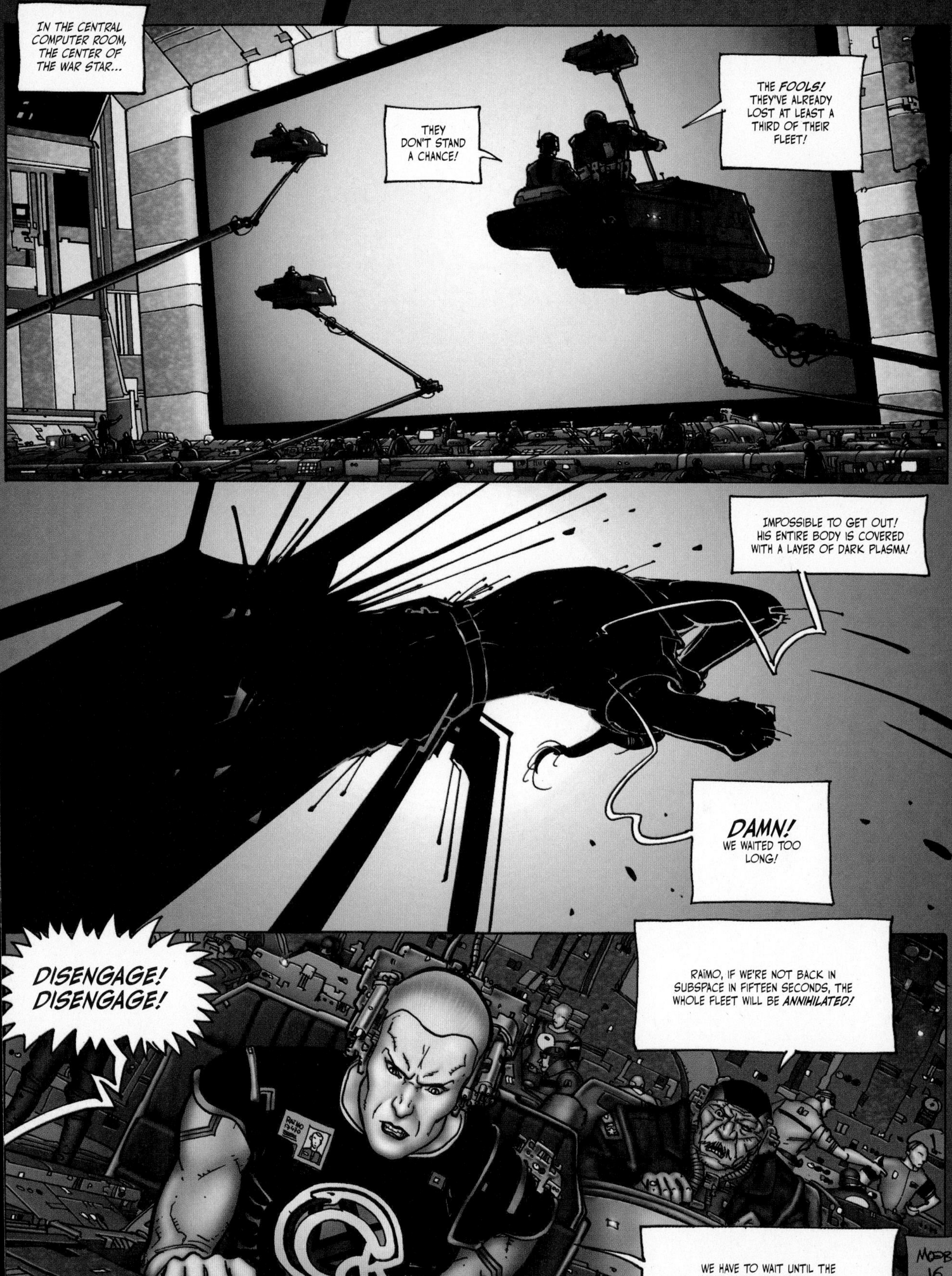

IN THE CENTRAL COMPUTER ROOM, THE CENTER OF THE WAR STAR...
THEY DON'T STAND A CHANCE!
THE *FOOLS!* THEY'VE ALREADY LOST AT LEAST A THIRD OF THEIR FLEET!
IMPOSSIBLE TO GET OUT! HIS ENTIRE BODY IS COVERED WITH A LAYER OF DARK PLASMA!
DAMN! WE WAITED TOO LONG!
DISENGAGE! DISENGAGE!
RAÏMO, IF WE'RE NOT BACK IN SUBSPACE IN FIFTEEN SECONDS, THE WHOLE FLEET WILL BE *ANNIHILATED!*
WE HAVE TO WAIT UNTIL THE VERY LAST SECOND! I HAVE *FAITH* IN THE INCAL!
MOEBIUS

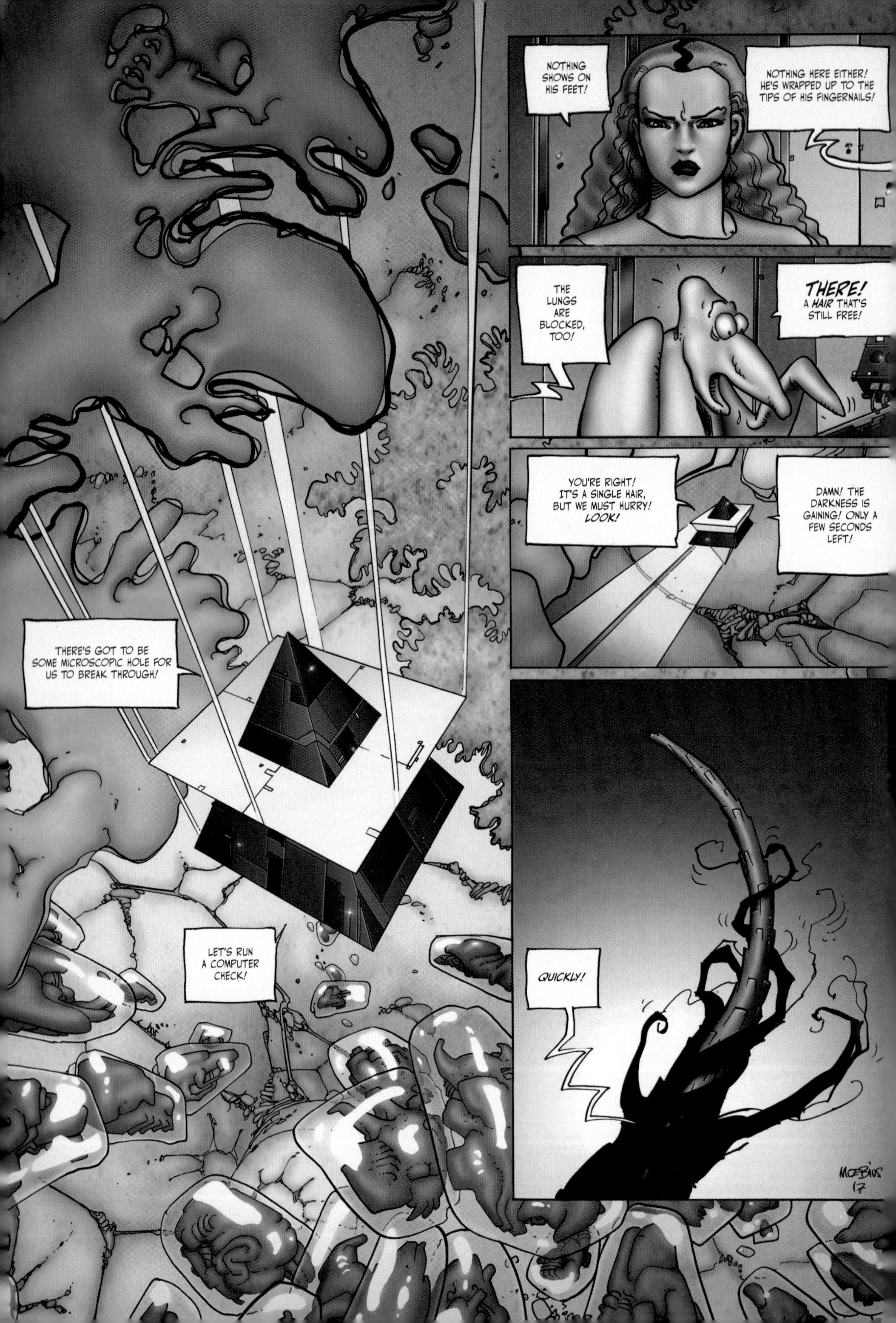
NOTHING SHOWS ON HIS FEET!
NOTHING HERE EITHER! HE'S WRAPPED UP TO THE TIPS OF HIS FINGERNAILS!
THE LUNGS ARE BLOCKED, TOO!
THERE! A HAIR THAT'S STILL FREE!
YOU'RE RIGHT! IT'S A SINGLE HAIR, BUT WE MUST HURRY! LOOK!
DAMN! THE DARKNESS IS GAINING! ONLY A FEW SECONDS LEFT!
THERE'S GOT TO BE SOME MICROSCOPIC HOLE FOR US TO BREAK THROUGH!
LET'S RUN A COMPUTER CHECK!
QUICKLY!
MOEBIUS
17

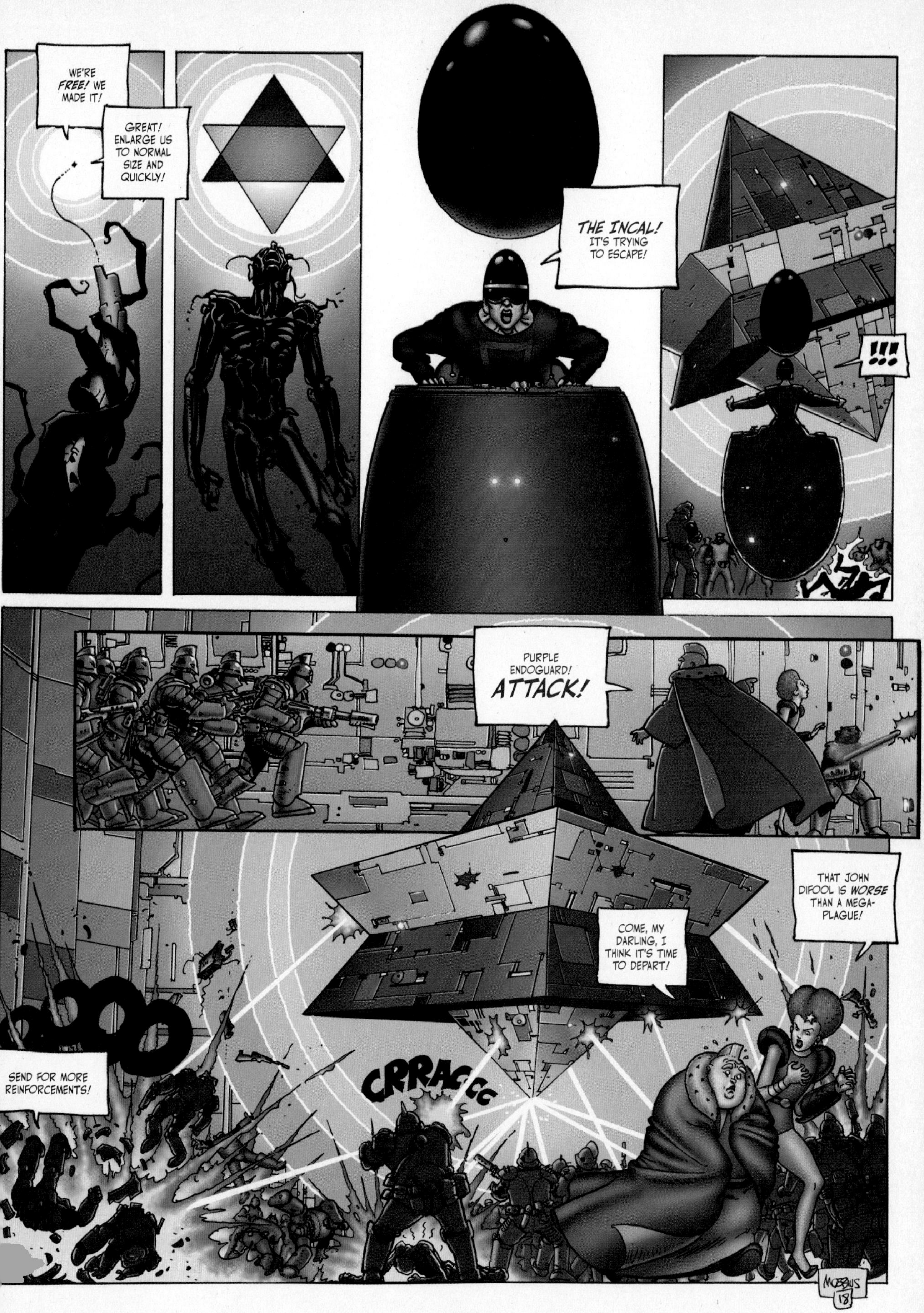
WE'RE FREE! WE MADE IT!
GREAT! ENLARGE US TO NORMAL SIZE AND QUICKLY!
THE INCAL! IT'S TRYING TO ESCAPE!
!!!
PURPLE ENDOGUARD! ATTACK!
THAT JOHN DIFOOL IS WORSE THAN A MEGA-PLAGUE!
COME, MY DARLING, I THINK IT'S TIME TO DEPART!
SEND FOR MORE REINFORCEMENTS!
CRRACCC
MOEBIUS 18

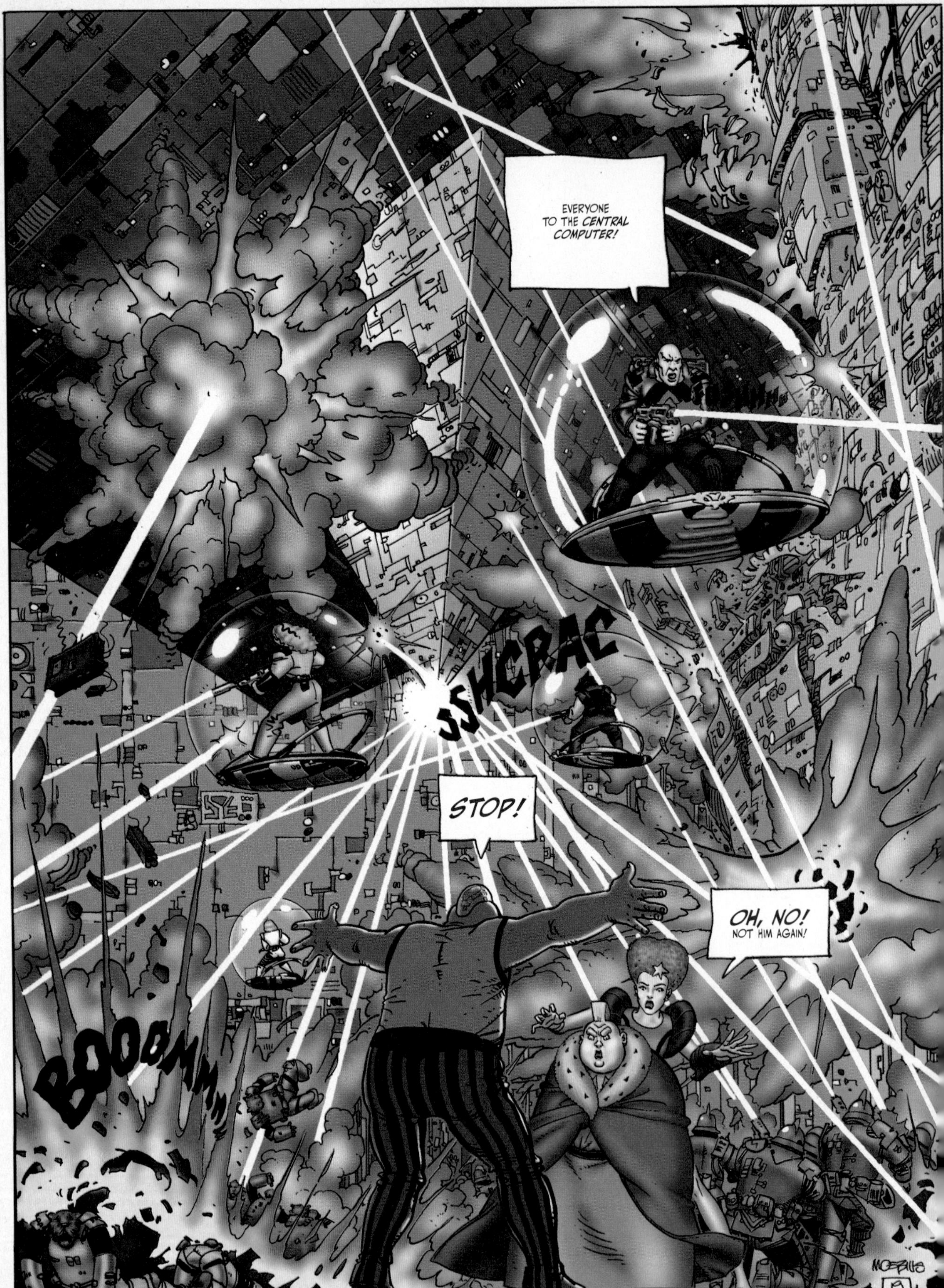
EVERYONE TO THE CENTRAL COMPUTER!
SSHCRAC
STOP!
OH, NO! NOT HIM AGAIN!
BOOOOMMM
MOEBIUS

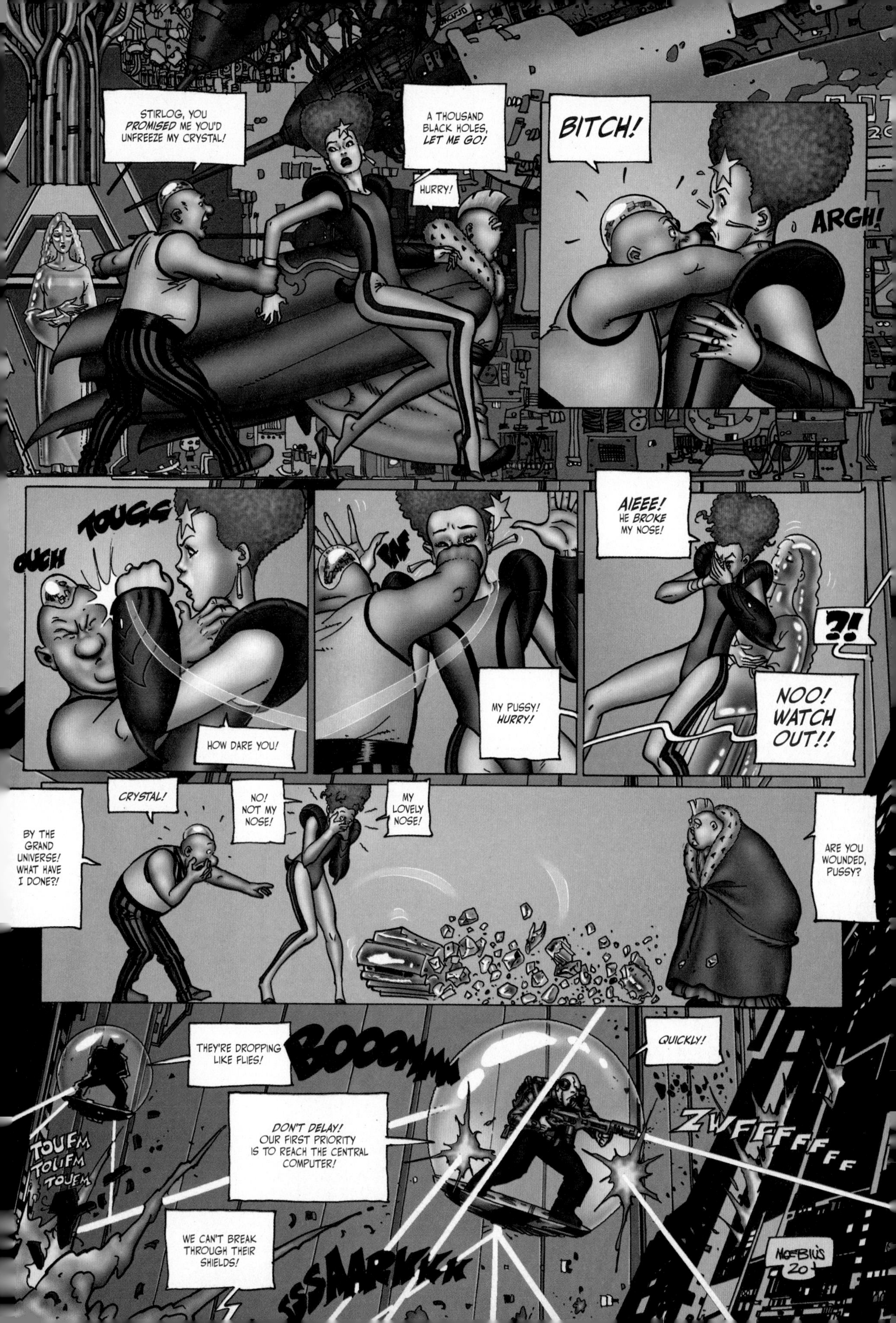
STIRLOG, YOU *PROMISED* ME YOU'D UNFREEZE MY CRYSTAL!
A THOUSAND BLACK HOLES, *LET ME GO!*
HURRY!
BITCH!
ARGH!
OUCH
TOUGG
HOW DARE YOU!
MY PUSSY! *HURRY!*
AIEEE! HE *BROKE* MY NOSE!
?!
NOO! WATCH OUT!!
BY THE GRAND UNIVERSE! WHAT HAVE I DONE?!
CRYSTAL!
NO! NOT MY NOSE!
MY LOVELY NOSE!
ARE YOU WOUNDED, PUSSY?
THEY'RE DROPPING LIKE FLIES!
BOOOMMM
QUICKLY!
DON'T DELAY! OUR FIRST PRIORITY IS TO REACH THE CENTRAL COMPUTER!
ZWFFFFFFFF
TOUFM TOUFM TOUFM
WE CAN'T BREAK THROUGH THEIR SHIELDS!
SSSAARKKKK
MOEBIUS 20

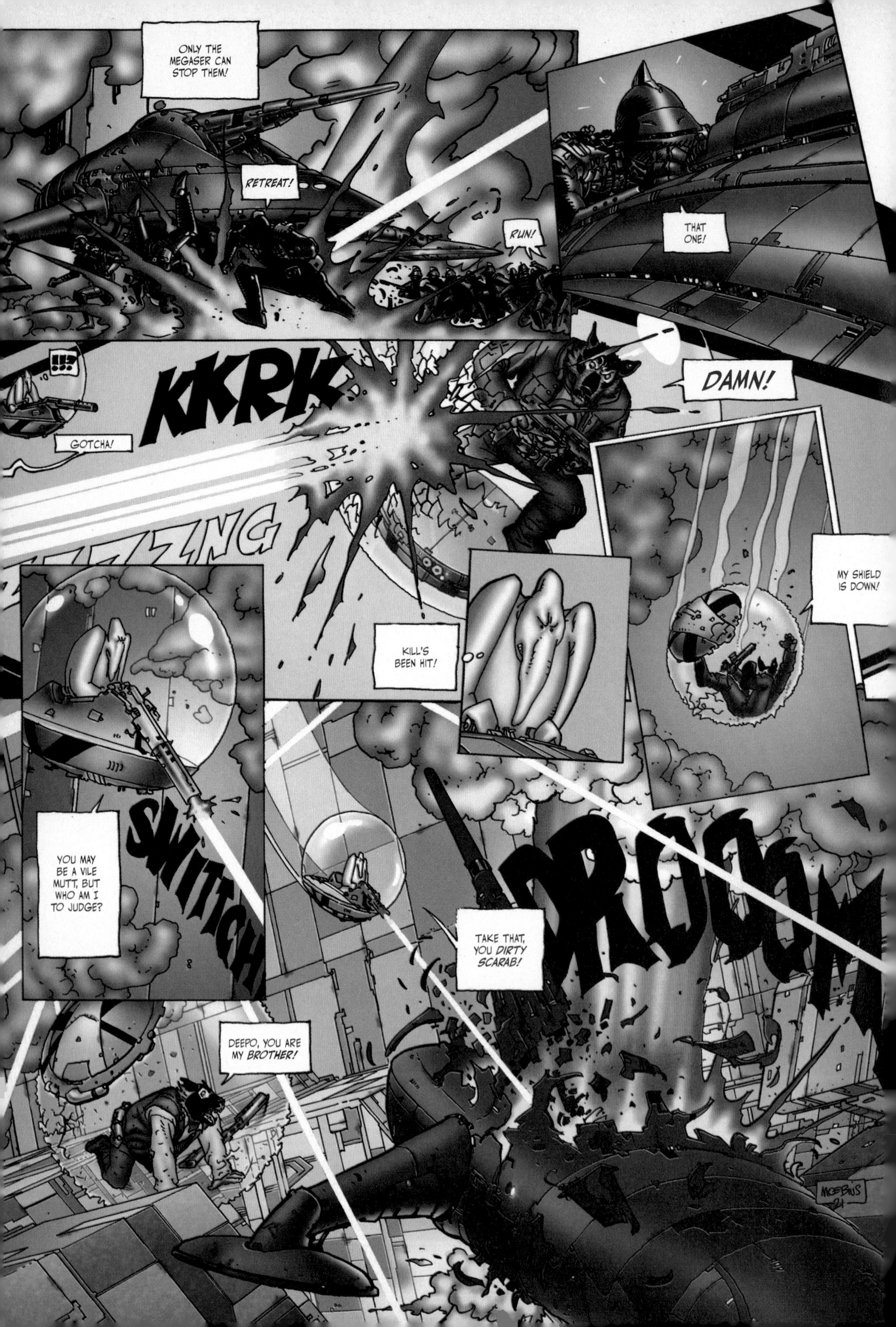
ONLY THE MEGASER CAN STOP THEM!
RETREAT!
RUN!
THAT ONE!
!!?
KKRK
DAMN!
GOTCHA!
ZZZZING
MY SHIELD IS DOWN!
KILL'S BEEN HIT!
SWITCH
YOU MAY BE A VILE MUTT, BUT WHO AM I TO JUDGE?
DROOOM
TAKE THAT, YOU DIRTY SCARAB!
DEEPO, YOU ARE MY BROTHER!
MOEBIUS

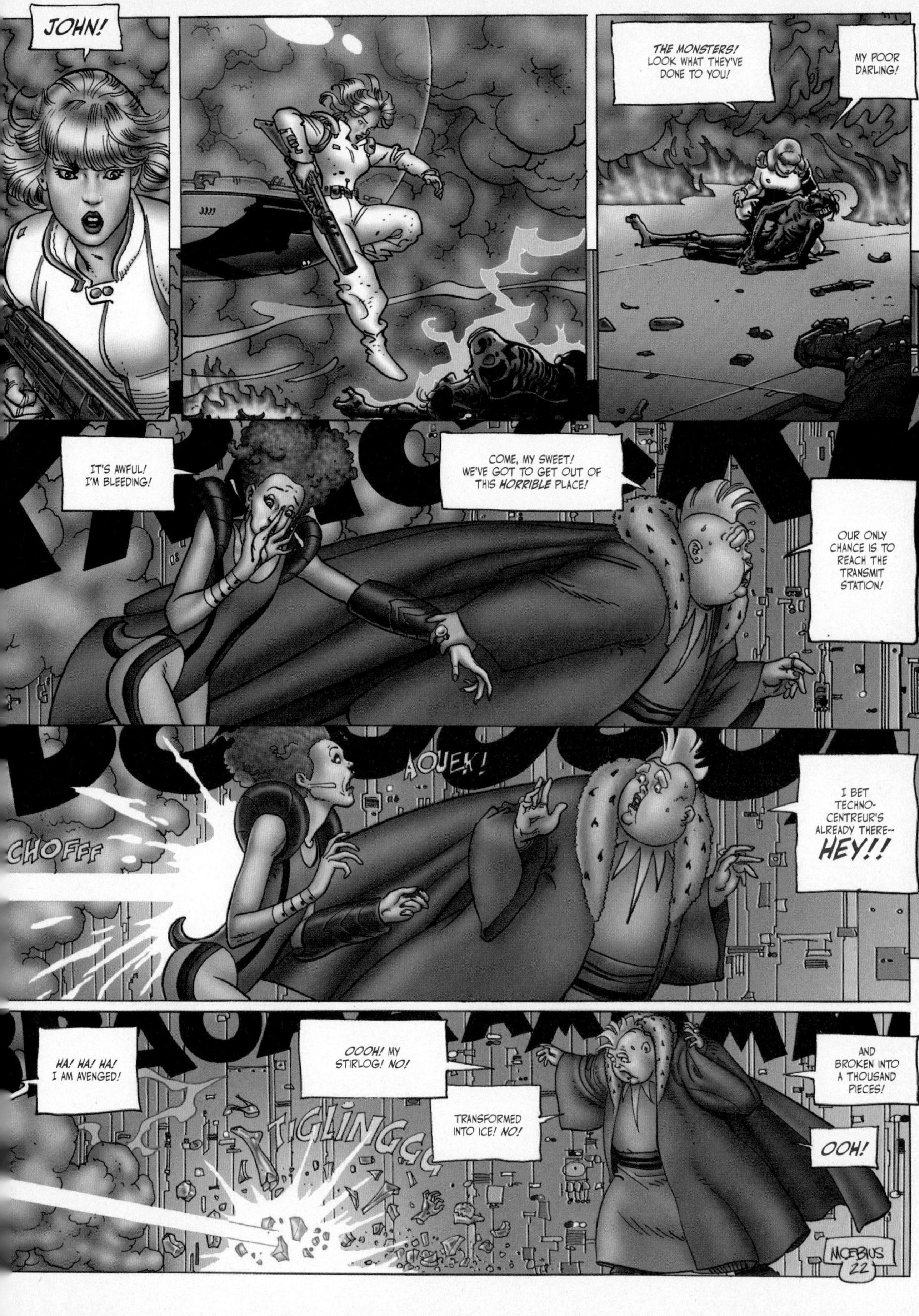
JOHN!
THE MONSTERS! LOOK WHAT THEY'VE DONE TO YOU!
MY POOR DARLING!
IT'S AWFUL! I'M BLEEDING!
COME, MY SWEET! WE'VE GOT TO GET OUT OF THIS HORRIBLE PLACE!
OUR ONLY CHANCE IS TO REACH THE TRANSMIT STATION!
CHOFFFF
AOUEK!
I BET TECHNO-CENTREUR'S ALREADY THERE-- HEY!!
HA! HA! HA! I AM AVENGED!
OOOH! MY STIRLOG! NO!
TRANSFORMED INTO ICE! NO!
TIGLINGGG
AND BROKEN INTO A THOUSAND PIECES!
OOH!
MOEBIUS 22

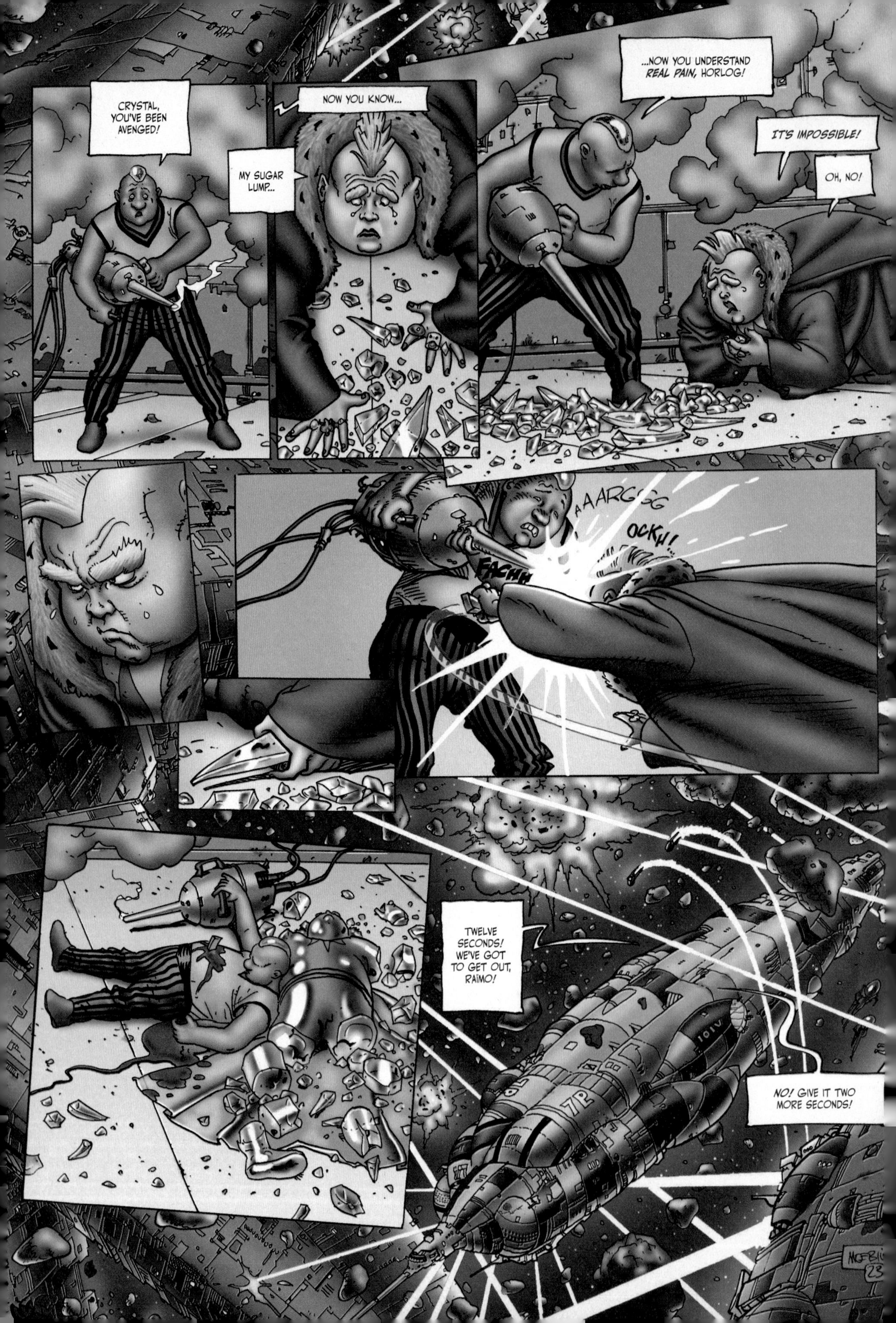
CRYSTAL, YOU'VE BEEN AVENGED!
NOW YOU KNOW...
MY SUGAR LUMP...
...NOW YOU UNDERSTAND REAL PAIN, HORLOG!
IT'S IMPOSSIBLE!
OH, NO!
AAARGGG
OCKH!
FACHH
TWELVE SECONDS! WE'VE GOT TO GET OUT, RAIMO!
NO! GIVE IT TWO MORE SECONDS!
23

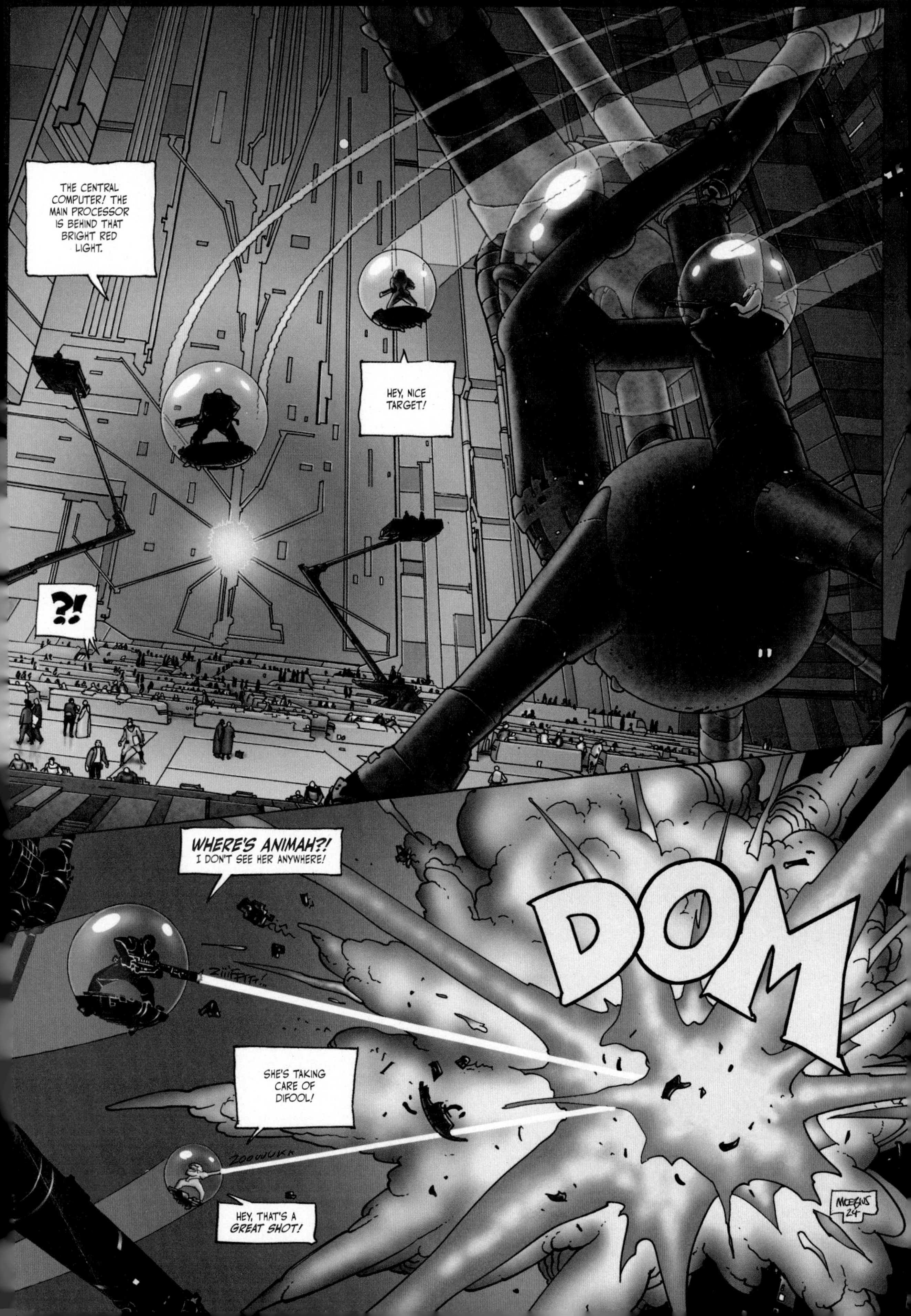
THE CENTRAL COMPUTER! THE MAIN PROCESSOR IS BEHIND THAT BRIGHT RED LIGHT.
HEY, NICE TARGET!
?!
WHERE'S ANIMAH?! I DON'T SEE HER ANYWHERE!
DOM
SHE'S TAKING CARE OF DIFOOL!
HEY, THAT'S A GREAT SHOT!
MOEBIUS 24

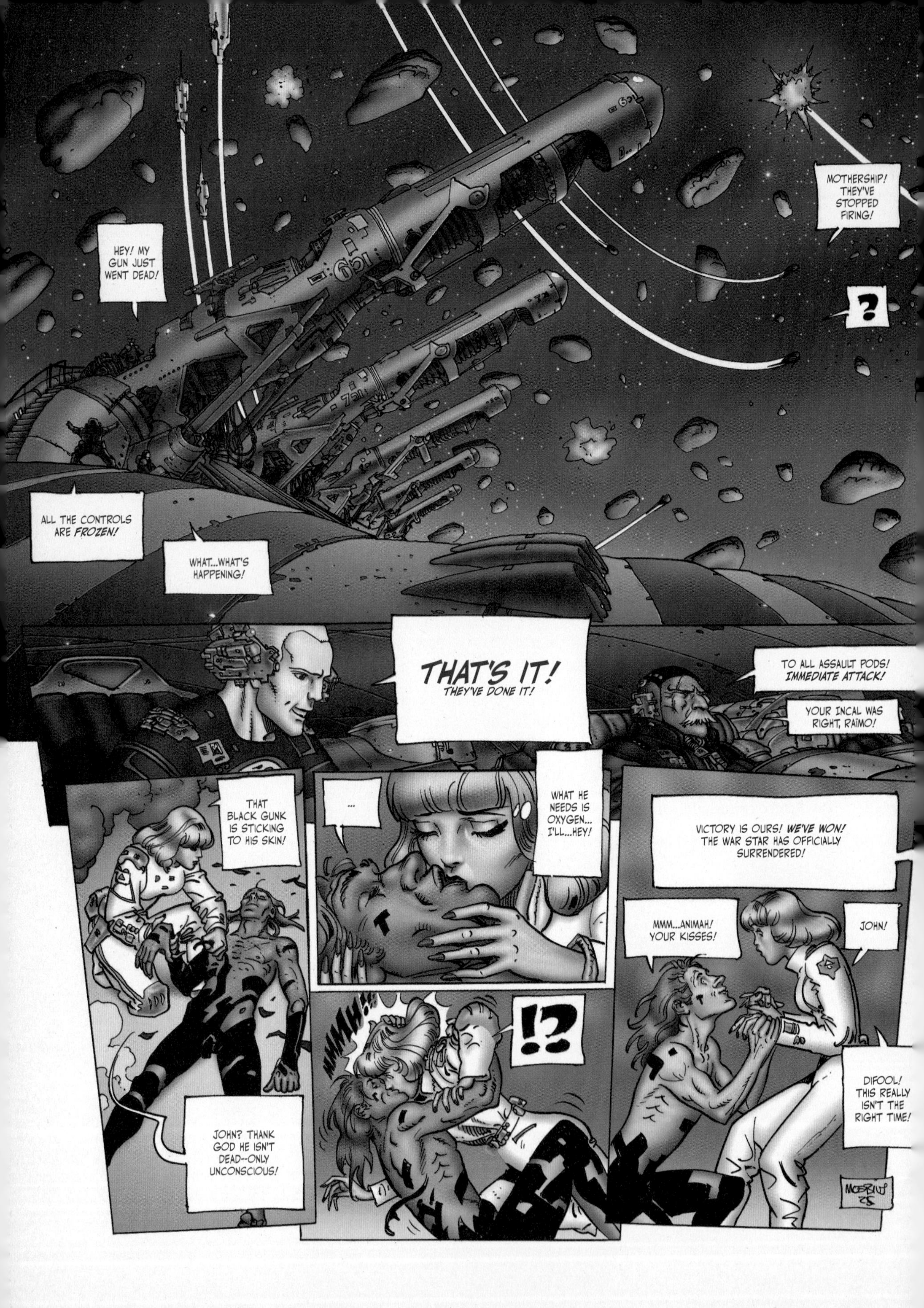
HEY! MY GUN JUST WENT DEAD!
MOTHERSHIP! THEY'VE STOPPED FIRING!
?
ALL THE CONTROLS ARE FROZEN!
WHAT...WHAT'S HAPPENING!
THAT'S IT! THEY'VE DONE IT!
TO ALL ASSAULT PODS! IMMEDIATE ATTACK!
YOUR INCAL WAS RIGHT, RAÏMO!
THAT BLACK GUNK IS STICKING TO HIS SKIN!
JOHN? THANK GOD HE ISN'T DEAD--ONLY UNCONSCIOUS!
...
WHAT HE NEEDS IS OXYGEN... I'LL...HEY!
!?
VICTORY IS OURS! WE'VE WON! THE WAR STAR HAS OFFICIALLY SURRENDERED!
MMM...ANIMAH! YOUR KISSES!
JOHN!
DIFOOL! THIS REALLY ISN'T THE RIGHT TIME!
MOEBIUS

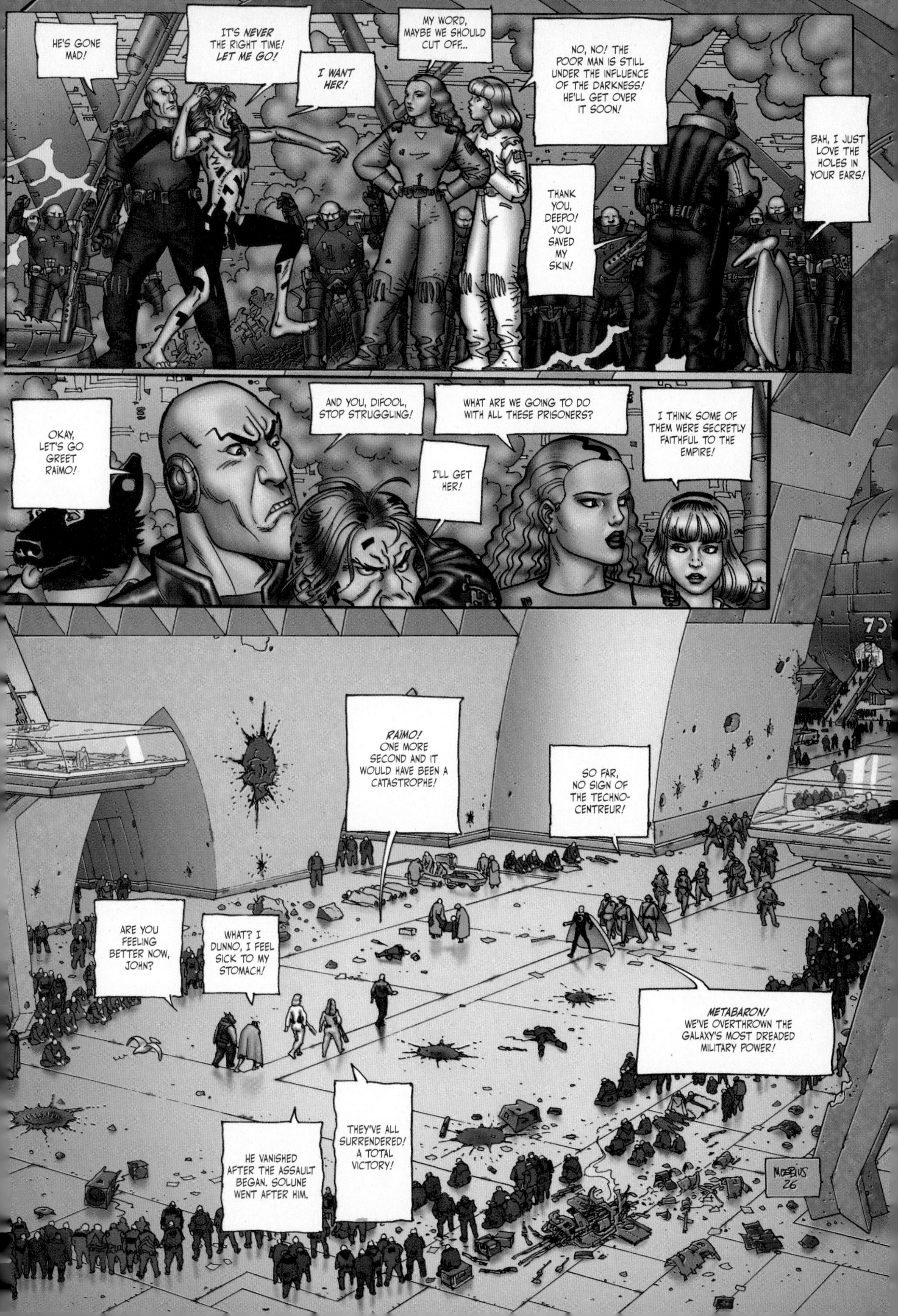
HE'S GONE MAD!
IT'S NEVER THE RIGHT TIME! LET ME GO!
I WANT HER!
MY WORD, MAYBE WE SHOULD CUT OFF...
NO, NO! THE POOR MAN IS STILL UNDER THE INFLUENCE OF THE DARKNESS! HE'LL GET OVER IT SOON!
THANK YOU, DEEPO! YOU SAVED MY SKIN!
BAH, I JUST LOVE THE HOLES IN YOUR EARS!
OKAY, LET'S GO GREET RAÏMO!
AND YOU, DIFOOL, STOP STRUGGLING!
I'LL GET HER!
WHAT ARE WE GOING TO DO WITH ALL THESE PRISONERS?
I THINK SOME OF THEM WERE SECRETLY FAITHFUL TO THE EMPIRE!
RAÏMO! ONE MORE SECOND AND IT WOULD HAVE BEEN A CATASTROPHE!
SO FAR, NO SIGN OF THE TECHNO-CENTREUR!
ARE YOU FEELING BETTER NOW, JOHN?
WHAT? I DUNNO, I FEEL SICK TO MY STOMACH!
METABARON! WE'VE OVERTHROWN THE GALAXY'S MOST DREADED MILITARY POWER!
HE VANISHED AFTER THE ASSAULT BEGAN. SOLUNE WENT AFTER HIM.
THEY'VE ALL SURRENDERED! A TOTAL VICTORY!
MOEBIUS 26

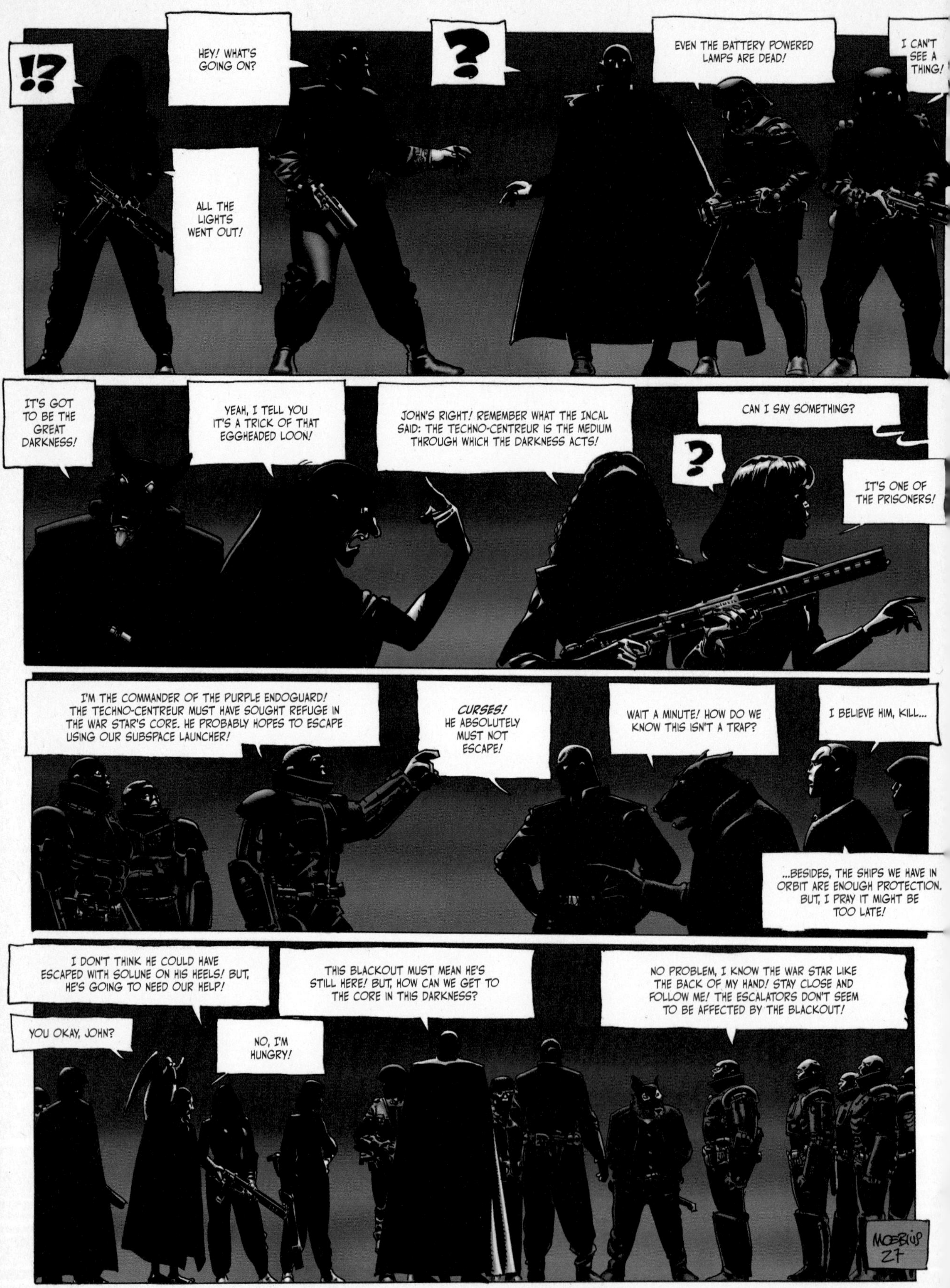
!?
HEY! WHAT'S GOING ON?
ALL THE LIGHTS WENT OUT!
?
EVEN THE BATTERY POWERED LAMPS ARE DEAD!
I CAN'T SEE A THING!
IT'S GOT TO BE THE GREAT DARKNESS!
YEAH, I TELL YOU IT'S A TRICK OF THAT EGGHEADED LOON!
JOHN'S RIGHT! REMEMBER WHAT THE INCAL SAID: THE TECHNO-CENTREUR IS THE MEDIUM THROUGH WHICH THE DARKNESS ACTS!
?
CAN I SAY SOMETHING?
IT'S ONE OF THE PRISONERS!
I'M THE COMMANDER OF THE PURPLE ENDOGUARD! THE TECHNO-CENTREUR MUST HAVE SOUGHT REFUGE IN THE WAR STAR'S CORE. HE PROBABLY HOPES TO ESCAPE USING OUR SUBSPACE LAUNCHER!
CURSES! HE ABSOLUTELY MUST NOT ESCAPE!
WAIT A MINUTE! HOW DO WE KNOW THIS ISN'T A TRAP?
I BELIEVE HIM, KILL...
...BESIDES, THE SHIPS WE HAVE IN ORBIT ARE ENOUGH PROTECTION. BUT, I PRAY IT MIGHT BE TOO LATE!
I DON'T THINK HE COULD HAVE ESCAPED WITH SOLUNE ON HIS HEELS! BUT, HE'S GOING TO NEED OUR HELP!
YOU OKAY, JOHN?
NO, I'M HUNGRY!
THIS BLACKOUT MUST MEAN HE'S STILL HERE! BUT, HOW CAN WE GET TO THE CORE IN THIS DARKNESS?
NO PROBLEM, I KNOW THE WAR STAR LIKE THE BACK OF MY HAND! STAY CLOSE AND FOLLOW ME! THE ESCALATORS DON'T SEEM TO BE AFFECTED BY THE BLACKOUT!
MOEBIUS 27

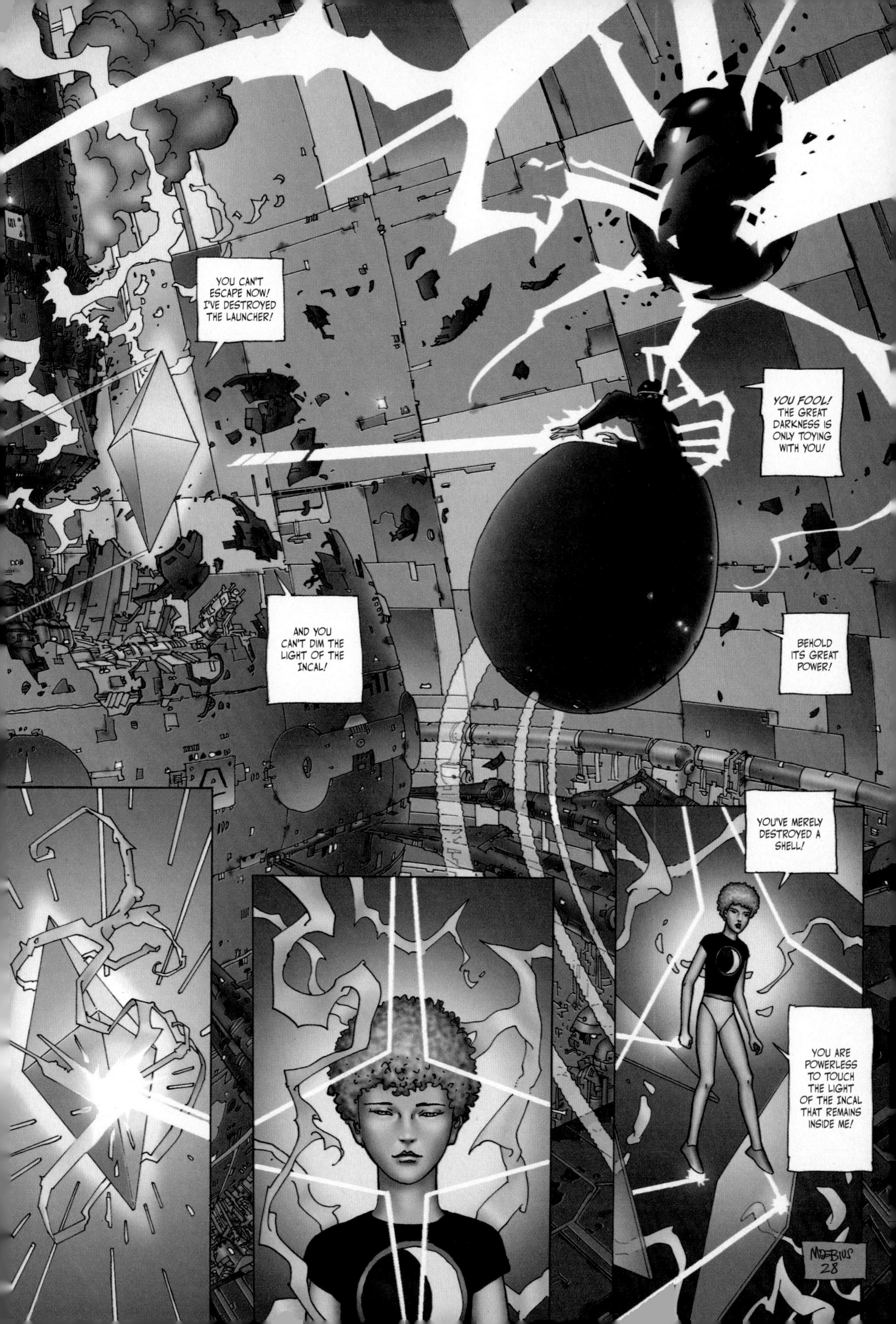
YOU CAN'T ESCAPE NOW! I'VE DESTROYED THE LAUNCHER!
YOU FOOL! THE GREAT DARKNESS IS ONLY TOYING WITH YOU!
AND YOU CAN'T DIM THE LIGHT OF THE INCAL!
BEHOLD ITS GREAT POWER!
YOU'VE MERELY DESTROYED A SHELL!
YOU ARE POWERLESS TO TOUCH THE LIGHT OF THE INCAL THAT REMAINS INSIDE ME!
MŒBIUS
28

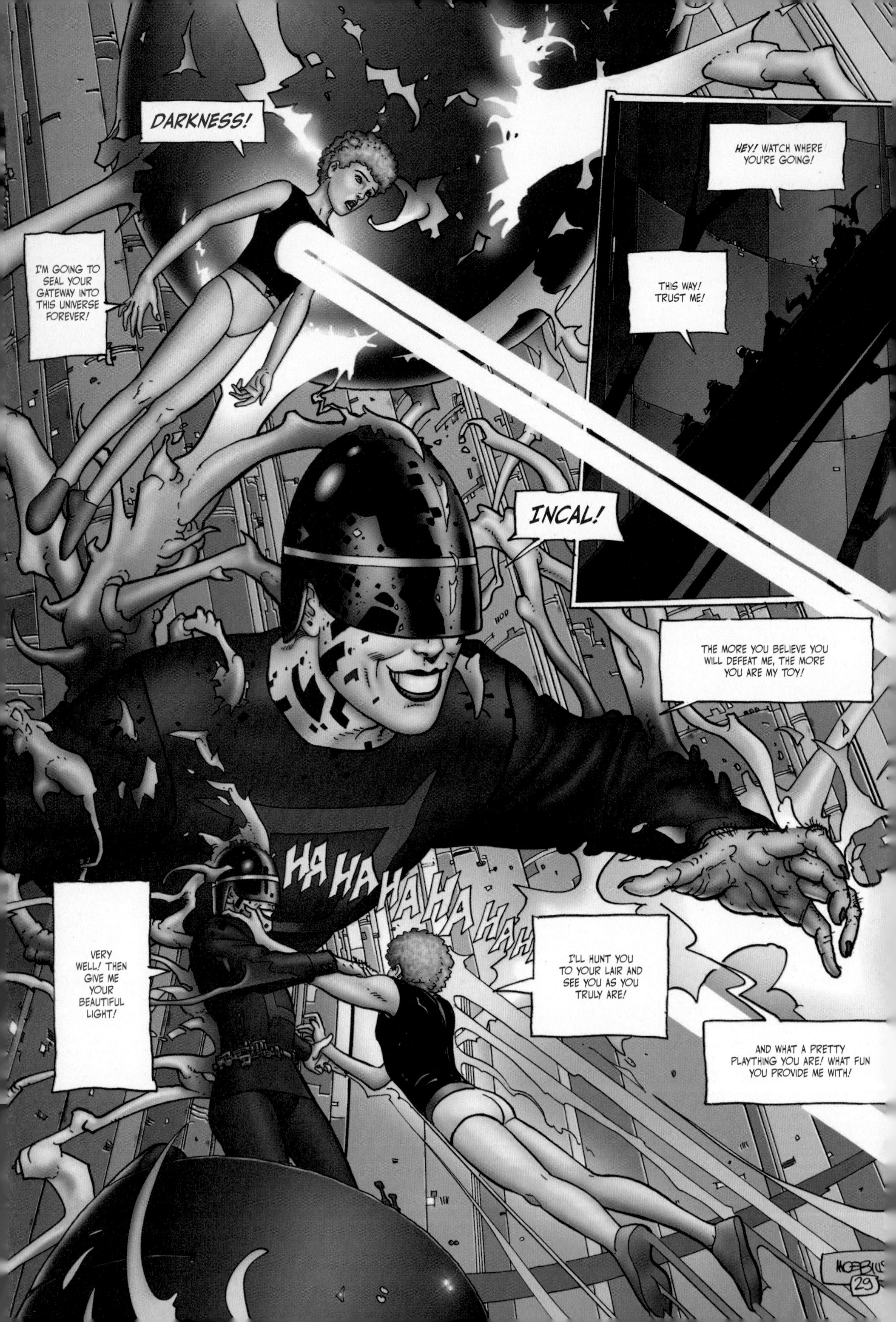
DARKNESS!
I'M GOING TO SEAL YOUR GATEWAY INTO THIS UNIVERSE FOREVER!
HEY! WATCH WHERE YOU'RE GOING!
THIS WAY! TRUST ME!
INCAL!
THE MORE YOU BELIEVE YOU WILL DEFEAT ME, THE MORE YOU ARE MY TOY!
HA HA HA HA HA HA HAH
VERY WELL! THEN GIVE ME YOUR BEAUTIFUL LIGHT!
I'LL HUNT YOU TO YOUR LAIR AND SEE YOU AS YOU TRULY ARE!
AND WHAT A PRETTY PLAYTHING YOU ARE! WHAT FUN YOU PROVIDE ME WITH!
MOEBIUS

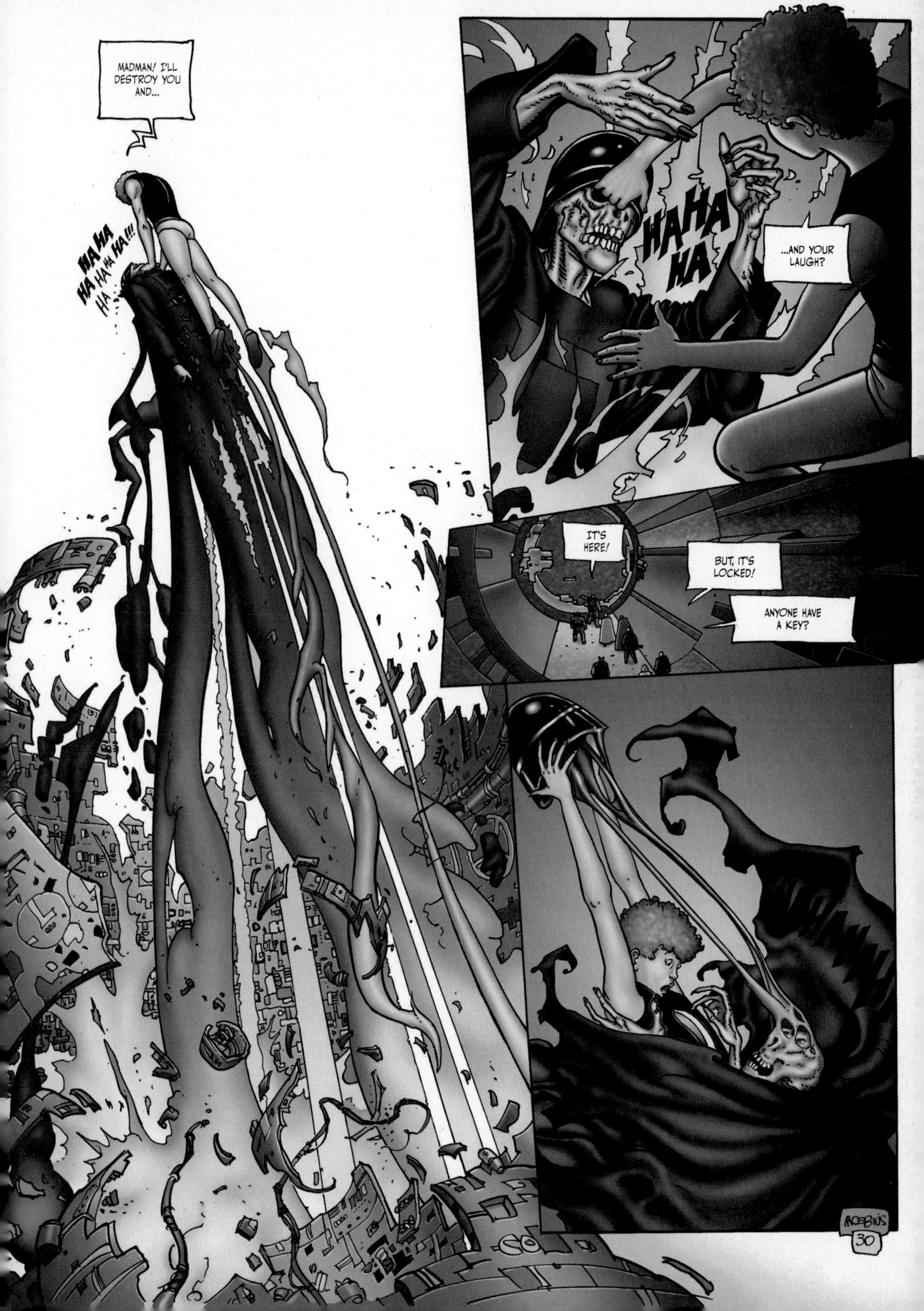
MADMAN! I'LL DESTROY YOU AND...
HA HA HA HA HA HA!!! HA
HA HA HA HA
...AND YOUR LAUGH?
IT'S HERE!
BUT, IT'S LOCKED!
ANYONE HAVE A KEY?
MOEBIUS

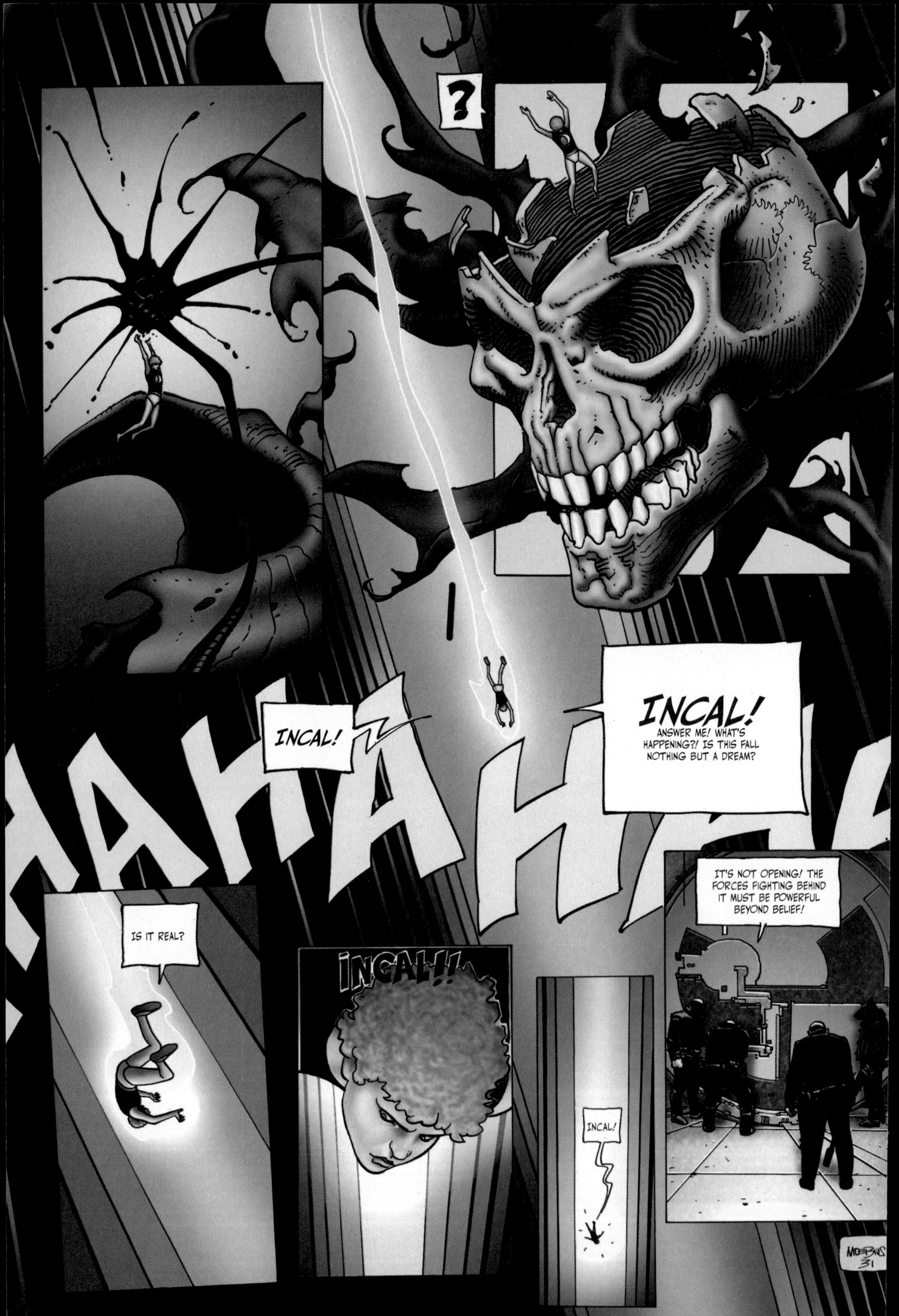
?
INCAL!
INCAL! ANSWER ME! WHAT'S HAPPENING?! IS THIS FALL NOTHING BUT A DREAM?
HAHAHA
IS IT REAL?
INCAL!!
INCAL!
IT'S NOT OPENING! THE FORCES FIGHTING BEHIND IT MUST BE POWERFUL BEYOND BELIEF!
MOEBIUS 31

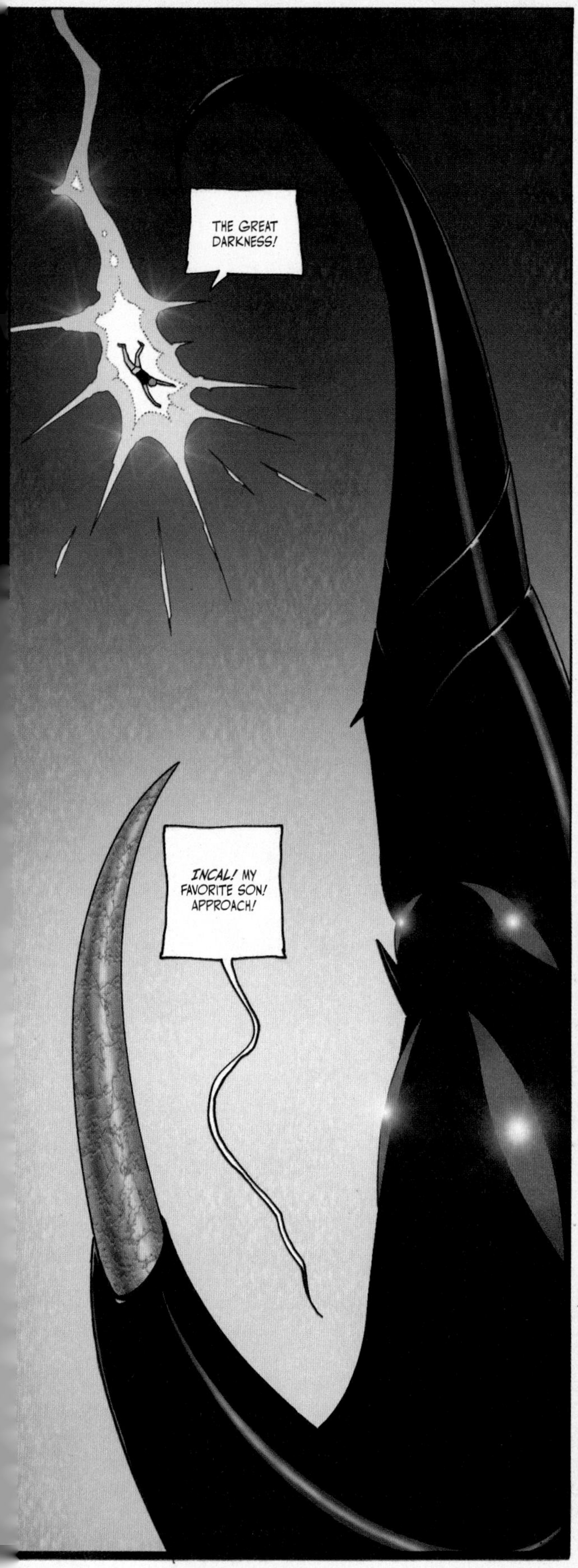
THE GREAT DARKNESS!
INCAL! MY FAVORITE SON! APPROACH!

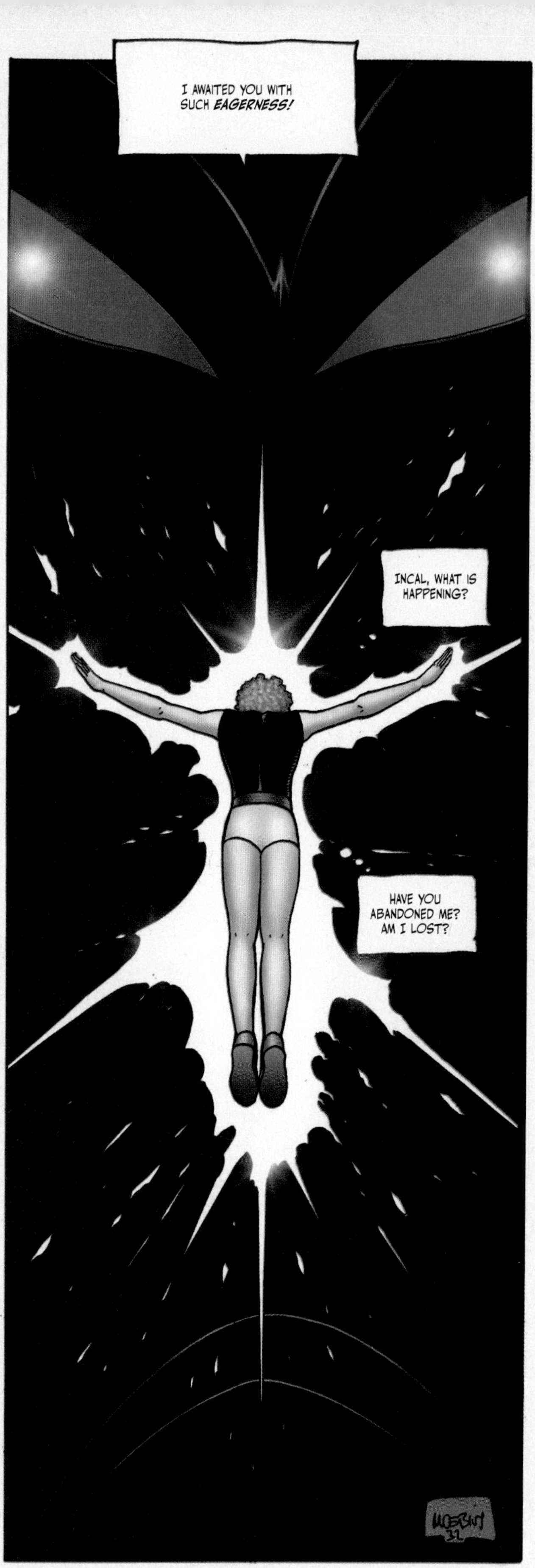
I AWAITED YOU WITH SUCH EAGERNESS!
INCAL, WHAT IS HAPPENING?
HAVE YOU ABANDONED ME? AM I LOST?

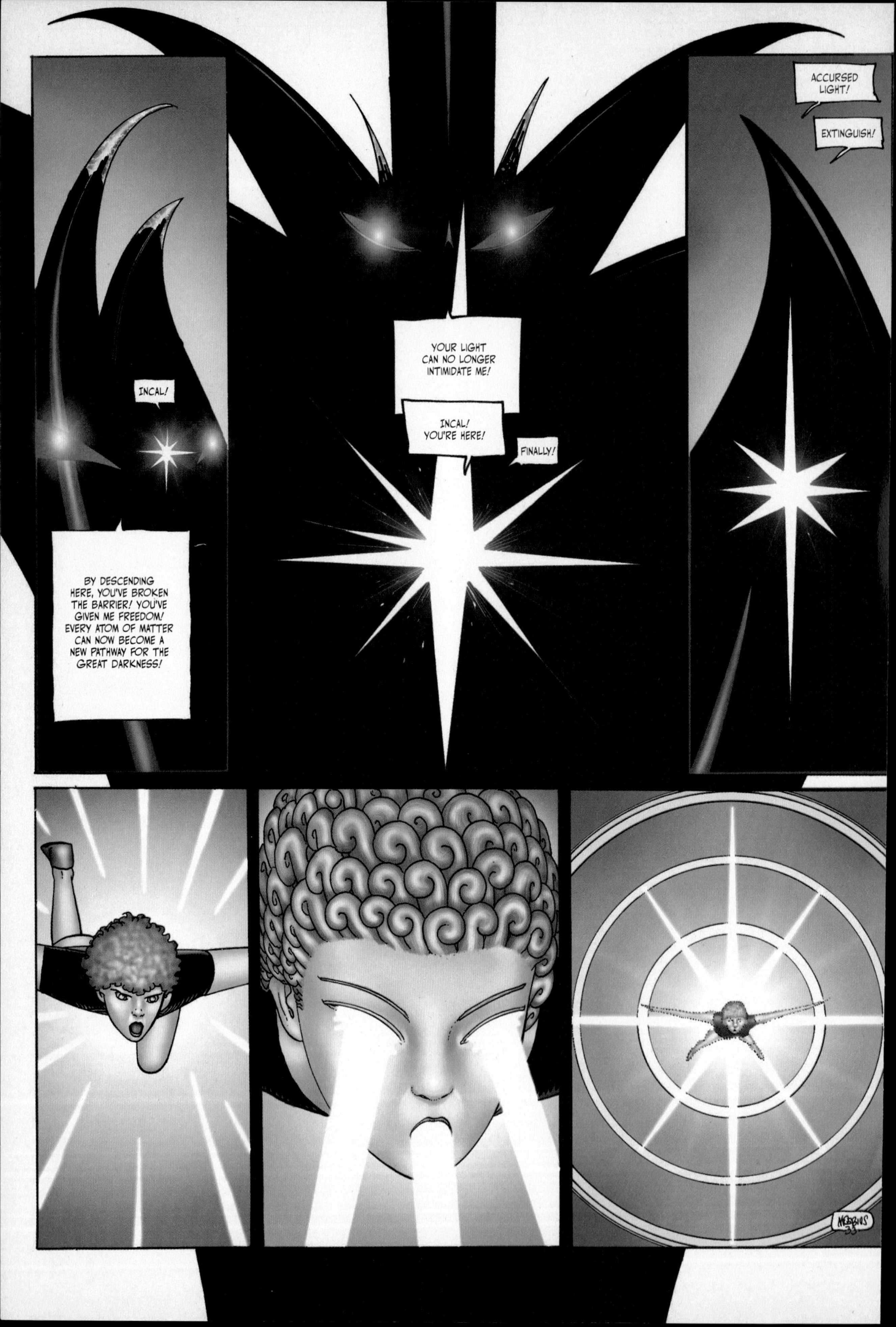

INCAL!
BY DESCENDING HERE, YOU'VE BROKEN THE BARRIER! YOU'VE GIVEN ME FREEDOM! EVERY ATOM OF MATTER CAN NOW BECOME A NEW PATHWAY FOR THE GREAT DARKNESS!
YOUR LIGHT CAN NO LONGER INTIMIDATE ME!
INCAL! YOU'RE HERE!
FINALLY!
ACCURSED LIGHT!
EXTINGUISH!
MŒBIUS

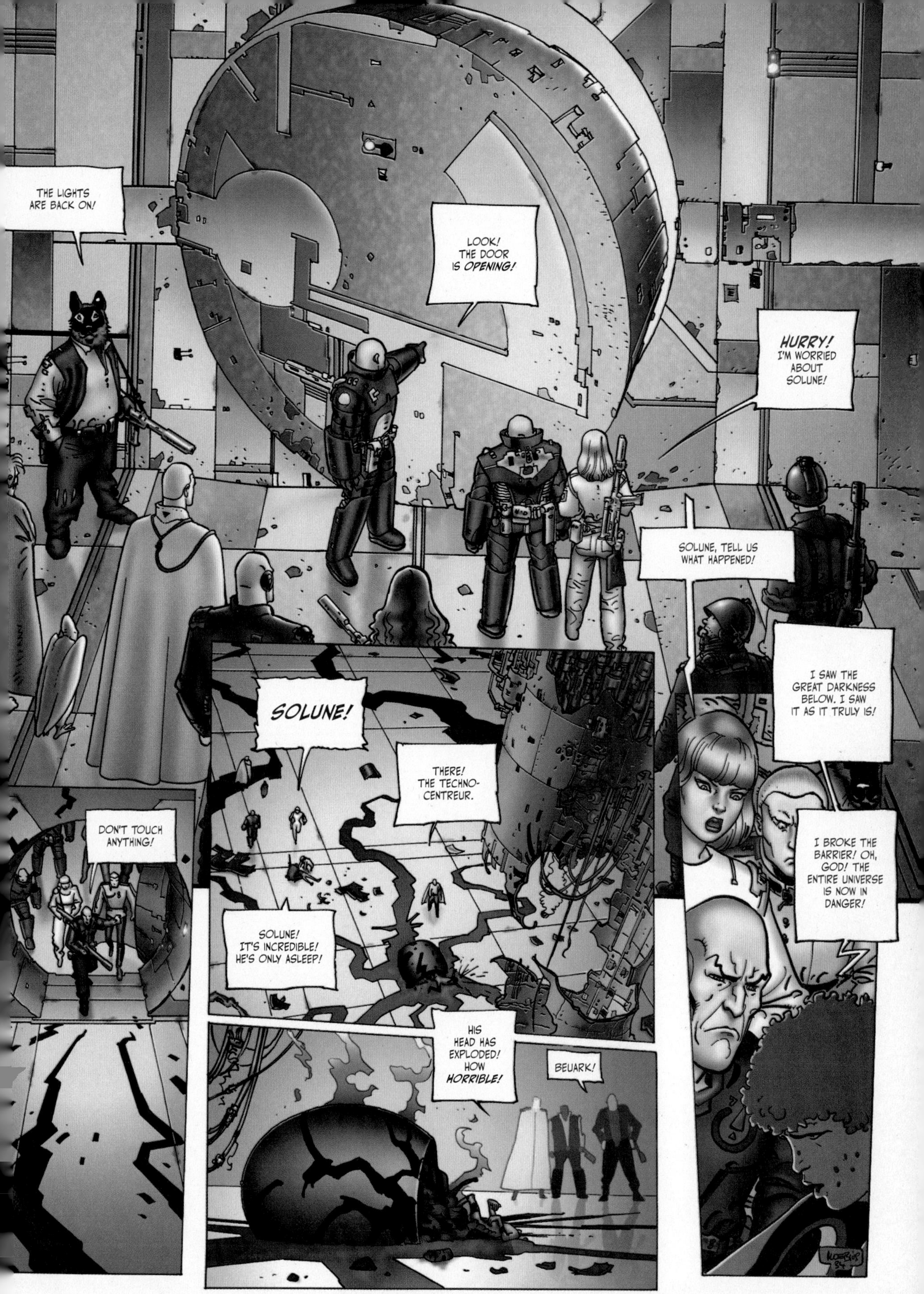
THE LIGHTS ARE BACK ON!
LOOK! THE DOOR IS *OPENING!*
HURRY! I'M WORRIED ABOUT SOLUNE!
SOLUNE, TELL US WHAT HAPPENED!
I SAW THE GREAT DARKNESS BELOW. I SAW IT AS IT TRULY IS!
I BROKE THE BARRIER! OH, GOD! THE ENTIRE UNIVERSE IS NOW IN DANGER!
DON'T TOUCH ANYTHING!
SOLUNE!
THERE! THE TECHNO-CENTREUR.
SOLUNE! IT'S INCREDIBLE! HE'S ONLY ASLEEP!
HIS HEAD HAS EXPLODED! HOW *HORRIBLE!*
BEUARK!

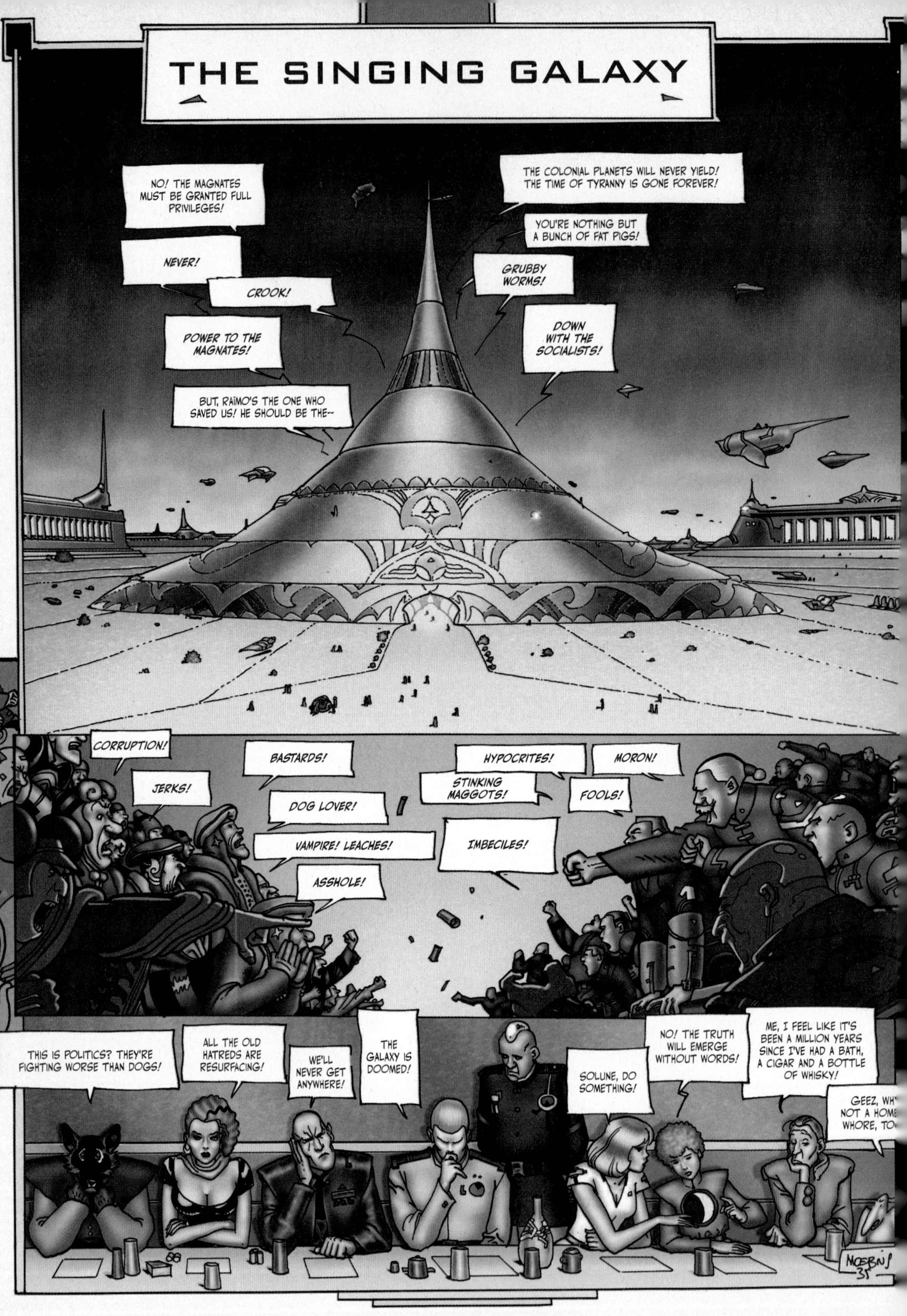

THE SINGING GALAXY
NO! THE MAGNATES MUST BE GRANTED FULL PRIVILEGES!
NEVER!
CROOK!
POWER TO THE MAGNATES!
BUT, RAÏMO'S THE ONE WHO SAVED US! HE SHOULD BE THE--
THE COLONIAL PLANETS WILL NEVER YIELD! THE TIME OF TYRANNY IS GONE FOREVER!
YOU'RE NOTHING BUT A BUNCH OF FAT PIGS!
GRUBBY WORMS!
DOWN WITH THE SOCIALISTS!
CORRUPTION!
JERKS!
BASTARDS!
DOG LOVER!
VAMPIRE! LEACHES!
ASSHOLE!
HYPOCRITES!
STINKING MAGGOTS!
IMBECILES!
MORON!
FOOLS!
THIS IS POLITICS? THEY'RE FIGHTING WORSE THAN DOGS!
ALL THE OLD HATREDS ARE RESURFACING!
WE'LL NEVER GET ANYWHERE!
THE GALAXY IS DOOMED!
SOLUNE, DO SOMETHING!
NO! THE TRUTH WILL EMERGE WITHOUT WORDS!
ME, I FEEL LIKE IT'S BEEN A MILLION YEARS SINCE I'VE HAD A BATH, A CIGAR AND A BOTTLE OF WHISKY!
GEEZ, WH
NOT A HOME
WHORE, TO
MOEBIUS

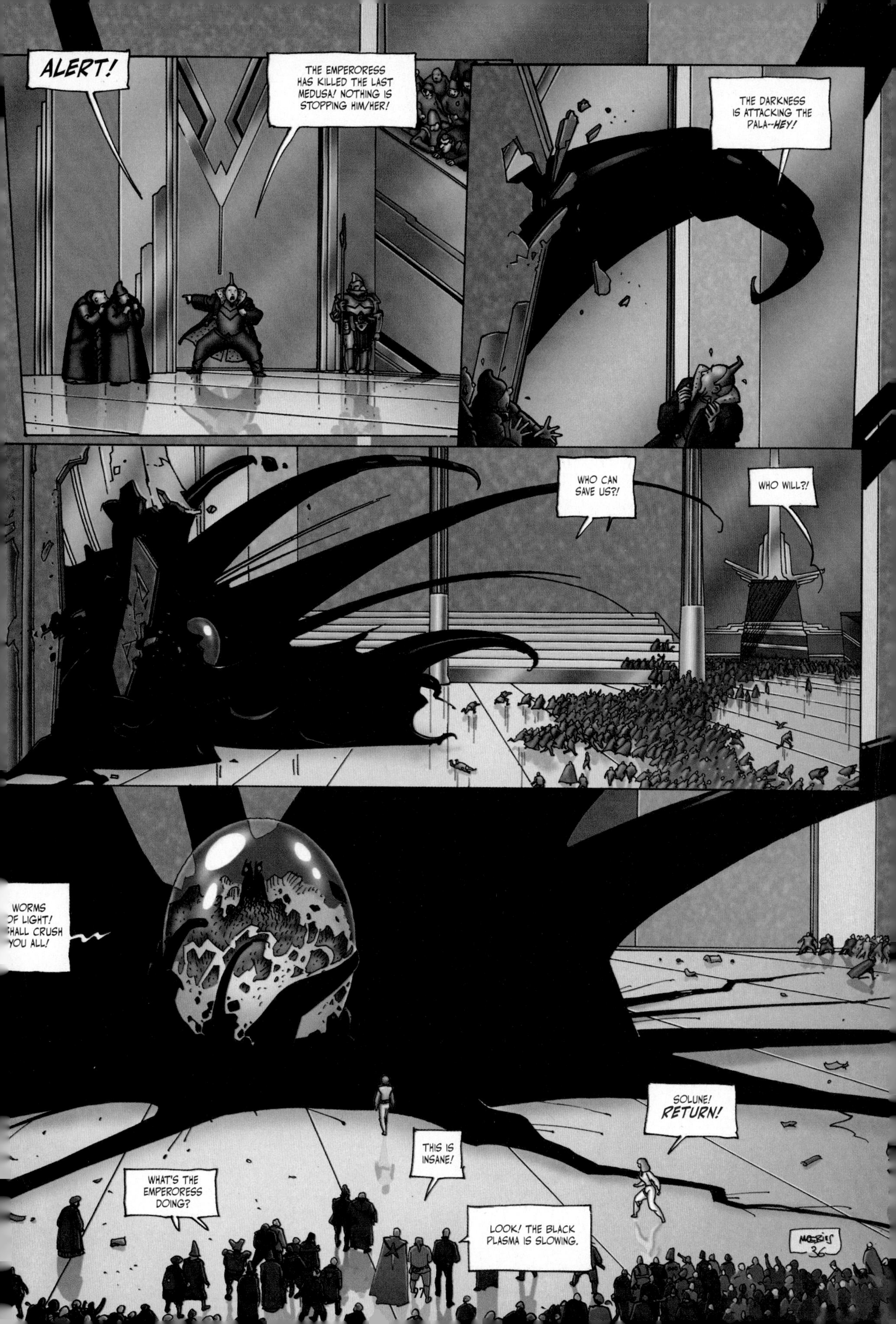

ALERT!
THE EMPERORESS HAS KILLED THE LAST MEDUSA! NOTHING IS STOPPING HIM/HER!
THE DARKNESS IS ATTACKING THE PALA--HEY!
WHO CAN SAVE US?!
WHO WILL?!
WORMS OF LIGHT! SHALL CRUSH YOU ALL!
SOLUNE! RETURN!
THIS IS INSANE!
WHAT'S THE EMPERORESS DOING?
LOOK! THE BLACK PLASMA IS SLOWING.
MOEBIUS 36

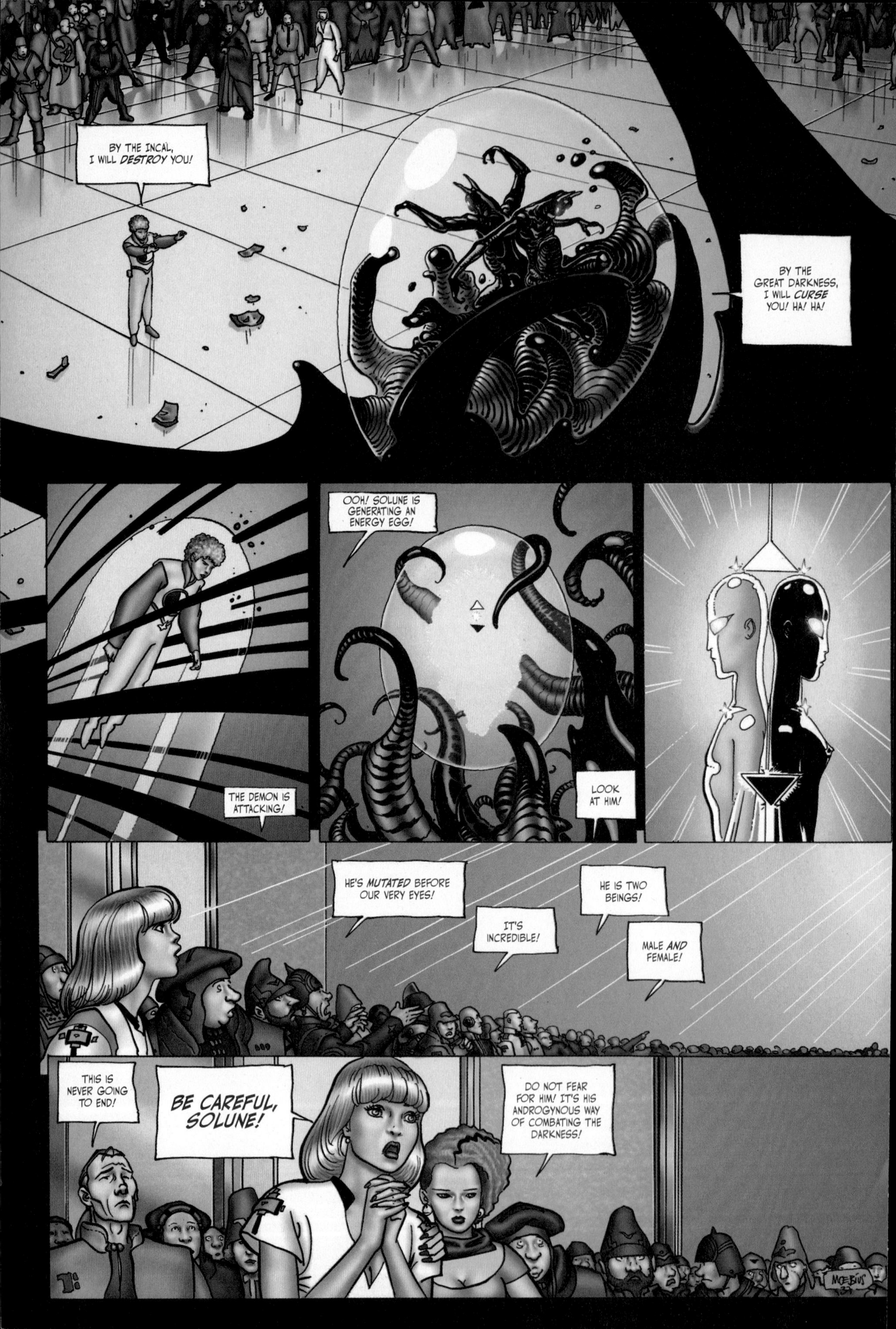
BY THE INCAL, I WILL DESTROY YOU!
BY THE GREAT DARKNESS, I WILL CURSE YOU! HA! HA!
THE DEMON IS ATTACKING!
OOH! SOLUNE IS GENERATING AN ENERGY EGG!
LOOK AT HIM!
HE'S MUTATED BEFORE OUR VERY EYES!
IT'S INCREDIBLE!
HE IS TWO BEINGS!
MALE AND FEMALE!
THIS IS NEVER GOING TO END!
BE CAREFUL, SOLUNE!
DO NOT FEAR FOR HIM! IT'S HIS ANDROGYNOUS WAY OF COMBATING THE DARKNESS!
MOEBIUS

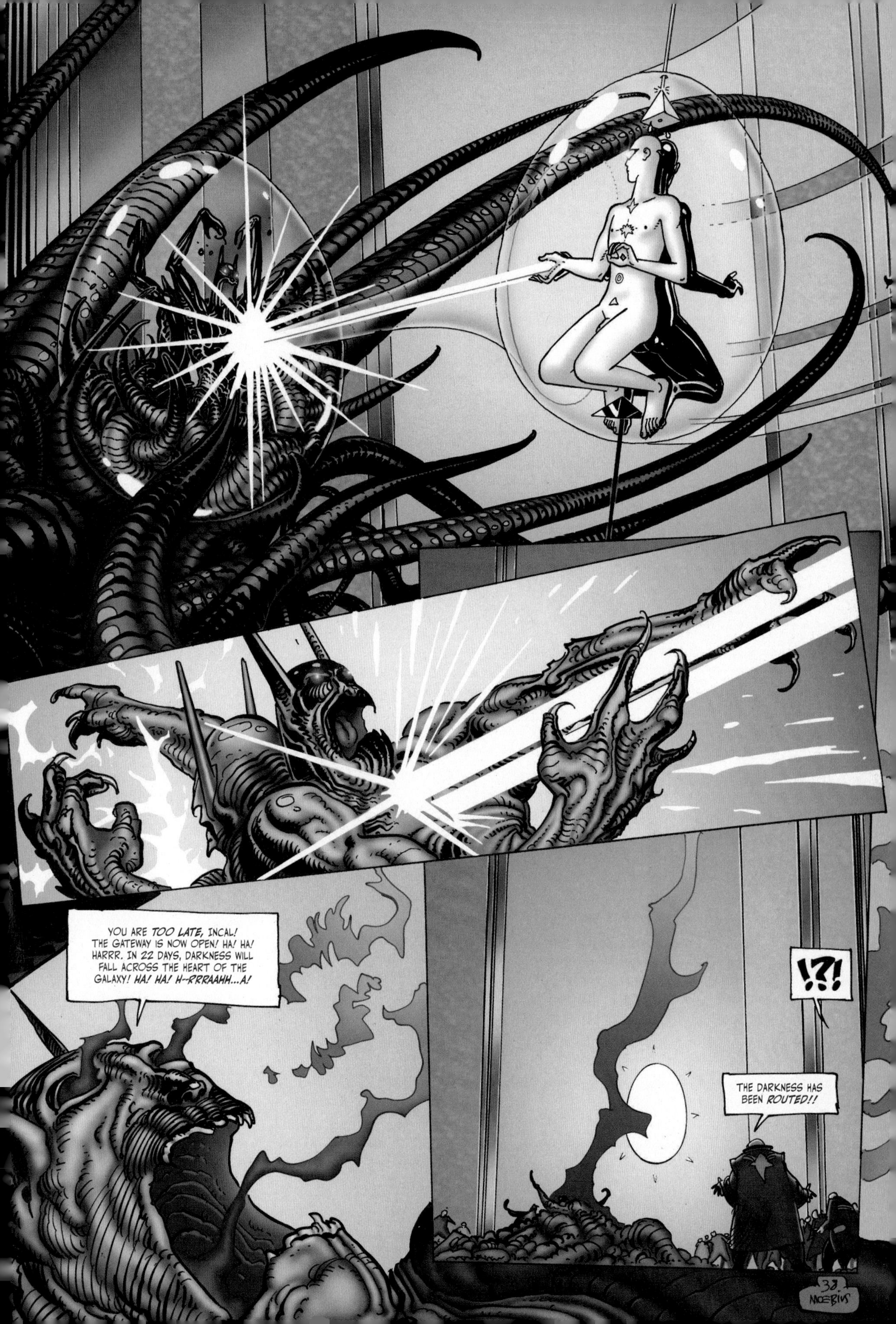
YOU ARE TOO LATE, INCAL! THE GATEWAY IS NOW OPEN! HA! HA! HARRR. IN 22 DAYS, DARKNESS WILL FALL ACROSS THE HEART OF THE GALAXY! HA! HA! H--RRRAAHH...A!
!?!
THE DARKNESS HAS BEEN ROUTED!!
38
MOEBIUS

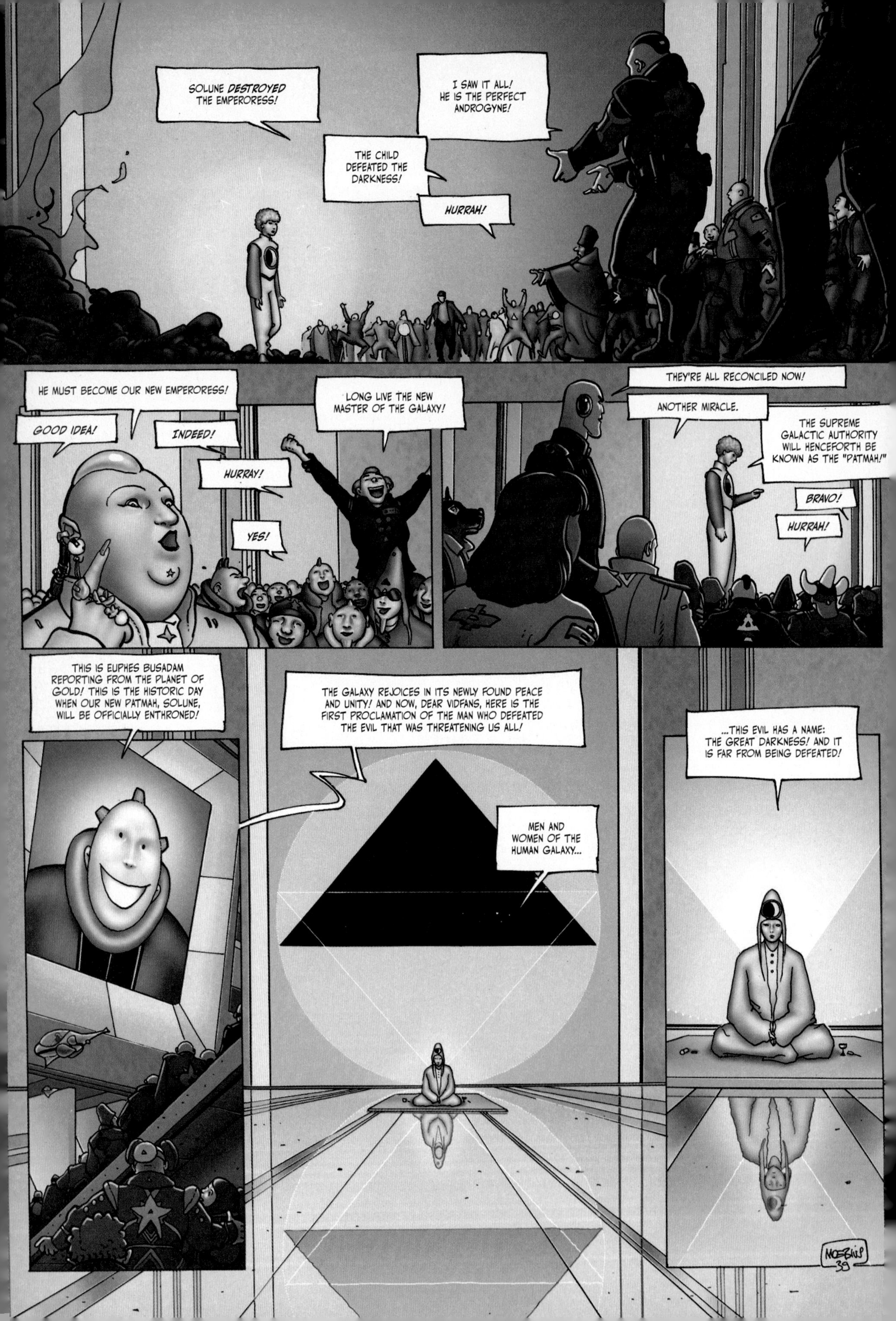
SOLUNE DESTROYED THE EMPERORESS!
I SAW IT ALL! HE IS THE PERFECT ANDROGYNE!
THE CHILD DEFEATED THE DARKNESS!
HURRAH!
HE MUST BECOME OUR NEW EMPERORESS!
GOOD IDEA!
INDEED!
HURRAY!
YES!
LONG LIVE THE NEW MASTER OF THE GALAXY!
THEY'RE ALL RECONCILED NOW!
ANOTHER MIRACLE.
THE SUPREME GALACTIC AUTHORITY WILL HENCEFORTH BE KNOWN AS THE "PATMAH!"
BRAVO!
HURRAH!
THIS IS EUPHES BUSADAM REPORTING FROM THE PLANET OF GOLD! THIS IS THE HISTORIC DAY WHEN OUR NEW PATMAH, SOLUNE, WILL BE OFFICIALLY ENTHRONED!
THE GALAXY REJOICES IN ITS NEWLY FOUND PEACE AND UNITY! AND NOW, DEAR VIDFANS, HERE IS THE FIRST PROCLAMATION OF THE MAN WHO DEFEATED THE EVIL THAT WAS THREATENING US ALL!
MEN AND WOMEN OF THE HUMAN GALAXY...
...THIS EVIL HAS A NAME: THE GREAT DARKNESS! AND IT IS FAR FROM BEING DEFEATED!
MOEBIUS

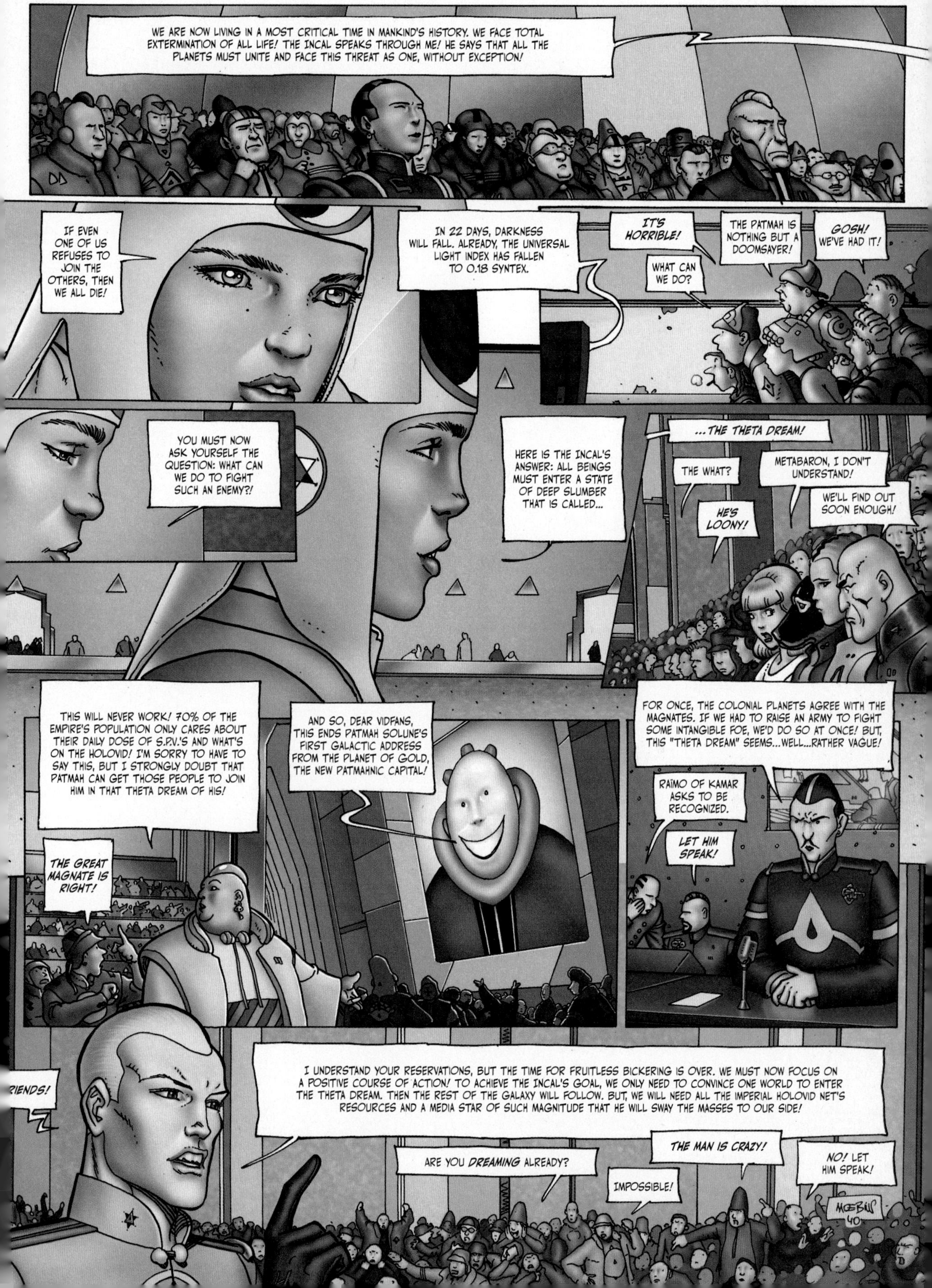

WE ARE NOW LIVING IN A MOST CRITICAL TIME IN MANKIND'S HISTORY. WE FACE TOTAL EXTERMINATION OF ALL LIFE! THE INCAL SPEAKS THROUGH ME! HE SAYS THAT ALL THE PLANETS MUST UNITE AND FACE THIS THREAT AS ONE, WITHOUT EXCEPTION!
IF EVEN ONE OF US REFUSES TO JOIN THE OTHERS, THEN WE ALL DIE!
IN 22 DAYS, DARKNESS WILL FALL. ALREADY, THE UNIVERSAL LIGHT INDEX HAS FALLEN TO 0.18 SYNTEX.
IT'S HORRIBLE!
WHAT CAN WE DO?
THE PATMAH IS NOTHING BUT A DOOMSAYER!
GOSH! WE'VE HAD IT!
YOU MUST NOW ASK YOURSELF THE QUESTION: WHAT CAN WE DO TO FIGHT SUCH AN ENEMY?!
HERE IS THE INCAL'S ANSWER: ALL BEINGS MUST ENTER A STATE OF DEEP SLUMBER THAT IS CALLED...
...THE THETA DREAM!
THE WHAT?
HE'S LOONY!
METABARON, I DON'T UNDERSTAND!
WE'LL FIND OUT SOON ENOUGH!
THIS WILL NEVER WORK! 70% OF THE EMPIRE'S POPULATION ONLY CARES ABOUT THEIR DAILY DOSE OF S.P.V.'S AND WHAT'S ON THE HOLOVID! I'M SORRY TO HAVE TO SAY THIS, BUT I STRONGLY DOUBT THAT PATMAH CAN GET THOSE PEOPLE TO JOIN HIM IN THAT THETA DREAM OF HIS!
THE GREAT MAGNATE IS RIGHT!
AND SO, DEAR VIDFANS, THIS ENDS PATMAH SOLUNE'S FIRST GALACTIC ADDRESS FROM THE PLANET OF GOLD, THE NEW PATMAHNIC CAPITAL!
FOR ONCE, THE COLONIAL PLANETS AGREE WITH THE MAGNATES. IF WE HAD TO RAISE AN ARMY TO FIGHT SOME INTANGIBLE FOE, WE'D DO SO AT ONCE! BUT, THIS "THETA DREAM" SEEMS...WELL...RATHER VAGUE!
RAÏMO OF KAMAR ASKS TO BE RECOGNIZED.
LET HIM SPEAK!
RIENDS!
I UNDERSTAND YOUR RESERVATIONS, BUT THE TIME FOR FRUITLESS BICKERING IS OVER. WE MUST NOW FOCUS ON A POSITIVE COURSE OF ACTION! TO ACHIEVE THE INCAL'S GOAL, WE ONLY NEED TO CONVINCE ONE WORLD TO ENTER THE THETA DREAM. THEN THE REST OF THE GALAXY WILL FOLLOW. BUT, WE WILL NEED ALL THE IMPERIAL HOLOVID NET'S RESOURCES AND A MEDIA STAR OF SUCH MAGNITUDE THAT HE WILL SWAY THE MASSES TO OUR SIDE!
ARE YOU DREAMING ALREADY?
THE MAN IS CRAZY!
IMPOSSIBLE!
NO! LET HIM SPEAK!
MOEBIUS
40

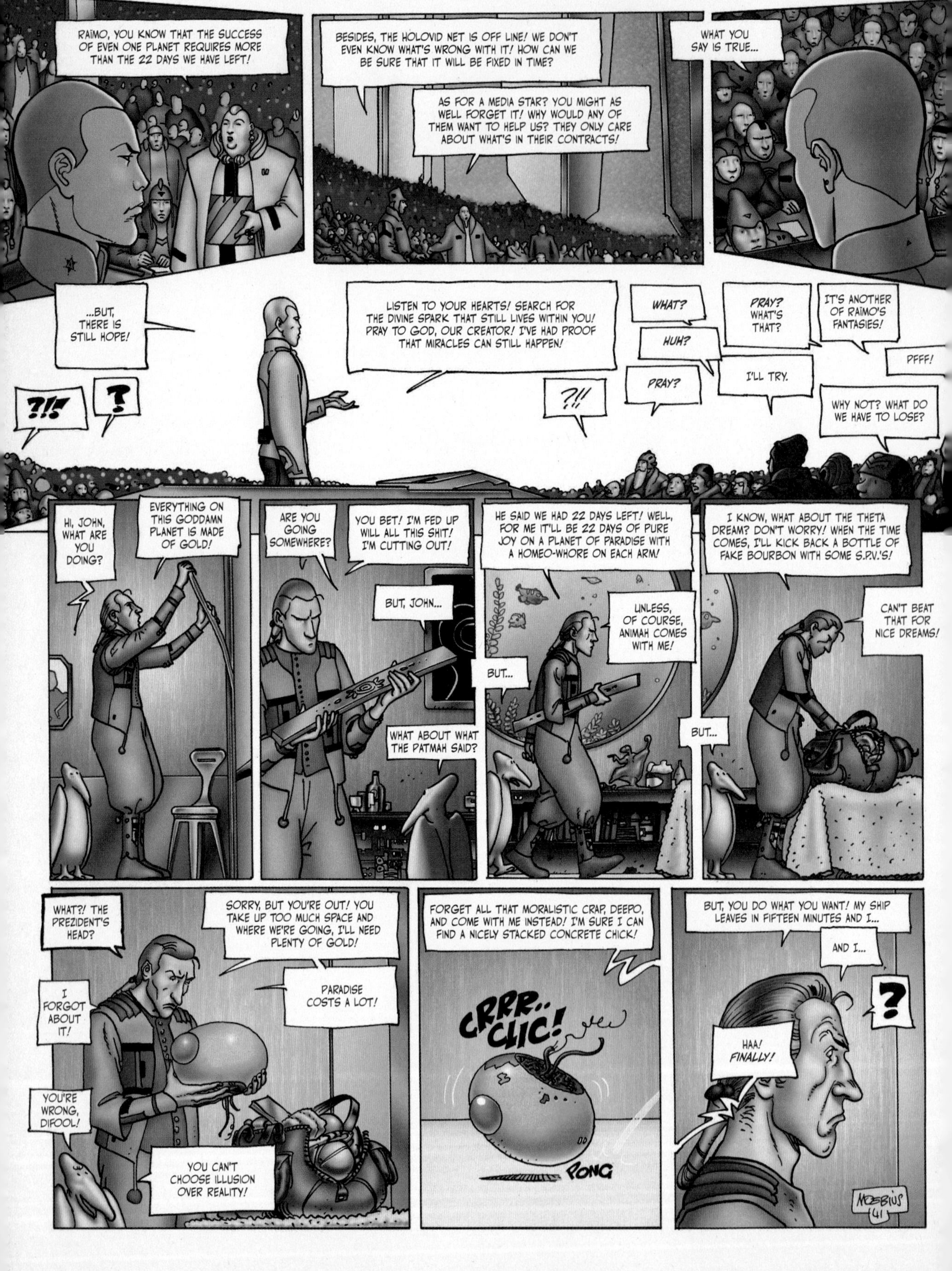
RAÏMO, YOU KNOW THAT THE SUCCESS OF EVEN ONE PLANET REQUIRES MORE THAN THE 22 DAYS WE HAVE LEFT!
BESIDES, THE HOLOVID NET IS OFF LINE! WE DON'T EVEN KNOW WHAT'S WRONG WITH IT! HOW CAN WE BE SURE THAT IT WILL BE FIXED IN TIME?
AS FOR A MEDIA STAR? YOU MIGHT AS WELL FORGET IT! WHY WOULD ANY OF THEM WANT TO HELP US? THEY ONLY CARE ABOUT WHAT'S IN THEIR CONTRACTS!
WHAT YOU SAY IS TRUE...
...BUT, THERE IS STILL HOPE!
?!!
?
LISTEN TO YOUR HEARTS! SEARCH FOR THE DIVINE SPARK THAT STILL LIVES WITHIN YOU! PRAY TO GOD, OUR CREATOR! I'VE HAD PROOF THAT MIRACLES CAN STILL HAPPEN!
?!!
WHAT?
HUH?
PRAY?
PRAY? WHAT'S THAT?
I'LL TRY.
IT'S ANOTHER OF RAÏMO'S FANTASIES!
PFFF!
WHY NOT? WHAT DO WE HAVE TO LOSE?
HI, JOHN, WHAT ARE YOU DOING?
EVERYTHING ON THIS GODDAMN PLANET IS MADE OF GOLD!
ARE YOU GOING SOMEWHERE?
YOU BET! I'M FED UP WILL ALL THIS SHIT! I'M CUTTING OUT!
BUT, JOHN...
WHAT ABOUT WHAT THE PATMAH SAID?
HE SAID WE HAD 22 DAYS LEFT! WELL, FOR ME IT'LL BE 22 DAYS OF PURE JOY ON A PLANET OF PARADISE WITH A HOMEO-WHORE ON EACH ARM!
BUT...
UNLESS, OF COURSE, ANIMAH COMES WITH ME!
I KNOW, WHAT ABOUT THE THETA DREAM? DON'T WORRY! WHEN THE TIME COMES, I'LL KICK BACK A BOTTLE OF FAKE BOURBON WITH SOME S.P.V.'S!
BUT...
CAN'T BEAT THAT FOR NICE DREAMS!
WHAT?! THE PREZIDENT'S HEAD?
I FORGOT ABOUT IT!
SORRY, BUT YOU'RE OUT! YOU TAKE UP TOO MUCH SPACE AND WHERE WE'RE GOING, I'LL NEED PLENTY OF GOLD!
PARADISE COSTS A LOT!
YOU'RE WRONG, DIFOOL!
YOU CAN'T CHOOSE ILLUSION OVER REALITY!
FORGET ALL THAT MORALISTIC CRAP, DEEPO, AND COME WITH ME INSTEAD! I'M SURE I CAN FIND A NICELY STACKED CONCRETE CHICK!
CRRR.. CLIC!
PONG
BUT, YOU DO WHAT YOU WANT! MY SHIP LEAVES IN FIFTEEN MINUTES AND I...
AND I...
?
HAA! FINALLY!
MOEBIUS 41

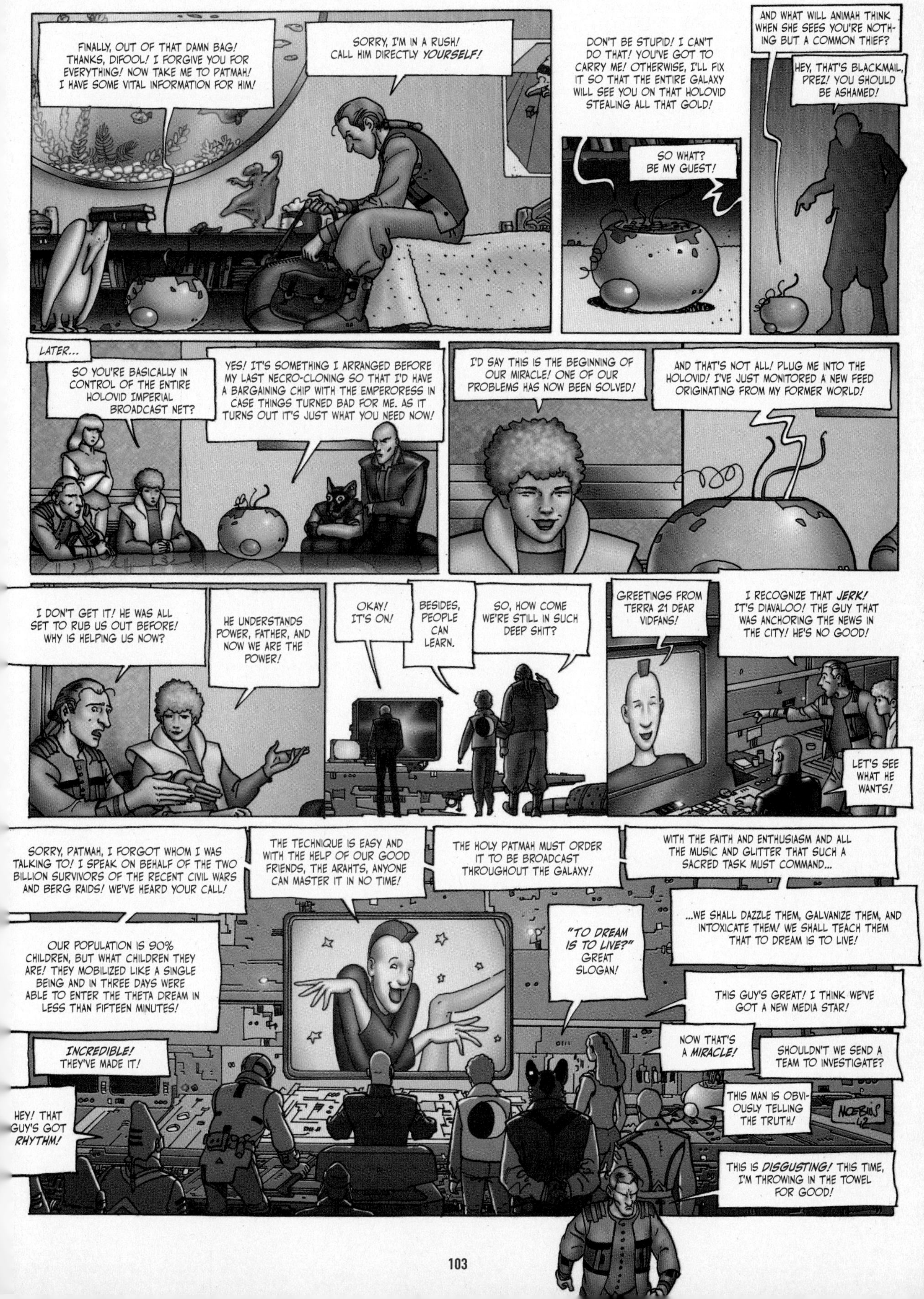

FINALLY, OUT OF THAT DAMN BAG! THANKS, DIFOOL! I FORGIVE YOU FOR EVERYTHING! NOW TAKE ME TO PATMAH! I HAVE SOME VITAL INFORMATION FOR HIM!
SORRY, I'M IN A RUSH! CALL HIM DIRECTLY YOURSELF!
DON'T BE STUPID! I CAN'T DO THAT! YOU'VE GOT TO CARRY ME! OTHERWISE, I'LL FIX IT SO THAT THE ENTIRE GALAXY WILL SEE YOU ON THAT HOLOVID STEALING ALL THAT GOLD!
SO WHAT? BE MY GUEST!
AND WHAT WILL ANIMAH THINK WHEN SHE SEES YOU'RE NOTHING BUT A COMMON THIEF?
HEY, THAT'S BLACKMAIL, PREZ! YOU SHOULD BE ASHAMED!
LATER...
SO YOU'RE BASICALLY IN CONTROL OF THE ENTIRE HOLOVID IMPERIAL BROADCAST NET?
YES! IT'S SOMETHING I ARRANGED BEFORE MY LAST NECRO-CLONING SO THAT I'D HAVE A BARGAINING CHIP WITH THE EMPERORESS IN CASE THINGS TURNED BAD FOR ME. AS IT TURNS OUT IT'S JUST WHAT YOU NEED NOW!
I'D SAY THIS IS THE BEGINNING OF OUR MIRACLE! ONE OF OUR PROBLEMS HAS NOW BEEN SOLVED!
AND THAT'S NOT ALL! PLUG ME INTO THE HOLOVID! I'VE JUST MONITORED A NEW FEED ORIGINATING FROM MY FORMER WORLD!
I DON'T GET IT! HE WAS ALL SET TO RUB US OUT BEFORE! WHY IS HELPING US NOW?
HE UNDERSTANDS POWER, FATHER, AND NOW WE ARE THE POWER!
OKAY! IT'S ON!
BESIDES, PEOPLE CAN LEARN.
SO, HOW COME WE'RE STILL IN SUCH DEEP SHIT?
GREETINGS FROM TERRA 21 DEAR VIDFANS!
I RECOGNIZE THAT JERK! IT'S DIAVALOO! THE GUY THAT WAS ANCHORING THE NEWS IN THE CITY! HE'S NO GOOD!
LET'S SEE WHAT HE WANTS!
SORRY, PATMAH, I FORGOT WHOM I WAS TALKING TO! I SPEAK ON BEHALF OF THE TWO BILLION SURVIVORS OF THE RECENT CIVIL WARS AND BERG RAIDS! WE'VE HEARD YOUR CALL!
THE TECHNIQUE IS EASY AND WITH THE HELP OF OUR GOOD FRIENDS, THE ARAHTS, ANYONE CAN MASTER IT IN NO TIME!
THE HOLY PATMAH MUST ORDER IT TO BE BROADCAST THROUGHOUT THE GALAXY!
WITH THE FAITH AND ENTHUSIASM AND ALL THE MUSIC AND GLITTER THAT SUCH A SACRED TASK MUST COMMAND...
...WE SHALL DAZZLE THEM, GALVANIZE THEM, AND INTOXICATE THEM! WE SHALL TEACH THEM THAT TO DREAM IS TO LIVE!
OUR POPULATION IS 90% CHILDREN, BUT WHAT CHILDREN THEY ARE! THEY MOBILIZED LIKE A SINGLE BEING AND IN THREE DAYS WERE ABLE TO ENTER THE THETA DREAM IN LESS THAN FIFTEEN MINUTES!
"TO DREAM IS TO LIVE?" GREAT SLOGAN!
THIS GUY'S GREAT! I THINK WE'VE GOT A NEW MEDIA STAR!
INCREDIBLE! THEY'VE MADE IT!
NOW THAT'S A MIRACLE!
SHOULDN'T WE SEND A TEAM TO INVESTIGATE?
HEY! THAT GUY'S GOT RHYTHM!
THIS MAN IS OBVIOUSLY TELLING THE TRUTH!
MOEBIUS 42
THIS IS DISGUSTING! THIS TIME, I'M THROWING IN THE TOWEL FOR GOOD!

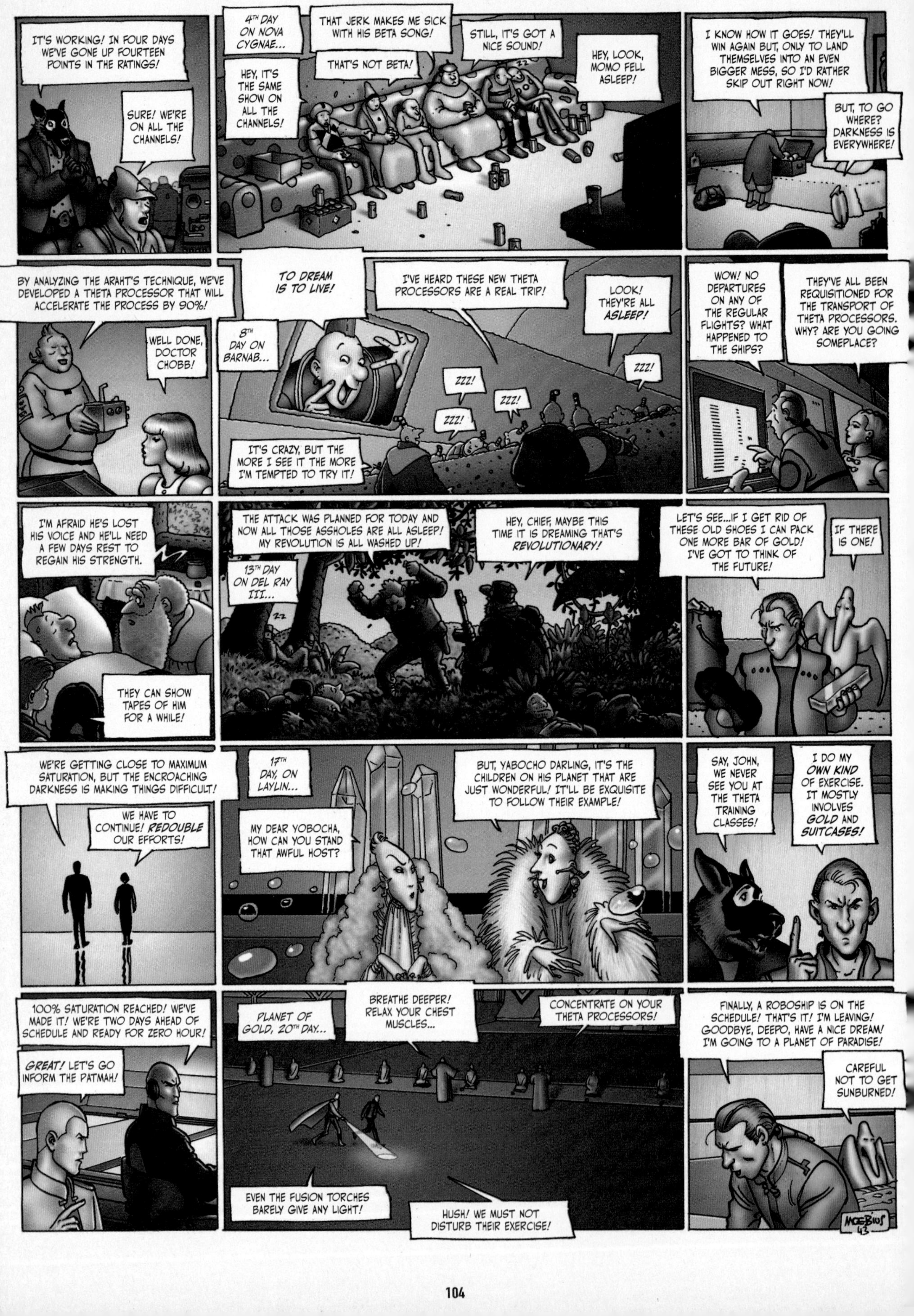
IT'S WORKING! IN FOUR DAYS WE'VE GONE UP FOURTEEN POINTS IN THE RATINGS!
SURE! WE'RE ON ALL THE CHANNELS!
4TH DAY ON NOVA CYGNAE...
THAT JERK MAKES ME SICK WITH HIS BETA SONG!
HEY, IT'S THE SAME SHOW ON ALL THE CHANNELS!
THAT'S NOT BETA!
STILL, IT'S GOT A NICE SOUND!
HEY, LOOK, MOMO FELL ASLEEP!
I KNOW HOW IT GOES! THEY'LL WIN AGAIN BUT, ONLY TO LAND THEMSELVES INTO AN EVEN BIGGER MESS, SO I'D RATHER SKIP OUT RIGHT NOW!
BUT, TO GO WHERE? DARKNESS IS EVERYWHERE!
BY ANALYZING THE ARAHT'S TECHNIQUE, WE'VE DEVELOPED A THETA PROCESSOR THAT WILL ACCELERATE THE PROCESS BY 90%!
WELL DONE, DOCTOR CHOBB!
TO DREAM IS TO LIVE!
8TH DAY ON BARNAB...
I'VE HEARD THESE NEW THETA PROCESSORS ARE A REAL TRIP!
LOOK! THEY'RE ALL ASLEEP!
ZZZ!
ZZZ!
ZZZ!
ZZZ!
IT'S CRAZY, BUT THE MORE I SEE IT THE MORE I'M TEMPTED TO TRY IT!
WOW! NO DEPARTURES ON ANY OF THE REGULAR FLIGHTS? WHAT HAPPENED TO THE SHIPS?
THEY'VE ALL BEEN REQUISITIONED FOR THE TRANSPORT OF THETA PROCESSORS. WHY? ARE YOU GOING SOMEPLACE?
I'M AFRAID HE'S LOST HIS VOICE AND HE'LL NEED A FEW DAYS REST TO REGAIN HIS STRENGTH.
THEY CAN SHOW TAPES OF HIM FOR A WHILE!
THE ATTACK WAS PLANNED FOR TODAY AND NOW ALL THOSE ASSHOLES ARE ALL ASLEEP! MY REVOLUTION IS ALL WASHED UP!
13TH DAY ON DEL RAY III...
HEY, CHIEF, MAYBE THIS TIME IT IS DREAMING THAT'S REVOLUTIONARY!
LET'S SEE...IF I GET RID OF THESE OLD SHOES I CAN PACK ONE MORE BAR OF GOLD! I'VE GOT TO THINK OF THE FUTURE!
IF THERE IS ONE!
WE'RE GETTING CLOSE TO MAXIMUM SATURATION, BUT THE ENCROACHING DARKNESS IS MAKING THINGS DIFFICULT!
WE HAVE TO CONTINUE! REDOUBLE OUR EFFORTS!
17TH DAY, ON LAYLIN...
MY DEAR YOBOCHA, HOW CAN YOU STAND THAT AWFUL HOST?
BUT, YABOCHO DARLING, IT'S THE CHILDREN ON HIS PLANET THAT ARE JUST WONDERFUL! IT'LL BE EXQUISITE TO FOLLOW THEIR EXAMPLE!
SAY, JOHN, WE NEVER SEE YOU AT THE THETA TRAINING CLASSES!
I DO MY OWN KIND OF EXERCISE. IT MOSTLY INVOLVES GOLD AND SUITCASES!
100% SATURATION REACHED! WE'VE MADE IT! WE'RE TWO DAYS AHEAD OF SCHEDULE AND READY FOR ZERO HOUR!
GREAT! LET'S GO INFORM THE PATMAH!
PLANET OF GOLD, 20TH DAY...
BREATHE DEEPER! RELAX YOUR CHEST MUSCLES...
CONCENTRATE ON YOUR THETA PROCESSORS!
EVEN THE FUSION TORCHES BARELY GIVE ANY LIGHT!
HUSH! WE MUST NOT DISTURB THEIR EXERCISE!
FINALLY, A ROBOSHIP IS ON THE SCHEDULE! THAT'S IT! I'M LEAVING! GOODBYE, DEEPO, HAVE A NICE DREAM! I'M GOING TO A PLANET OF PARADISE!
CAREFUL NOT TO GET SUNBURNED!

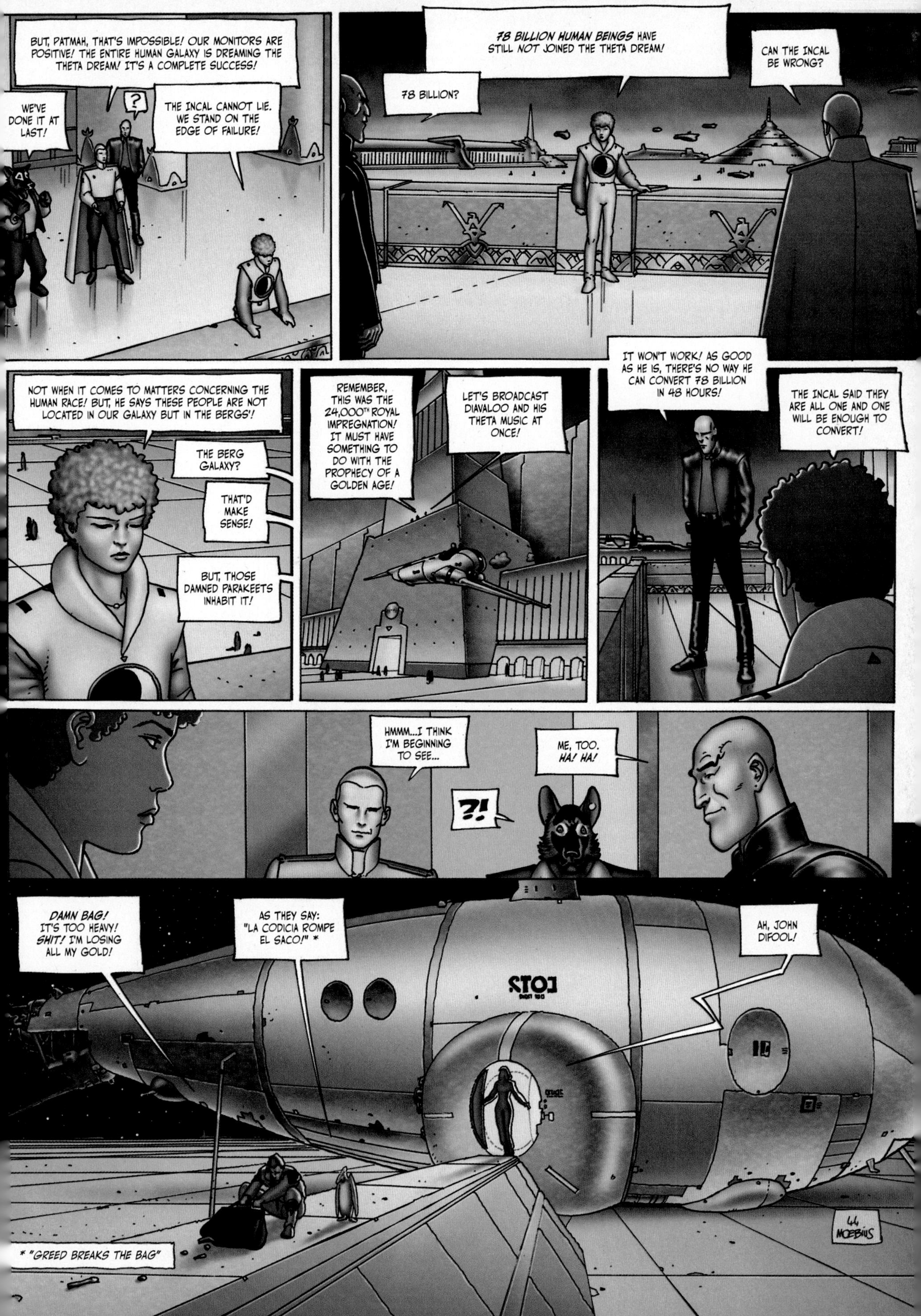

BUT, PATMAH, THAT'S IMPOSSIBLE! OUR MONITORS ARE POSITIVE! THE ENTIRE HUMAN GALAXY IS DREAMING THE THETA DREAM! IT'S A COMPLETE SUCCESS!
WE'VE DONE IT AT LAST!
?
THE INCAL CANNOT LIE. WE STAND ON THE EDGE OF FAILURE!
78 BILLION HUMAN BEINGS HAVE STILL NOT JOINED THE THETA DREAM!
78 BILLION?
CAN THE INCAL BE WRONG?
NOT WHEN IT COMES TO MATTERS CONCERNING THE HUMAN RACE! BUT, HE SAYS THESE PEOPLE ARE NOT LOCATED IN OUR GALAXY BUT IN THE BERGS'!
THE BERG GALAXY?
THAT'D MAKE SENSE!
BUT, THOSE DAMNED PARAKEETS INHABIT IT!
REMEMBER, THIS WAS THE 24,000TH ROYAL IMPREGNATION! IT MUST HAVE SOMETHING TO DO WITH THE PROPHECY OF A GOLDEN AGE!
LET'S BROADCAST DIAVALOO AND HIS THETA MUSIC AT ONCE!
IT WON'T WORK! AS GOOD AS HE IS, THERE'S NO WAY HE CAN CONVERT 78 BILLION IN 48 HOURS!
THE INCAL SAID THEY ARE ALL ONE AND ONE WILL BE ENOUGH TO CONVERT!
HMMM...I THINK I'M BEGINNING TO SEE...
?!
ME, TOO. HA! HA!
DAMN BAG! IT'S TOO HEAVY! SHIT! I'M LOSING ALL MY GOLD!
AS THEY SAY: "LA CODICIA ROMPE EL SACO!" *
AH, JOHN DIFOOL!
MOEBIUS

* "GREED BREAKS THE BAG"

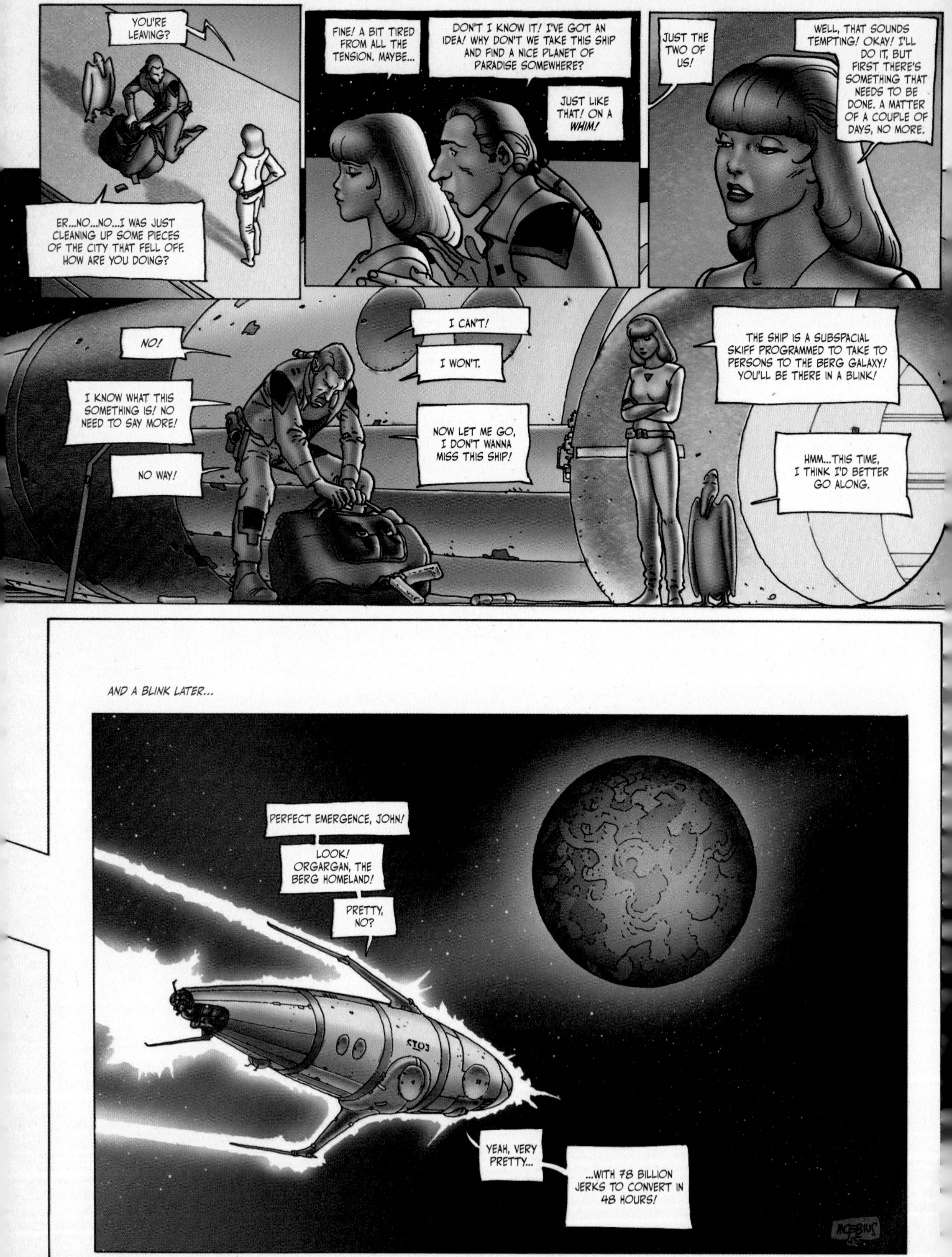
YOU'RE LEAVING?
ER...NO...NO...I WAS JUST CLEANING UP SOME PIECES OF THE CITY THAT FELL OFF. HOW ARE YOU DOING?
FINE! A BIT TIRED FROM ALL THE TENSION. MAYBE...
DON'T I KNOW IT! I'VE GOT AN IDEA! WHY DON'T WE TAKE THIS SHIP AND FIND A NICE PLANET OF PARADISE SOMEWHERE?
JUST LIKE THAT! ON A *WHIM!*
JUST THE TWO OF US!
WELL, THAT SOUNDS TEMPTING! OKAY! I'LL DO IT, BUT FIRST THERE'S SOMETHING THAT NEEDS TO BE DONE. A MATTER OF A COUPLE OF DAYS, NO MORE.
NO!
I KNOW WHAT THIS SOMETHING IS! NO NEED TO SAY MORE!
NO WAY!
I CAN'T!
I WON'T.
NOW LET ME GO, I DON'T WANNA MISS THIS SHIP!
THE SHIP IS A SUBSPACIAL SKIFF PROGRAMMED TO TAKE TO PERSONS TO THE BERG GALAXY! YOU'LL BE THERE IN A BLINK!
HMM...THIS TIME, I THINK I'D BETTER GO ALONG.
AND A BLINK LATER...
PERFECT EMERGENCE, JOHN!
LOOK! ORGARGAN, THE BERG HOMELAND!
PRETTY, NO?
YEAH, VERY PRETTY...
...WITH 78 BILLION JERKS TO CONVERT IN 48 HOURS!

78 BILLION IN 1

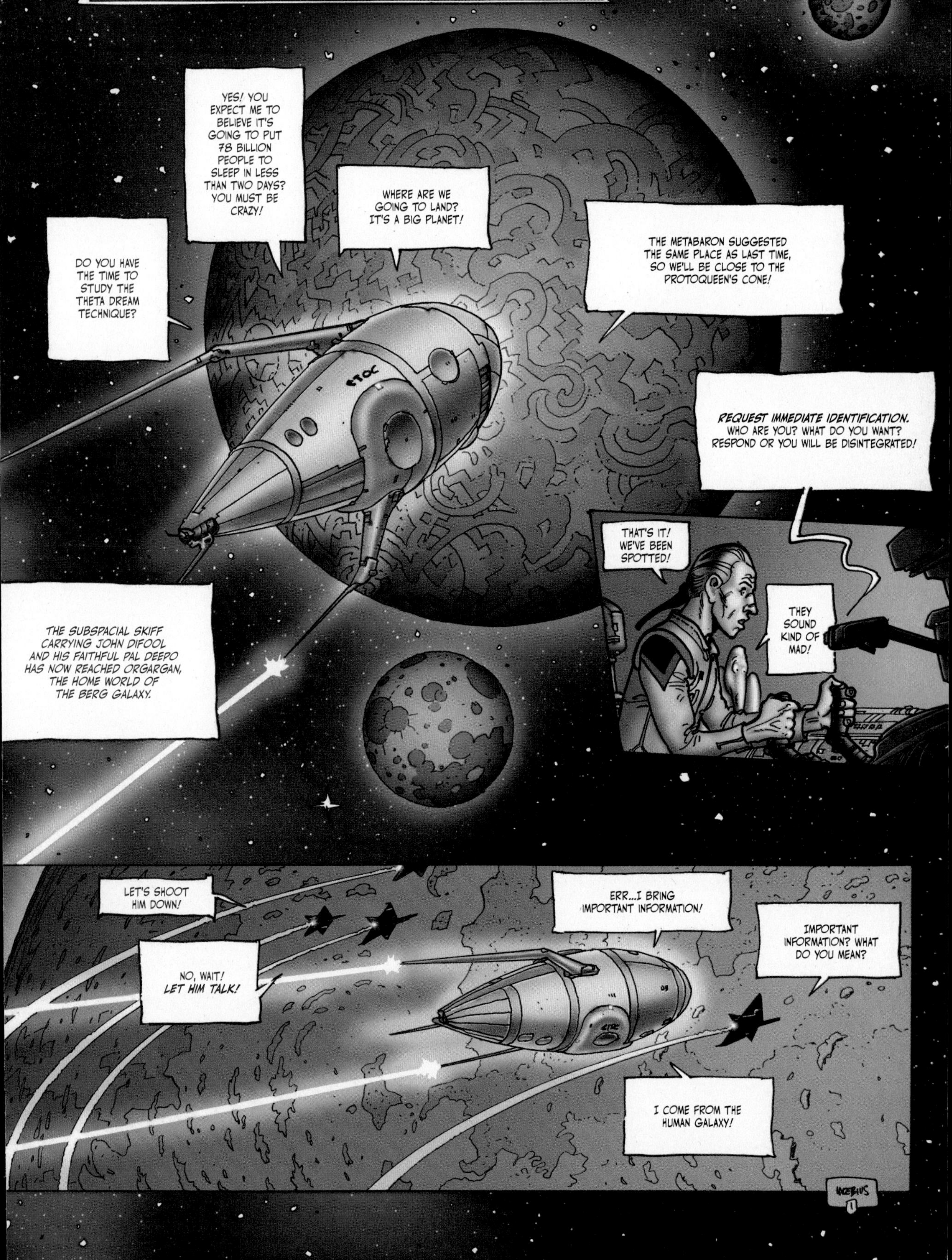
THE SUBSPACIAL SKIFF CARRYING JOHN DIFOOL AND HIS FAITHFUL PAL DEEPO HAS NOW REACHED ORGARGAN, THE HOME WORLD OF THE BERG GALAXY.
DO YOU HAVE THE TIME TO STUDY THE THETA DREAM TECHNIQUE?
YES! YOU EXPECT ME TO BELIEVE IT'S GOING TO PUT 78 BILLION PEOPLE TO SLEEP IN LESS THAN TWO DAYS? YOU MUST BE CRAZY!
WHERE ARE WE GOING TO LAND? IT'S A BIG PLANET!
THE METABARON SUGGESTED THE SAME PLACE AS LAST TIME, SO WE'LL BE CLOSE TO THE PROTOQUEEN'S CONE!
REQUEST IMMEDIATE IDENTIFICATION. WHO ARE YOU? WHAT DO YOU WANT? RESPOND OR YOU WILL BE DISINTEGRATED!
THAT'S IT! WE'VE BEEN SPOTTED!
THEY SOUND KIND OF MAD!
LET'S SHOOT HIM DOWN!
NO, WAIT! *LET HIM TALK!*
ERR...I BRING IMPORTANT INFORMATION!
IMPORTANT INFORMATION? WHAT DO YOU MEAN?
I COME FROM THE HUMAN GALAXY!

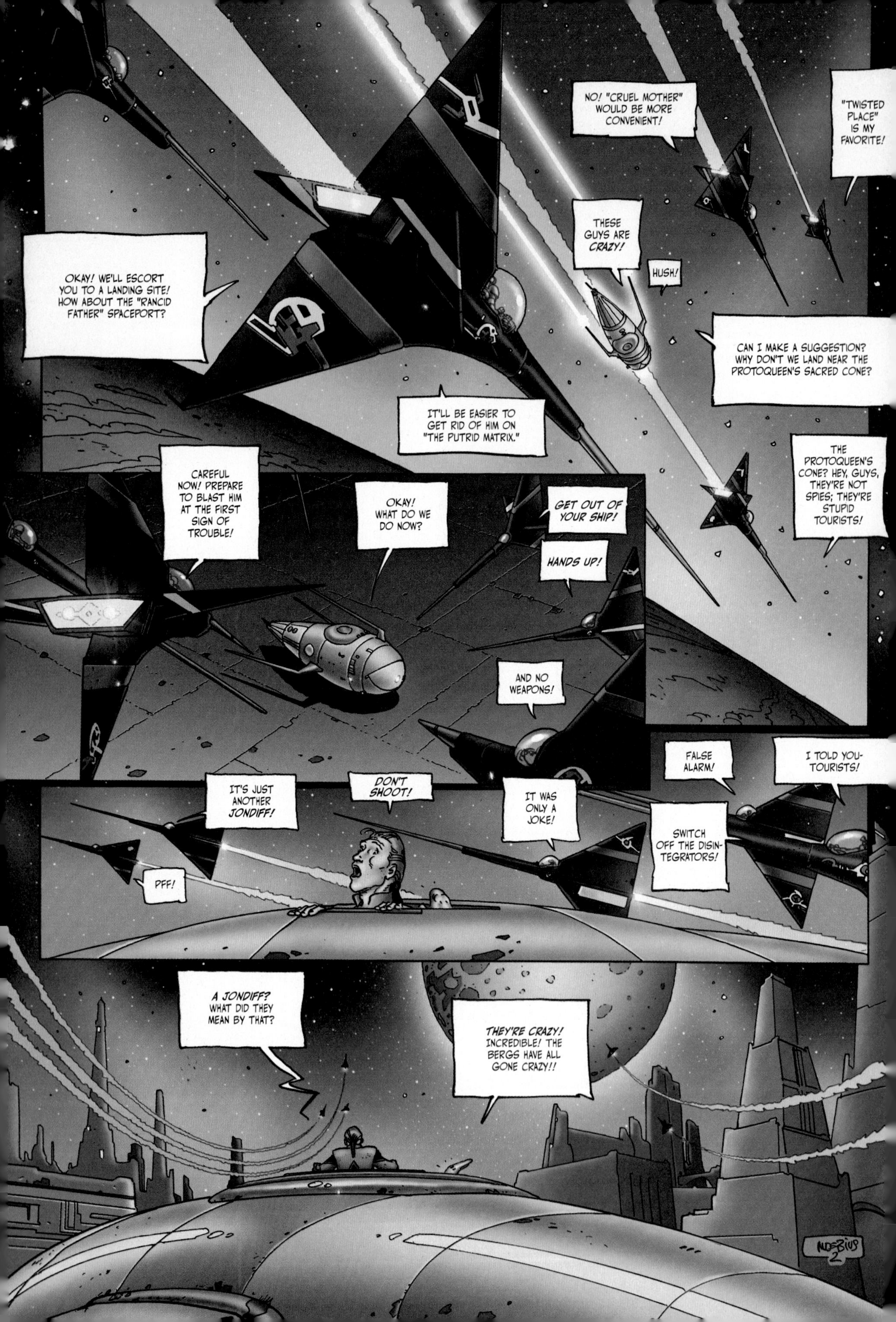

OKAY! WE'LL ESCORT YOU TO A LANDING SITE! HOW ABOUT THE "RANCID FATHER" SPACEPORT?
IT'LL BE EASIER TO GET RID OF HIM ON "THE PUTRID MATRIX."
NO! "CRUEL MOTHER" WOULD BE MORE CONVENIENT!
"TWISTED PLACE" IS MY FAVORITE!
THESE GUYS ARE CRAZY!
HUSH!
CAN I MAKE A SUGGESTION? WHY DON'T WE LAND NEAR THE PROTOQUEEN'S SACRED CONE?
THE PROTOQUEEN'S CONE? HEY, GUYS, THEY'RE NOT SPIES; THEY'RE STUPID TOURISTS!
CAREFUL NOW! PREPARE TO BLAST HIM AT THE FIRST SIGN OF TROUBLE!
OKAY! WHAT DO WE DO NOW?
GET OUT OF YOUR SHIP!
HANDS UP!
AND NO WEAPONS!
IT'S JUST ANOTHER JONDIFF!
DON'T SHOOT!
PFF!
IT WAS ONLY A JOKE!
FALSE ALARM!
I TOLD YOU- TOURISTS!
SWITCH OFF THE DISIN- TEGRATORS!
A JONDIFF? WHAT DID THEY MEAN BY THAT?
THEY'RE CRAZY! INCREDIBLE! THE BERGS HAVE ALL GONE CRAZY!!
MOEBIUS 2

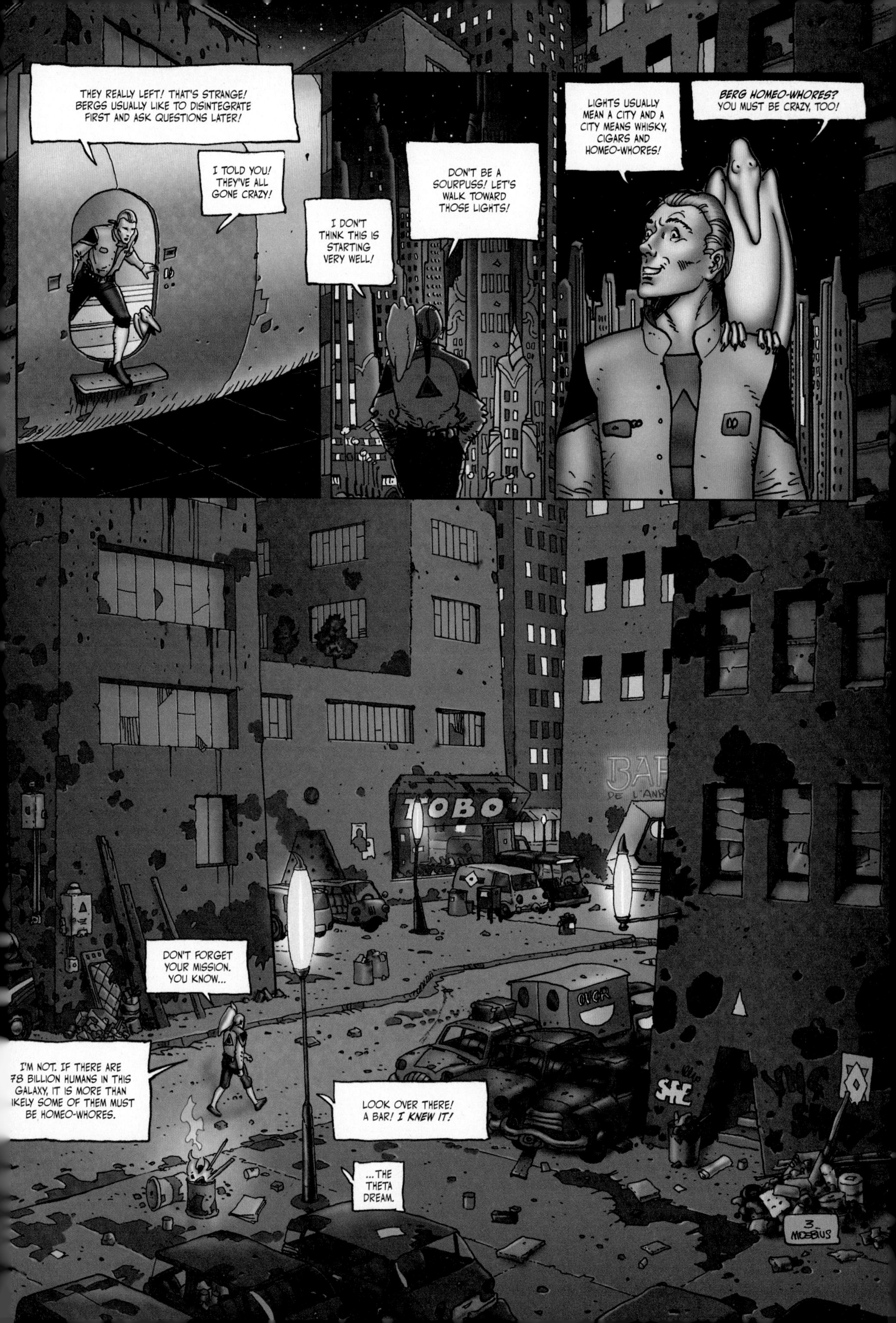
THEY REALLY LEFT! THAT'S STRANGE! BERGS USUALLY LIKE TO DISINTEGRATE FIRST AND ASK QUESTIONS LATER!
I TOLD YOU! THEY'VE ALL GONE CRAZY!
I DON'T THINK THIS IS STARTING VERY WELL!
DON'T BE A SOURPUSS! LET'S WALK TOWARD THOSE LIGHTS!
LIGHTS USUALLY MEAN A CITY AND A CITY MEANS WHISKY, CIGARS AND HOMEO-WHORES!
BERG HOMEO-WHORES? YOU MUST BE CRAZY, TOO!
TOBO
BAR
DE L'ANR
DON'T FORGET YOUR MISSION. YOU KNOW...
I'M NOT. IF THERE ARE 78 BILLION HUMANS IN THIS GALAXY, IT IS MORE THAN IKELY SOME OF THEM MUST BE HOMEO-WHORES.
LOOK OVER THERE! A BAR! I KNEW IT!
...THE THETA DREAM.
3
MOEBIUS

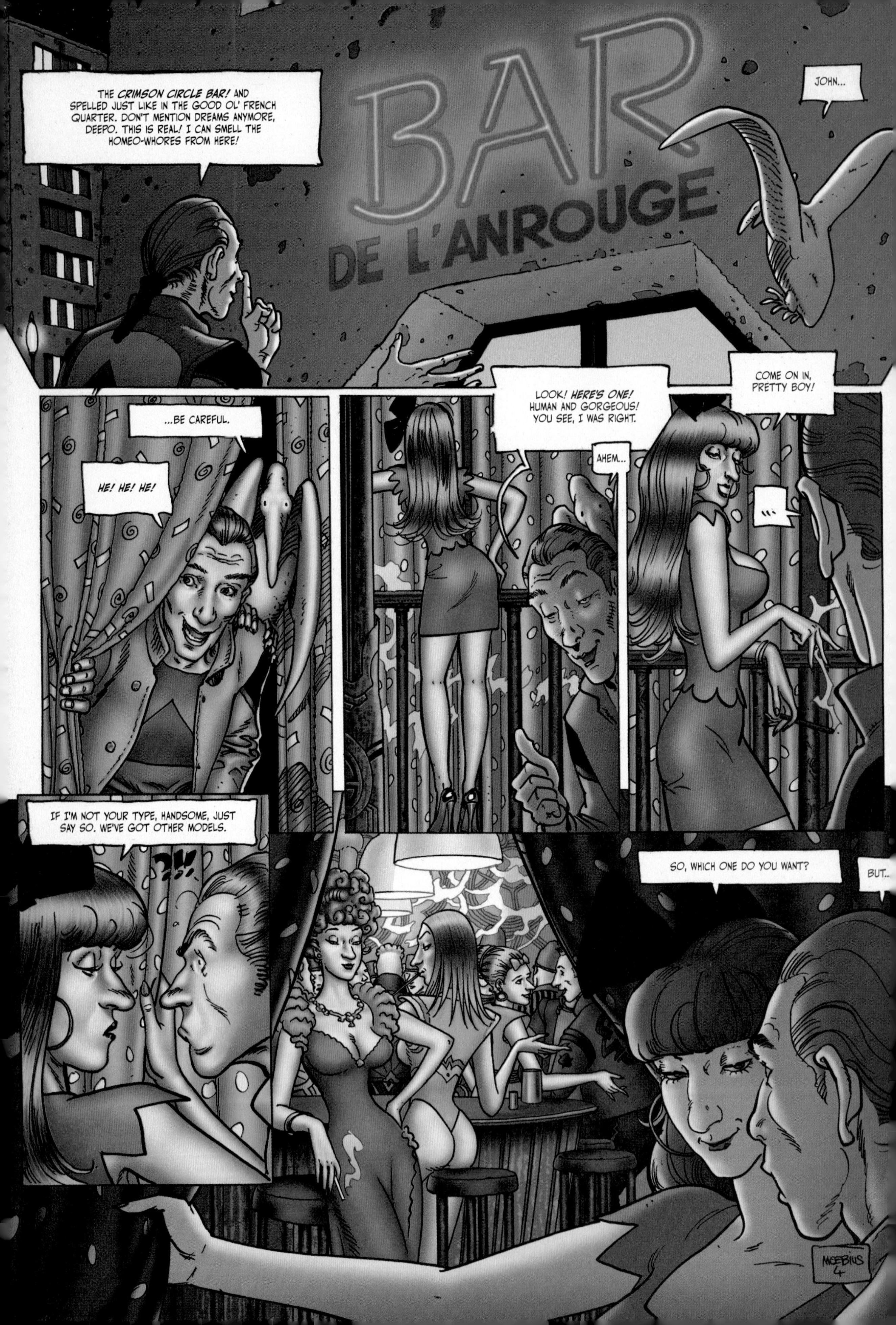

THE CRIMSON CIRCLE BAR! AND SPELLED JUST LIKE IN THE GOOD OL' FRENCH QUARTER. DON'T MENTION DREAMS ANYMORE, DEEPO. THIS IS REAL! I CAN SMELL THE HOMEO-WHORES FROM HERE!
BAR DE L'ANROUGE
JOHN...
...BE CAREFUL.
HE! HE! HE!
LOOK! HERE'S ONE! HUMAN AND GORGEOUS! YOU SEE, I WAS RIGHT.
AHEM...
COME ON IN, PRETTY BOY!
...
IF I'M NOT YOUR TYPE, HANDSOME, JUST SAY SO. WE'VE GOT OTHER MODELS.
SO, WHICH ONE DO YOU WANT?
BUT...
MOEBIUS

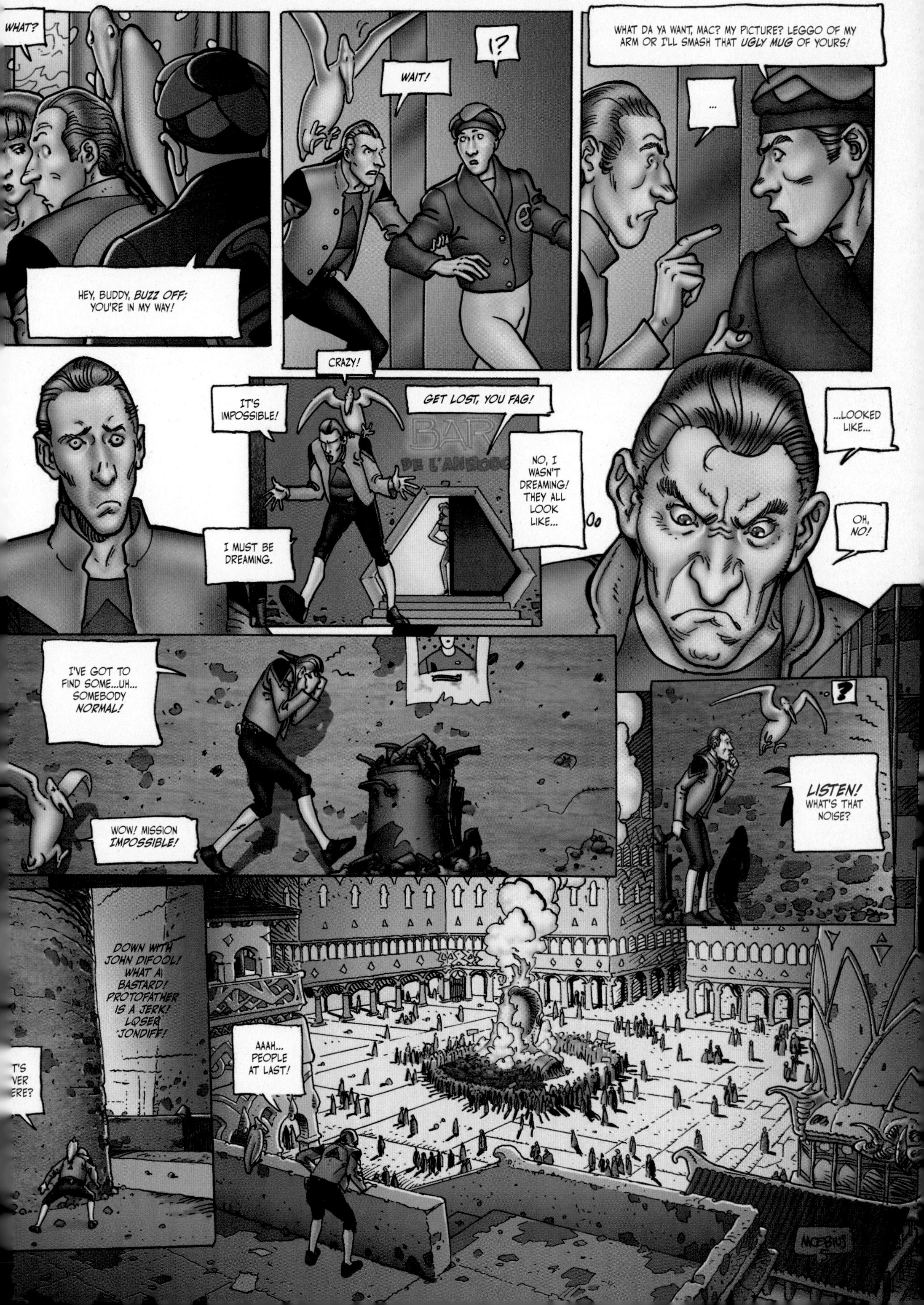

WHAT?
HEY, BUDDY, BUZZ OFF; YOU'RE IN MY WAY!
WAIT!
!?
WHAT DA YA WANT, MAC? MY PICTURE? LEGGO OF MY ARM OR I'LL SMASH THAT UGLY MUG OF YOURS!
...
CRAZY!
IT'S IMPOSSIBLE!
GET LOST, YOU FAG!
BAR DE L'AN
I MUST BE DREAMING.
NO, I WASN'T DREAMING! THEY ALL LOOK LIKE...
...LOOKED LIKE...
OH, NO!
I'VE GOT TO FIND SOME...UH... SOMEBODY NORMAL!
WOW! MISSION IMPOSSIBLE!
?
LISTEN! WHAT'S THAT NOISE?
DOWN WITH JOHN DIFOOL! WHAT A BASTARD! PROTOFATHER IS A JERK! LOSER JONDIFF!
AAAH... PEOPLE AT LAST!
MOEBIUS

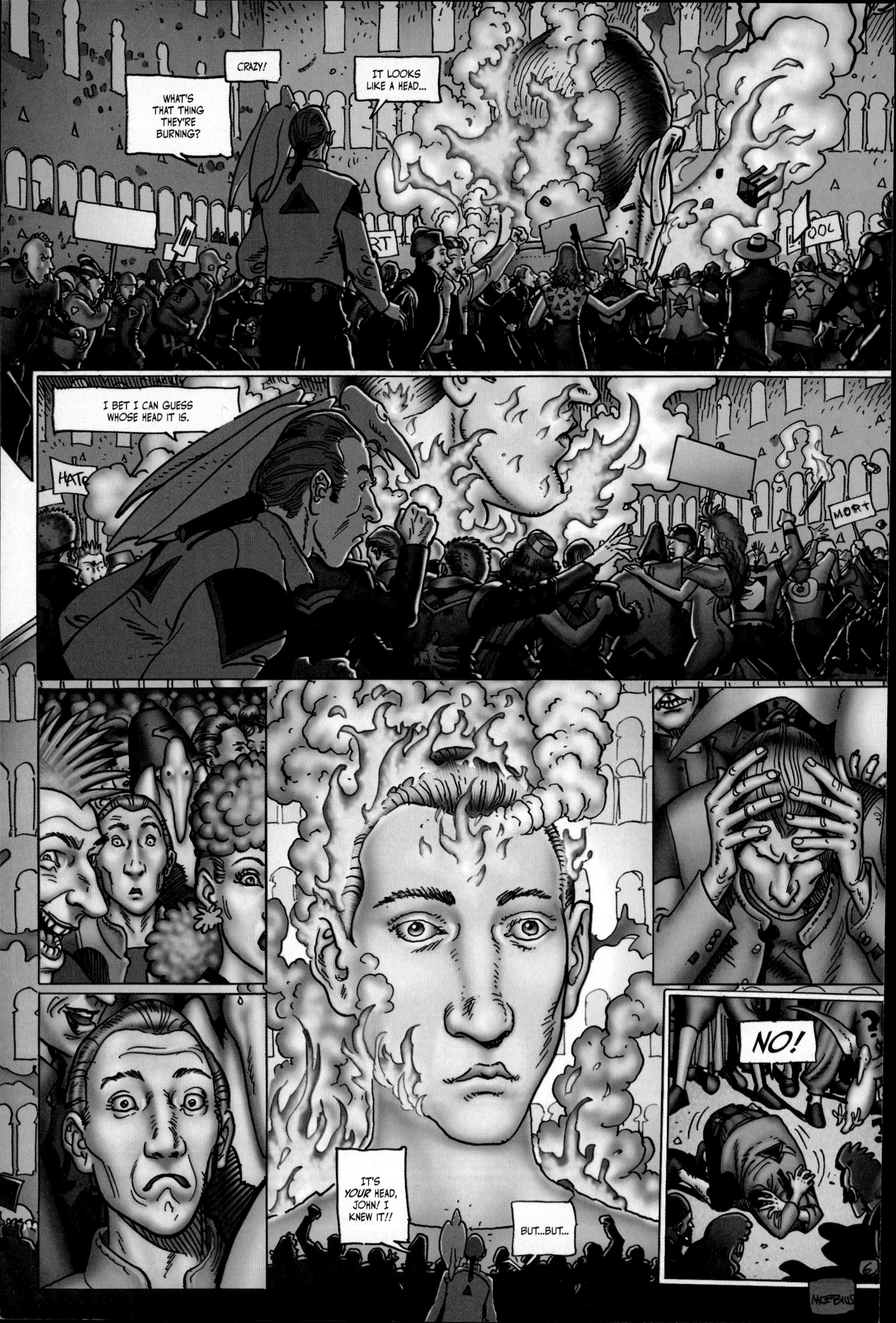
WHAT'S THAT THING THEY'RE BURNING?
CRAZY!
IT LOOKS LIKE A HEAD...
I BET I CAN GUESS WHOSE HEAD IT IS.
HATO
MORT
IT'S YOUR HEAD, JOHN! I KNEW IT!!
BUT...BUT...
NO!
MŒBIUS

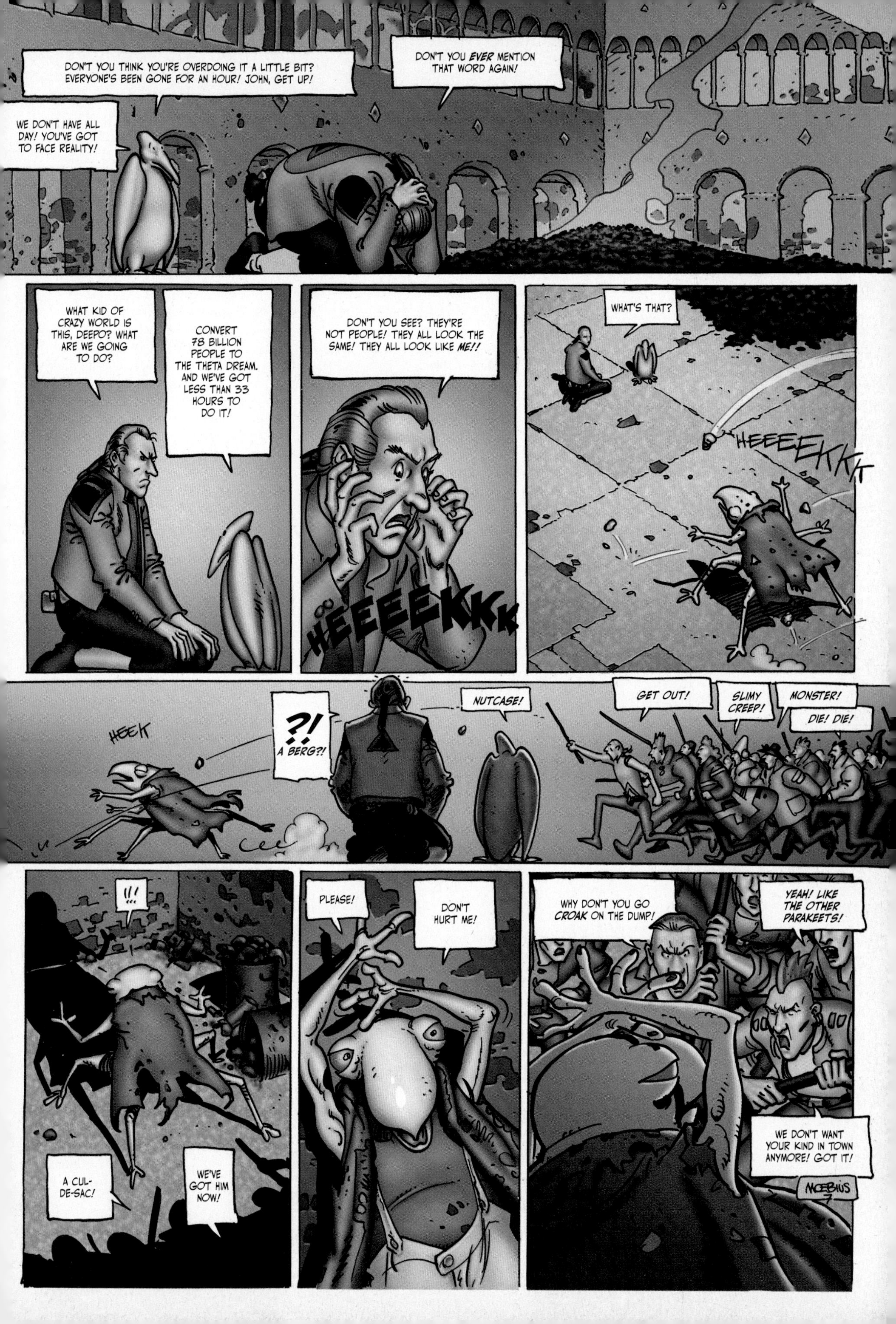
DON'T YOU THINK YOU'RE OVERDOING IT A LITTLE BIT? EVERYONE'S BEEN GONE FOR AN HOUR! JOHN, GET UP!
WE DON'T HAVE ALL DAY! YOU'VE GOT TO FACE REALITY!
DON'T YOU *EVER* MENTION THAT WORD AGAIN!
WHAT KID OF CRAZY WORLD IS THIS, DEEPO? WHAT ARE WE GOING TO DO?
CONVERT 78 BILLION PEOPLE TO THE THETA DREAM. AND WE'VE GOT LESS THAN 33 HOURS TO DO IT!
DON'T YOU SEE? THEY'RE NOT PEOPLE! THEY ALL LOOK THE SAME! THEY ALL LOOK LIKE *ME!!*
HEEEEKKK
WHAT'S THAT?
HEEEEKKK
HEEK
?! A BERG?!
NUTCASE!
GET OUT!
SLIMY CREEP!
MONSTER!
DIE! DIE!
!!!
A CUL-DE-SAC!
WE'VE GOT HIM NOW!
PLEASE!
DON'T HURT ME!
WHY DON'T YOU GO *CROAK* ON THE DUMP!
YEAH! LIKE THE OTHER PARAKEETS!
WE DON'T WANT YOUR KIND IN TOWN ANYMORE! GOT IT!
MOEBIUS

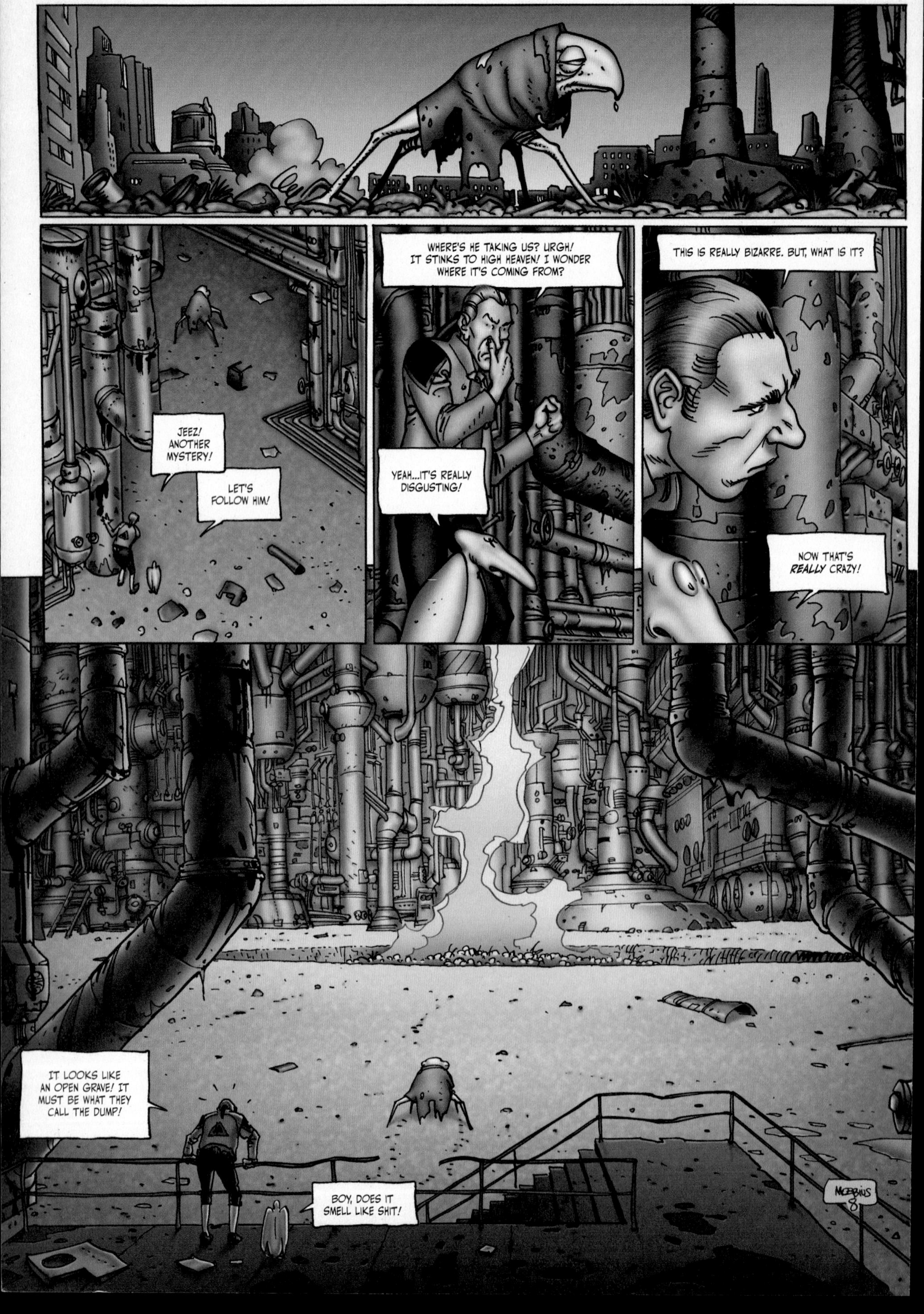

JEEZ! ANOTHER MYSTERY!
LET'S FOLLOW HIM!
WHERE'S HE TAKING US? URGH! IT STINKS TO HIGH HEAVEN! I WONDER WHERE IT'S COMING FROM?
YEAH...IT'S REALLY DISGUSTING!
THIS IS REALLY BIZARRE. BUT, WHAT IS IT?
NOW THAT'S REALLY CRAZY!
IT LOOKS LIKE AN OPEN GRAVE! IT MUST BE WHAT THEY CALL THE DUMP!
BOY, DOES IT SMELL LIKE SHIT!
MOEBIUS 8

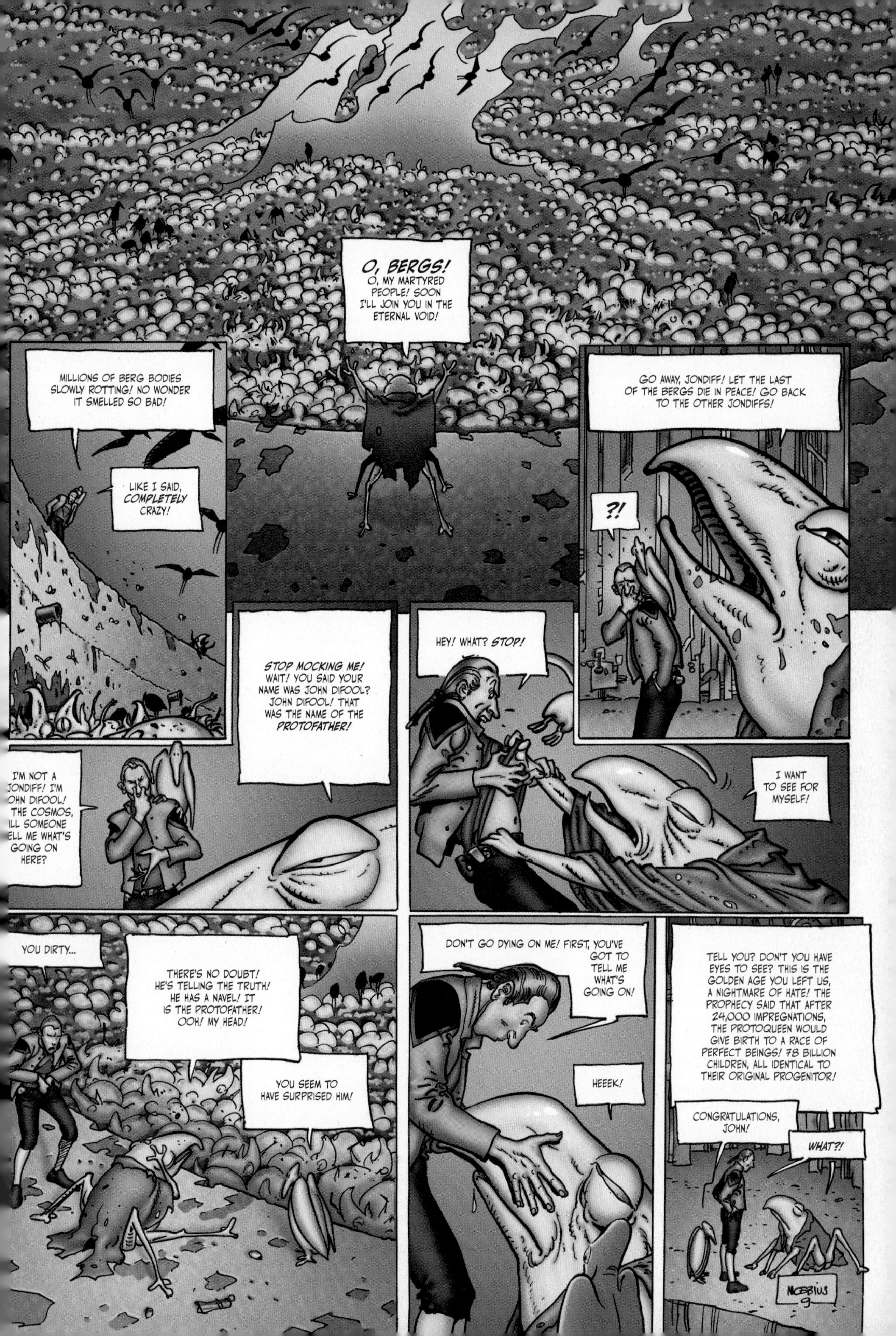
O, BERGS! O, MY MARTYRED PEOPLE! SOON I'LL JOIN YOU IN THE ETERNAL VOID!
MILLIONS OF BERG BODIES SLOWLY ROTTING! NO WONDER IT SMELLED SO BAD!
LIKE I SAID, COMPLETELY CRAZY!
GO AWAY, JONDIFF! LET THE LAST OF THE BERGS DIE IN PEACE! GO BACK TO THE OTHER JONDIFFS!
?!
I'M NOT A JONDIFF! I'M JOHN DIFOOL! THE COSMOS, ILL SOMEONE ELL ME WHAT'S GOING ON HERE?
STOP MOCKING ME! WAIT! YOU SAID YOUR NAME WAS JOHN DIFOOL? JOHN DIFOOL! THAT WAS THE NAME OF THE PROTOFATHER!
HEY! WHAT? STOP!
I WANT TO SEE FOR MYSELF!
YOU DIRTY...
THERE'S NO DOUBT! HE'S TELLING THE TRUTH! HE HAS A NAVEL! IT IS THE PROTOFATHER! OOH! MY HEAD!
YOU SEEM TO HAVE SURPRISED HIM!
DON'T GO DYING ON ME! FIRST, YOU'VE GOT TO TELL ME WHAT'S GOING ON!
HEEEK!
TELL YOU? DON'T YOU HAVE EYES TO SEE? THIS IS THE GOLDEN AGE YOU LEFT US, A NIGHTMARE OF HATE! THE PROPHECY SAID THAT AFTER 24,000 IMPREGNATIONS, THE PROTOQUEEN WOULD GIVE BIRTH TO A RACE OF PERFECT BEINGS! 78 BILLION CHILDREN, ALL IDENTICAL TO THEIR ORIGINAL PROGENITOR!
CONGRATULATIONS, JOHN!
WHAT?!
MŒBIUS 9

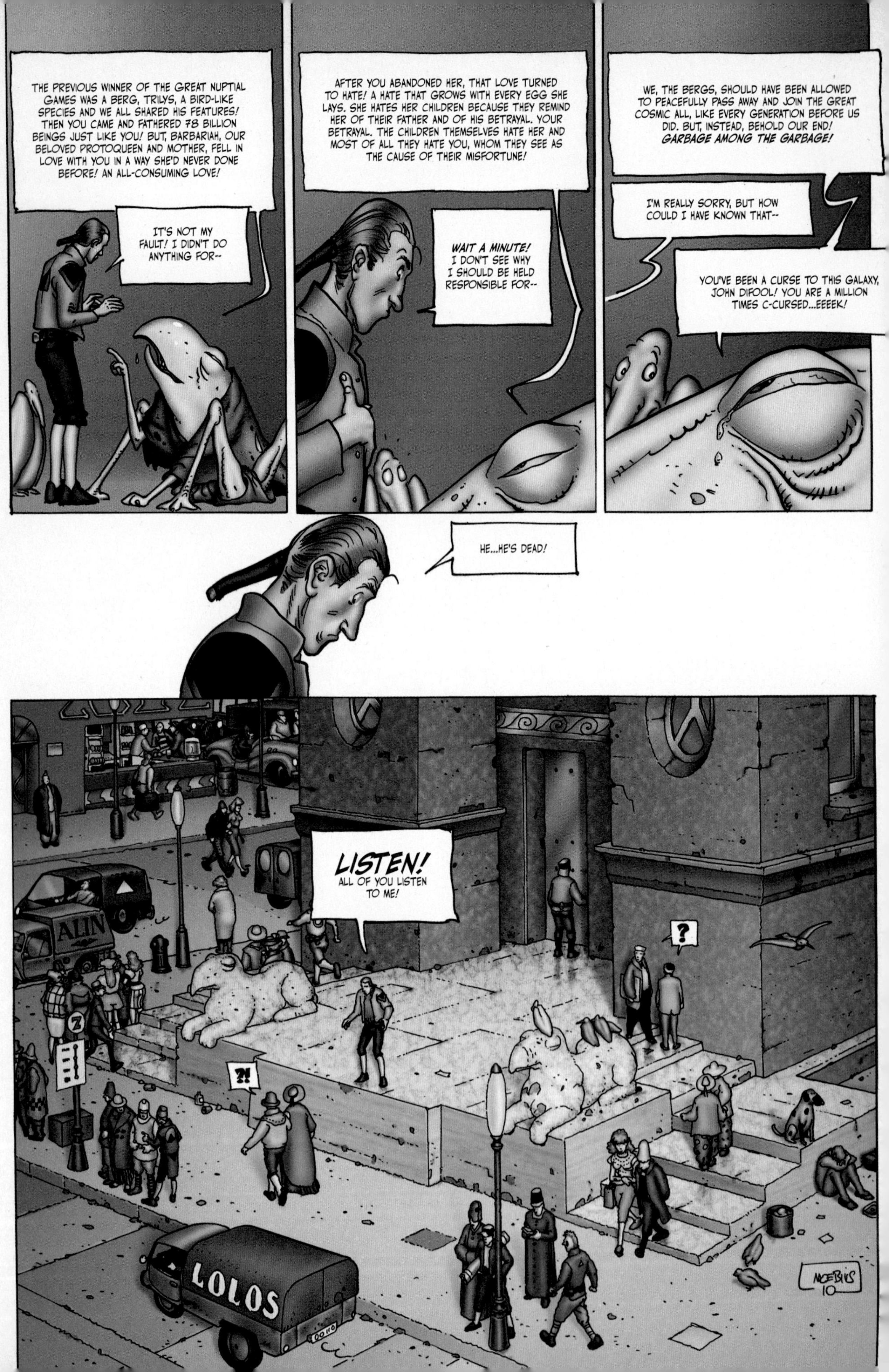
THE PREVIOUS WINNER OF THE GREAT NUPTIAL GAMES WAS A BERG, TRILYS, A BIRD-LIKE SPECIES AND WE ALL SHARED HIS FEATURES! THEN YOU CAME AND FATHERED 78 BILLION BEINGS JUST LIKE YOU! BUT, BARBARIAH, OUR BELOVED PROTOQUEEN AND MOTHER, FELL IN LOVE WITH YOU IN A WAY SHE'D NEVER DONE BEFORE! AN ALL-CONSUMING LOVE!
IT'S NOT MY FAULT! I DIDN'T DO ANYTHING FOR--
AFTER YOU ABANDONED HER, THAT LOVE TURNED TO HATE! A HATE THAT GROWS WITH EVERY EGG SHE LAYS. SHE HATES HER CHILDREN BECAUSE THEY REMIND HER OF THEIR FATHER AND OF HIS BETRAYAL. YOUR BETRAYAL. THE CHILDREN THEMSELVES HATE HER AND MOST OF ALL THEY HATE YOU, WHOM THEY SEE AS THE CAUSE OF THEIR MISFORTUNE!
WAIT A MINUTE! I DON'T SEE WHY I SHOULD BE HELD RESPONSIBLE FOR--
WE, THE BERGS, SHOULD HAVE BEEN ALLOWED TO PEACEFULLY PASS AWAY AND JOIN THE GREAT COSMIC ALL, LIKE EVERY GENERATION BEFORE US DID. BUT, INSTEAD, BEHOLD OUR END! GARBAGE AMONG THE GARBAGE!
I'M REALLY SORRY, BUT HOW COULD I HAVE KNOWN THAT--
YOU'VE BEEN A CURSE TO THIS GALAXY, JOHN DIFOOL! YOU ARE A MILLION TIMES C-CURSED...EEEEK!
HE...HE'S DEAD!
LISTEN! ALL OF YOU LISTEN TO ME!
ALIN
?
?!
LOLOS
MOEBIUS 10

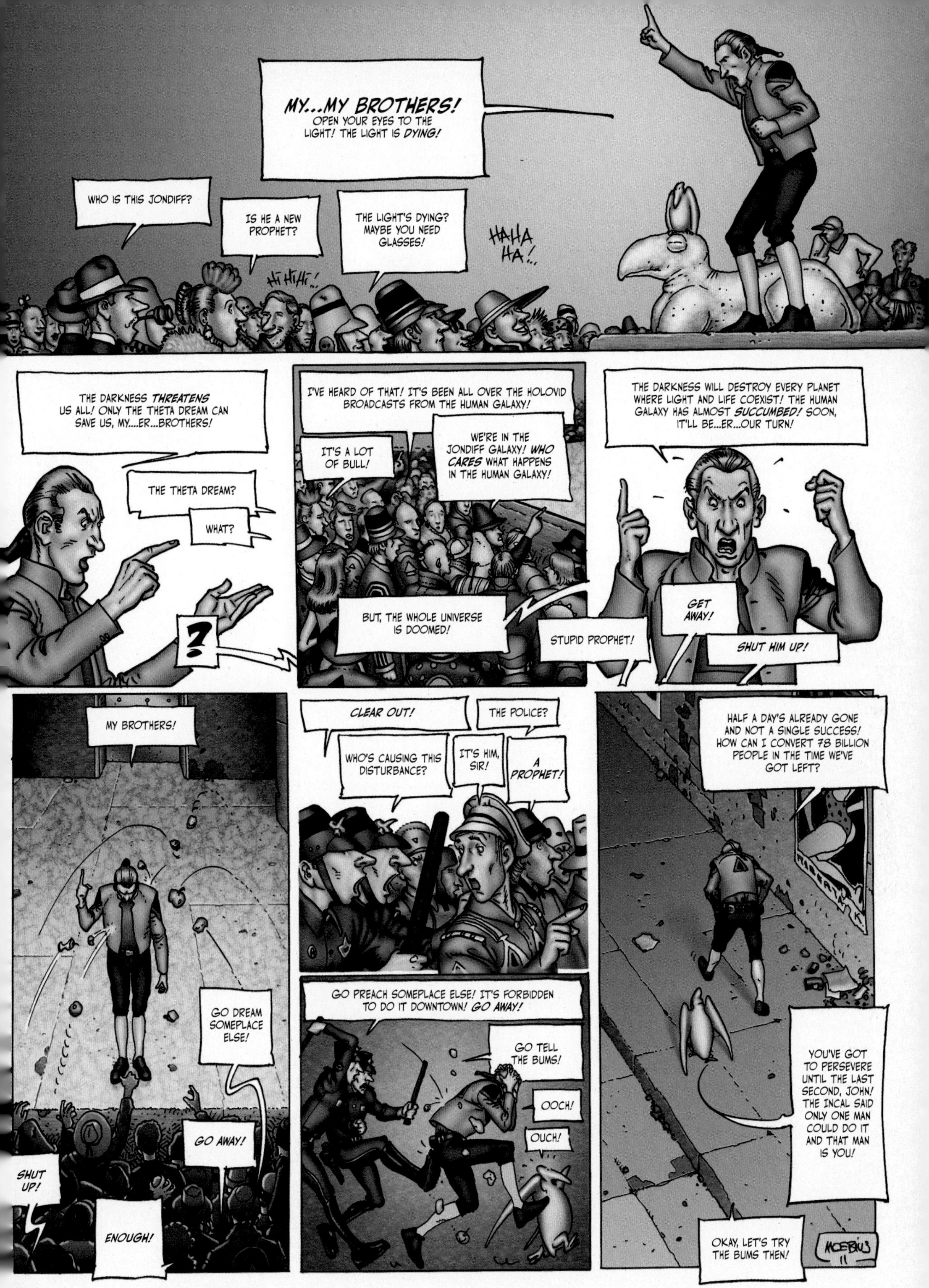
MY...MY BROTHERS!
OPEN YOUR EYES TO THE LIGHT! THE LIGHT IS DYING!
WHO IS THIS JONDIFF?
IS HE A NEW PROPHET?
HI HI HI!
THE LIGHT'S DYING? MAYBE YOU NEED GLASSES!
HA HA HA!
THE DARKNESS THREATENS US ALL! ONLY THE THETA DREAM CAN SAVE US, MY....ER...BROTHERS!
THE THETA DREAM?
WHAT?
?
I'VE HEARD OF THAT! IT'S BEEN ALL OVER THE HOLOVID BROADCASTS FROM THE HUMAN GALAXY!
IT'S A LOT OF BULL!
WE'RE IN THE JONDIFF GALAXY! WHO CARES WHAT HAPPENS IN THE HUMAN GALAXY!
BUT, THE WHOLE UNIVERSE IS DOOMED!
THE DARKNESS WILL DESTROY EVERY PLANET WHERE LIGHT AND LIFE COEXIST! THE HUMAN GALAXY HAS ALMOST SUCCUMBED! SOON, IT'LL BE...ER...OUR TURN!
STUPID PROPHET!
GET AWAY!
SHUT HIM UP!
MY BROTHERS!
GO DREAM SOMEPLACE ELSE!
GO AWAY!
SHUT UP!
ENOUGH!
CLEAR OUT!
THE POLICE?
WHO'S CAUSING THIS DISTURBANCE?
IT'S HIM, SIR!
A PROPHET!
GO PREACH SOMEPLACE ELSE! IT'S FORBIDDEN TO DO IT DOWNTOWN! GO AWAY!
GO TELL THE BUMS!
OOCH!
OUCH!
HALF A DAY'S ALREADY GONE AND NOT A SINGLE SUCCESS! HOW CAN I CONVERT 78 BILLION PEOPLE IN THE TIME WE'VE GOT LEFT?
YOU'VE GOT TO PERSEVERE UNTIL THE LAST SECOND, JOHN! THE INCAL SAID ONLY ONE MAN COULD DO IT AND THAT MAN IS YOU!
OKAY, LET'S TRY THE BUMS THEN!
MOEBIUS 11

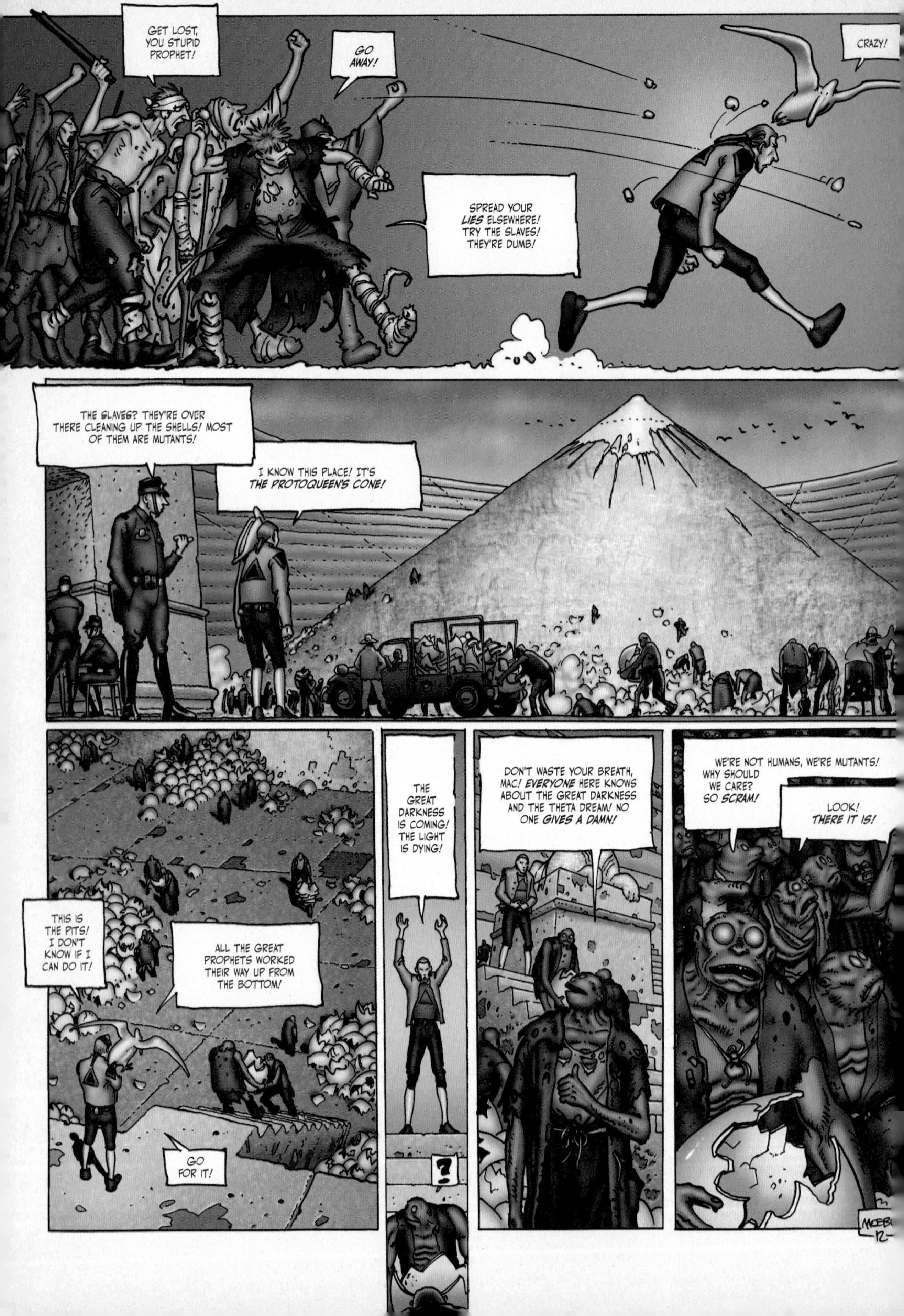
GET LOST, YOU STUPID PROPHET!
GO AWAY!
SPREAD YOUR LIES ELSEWHERE! TRY THE SLAVES! THEY'RE DUMB!
CRAZY!
THE SLAVES? THEY'RE OVER THERE CLEANING UP THE SHELLS! MOST OF THEM ARE MUTANTS!
I KNOW THIS PLACE! IT'S THE PROTOQUEEN'S CONE!
THIS IS THE PITS! I DON'T KNOW IF I CAN DO IT!
ALL THE GREAT PROPHETS WORKED THEIR WAY UP FROM THE BOTTOM!
GO FOR IT!
THE GREAT DARKNESS IS COMING! THE LIGHT IS DYING!
?
DON'T WASTE YOUR BREATH, MAC! EVERYONE HERE KNOWS ABOUT THE GREAT DARKNESS AND THE THETA DREAM! NO ONE GIVES A DAMN!
WE'RE NOT HUMANS, WE'RE MUTANTS! WHY SHOULD WE CARE? SO SCRAM!
LOOK! THERE IT IS!

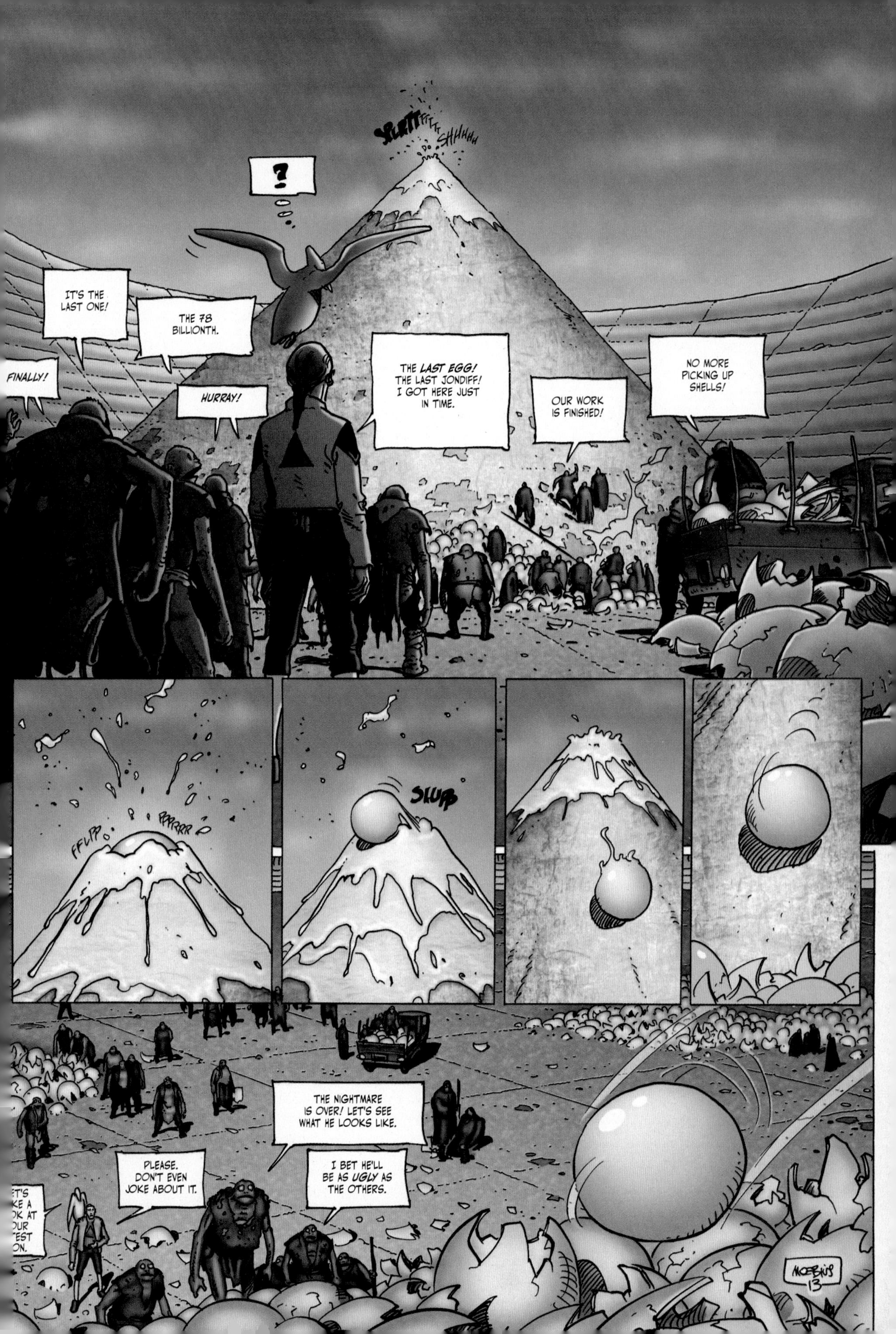

SHHHhhh
?
IT'S THE LAST ONE!
THE 78 BILLIONTH.
FINALLY!
HURRAY!
THE LAST EGG! THE LAST JONDIFF! I GOT HERE JUST IN TIME.
OUR WORK IS FINISHED!
NO MORE PICKING UP SHELLS!
FFLIPP
PPPRRRR
SLUPP
THE NIGHTMARE IS OVER! LET'S SEE WHAT HE LOOKS LIKE.
PLEASE. DON'T EVEN JOKE ABOUT IT.
I BET HE'LL BE AS UGLY AS THE OTHERS.
ET'S KE A OK AT OUR TEST ON.
MOEBIUS 13

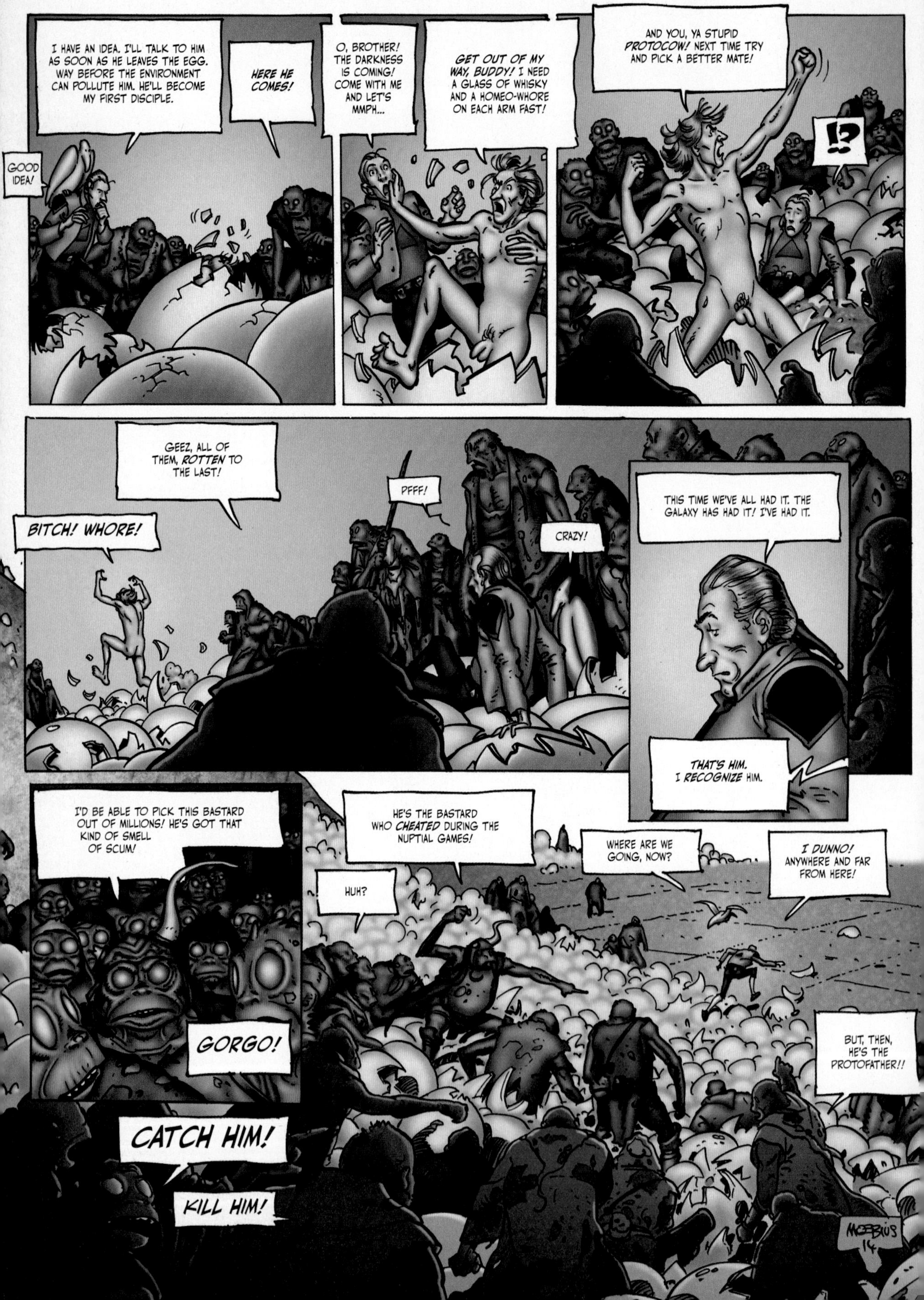
I HAVE AN IDEA. I'LL TALK TO HIM AS SOON AS HE LEAVES THE EGG. WAY BEFORE THE ENVIRONMENT CAN POLLUTE HIM. HE'LL BECOME MY FIRST DISCIPLE.
HERE HE COMES!
GOOD IDEA!
O, BROTHER! THE DARKNESS IS COMING! COME WITH ME AND LET'S MMPH...
GET OUT OF MY WAY, BUDDY! I NEED A GLASS OF WHISKY AND A HOMEO-WHORE ON EACH ARM FAST!
AND YOU, YA STUPID PROTOCOW! NEXT TIME TRY AND PICK A BETTER MATE!
!?
GEEZ, ALL OF THEM, ROTTEN TO THE LAST!
BITCH! WHORE!
PFFF!
CRAZY!
THIS TIME WE'VE ALL HAD IT. THE GALAXY HAS HAD IT! I'VE HAD IT.
THAT'S HIM. I RECOGNIZE HIM.
I'D BE ABLE TO PICK THIS BASTARD OUT OF MILLIONS! HE'S GOT THAT KIND OF SMELL OF SCUM!
GORGO!
HE'S THE BASTARD WHO CHEATED DURING THE NUPTIAL GAMES!
HUH?
WHERE ARE WE GOING, NOW?
I DUNNO! ANYWHERE AND FAR FROM HERE!
BUT, THEN, HE'S THE PROTOFATHER!!
CATCH HIM!
KILL HIM!

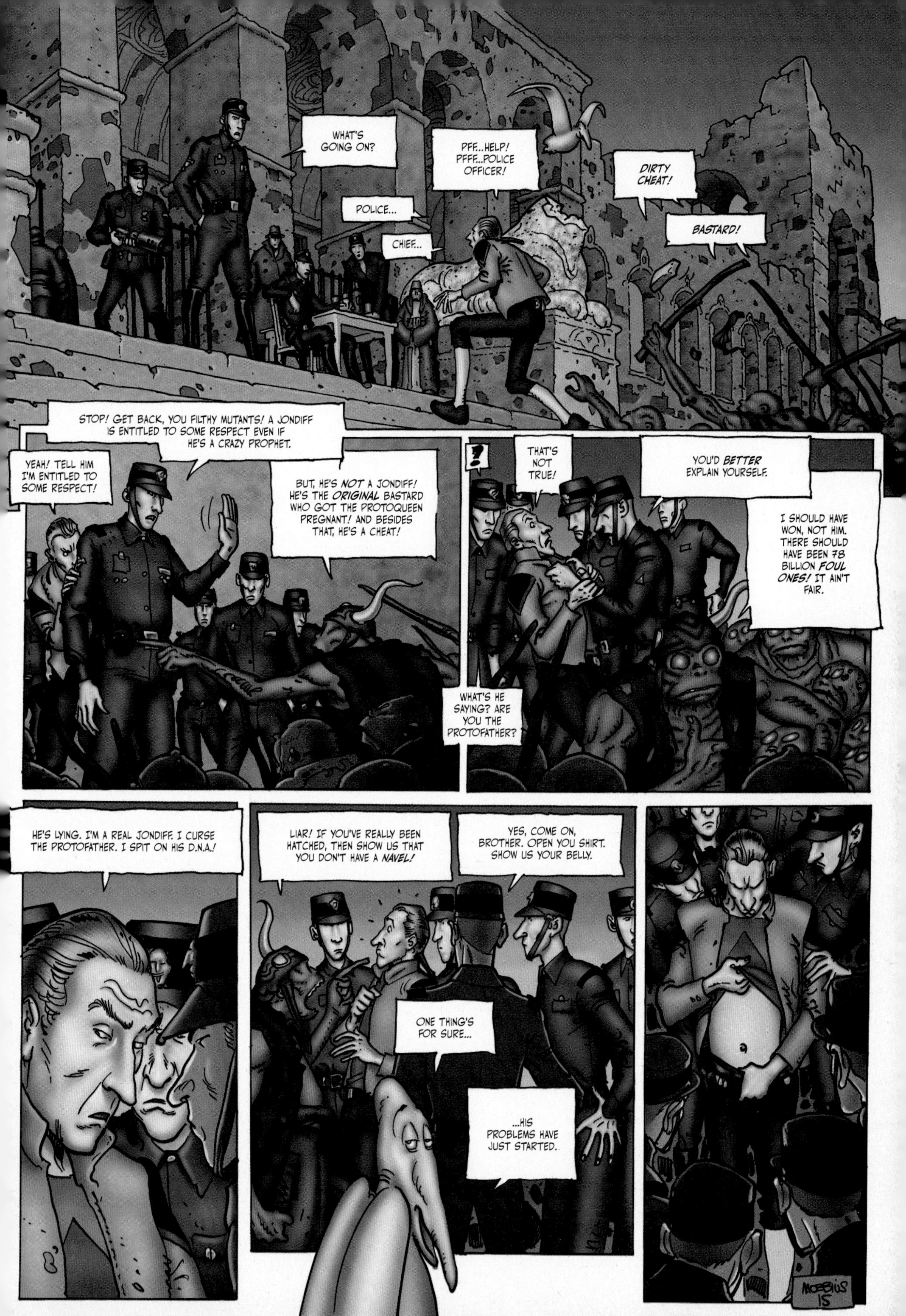
WHAT'S GOING ON?
PFF...HELP! PFFF...POLICE OFFICER!
DIRTY CHEAT!
POLICE...
CHIEF...
BASTARD!
STOP! GET BACK, YOU FILTHY MUTANTS! A JONDIFF IS ENTITLED TO SOME RESPECT EVEN IF HE'S A CRAZY PROPHET.
YEAH! TELL HIM I'M ENTITLED TO SOME RESPECT!
BUT, HE'S NOT A JONDIFF! HE'S THE ORIGINAL BASTARD WHO GOT THE PROTOQUEEN PREGNANT! AND BESIDES THAT, HE'S A CHEAT!
!
THAT'S NOT TRUE!
YOU'D BETTER EXPLAIN YOURSELF.
I SHOULD HAVE WON, NOT HIM. THERE SHOULD HAVE BEEN 78 BILLION FOUL ONES! IT AIN'T FAIR.
WHAT'S HE SAYING? ARE YOU THE PROTOFATHER?
HE'S LYING. I'M A REAL JONDIFF. I CURSE THE PROTOFATHER. I SPIT ON HIS D.N.A.!
LIAR! IF YOU'VE REALLY BEEN HATCHED, THEN SHOW US THAT YOU DON'T HAVE A NAVEL!
YES, COME ON, BROTHER. OPEN YOU SHIRT. SHOW US YOUR BELLY.
ONE THING'S FOR SURE...
...HIS PROBLEMS HAVE JUST STARTED.
MOEBIUS 15

CROSS

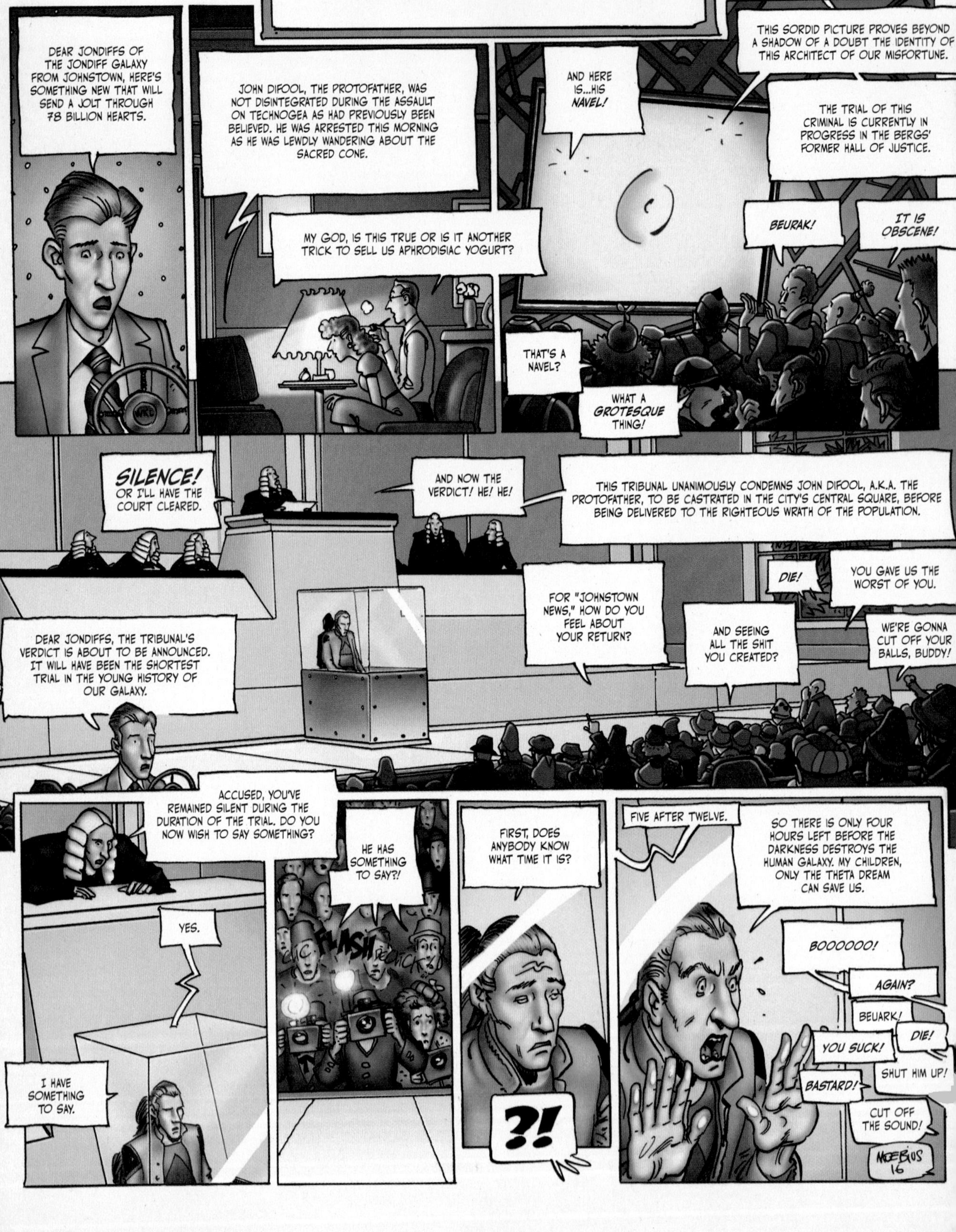
DEAR JONDIFFS OF THE JONDIFF GALAXY FROM JOHNSTOWN, HERE'S SOMETHING NEW THAT WILL SEND A JOLT THROUGH 78 BILLION HEARTS.
JOHN DIFOOL, THE PROTOFATHER, WAS NOT DISINTEGRATED DURING THE ASSAULT ON TECHNOGEA AS HAD PREVIOUSLY BEEN BELIEVED. HE WAS ARRESTED THIS MORNING AS HE WAS LEWDLY WANDERING ABOUT THE SACRED CONE.
MY GOD, IS THIS TRUE OR IS IT ANOTHER TRICK TO SELL US APHRODISIAC YOGURT?
AND HERE IS...HIS NAVEL!
THIS SORDID PICTURE PROVES BEYOND A SHADOW OF A DOUBT THE IDENTITY OF THIS ARCHITECT OF OUR MISFORTUNE.
THE TRIAL OF THIS CRIMINAL IS CURRENTLY IN PROGRESS IN THE BERGS' FORMER HALL OF JUSTICE.
BEURAK!
IT IS OBSCENE!
THAT'S A NAVEL?
WHAT A GROTESQUE THING!
SILENCE! OR I'LL HAVE THE COURT CLEARED.
AND NOW THE VERDICT! HE! HE!
THIS TRIBUNAL UNANIMOUSLY CONDEMNS JOHN DIFOOL, A.K.A. THE PROTOFATHER, TO BE CASTRATED IN THE CITY'S CENTRAL SQUARE, BEFORE BEING DELIVERED TO THE RIGHTEOUS WRATH OF THE POPULATION.
DEAR JONDIFFS, THE TRIBUNAL'S VERDICT IS ABOUT TO BE ANNOUNCED. IT WILL HAVE BEEN THE SHORTEST TRIAL IN THE YOUNG HISTORY OF OUR GALAXY.
FOR "JOHNSTOWN NEWS," HOW DO YOU FEEL ABOUT YOUR RETURN?
AND SEEING ALL THE SHIT YOU CREATED?
DIE!
YOU GAVE US THE WORST OF YOU.
WE'RE GONNA CUT OFF YOUR BALLS, BUDDY!
ACCUSED, YOU'VE REMAINED SILENT DURING THE DURATION OF THE TRIAL. DO YOU NOW WISH TO SAY SOMETHING?
YES.
I HAVE SOMETHING TO SAY.
HE HAS SOMETHING TO SAY?!
FLASH
FIRST, DOES ANYBODY KNOW WHAT TIME IT IS?
?!
FIVE AFTER TWELVE.
SO THERE IS ONLY FOUR HOURS LEFT BEFORE THE DARKNESS DESTROYS THE HUMAN GALAXY. MY CHILDREN, ONLY THE THETA DREAM CAN SAVE US.
BOOOOOO!
AGAIN?
BEUARK!
DIE!
YOU SUCK!
SHUT HIM UP!
BASTARD!
CUT OFF THE SOUND!
MOEBIUS 16

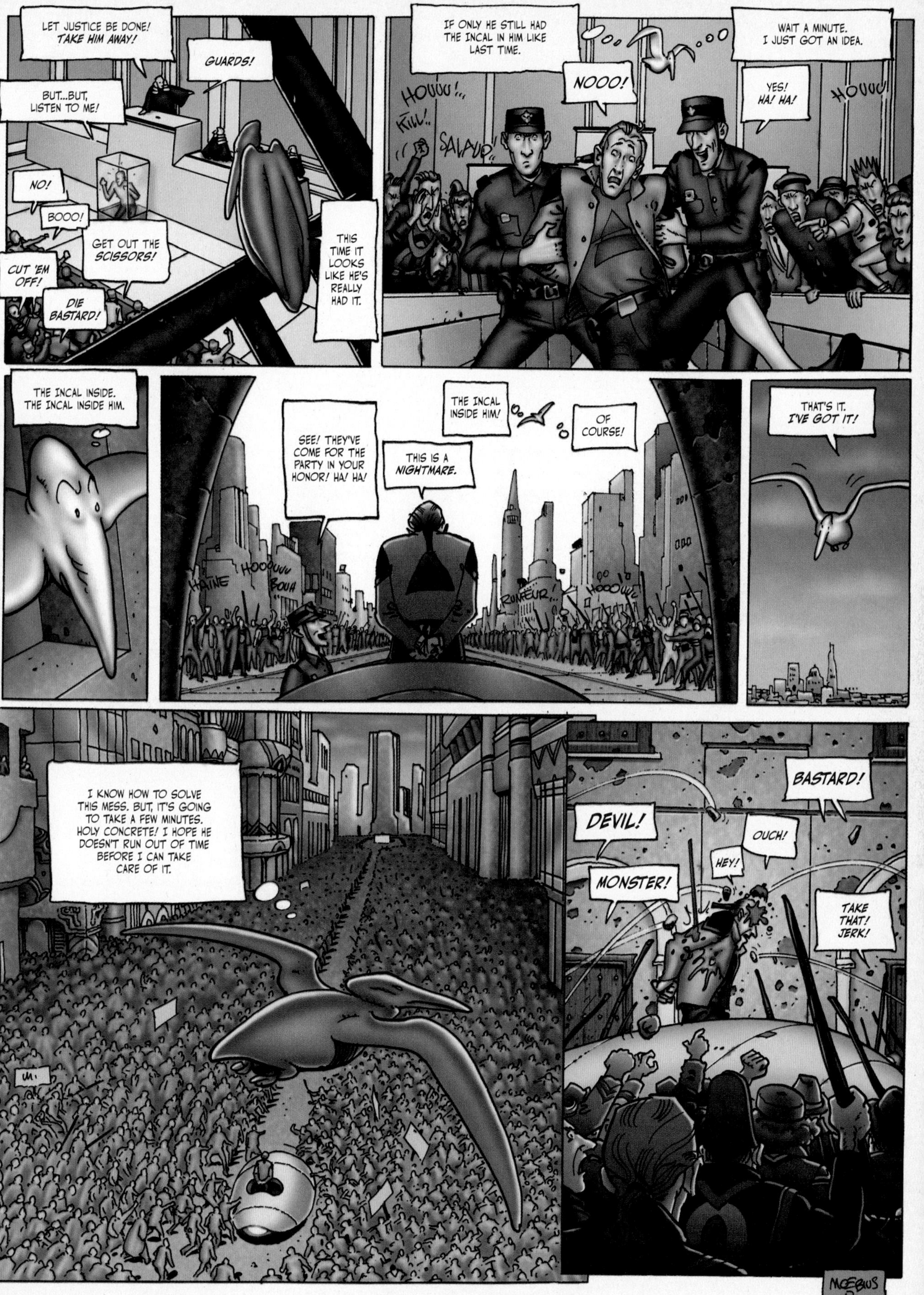
LET JUSTICE BE DONE! TAKE HIM AWAY!
GUARDS!
BUT...BUT, LISTEN TO ME!
NO!
BOOO!
GET OUT THE SCISSORS!
CUT 'EM OFF!
DIE BASTARD!
THIS TIME IT LOOKS LIKE HE'S REALLY HAD IT.
IF ONLY HE STILL HAD THE INCAL IN HIM LIKE LAST TIME.
NOOO!
WAIT A MINUTE. I JUST GOT AN IDEA.
YES! HA! HA!
HOUUU!..
KILL!..
SALAUD!
HOUUU
THE INCAL INSIDE. THE INCAL INSIDE HIM.
SEE! THEY'VE COME FOR THE PARTY IN YOUR HONOR! HA! HA!
THIS IS A NIGHTMARE.
THE INCAL INSIDE HIM!
OF COURSE!
HAINE
HOOOUUU
BOUH
RUNFEUR!..
HOOOUUU
THAT'S IT. I'VE GOT IT!
I KNOW HOW TO SOLVE THIS MESS. BUT, IT'S GOING TO TAKE A FEW MINUTES. HOLY CONCRETE! I HOPE HE DOESN'T RUN OUT OF TIME BEFORE I CAN TAKE CARE OF IT.
BASTARD!
DEVIL!
OUCH!
HEY!
MONSTER!
TAKE THAT! JERK!
MŒBIUS 17

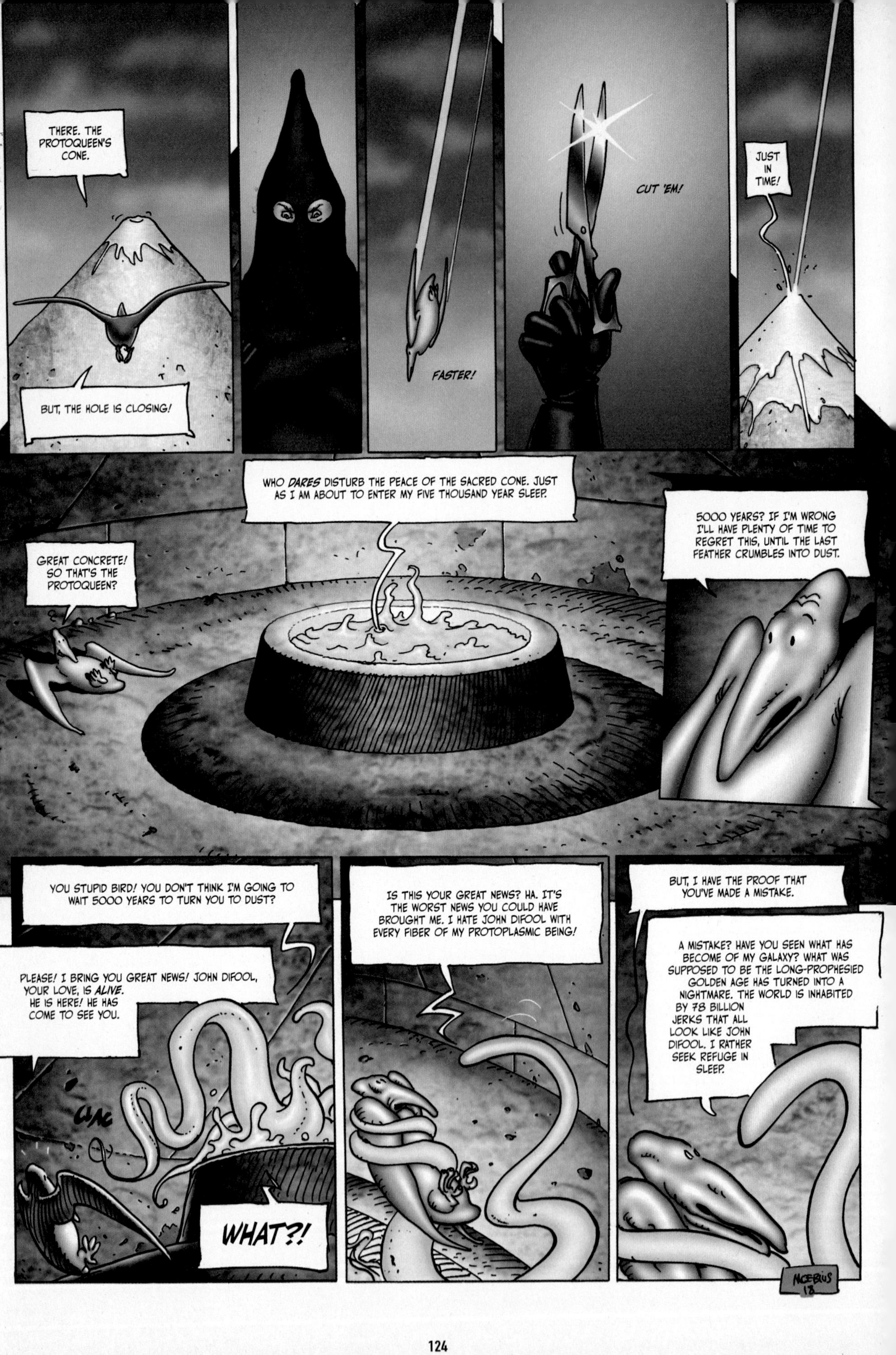

THERE. THE PROTOQUEEN'S CONE.
BUT, THE HOLE IS CLOSING!
FASTER!
CUT 'EM!
JUST IN TIME!
WHO DARES DISTURB THE PEACE OF THE SACRED CONE. JUST AS I AM ABOUT TO ENTER MY FIVE THOUSAND YEAR SLEEP.
GREAT CONCRETE! SO THAT'S THE PROTOQUEEN?
5000 YEARS? IF I'M WRONG I'LL HAVE PLENTY OF TIME TO REGRET THIS, UNTIL THE LAST FEATHER CRUMBLES INTO DUST.
YOU STUPID BIRD! YOU DON'T THINK I'M GOING TO WAIT 5000 YEARS TO TURN YOU TO DUST?
PLEASE! I BRING YOU GREAT NEWS! JOHN DIFOOL, YOUR LOVE, IS ALIVE. HE IS HERE! HE HAS COME TO SEE YOU.
WHAT?!
IS THIS YOUR GREAT NEWS? HA. IT'S THE WORST NEWS YOU COULD HAVE BROUGHT ME. I HATE JOHN DIFOOL WITH EVERY FIBER OF MY PROTOPLASMIC BEING!
BUT, I HAVE THE PROOF THAT YOU'VE MADE A MISTAKE.
A MISTAKE? HAVE YOU SEEN WHAT HAS BECOME OF MY GALAXY? WHAT WAS SUPPOSED TO BE THE LONG-PROPHESIED GOLDEN AGE HAS TURNED INTO A NIGHTMARE. THE WORLD IS INHABITED BY 78 BILLION JERKS THAT ALL LOOK LIKE JOHN DIFOOL. I RATHER SEEK REFUGE IN SLEEP.

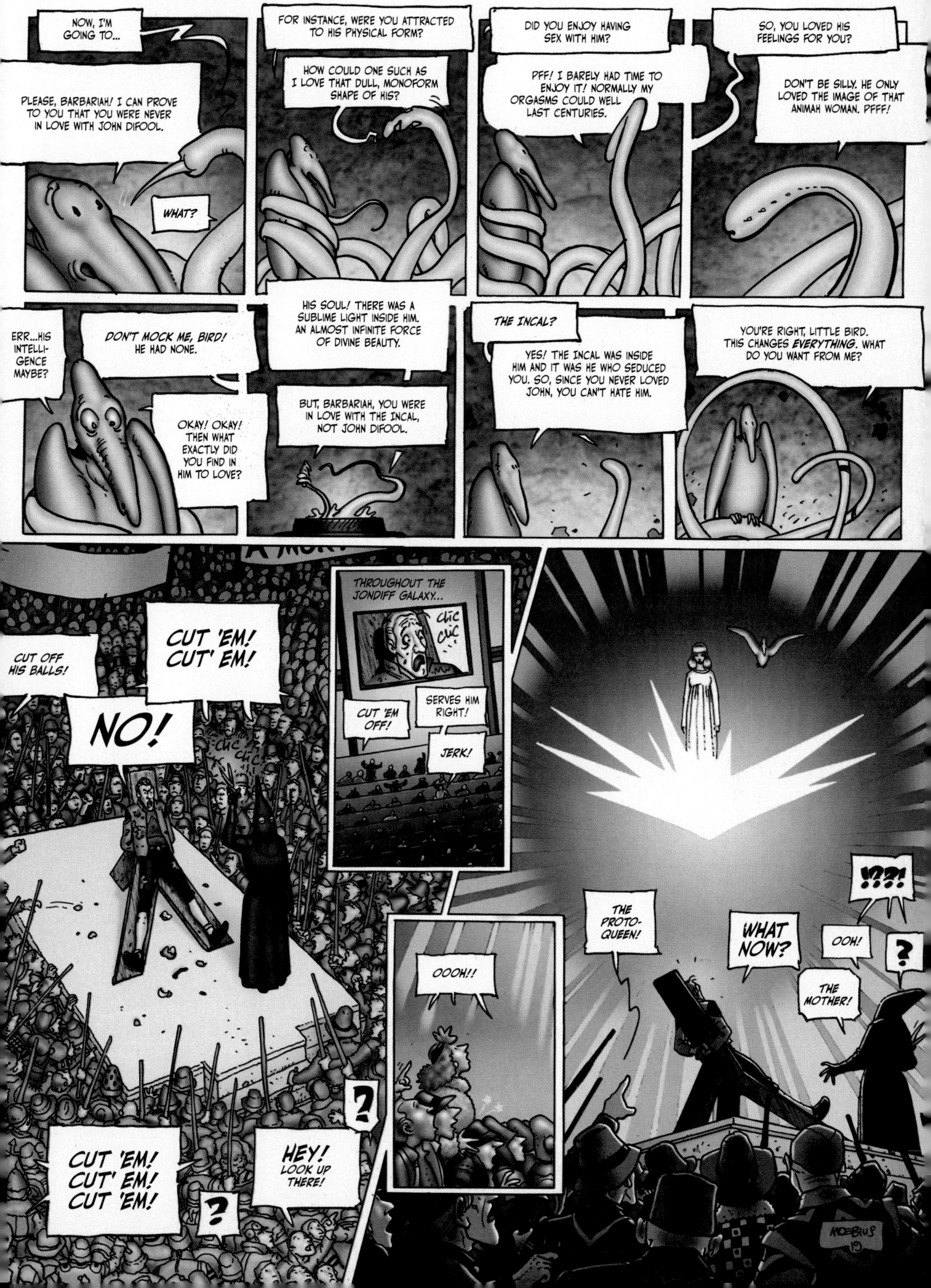
NOW, I'M GOING TO...
PLEASE, BARBARIAH! I CAN PROVE TO YOU THAT YOU WERE NEVER IN LOVE WITH JOHN DIFOOL.
WHAT?
FOR INSTANCE, WERE YOU ATTRACTED TO HIS PHYSICAL FORM?
HOW COULD ONE SUCH AS I LOVE THAT DULL, MONOFORM SHAPE OF HIS?
DID YOU ENJOY HAVING SEX WITH HIM?
PFF! I BARELY HAD TIME TO ENJOY IT! NORMALLY MY ORGASMS COULD WELL LAST CENTURIES.
SO, YOU LOVED HIS FEELINGS FOR YOU?
DON'T BE SILLY. HE ONLY LOVED THE IMAGE OF THAT ANIMAH WOMAN. PFFF!
ERR...HIS INTELLI-GENCE MAYBE?
DON'T MOCK ME, BIRD! HE HAD NONE.
OKAY! OKAY! THEN WHAT EXACTLY DID YOU FIND IN HIM TO LOVE?
HIS SOUL! THERE WAS A SUBLIME LIGHT INSIDE HIM. AN ALMOST INFINITE FORCE OF DIVINE BEAUTY.
BUT, BARBARIAH, YOU WERE IN LOVE WITH THE INCAL, NOT JOHN DIFOOL.
THE INCAL?
YES! THE INCAL WAS INSIDE HIM AND IT WAS HE WHO SEDUCED YOU. SO, SINCE YOU NEVER LOVED JOHN, YOU CAN'T HATE HIM.
YOU'RE RIGHT, LITTLE BIRD. THIS CHANGES EVERYTHING. WHAT DO YOU WANT FROM ME?
CUT OFF HIS BALLS!
CUT 'EM! CUT' EM!
NO!
CLIC CLIC
CUT 'EM! CUT' EM! CUT 'EM!
?
HEY! LOOK UP THERE!
?
THROUGHOUT THE JONDIFF GALAXY...
CLIC CLIC
CUT 'EM OFF!
SERVES HIM RIGHT!
JERK!
OOOH!!
THE PROTO-QUEEN!
WHAT NOW?
!???!
OOH!
?
THE MOTHER!
MOEBIUS

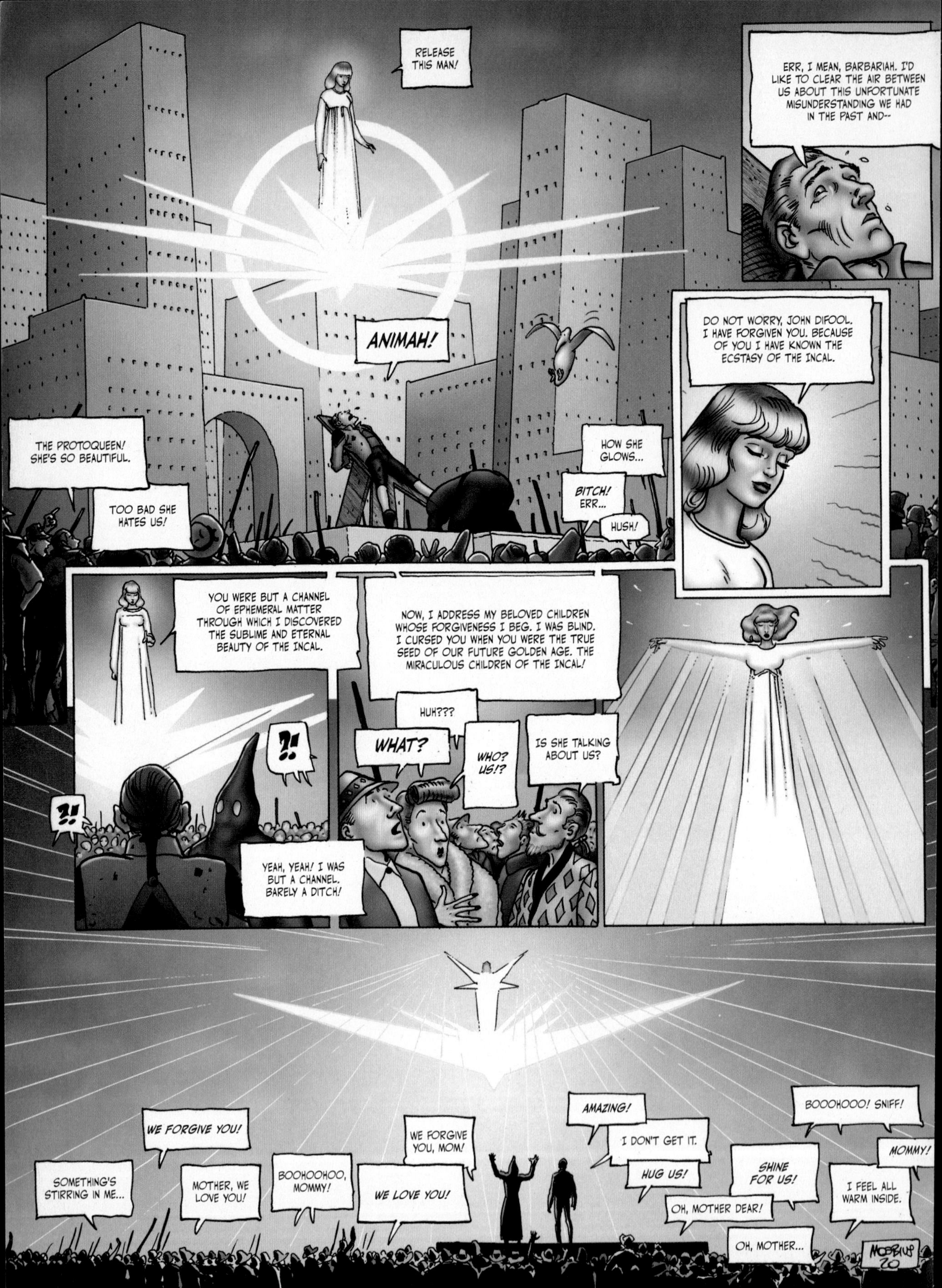
RELEASE THIS MAN!
ERR, I MEAN, BARBARIAH. I'D LIKE TO CLEAR THE AIR BETWEEN US ABOUT THIS UNFORTUNATE MISUNDERSTANDING WE HAD IN THE PAST AND--
ANIMAH!
DO NOT WORRY, JOHN DIFOOL. I HAVE FORGIVEN YOU. BECAUSE OF YOU I HAVE KNOWN THE ECSTASY OF THE INCAL.
THE PROTOQUEEN! SHE'S SO BEAUTIFUL.
TOO BAD SHE HATES US!
HOW SHE GLOWS...
BITCH! ERR...
HUSH!
YOU WERE BUT A CHANNEL OF EPHEMERAL MATTER THROUGH WHICH I DISCOVERED THE SUBLIME AND ETERNAL BEAUTY OF THE INCAL.
?!
?!
YEAH, YEAH! I WAS BUT A CHANNEL. BARELY A DITCH!
NOW, I ADDRESS MY BELOVED CHILDREN WHOSE FORGIVENESS I BEG. I WAS BLIND. I CURSED YOU WHEN YOU WERE THE TRUE SEED OF OUR FUTURE GOLDEN AGE. THE MIRACULOUS CHILDREN OF THE INCAL!
HUH???
WHAT?
WHO? US!?
IS SHE TALKING ABOUT US?
SOMETHING'S STIRRING IN ME...
WE FORGIVE YOU!
MOTHER, WE LOVE YOU!
BOOHOOHOO, MOMMY!
WE FORGIVE YOU, MOM!
WE LOVE YOU!
AMAZING!
I DON'T GET IT.
HUG US!
SHINE FOR US!
OH, MOTHER DEAR!
BOOOHOOO! SNIFF!
MOMMY!
I FEEL ALL WARM INSIDE.
OH, MOTHER...
MOEBIUS 20

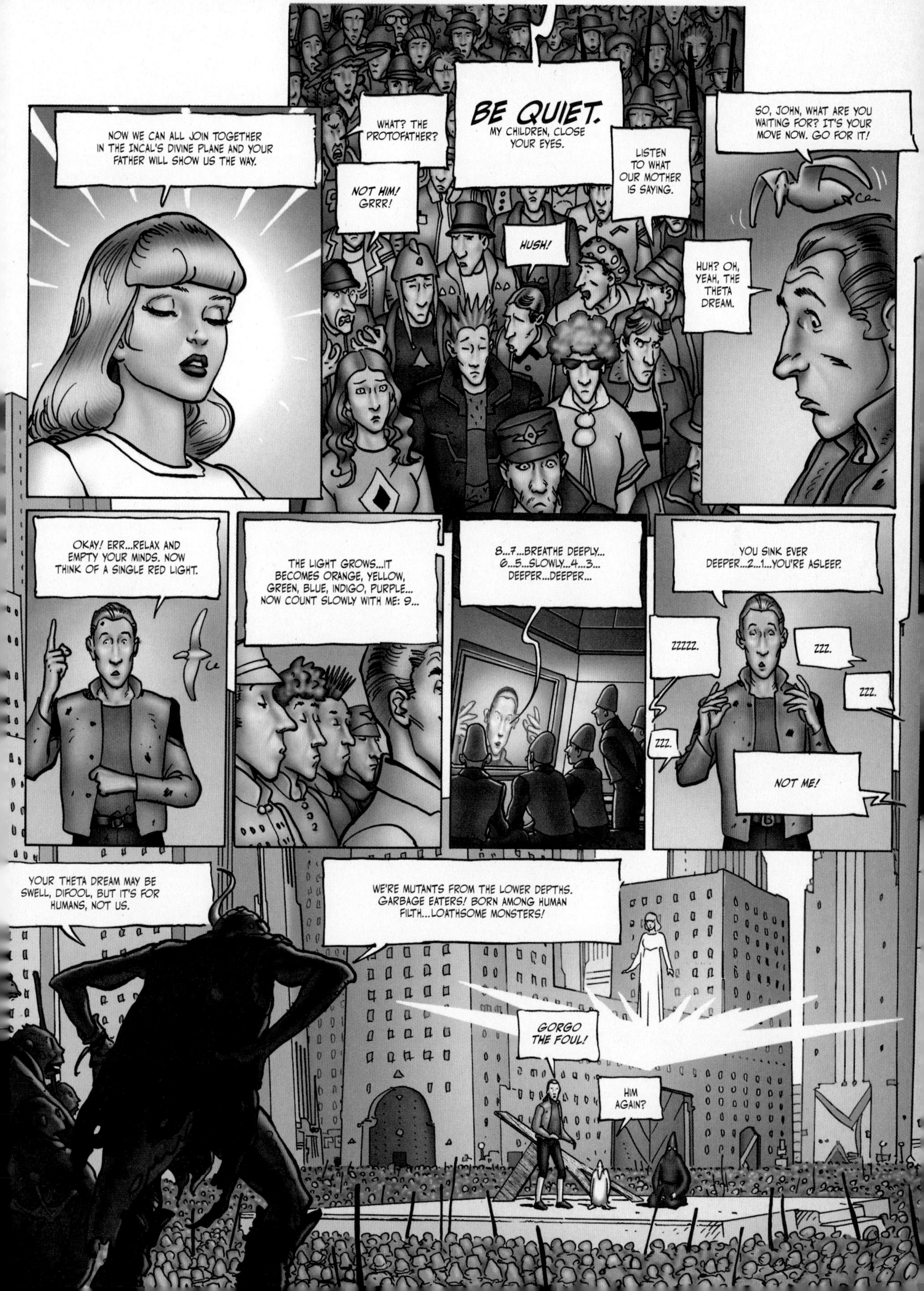
NOW WE CAN ALL JOIN TOGETHER IN THE INCAL'S DIVINE PLANE AND YOUR FATHER WILL SHOW US THE WAY.
WHAT? THE PROTOFATHER?
NOT HIM! GRRR!
BE QUIET.
MY CHILDREN, CLOSE YOUR EYES.
LISTEN TO WHAT OUR MOTHER IS SAYING.
HUSH!
SO, JOHN, WHAT ARE YOU WAITING FOR? IT'S YOUR MOVE NOW. GO FOR IT!
HUH? OH, YEAH, THE THETA DREAM.
OKAY! ERR...RELAX AND EMPTY YOUR MINDS. NOW THINK OF A SINGLE RED LIGHT.
THE LIGHT GROWS...IT BECOMES ORANGE, YELLOW, GREEN, BLUE, INDIGO, PURPLE... NOW COUNT SLOWLY WITH ME: 9...
8...7...BREATHE DEEPLY... 6...5...SLOWLY...4...3... DEEPER...DEEPER...
YOU SINK EVER DEEPER...2...1...YOU'RE ASLEEP.
ZZZZZ.
ZZZ.
ZZZ.
ZZZ.
NOT ME!
YOUR THETA DREAM MAY BE SWELL, DIFOOL, BUT IT'S FOR HUMANS, NOT US.
WE'RE MUTANTS FROM THE LOWER DEPTHS. GARBAGE EATERS! BORN AMONG HUMAN FILTH...LOATHSOME MONSTERS!
GORGO THE FOUL!
HIM AGAIN?

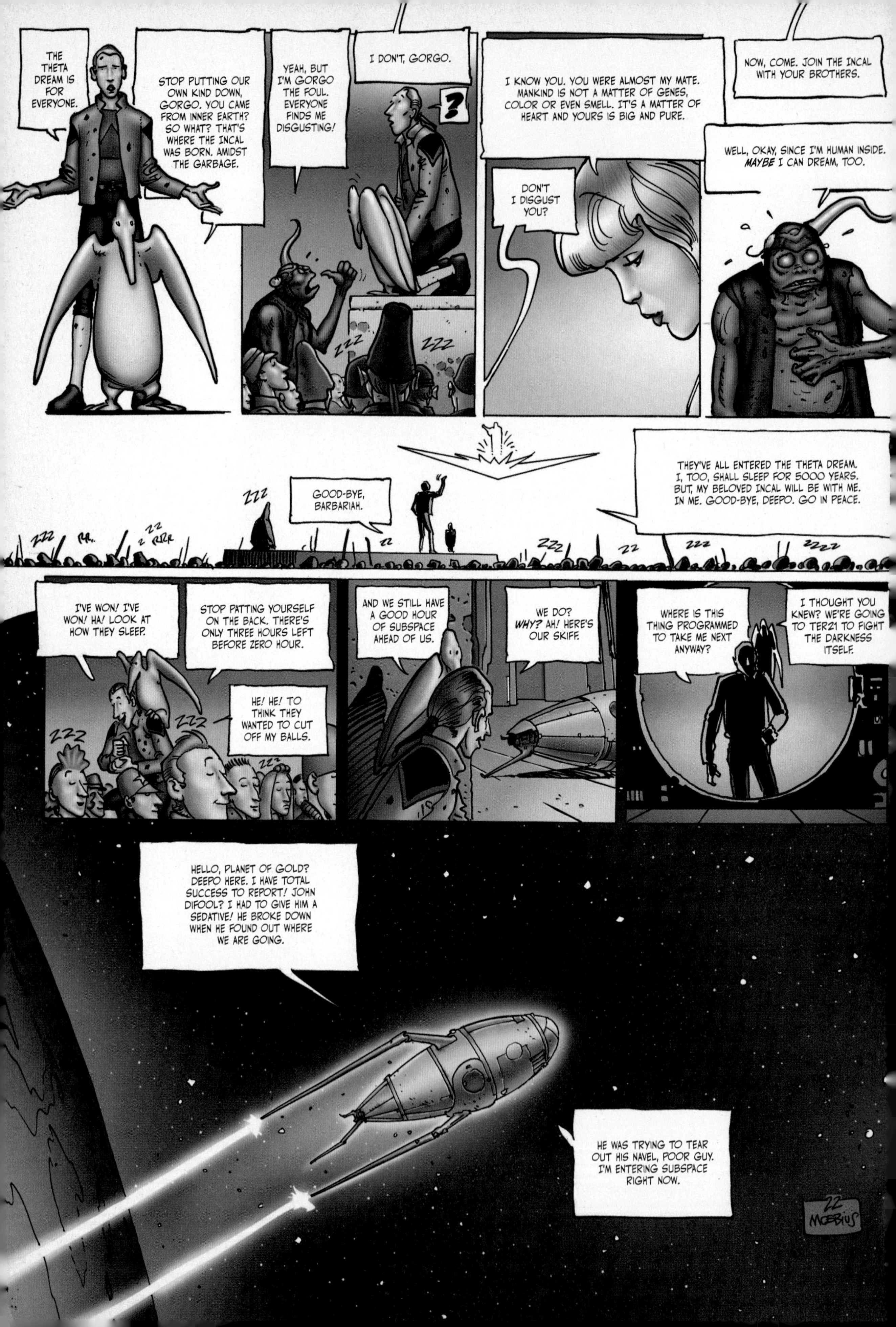
THE THETA DREAM IS FOR EVERYONE.
STOP PUTTING OUR OWN KIND DOWN, GORGO. YOU CAME FROM INNER EARTH? SO WHAT? THAT'S WHERE THE INCAL WAS BORN. AMIDST THE GARBAGE.
YEAH, BUT I'M GORGO THE FOUL. EVERYONE FINDS ME DISGUSTING!
I DON'T, GORGO.
?
ZZZ
ZZZ
DON'T I DISGUST YOU?
I KNOW YOU. YOU WERE ALMOST MY MATE. MANKIND IS NOT A MATTER OF GENES, COLOR OR EVEN SMELL. IT'S A MATTER OF HEART AND YOURS IS BIG AND PURE.
NOW, COME. JOIN THE INCAL WITH YOUR BROTHERS.
WELL, OKAY, SINCE I'M HUMAN INSIDE. MAYBE I CAN DREAM, TOO.
ZZZ
GOOD-BYE, BARBARIAH.
THEY'VE ALL ENTERED THE THETA DREAM. I, TOO, SHALL SLEEP FOR 5000 YEARS. BUT, MY BELOVED INCAL WILL BE WITH ME. IN ME. GOOD-BYE, DEEPO. GO IN PEACE.
I'VE WON! I'VE WON! HA! LOOK AT HOW THEY SLEEP.
STOP PATTING YOURSELF ON THE BACK. THERE'S ONLY THREE HOURS LEFT BEFORE ZERO HOUR.
HE! HE! TO THINK THEY WANTED TO CUT OFF MY BALLS.
ZZZ
AND WE STILL HAVE A GOOD HOUR OF SUBSPACE AHEAD OF US.
WE DO? WHY? AH! HERE'S OUR SKIFF.
WHERE IS THIS THING PROGRAMMED TO TAKE ME NEXT ANYWAY?
I THOUGHT YOU KNEW? WE'RE GOING TO TER21 TO FIGHT THE DARKNESS ITSELF.
HELLO, PLANET OF GOLD? DEEPO HERE. I HAVE TOTAL SUCCESS TO REPORT! JOHN DIFOOL? I HAD TO GIVE HIM A SEDATIVE! HE BROKE DOWN WHEN HE FOUND OUT WHERE WE ARE GOING.
HE WAS TRYING TO TEAR OUT HIS NAVEL, POOR GUY. I'M ENTERING SUBSPACE RIGHT NOW.
22
MOEBIUS

THE CIRCLES OF NIGHTMARE

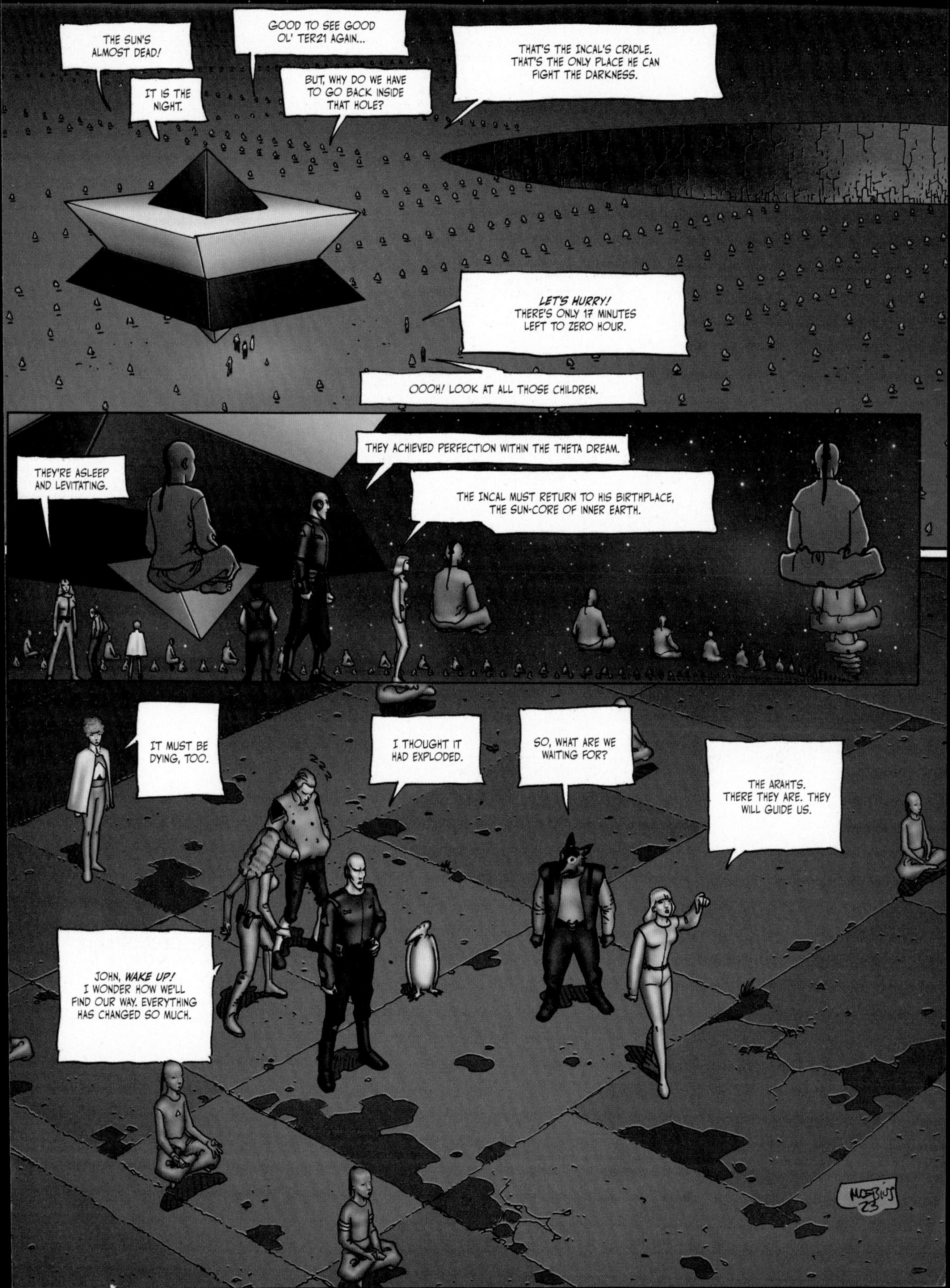

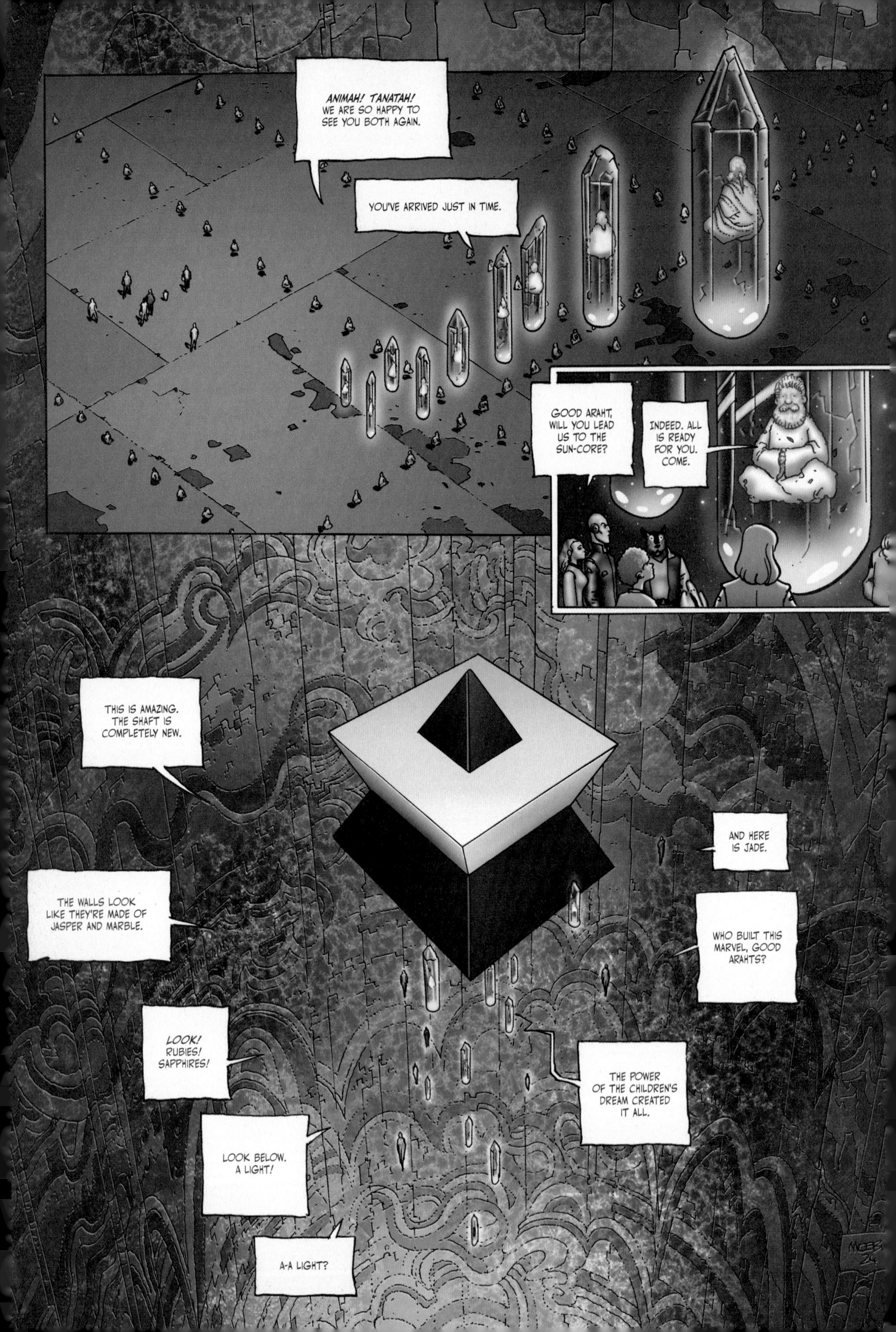
ANIMAH! TANATAH! WE ARE SO HAPPY TO SEE YOU BOTH AGAIN.
YOU'VE ARRIVED JUST IN TIME.
GOOD ARAHT, WILL YOU LEAD US TO THE SUN-CORE?
INDEED. ALL IS READY FOR YOU. COME.
THIS IS AMAZING. THE SHAFT IS COMPLETELY NEW.
AND HERE IS JADE.
THE WALLS LOOK LIKE THEY'RE MADE OF JASPER AND MARBLE.
WHO BUILT THIS MARVEL, GOOD ARAHTS?
LOOK! RUBIES! SAPPHIRES!
THE POWER OF THE CHILDREN'S DREAM CREATED IT ALL.
LOOK BELOW. A LIGHT!
A-A LIGHT?

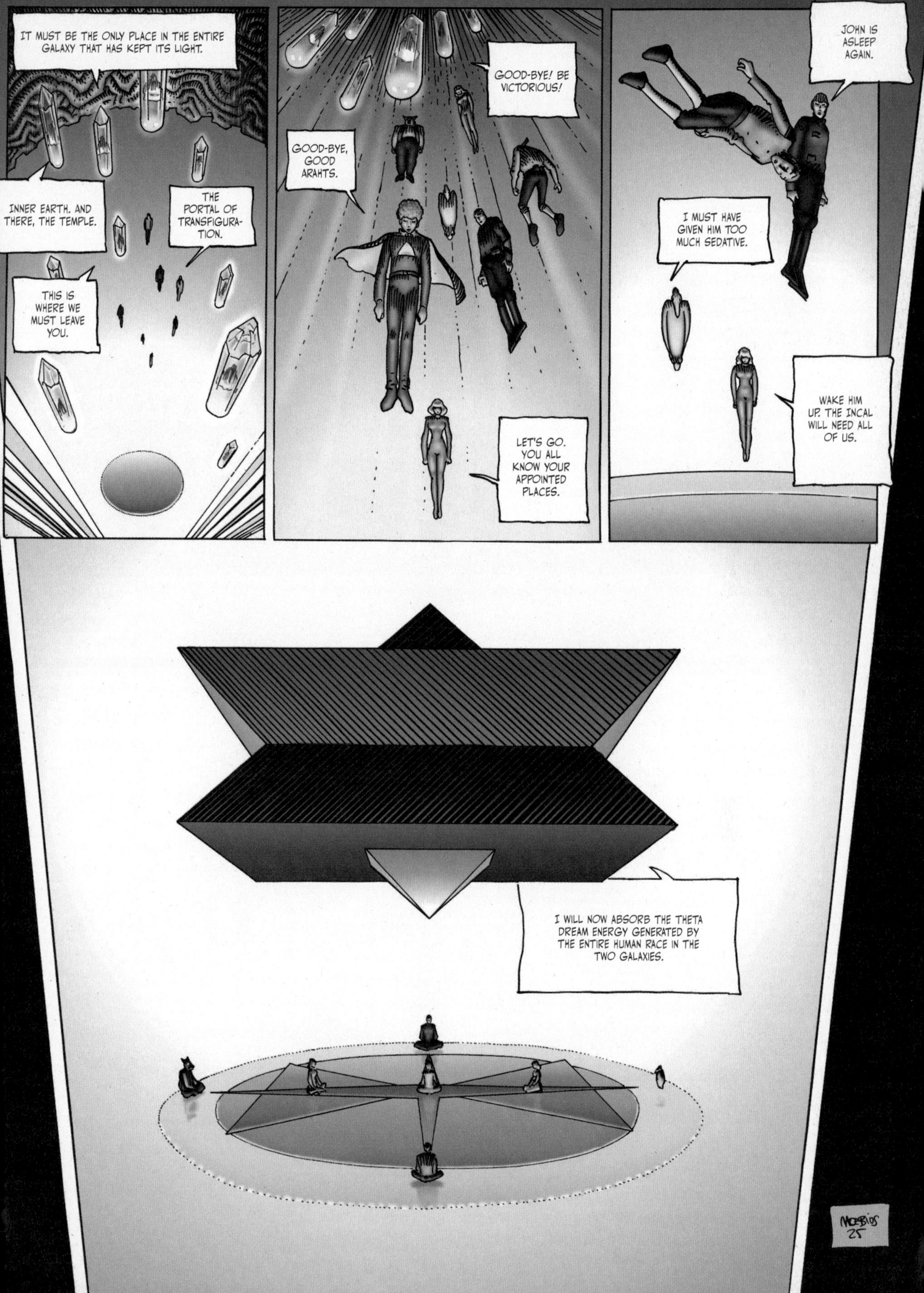

IT MUST BE THE ONLY PLACE IN THE ENTIRE GALAXY THAT HAS KEPT ITS LIGHT.
INNER EARTH. AND THERE, THE TEMPLE.
THE PORTAL OF TRANSFIGURATION.
THIS IS WHERE WE MUST LEAVE YOU.
GOOD-BYE! BE VICTORIOUS!
GOOD-BYE, GOOD ARAHTS.
LET'S GO. YOU ALL KNOW YOUR APPOINTED PLACES.
JOHN IS ASLEEP AGAIN.
I MUST HAVE GIVEN HIM TOO MUCH SEDATIVE.
WAKE HIM UP. THE INCAL WILL NEED ALL OF US.
I WILL NOW ABSORB THE THETA DREAM ENERGY GENERATED BY THE ENTIRE HUMAN RACE IN THE TWO GALAXIES.
MOEBIUS 25

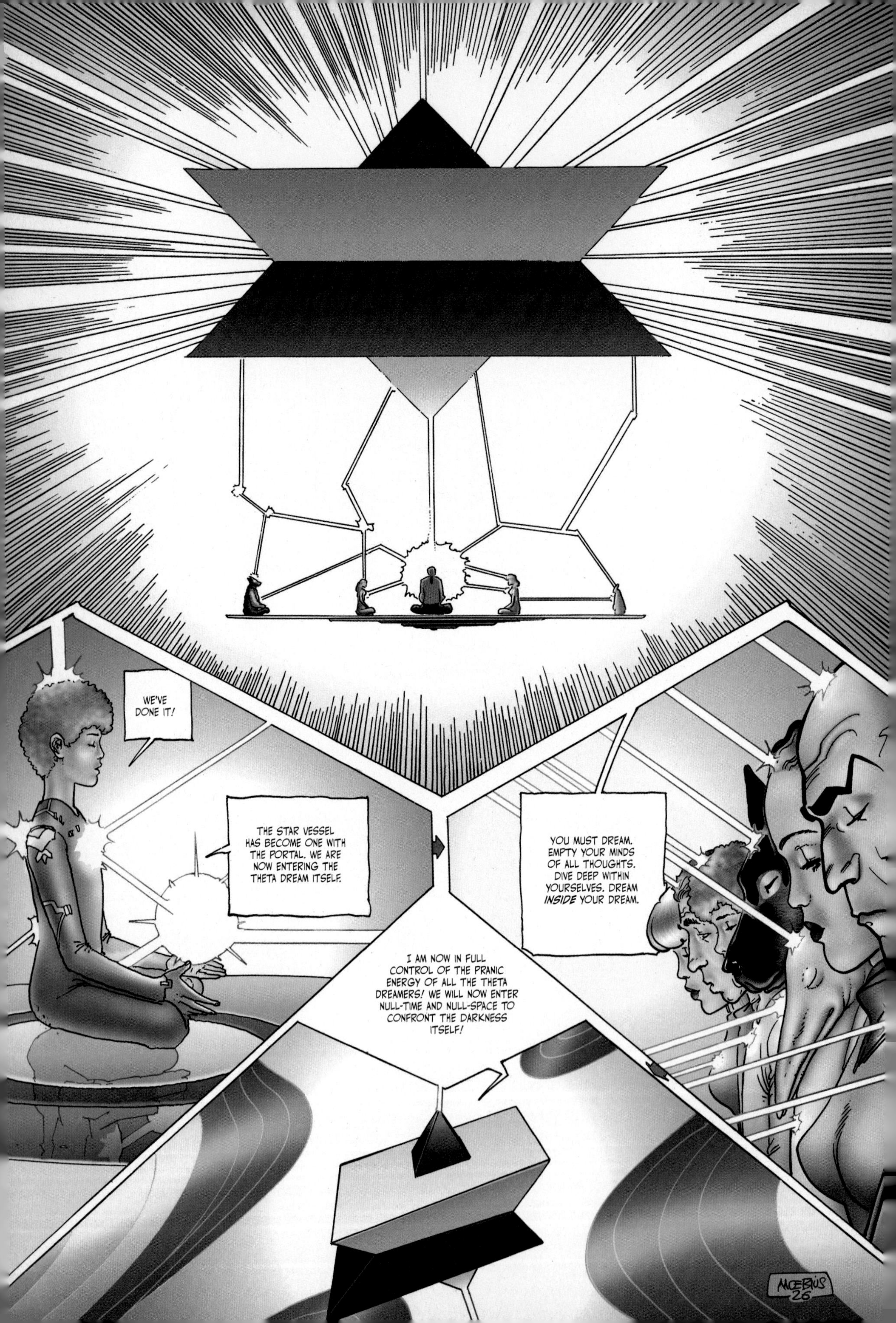
WE'VE DONE IT!
THE STAR VESSEL HAS BECOME ONE WITH THE PORTAL. WE ARE NOW ENTERING THE THETA DREAM ITSELF.
YOU MUST DREAM. EMPTY YOUR MINDS OF ALL THOUGHTS. DIVE DEEP WITHIN YOURSELVES. DREAM *INSIDE* YOUR DREAM.
I AM NOW IN FULL CONTROL OF THE PRANIC ENERGY OF ALL THE THETA DREAMERS! WE WILL NOW ENTER NULL-TIME AND NULL-SPACE TO CONFRONT THE DARKNESS ITSELF!
MOEBIUS '25

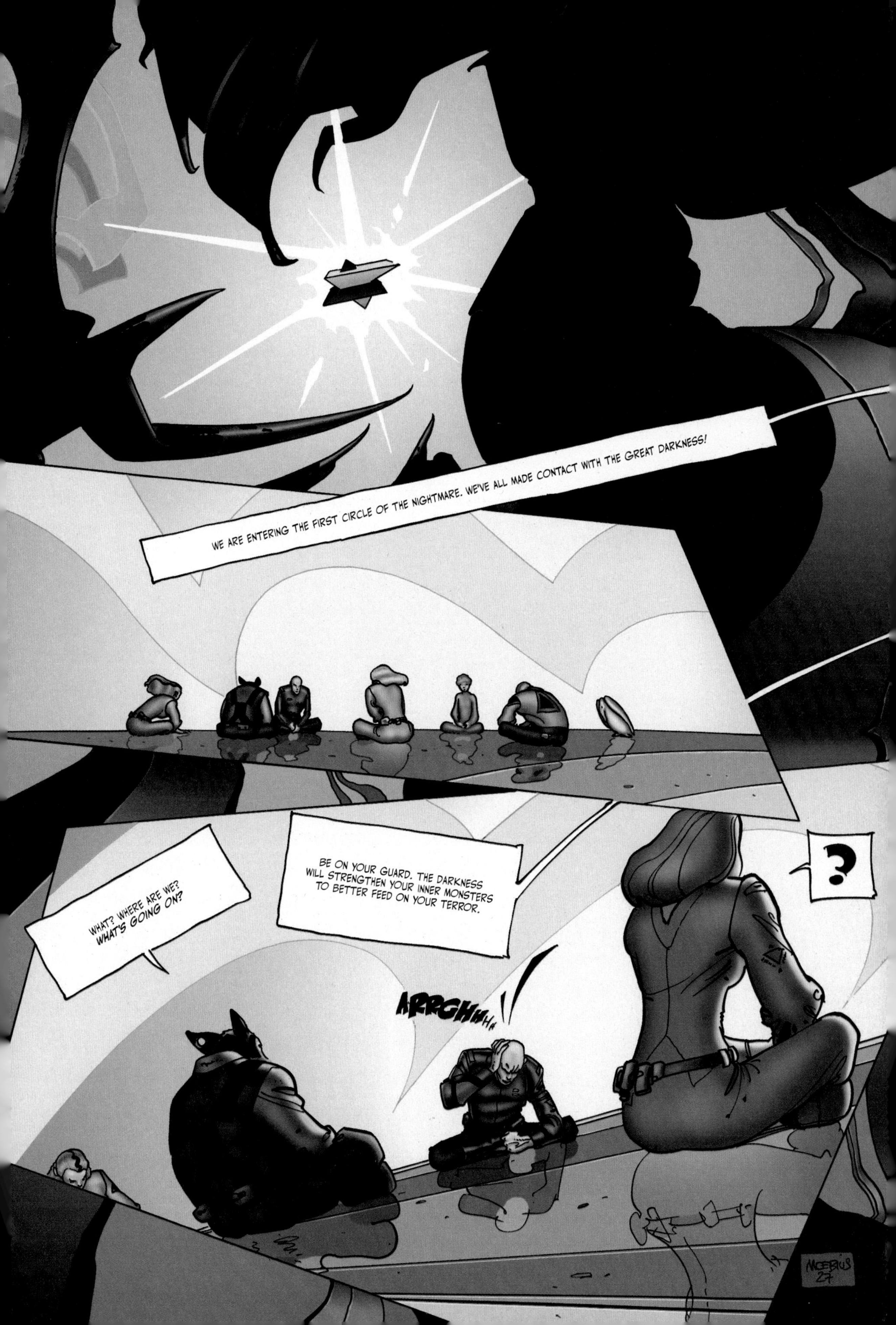
WE ARE ENTERING THE FIRST CIRCLE OF THE NIGHTMARE. WE'VE ALL MADE CONTACT WITH THE GREAT DARKNESS!
WHAT? WHERE ARE WE? WHAT'S GOING ON?
BE ON YOUR GUARD. THE DARKNESS WILL STRENGTHEN YOUR INNER MONSTERS TO BETTER FEED ON YOUR TERROR.
?
ARRGHHHH!!
MOEBIUS

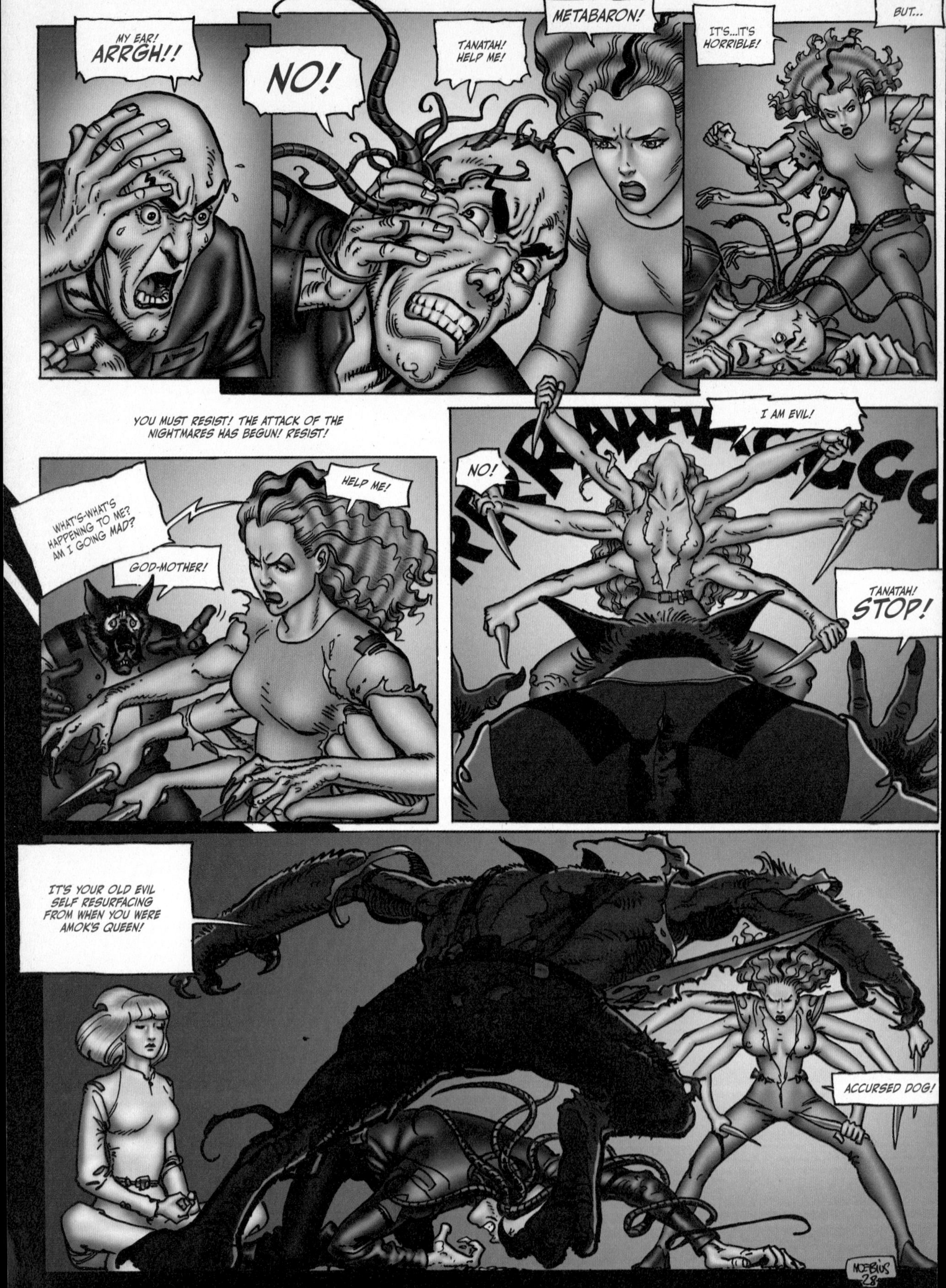
MY EAR! ARRGH!!
NO!
TANATAH! HELP ME!
METABARON!
IT'S...IT'S HORRIBLE!
BUT...
YOU MUST RESIST! THE ATTACK OF THE NIGHTMARES HAS BEGUN! RESIST!
HELP ME!
WHAT'S-WHAT'S HAPPENING TO ME? AM I GOING MAD?
GOD-MOTHER!
I AM EVIL!
NO!
RRRAAARGGGG
TANATAH! STOP!
IT'S YOUR OLD EVIL SELF RESURFACING FROM WHEN YOU WERE AMOK'S QUEEN!
ACCURSED DOG!
MOEBIUS
28

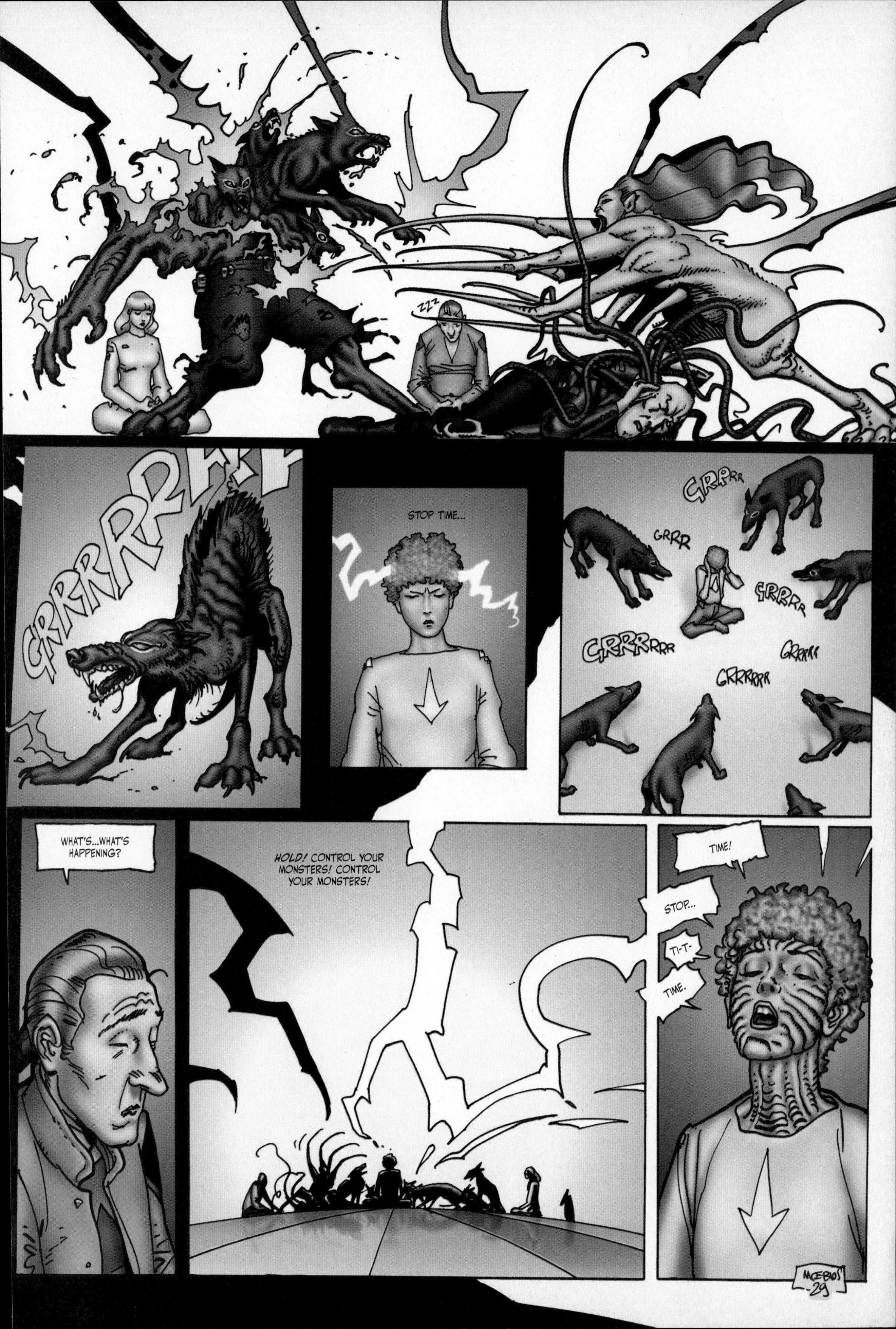
ZZZ
GRRRRRRAA
STOP TIME...
GRRrrr
GRRR
GRRRRR
GRRRRrrr
GRRRRR
GRRRRRRR
WHAT'S...WHAT'S HAPPENING?
HOLD! CONTROL YOUR MONSTERS! CONTROL YOUR MONSTERS!
TIME!
STOP...
TI-T-
TIME.

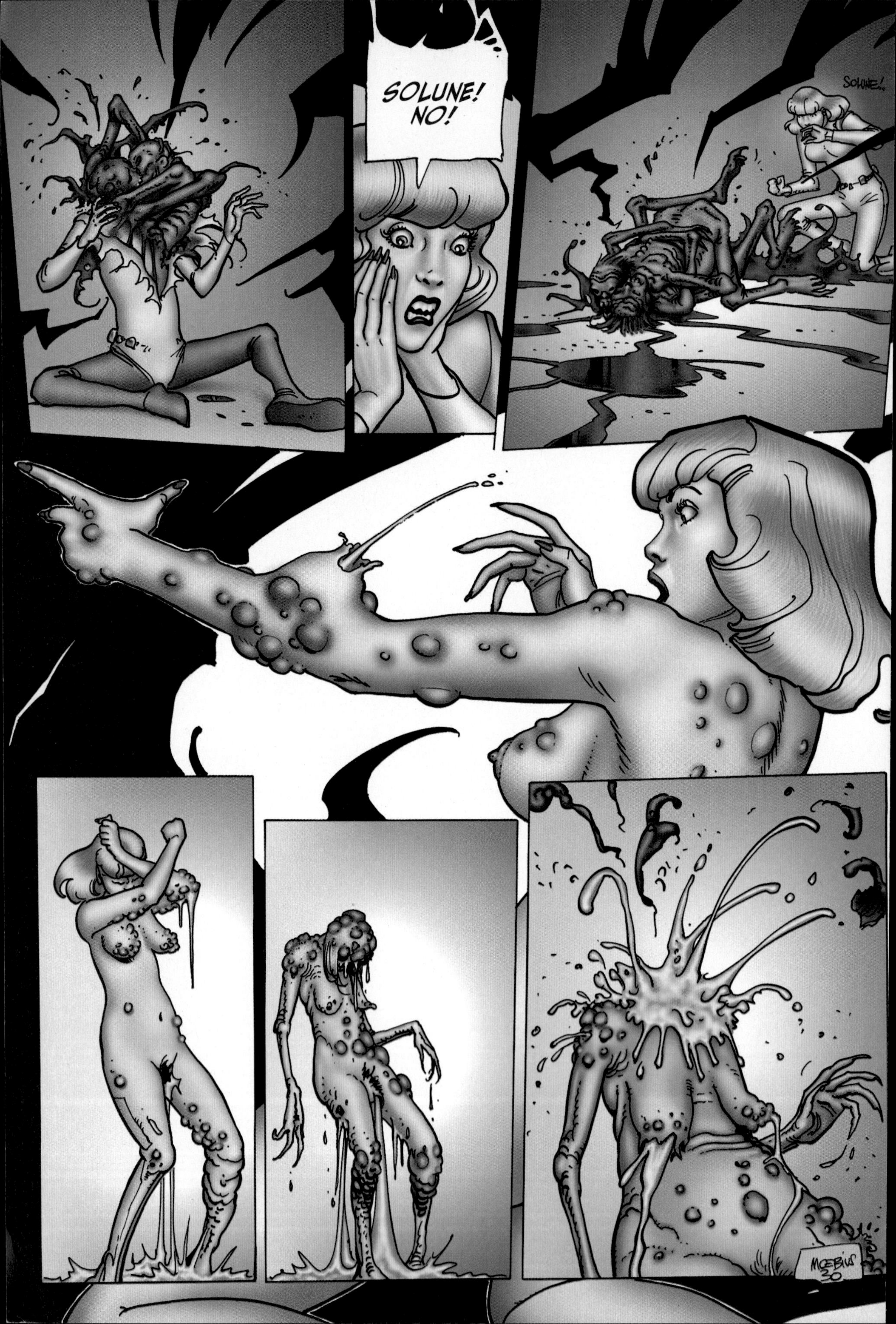
SOLUNE! NO!
SOLUNE!...
MŒBIUS
30

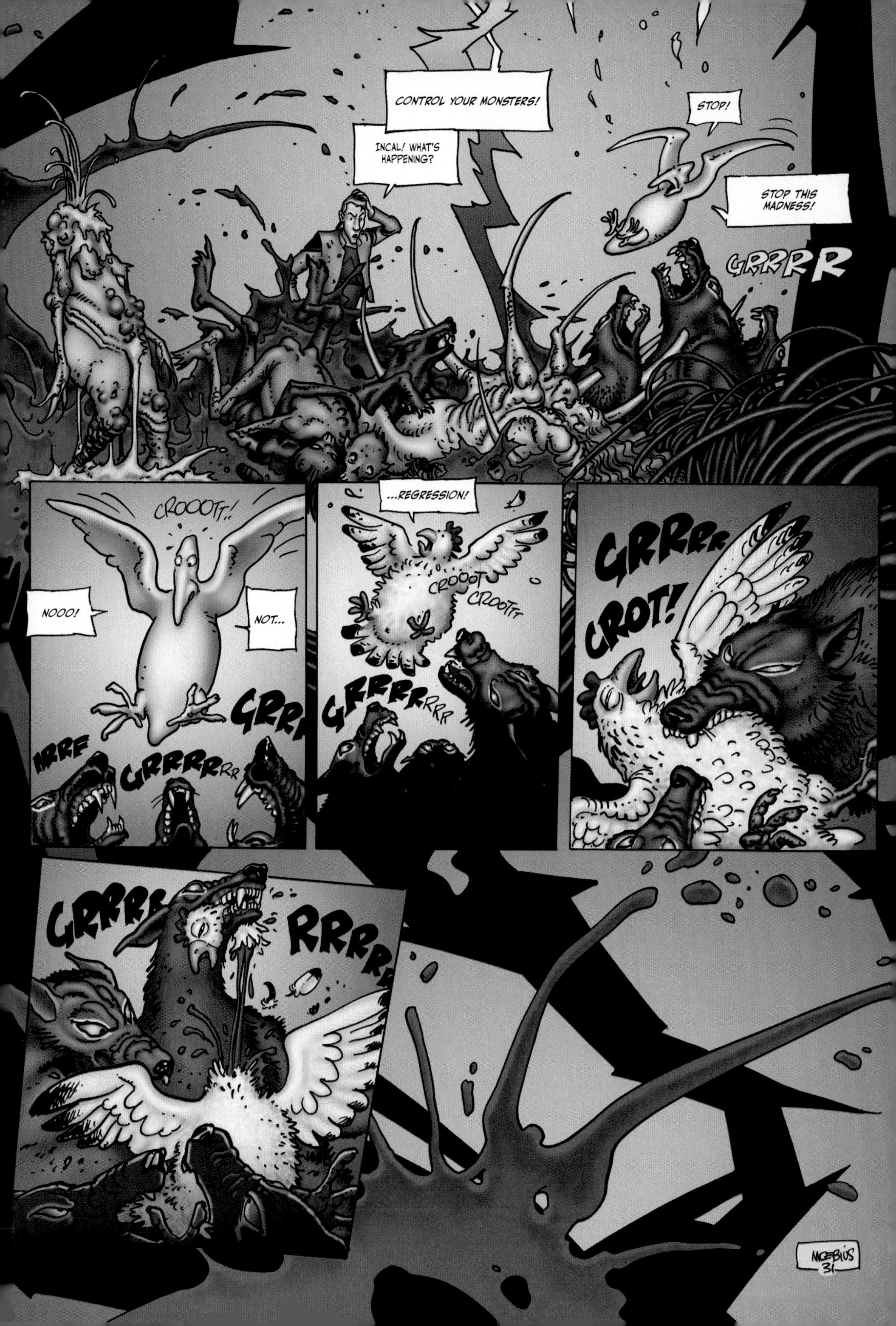
CONTROL YOUR MONSTERS!
INCAL! WHAT'S HAPPENING?
STOP!
STOP THIS MADNESS!
GRRRR
CROOOTT..!
NOOO!
NOT...
GRRR
HRRF
GRRRRRR
...REGRESSION!
CROOOT
CROOTTT
GRRRRRRR
GRRRR
CROT!
GRRRR
RRRRR
MŒBIUS 31

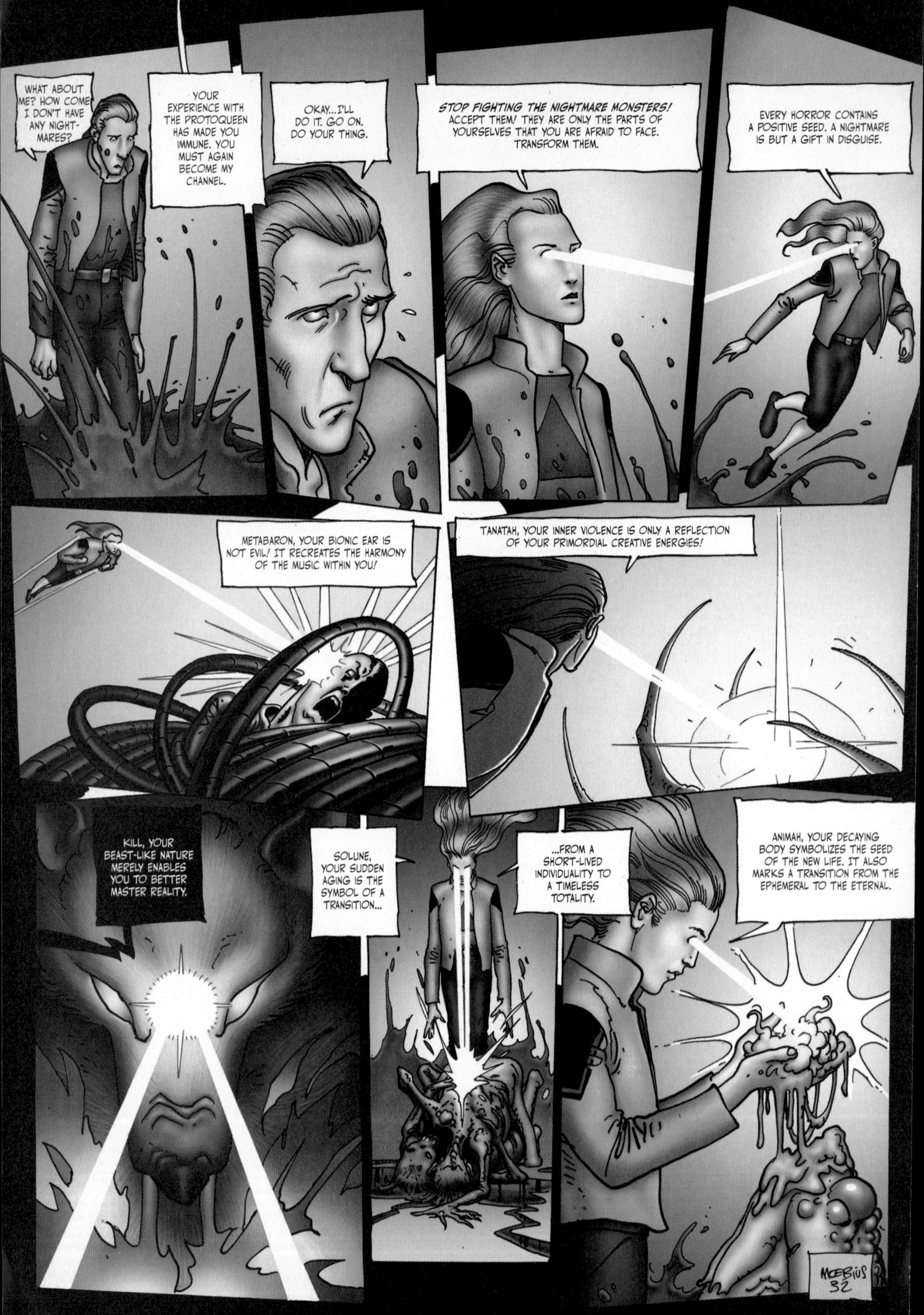
WHAT ABOUT ME? HOW COME I DON'T HAVE ANY NIGHT-MARES?
YOUR EXPERIENCE WITH THE PROTOQUEEN HAS MADE YOU IMMUNE. YOU MUST AGAIN BECOME MY CHANNEL.
OKAY...I'LL DO IT. GO ON. DO YOUR THING.
STOP FIGHTING THE NIGHTMARE MONSTERS! ACCEPT THEM! THEY ARE ONLY THE PARTS OF YOURSELVES THAT YOU ARE AFRAID TO FACE. TRANSFORM THEM.
EVERY HORROR CONTAINS A POSITIVE SEED. A NIGHTMARE IS BUT A GIFT IN DISGUISE.
METABARON, YOUR BIONIC EAR IS NOT EVIL! IT RECREATES THE HARMONY OF THE MUSIC WITHIN YOU!
TANATAH, YOUR INNER VIOLENCE IS ONLY A REFLECTION OF YOUR PRIMORDIAL CREATIVE ENERGIES!
KILL, YOUR BEAST-LIKE NATURE MERELY ENABLES YOU TO BETTER MASTER REALITY.
SOLUNE, YOUR SUDDEN AGING IS THE SYMBOL OF A TRANSITION...
...FROM A SHORT-LIVED INDIVIDUALITY TO A TIMELESS TOTALITY.
ANIMAH, YOUR DECAYING BODY SYMBOLIZES THE SEED OF THE NEW LIFE. IT ALSO MARKS A TRANSITION FROM THE EPHEMERAL TO THE ETERNAL.
MOEBIUS 32

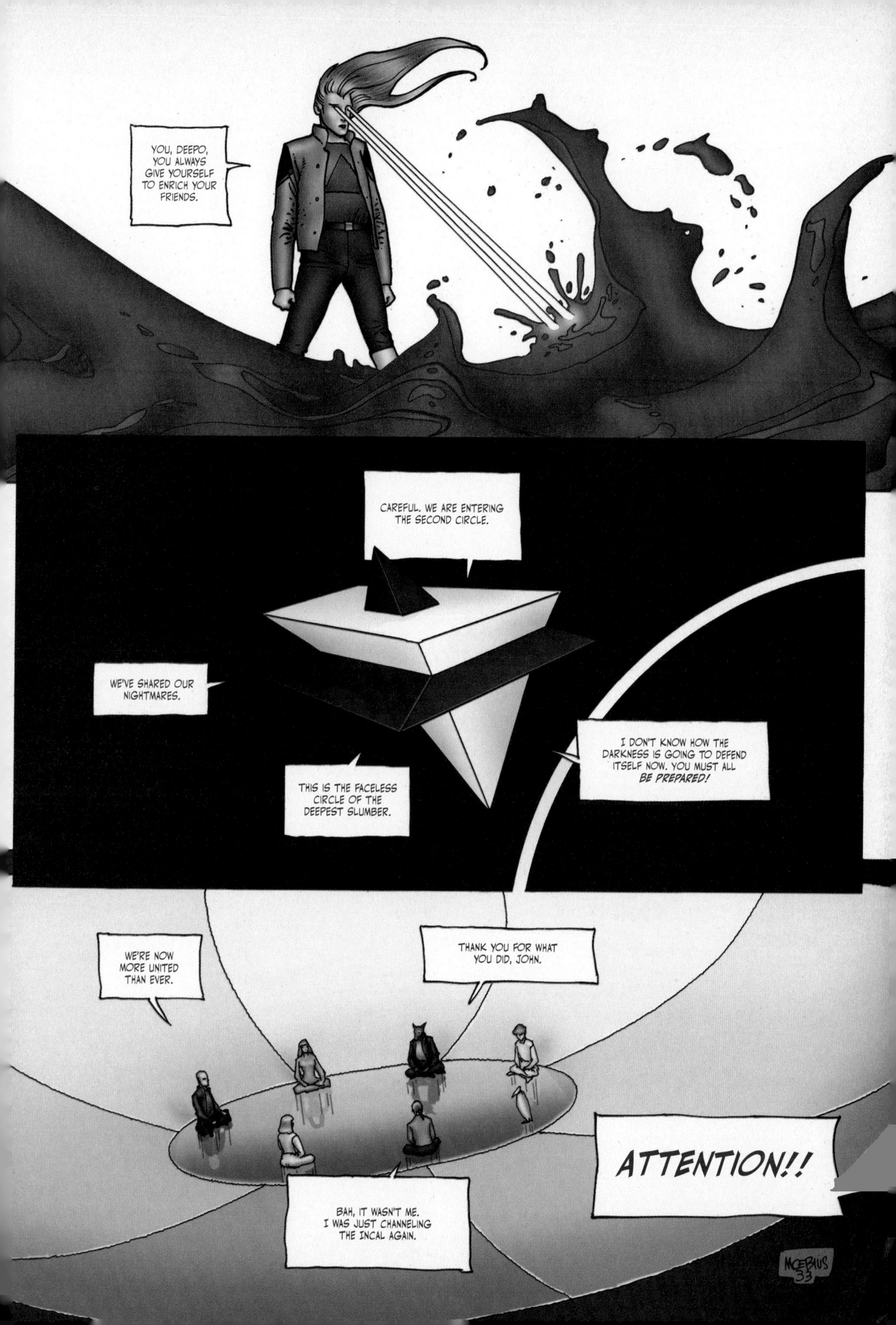
YOU, DEEPO, YOU ALWAYS GIVE YOURSELF TO ENRICH YOUR FRIENDS.
CAREFUL. WE ARE ENTERING THE SECOND CIRCLE.
WE'VE SHARED OUR NIGHTMARES.
THIS IS THE FACELESS CIRCLE OF THE DEEPEST SLUMBER.
I DON'T KNOW HOW THE DARKNESS IS GOING TO DEFEND ITSELF NOW. YOU MUST ALL *BE PREPARED!*
WE'RE NOW MORE UNITED THAN EVER.
THANK YOU FOR WHAT YOU DID, JOHN.
BAH, IT WASN'T ME. I WAS JUST CHANNELING THE INCAL AGAIN.
ATTENTION!!
MŒBIUS 33

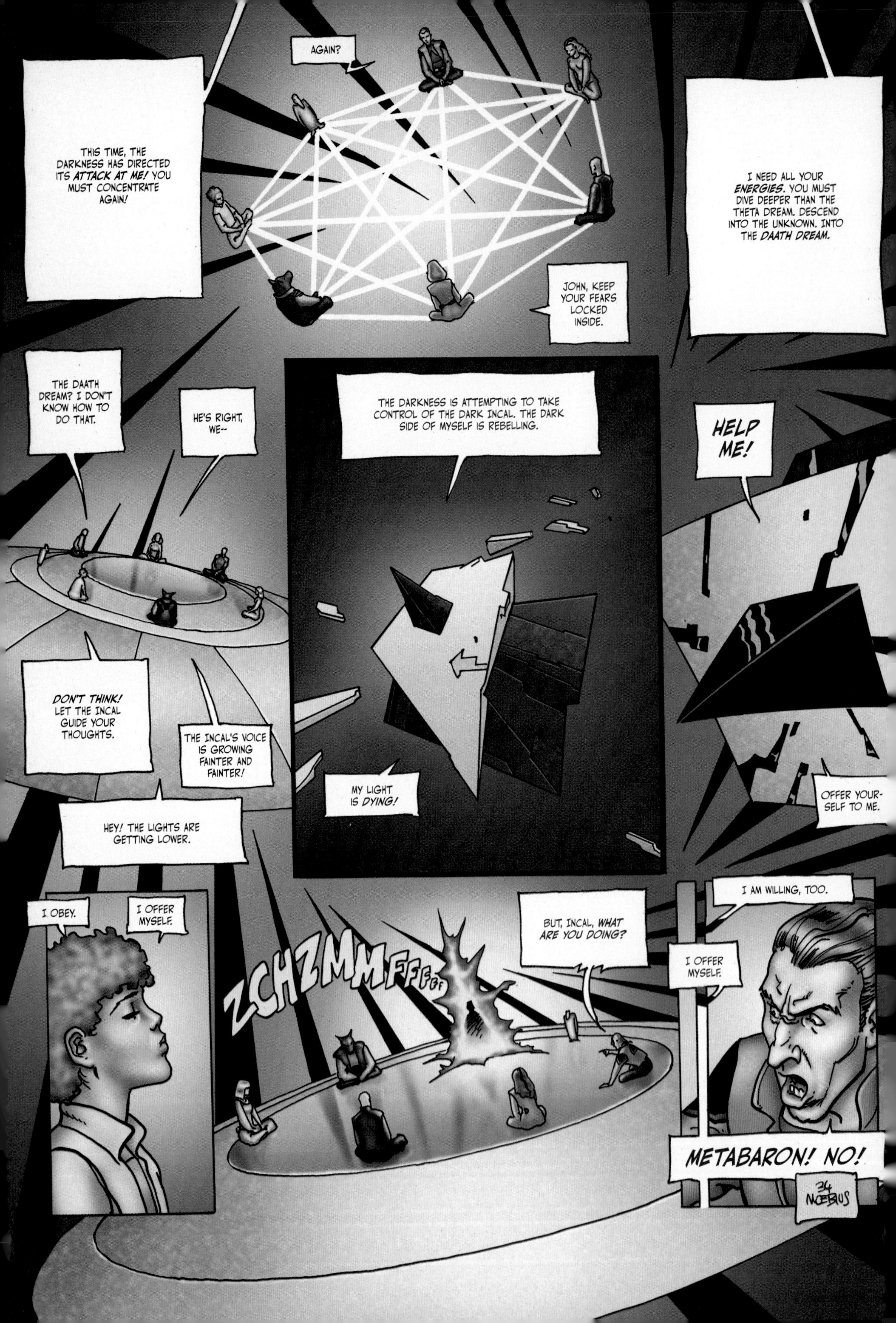

THIS TIME, THE DARKNESS HAS DIRECTED ITS *ATTACK AT ME!* YOU MUST CONCENTRATE AGAIN!
AGAIN?
I NEED ALL YOUR *ENERGIES*. YOU MUST DIVE DEEPER THAN THE THETA DREAM. DESCEND INTO THE UNKNOWN. INTO THE *DAATH DREAM*.
JOHN, KEEP YOUR FEARS LOCKED INSIDE.
THE DAATH DREAM? I DON'T KNOW HOW TO DO THAT.
HE'S RIGHT, WE--
DON'T THINK! LET THE INCAL GUIDE YOUR THOUGHTS.
THE INCAL'S VOICE IS GROWING FAINTER AND FAINTER!
HEY! THE LIGHTS ARE GETTING LOWER.
THE DARKNESS IS ATTEMPTING TO TAKE CONTROL OF THE DARK INCAL. THE DARK SIDE OF MYSELF IS REBELLING.
MY LIGHT IS *DYING!*
HELP ME!
OFFER YOURSELF TO ME.
I OBEY.
I OFFER MYSELF.
ZCHZMMFFFFF
BUT, INCAL, *WHAT ARE YOU DOING?*
I AM WILLING, TOO.
I OFFER MYSELF.
METABARON! NO!
34
MOEBIUS

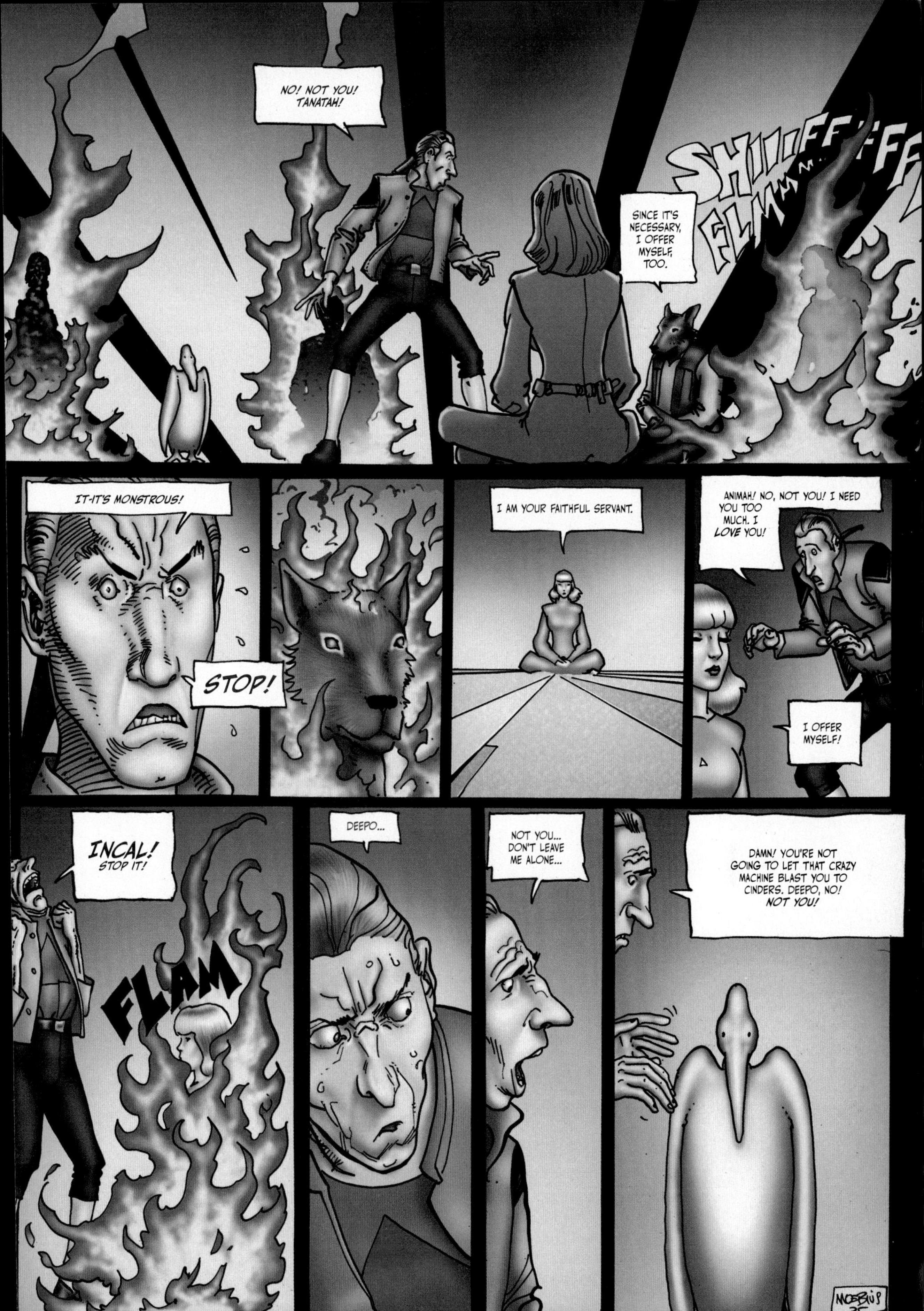

NO! NOT YOU! TANATAH!
SINCE IT'S NECESSARY, I OFFER MYSELF, TOO.
SHIIIFFFFFFF
FLMMMM
IT-IT'S MONSTROUS!
STOP!
I AM YOUR FAITHFUL SERVANT.
ANIMAH! NO, NOT YOU! I NEED YOU TOO MUCH. I LOVE YOU!
I OFFER MYSELF!
INCAL! STOP IT!
FLAM
DEEPO...
NOT YOU... DON'T LEAVE ME ALONE...
DAMN! YOU'RE NOT GOING TO LET THAT CRAZY MACHINE BLAST YOU TO CINDERS. DEEPO, NO! NOT YOU!
MOEBIUS

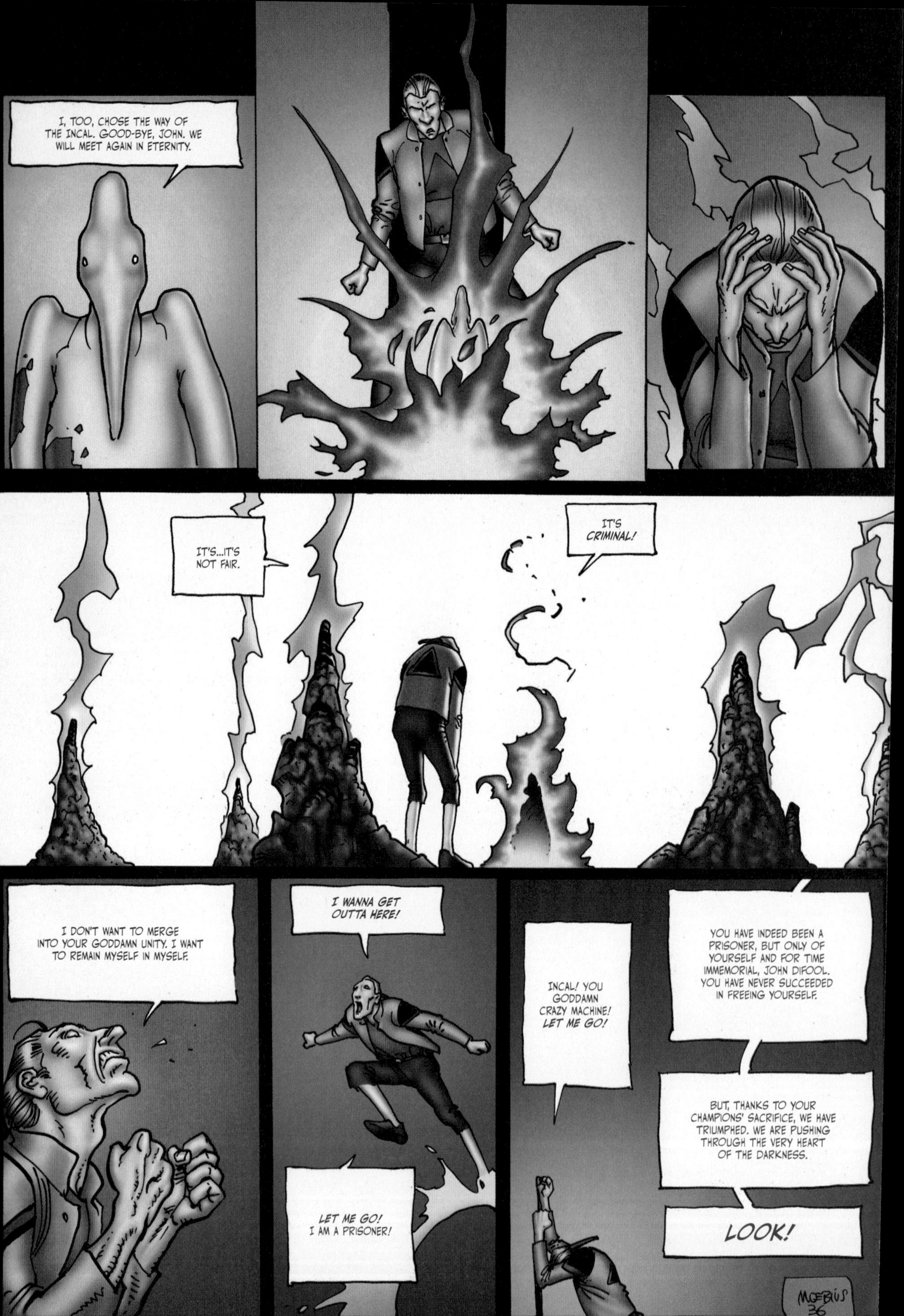
I, TOO, CHOSE THE WAY OF THE INCAL. GOOD-BYE, JOHN. WE WILL MEET AGAIN IN ETERNITY.
IT'S...IT'S NOT FAIR.
IT'S CRIMINAL!
I DON'T WANT TO MERGE INTO YOUR GODDAMN UNITY. I WANT TO REMAIN MYSELF IN MYSELF.
I WANNA GET OUTTA HERE!
LET ME GO! I AM A PRISONER!
INCAL! YOU GODDAMN CRAZY MACHINE! LET ME GO!
YOU HAVE INDEED BEEN A PRISONER, BUT ONLY OF YOURSELF AND FOR TIME IMMEMORIAL, JOHN DIFOOL. YOU HAVE NEVER SUCCEEDED IN FREEING YOURSELF.
BUT, THANKS TO YOUR CHAMPIONS' SACRIFICE, WE HAVE TRIUMPHED. WE ARE PUSHING THROUGH THE VERY HEART OF THE DARKNESS.
LOOK!
MOEBIUS
36

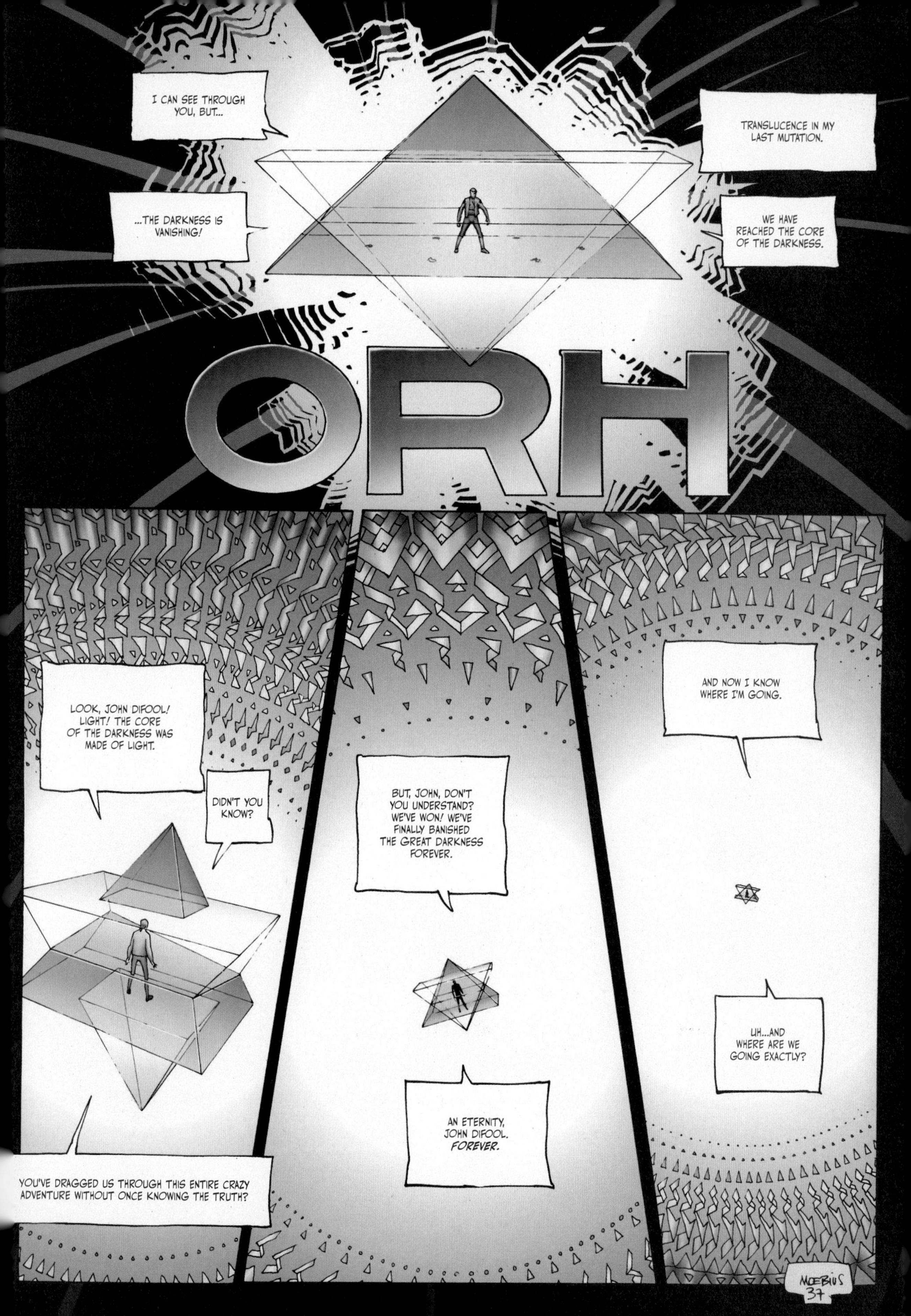
I CAN SEE THROUGH YOU, BUT...
TRANSLUCENCE IN MY LAST MUTATION.
...THE DARKNESS IS VANISHING!
WE HAVE REACHED THE CORE OF THE DARKNESS.
ORH
LOOK, JOHN DIFOOL! LIGHT! THE CORE OF THE DARKNESS WAS MADE OF LIGHT.
DIDN'T YOU KNOW?
YOU'VE DRAGGED US THROUGH THIS ENTIRE CRAZY ADVENTURE WITHOUT ONCE KNOWING THE TRUTH?
BUT, JOHN, DON'T YOU UNDERSTAND? WE'VE WON! WE'VE FINALLY BANISHED THE GREAT DARKNESS FOREVER.
AN ETERNITY, JOHN DIFOOL. *FOREVER.*
AND NOW I KNOW WHERE I'M GOING.
UH...AND WHERE ARE WE GOING EXACTLY?
MOEBIUS

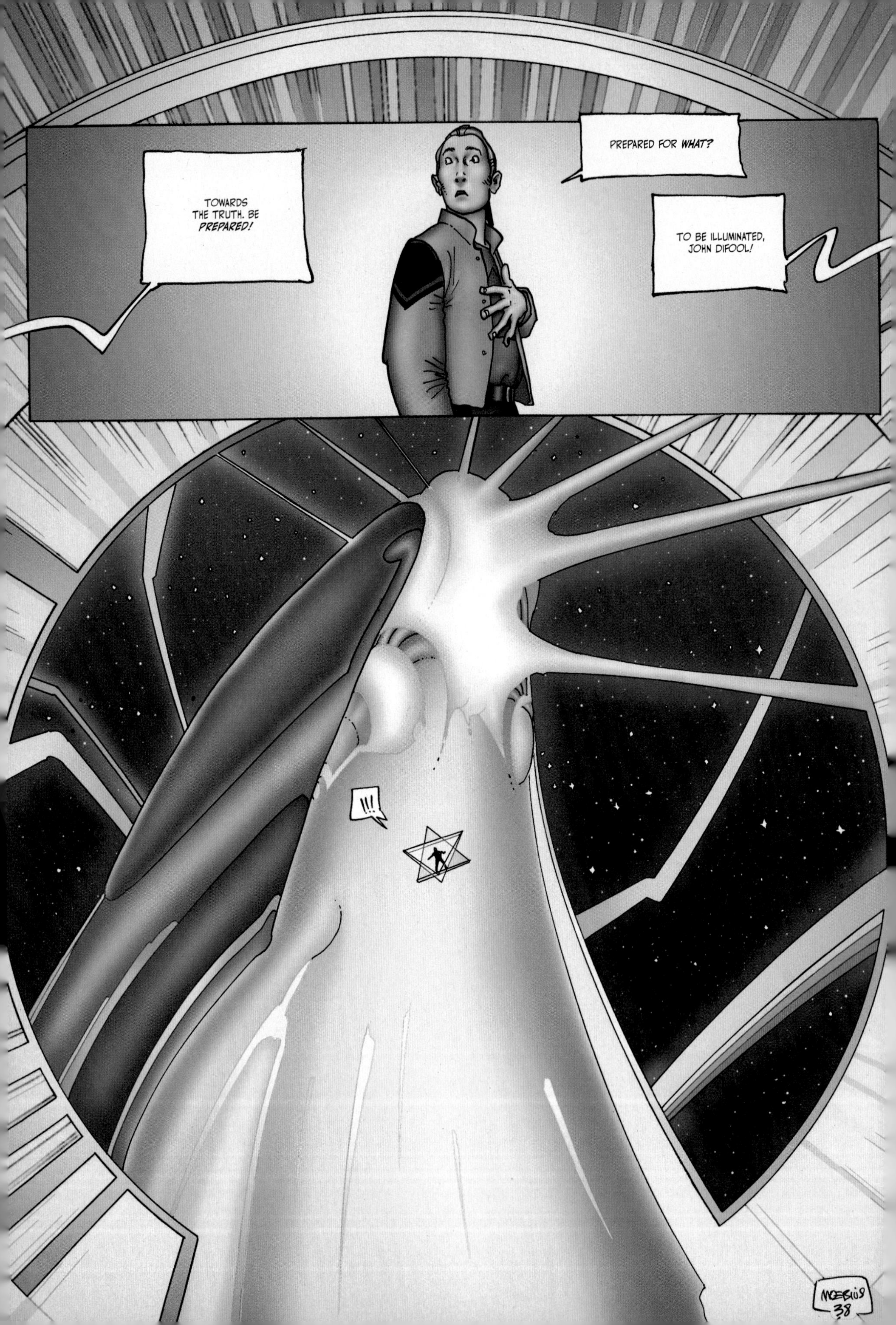
TOWARDS THE TRUTH. BE PREPARED!
PREPARED FOR WHAT?
TO BE ILLUMINATED, JOHN DIFOOL!
!!!
MOEBIUS 38

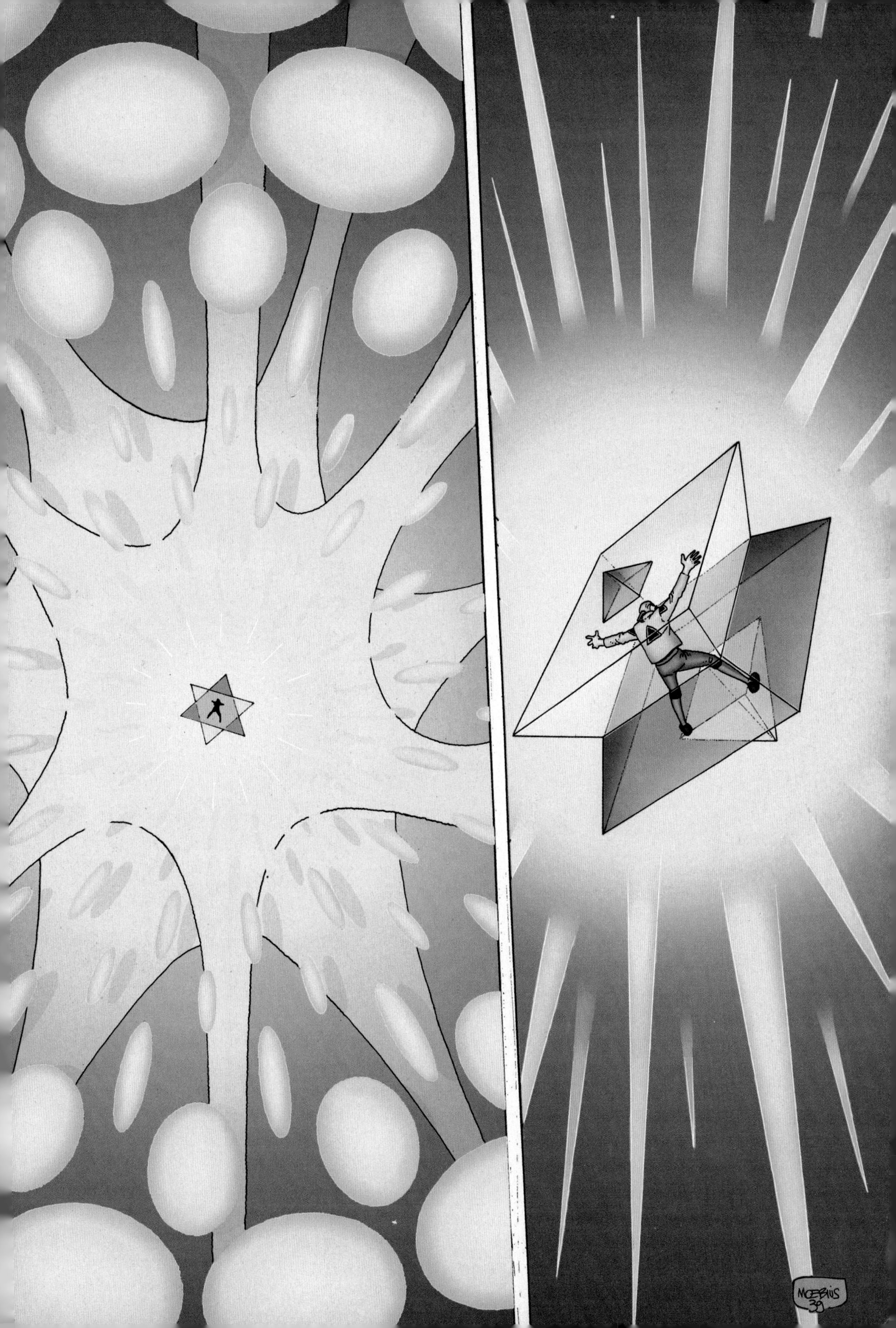
MOEBIUS
39

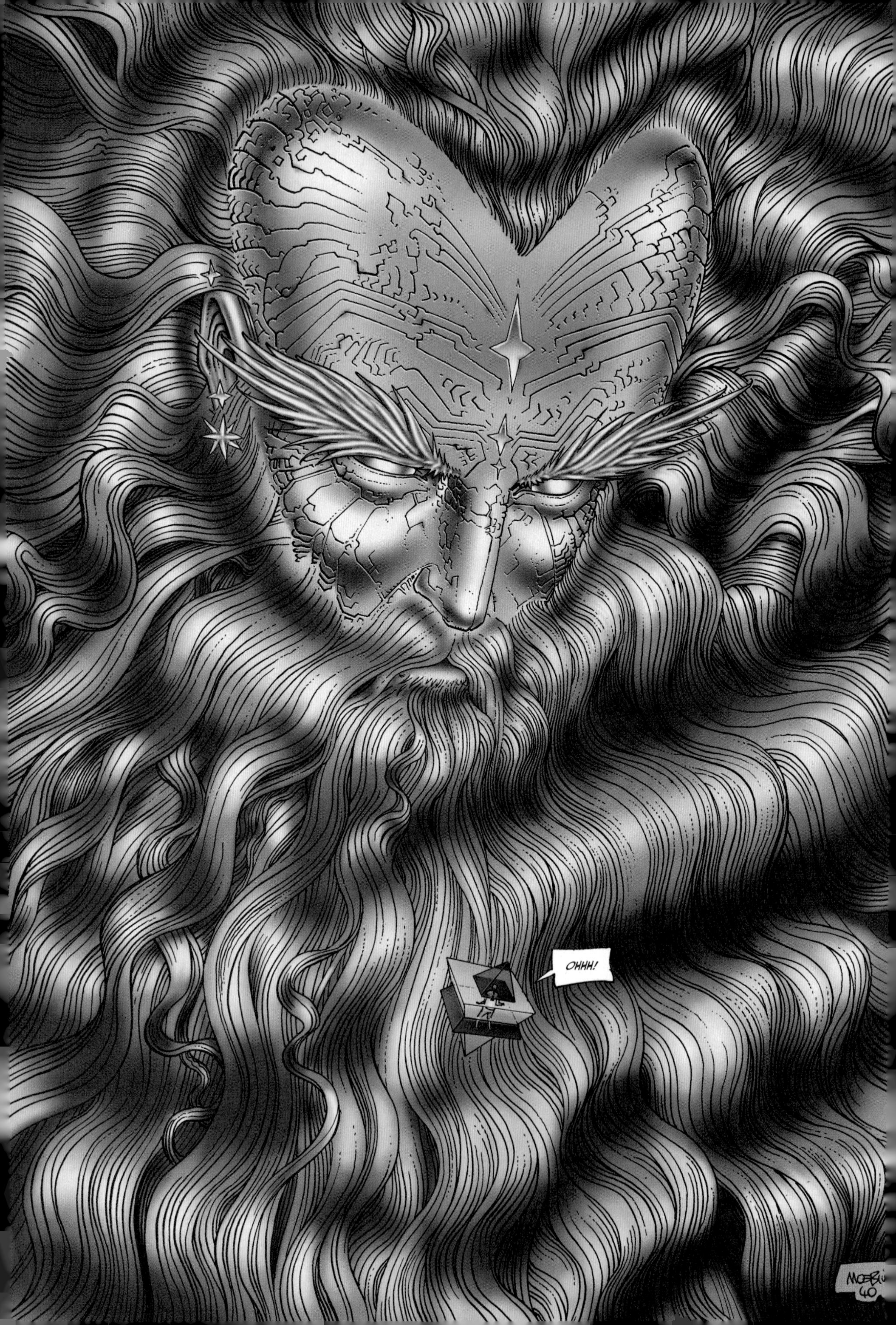
OHHH!

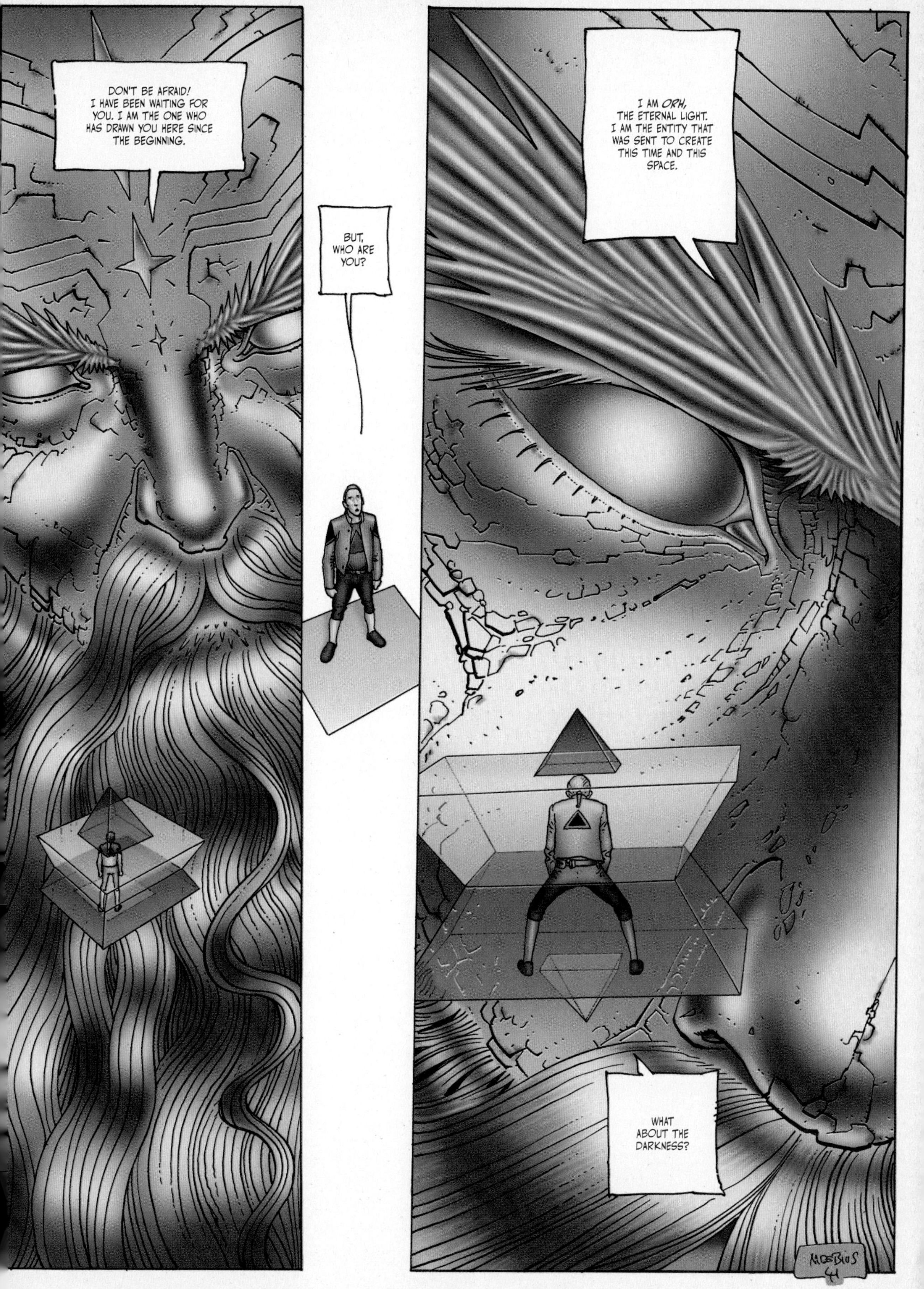
DON'T BE AFRAID! I HAVE BEEN WAITING FOR YOU. I AM THE ONE WHO HAS DRAWN YOU HERE SINCE THE BEGINNING.
BUT, WHO ARE YOU?
I AM *ORH*, THE ETERNAL LIGHT. I AM THE ENTITY THAT WAS SENT TO CREATE THIS TIME AND THIS SPACE.
WHAT ABOUT THE DARKNESS?

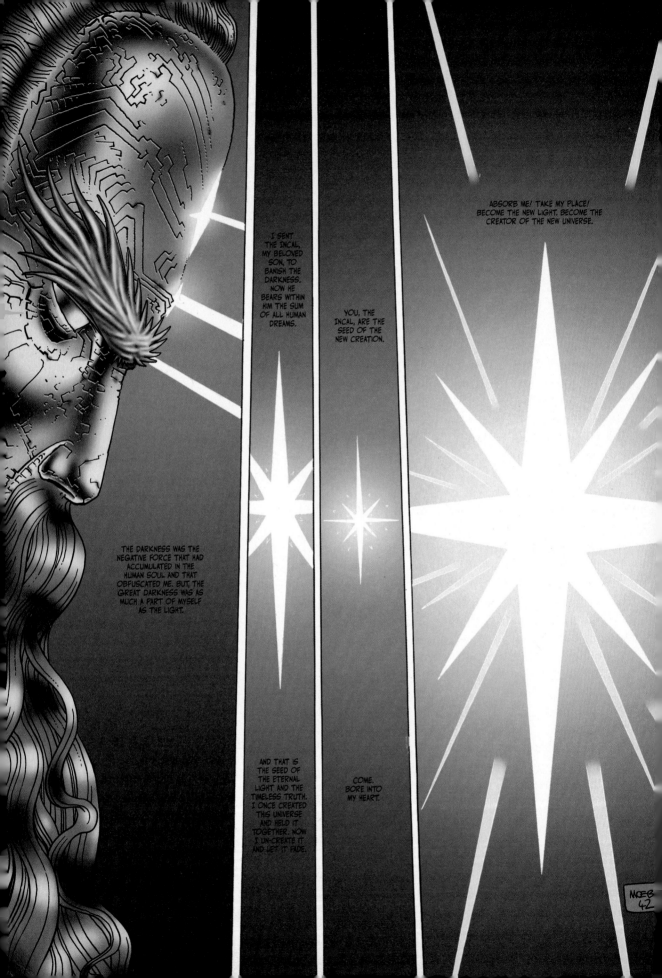

ABSORB ME! TAKE MY PLACE! BECOME THE NEW LIGHT. BECOME THE CREATOR OF THE NEW UNIVERSE.

I SENT THE INCAL, MY BELOVED SON, TO BANISH THE DARKNESS. NOW HE BEARS WITHIN HIM THE SUM OF ALL HUMAN DREAMS.

YOU, THE INCAL, ARE THE SEED OF THE NEW CREATION.

THE DARKNESS WAS THE NEGATIVE FORCE THAT HAD ACCUMULATED IN THE HUMAN SOUL AND THAT OBFUSCATED ME. BUT, THE GREAT DARKNESS WAS AS MUCH A PART OF MYSELF AS THE LIGHT.

AND THAT IS THE SEED OF THE ETERNAL LIGHT AND THE TIMELESS TRUTH. I ONCE CREATED THIS UNIVERSE AND HELD IT TOGETHER. NOW I UN-CREATE IT AND LET IT FADE.

COME. BORE INTO MY HEART.

MŒB
42

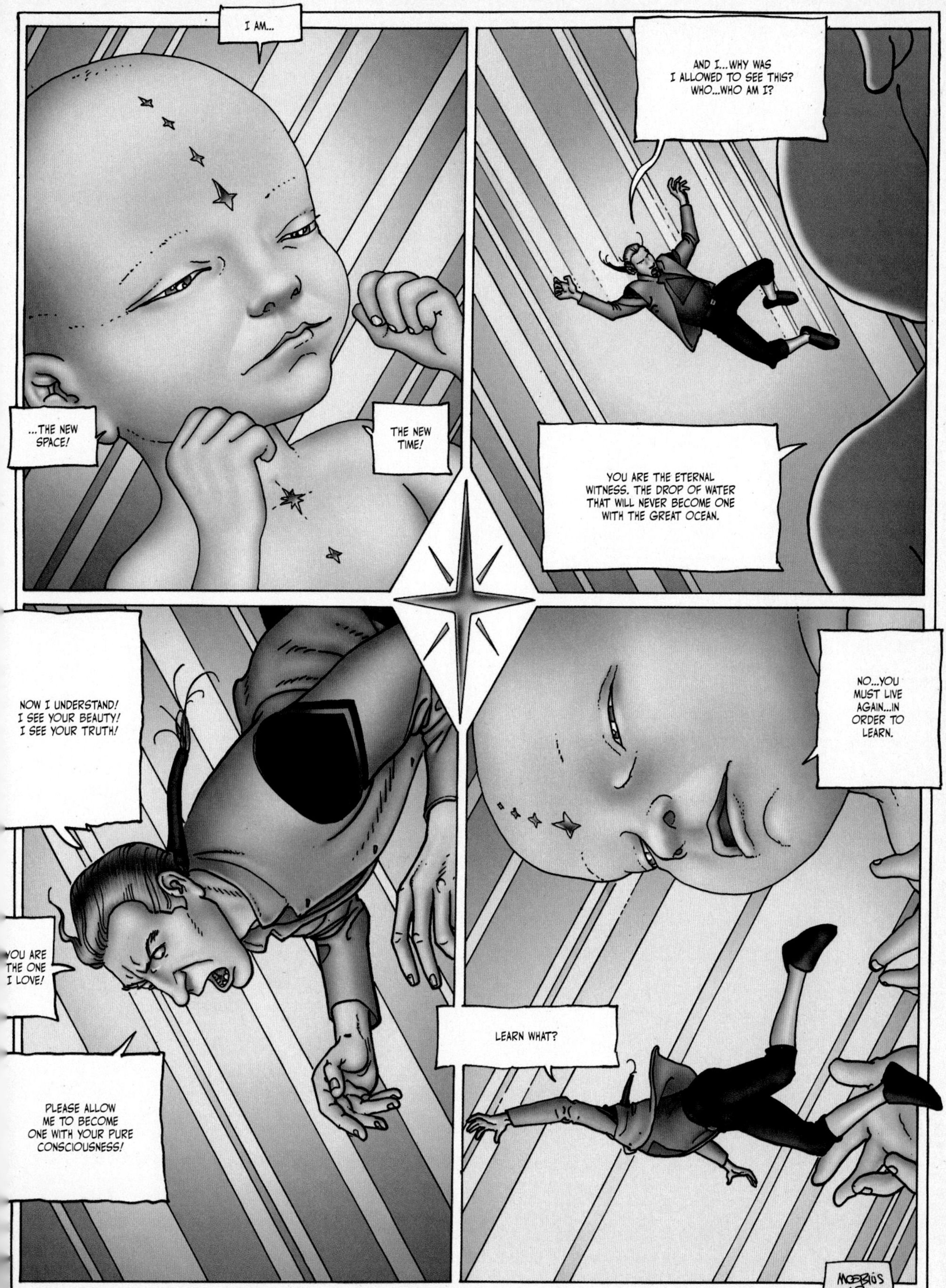
I AM...
...THE NEW SPACE!
THE NEW TIME!
AND I...WHY WAS I ALLOWED TO SEE THIS? WHO...WHO AM I?
YOU ARE THE ETERNAL WITNESS. THE DROP OF WATER THAT WILL NEVER BECOME ONE WITH THE GREAT OCEAN.
NOW I UNDERSTAND! I SEE YOUR BEAUTY! I SEE YOUR TRUTH!
YOU ARE THE ONE I LOVE!
PLEASE ALLOW ME TO BECOME ONE WITH YOUR PURE CONSCIOUSNESS!
NO...YOU MUST LIVE AGAIN...IN ORDER TO LEARN.
LEARN WHAT?
MOEBIUS 43

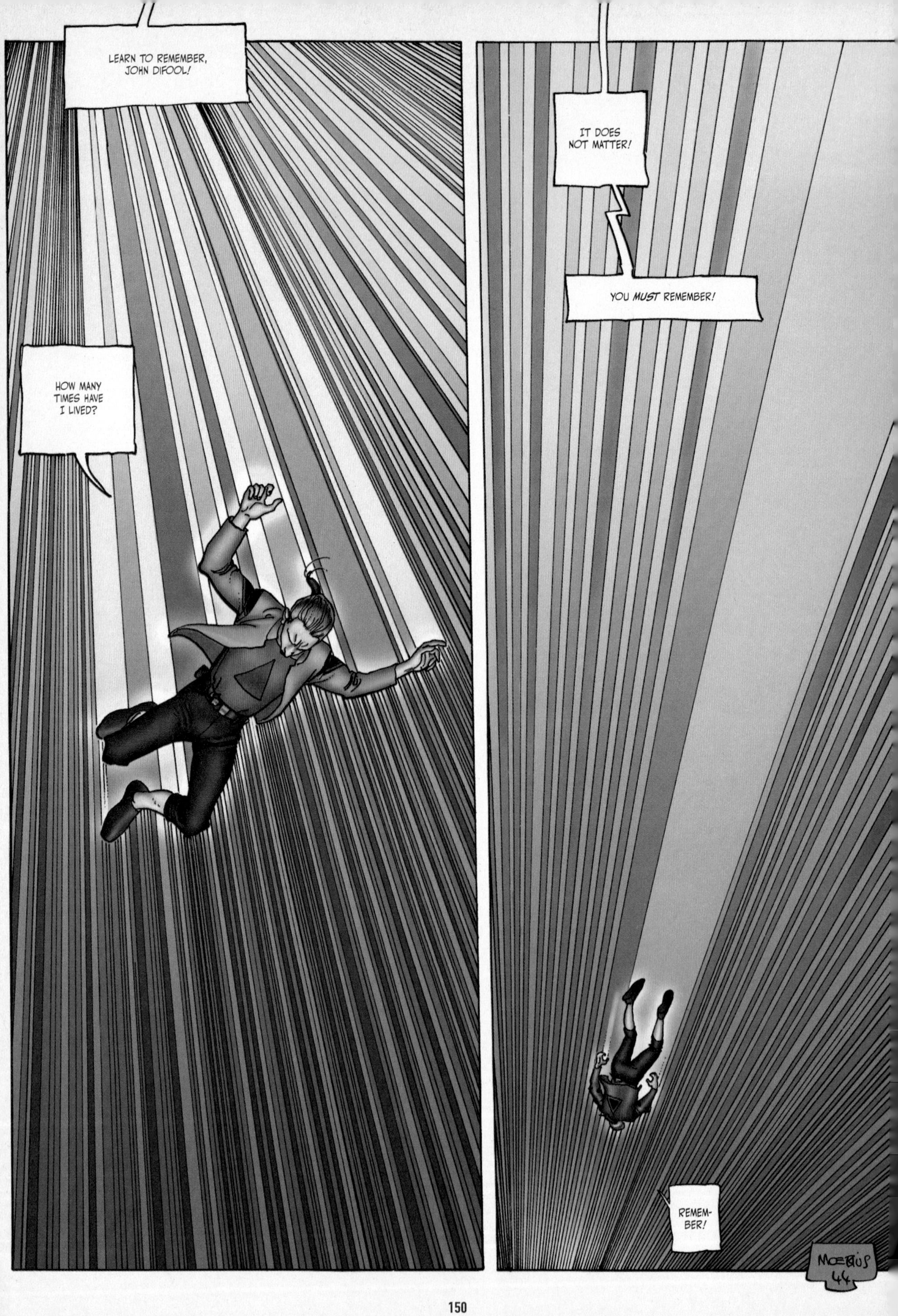
LEARN TO REMEMBER, JOHN DIFOOL!
HOW MANY TIMES HAVE I LIVED?
IT DOES NOT MATTER!
YOU MUST REMEMBER!
REMEM-BER!
MOEBIUS 44

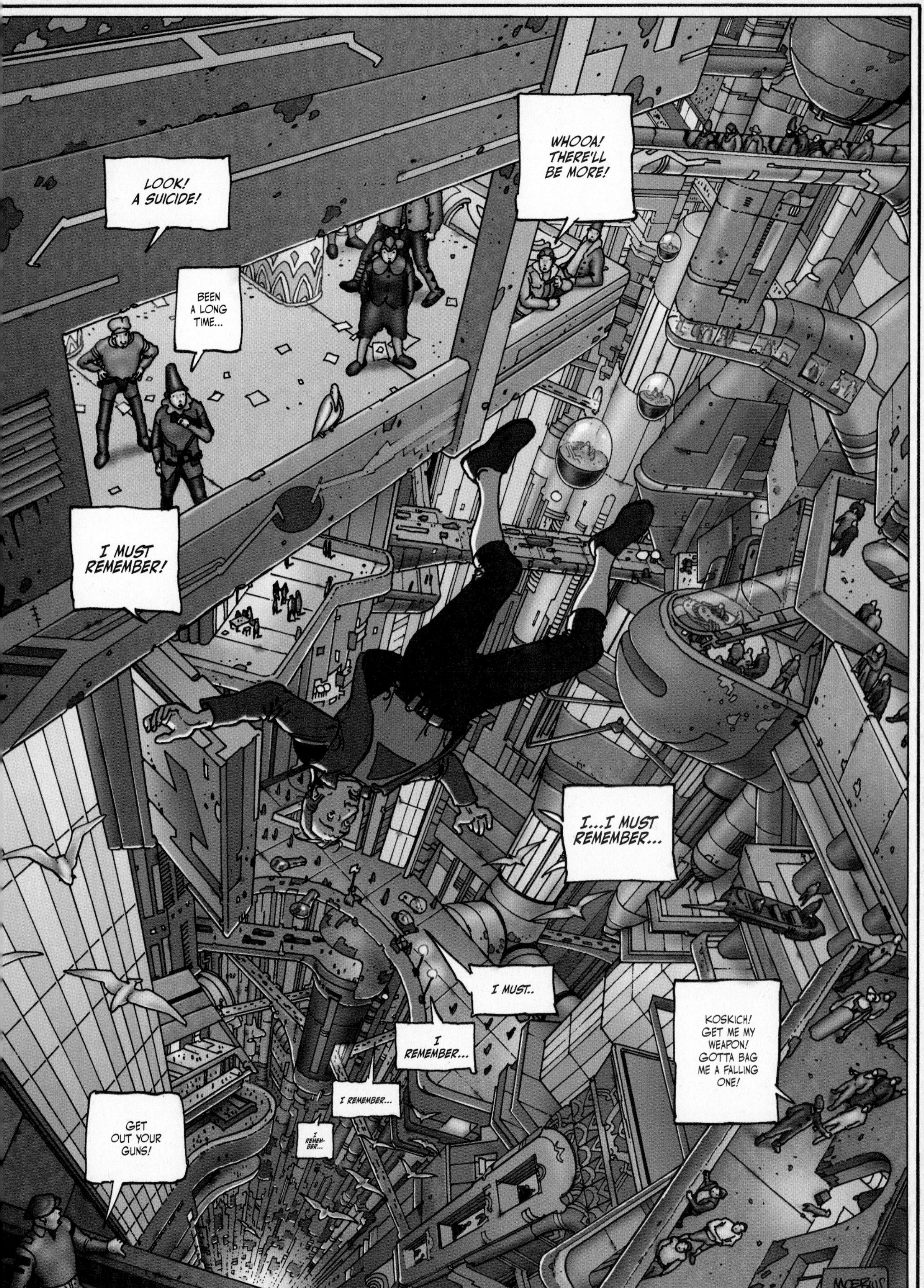
LOOK! A SUICIDE!
WHOOA! THERE'LL BE MORE!
BEEN A LONG TIME...
I MUST REMEMBER!
I...I MUST REMEMBER...
I MUST..
I REMEMBER...
I REMEMBER...
I REMEMBER...
KOSKICH! GET ME MY WEAPON! GOTTA BAG ME A FALLING ONE!
GET OUT YOUR GUNS!

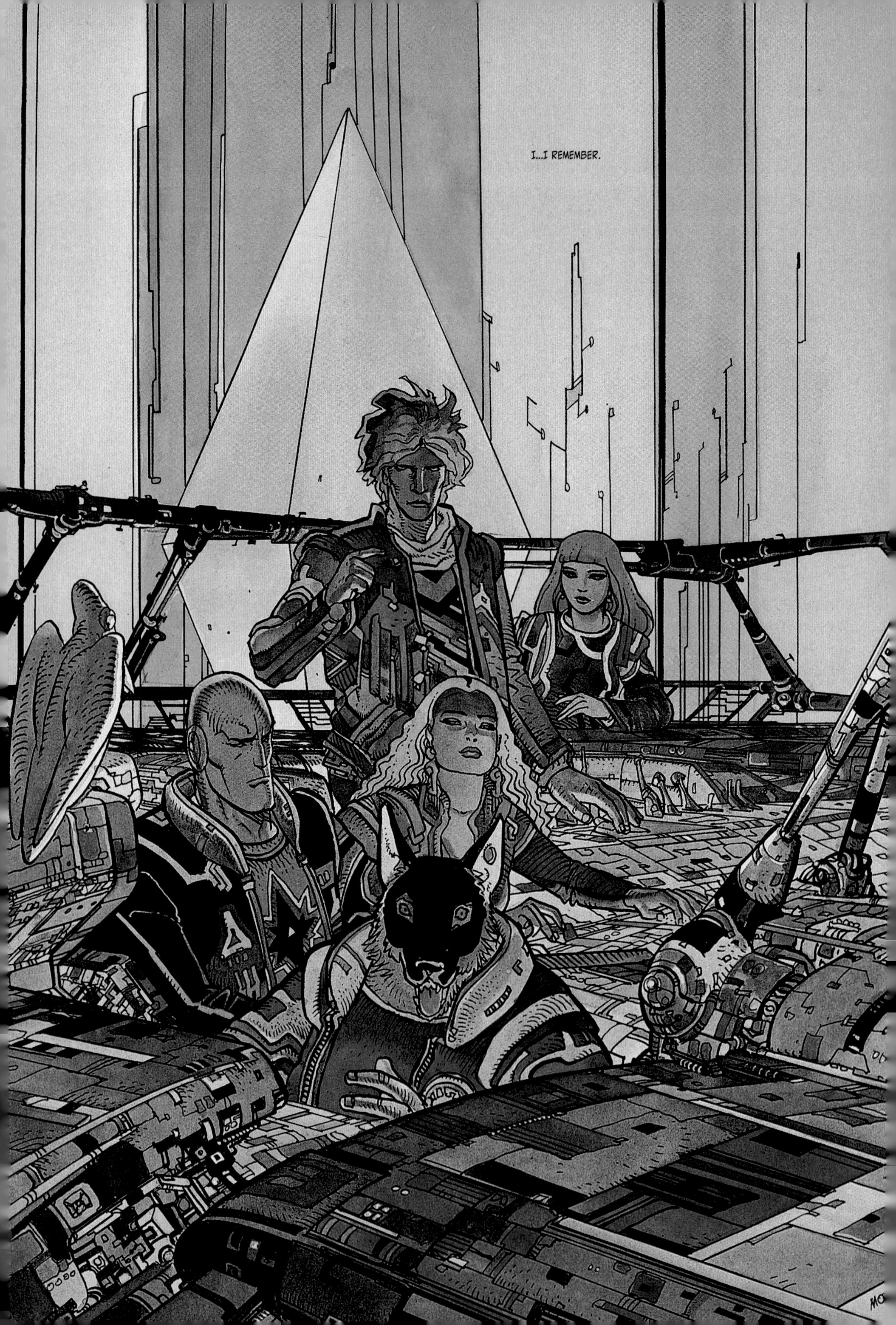
I...I REMEMBER.

THE INCAL:
The Original Covers

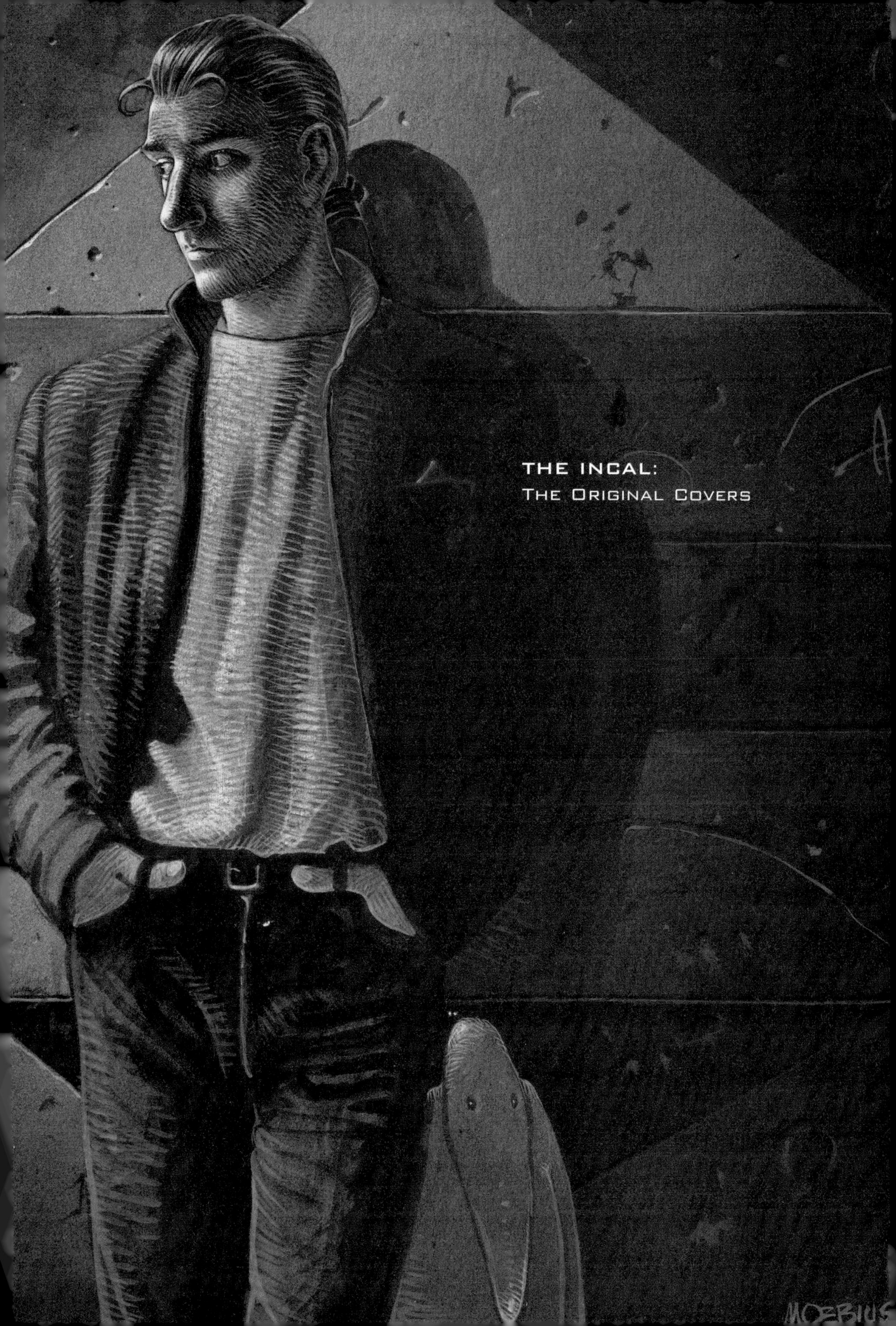
MOEBIUS

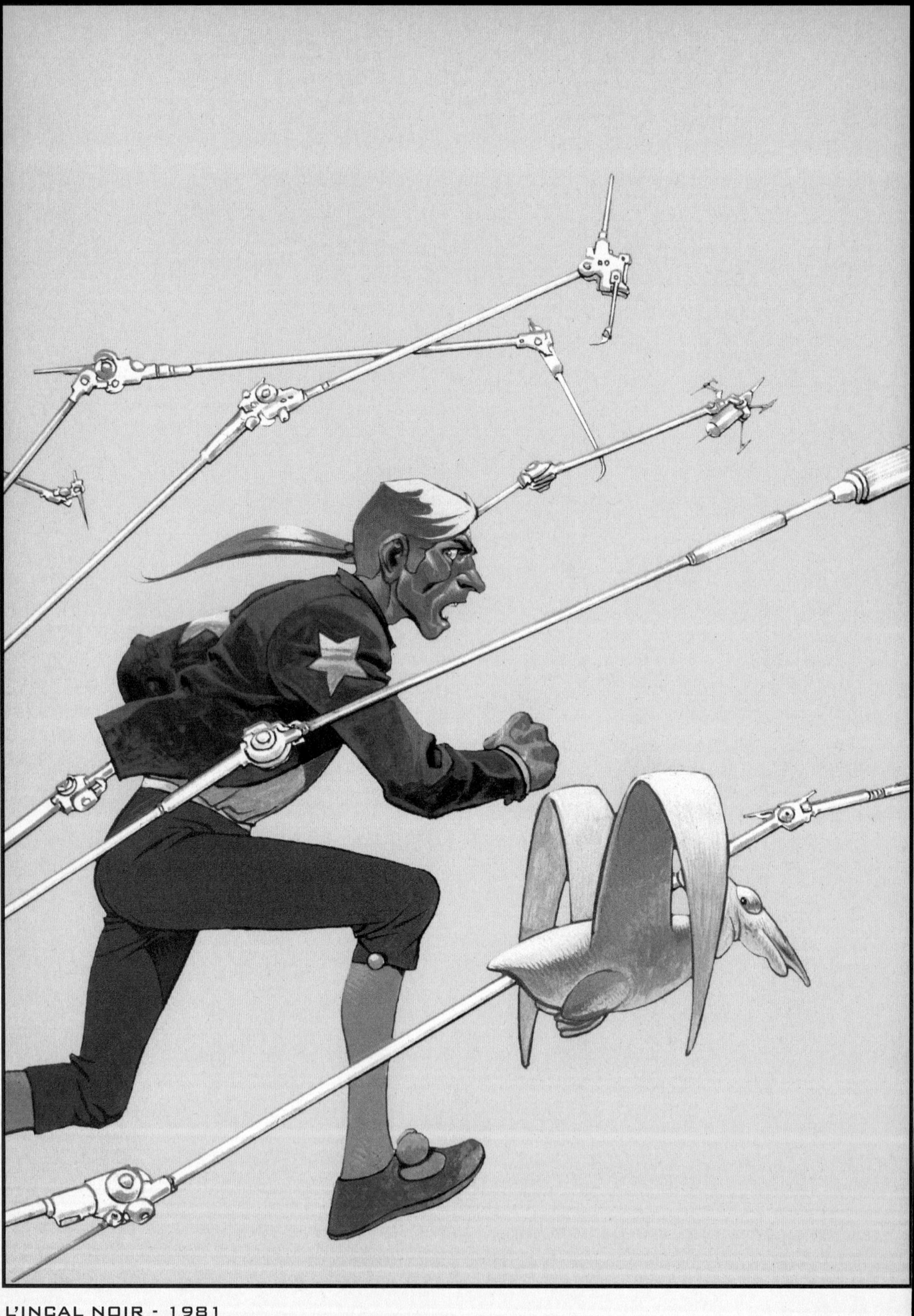

L'INCAL NOIR - 1981

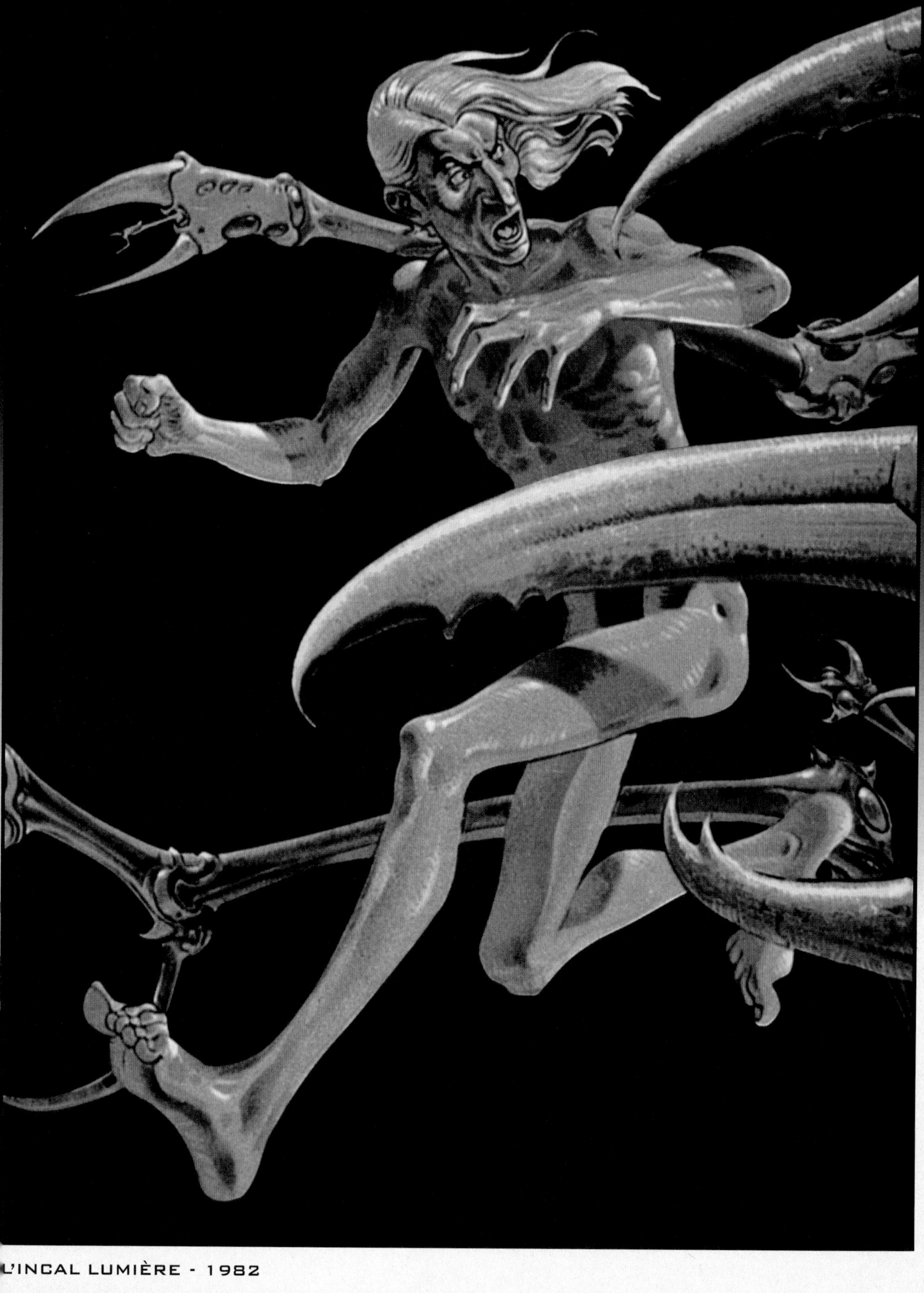

L'INCAL LUMIÈRE - 1982

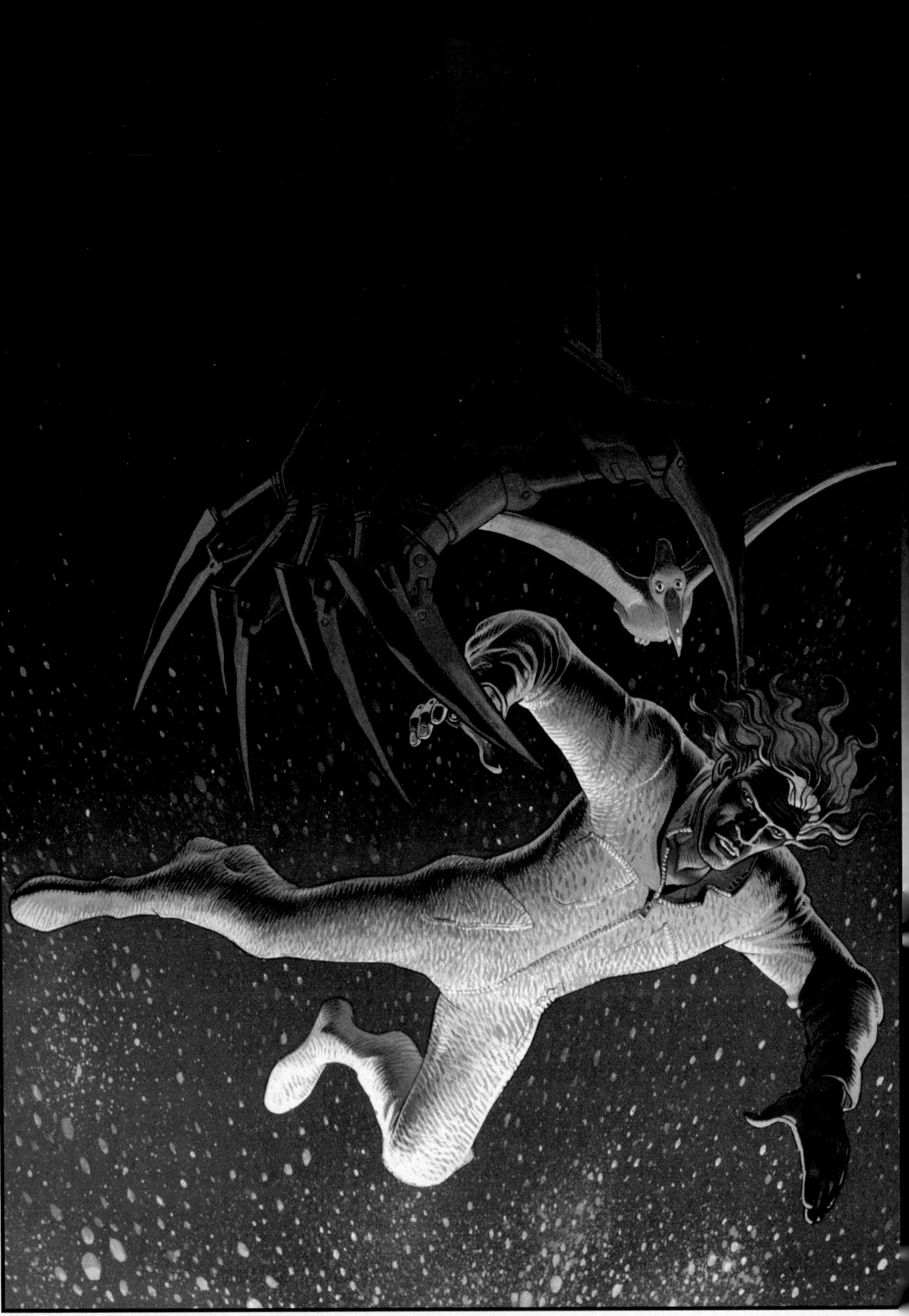

CE QUI EST EN BAS - 1983

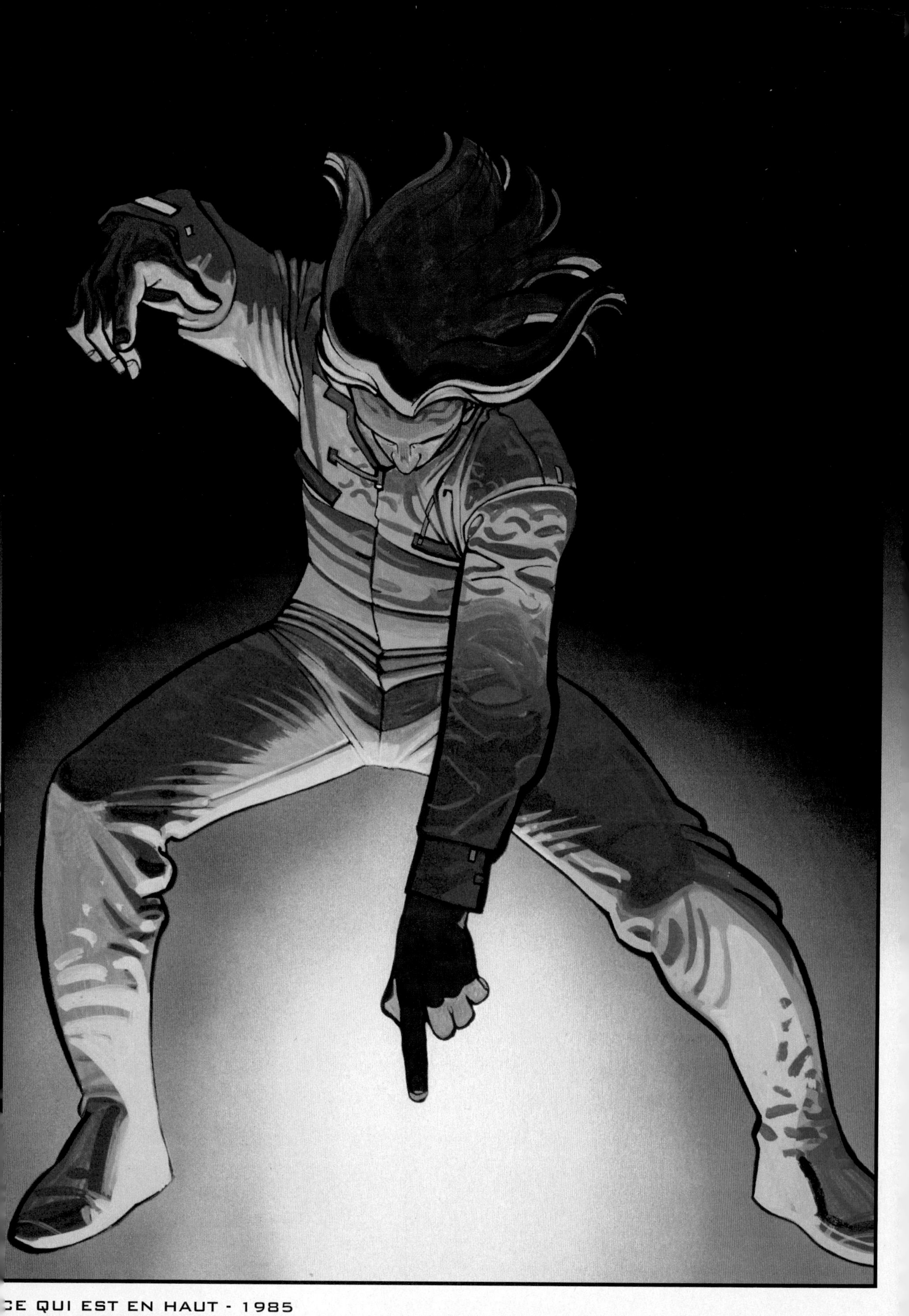

CE QUI EST EN HAUT - 1985

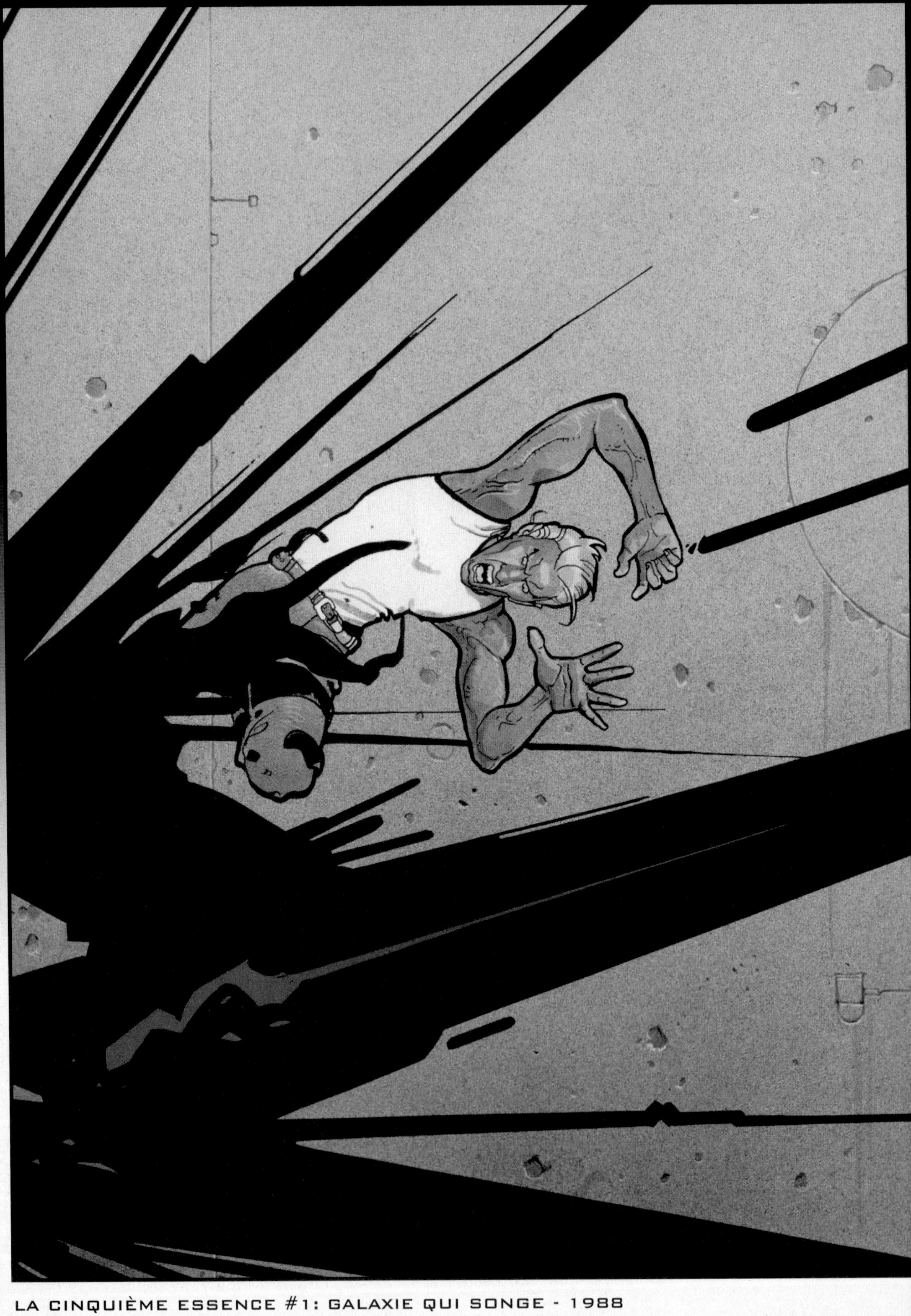

LA CINQUIÈME ESSENCE #1: GALAXIE QUI SONGE - 1988

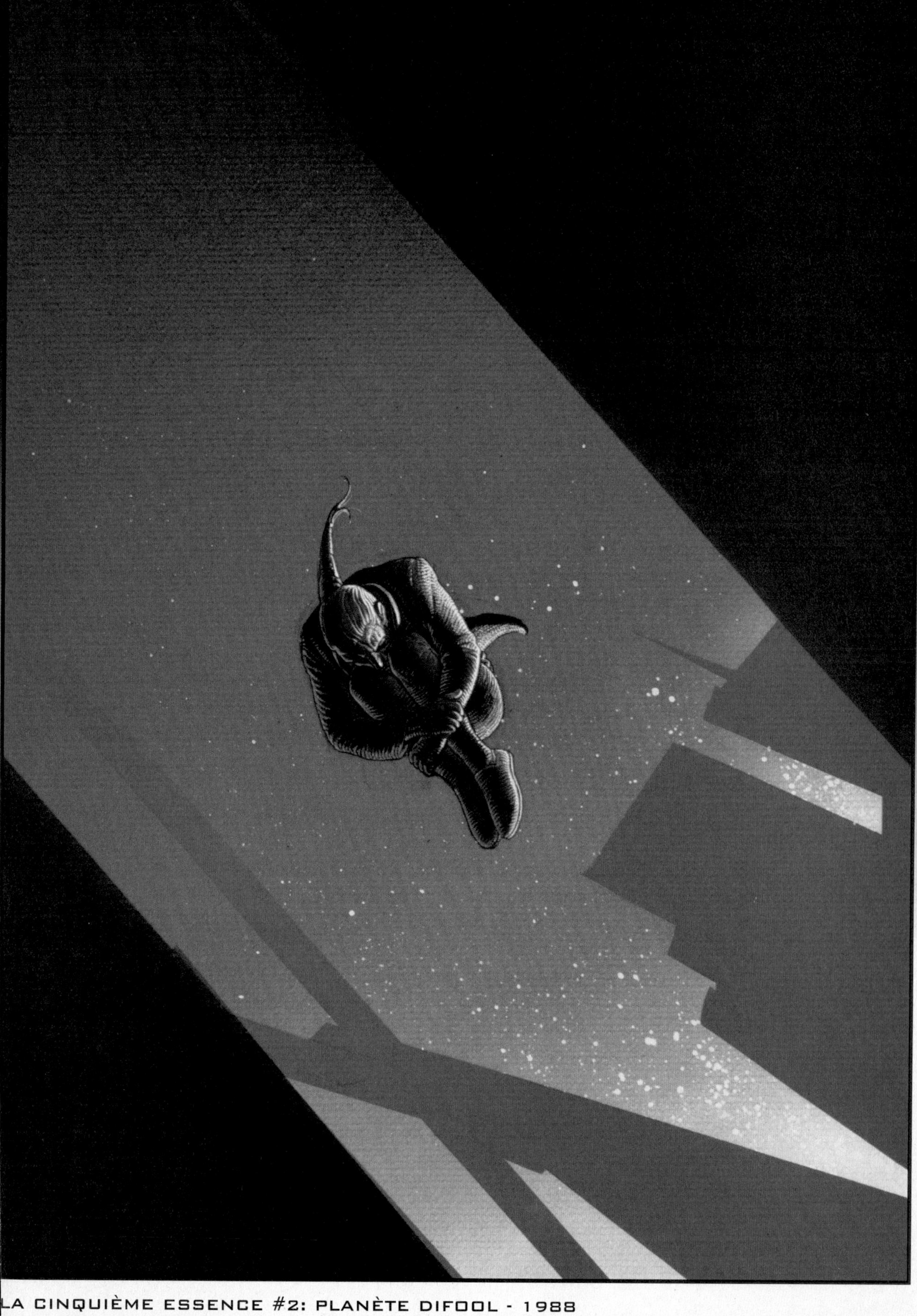

LA CINQUIÈME ESSENCE #2: PLANÈTE DIFOOL - 1988

HUMANOIDS/DC COMICS
MORE WILD TALES FROM THE UNTAMED MIND OF ACCLAIMED WRITER AND FILMMAKER ALEXANDRO JODOROWSKY

THE INCAL: THE EPIC CONSPIRACY
Illustrated by Moebius
One of comics' greatest masterpieces. A tale of comical and cosmic proportions that has John DiFool, a hard-luck detective, fighting for the universe's survival.

THE METABARONS #1: OTHON & HONORATA
Illustrated by Juan Gimenez
The bloodline of the universe's greatest warrior starts here. Othon, the first Metabaron, fights against the forces of a corrupt and terror-filled universe.

THE METABARONS #2: AGHNAR & ODA
Illustrated by Juan Gimenez
The saga of the Metabaron continues. The latest Metabaron faces danger and heartbreak as he inherits the dreadful mantle of the universe's greatest warrior at the cost of his future, his life and his soul.

THE METABARONS #3: STEELHEAD & DOÑA VICENTA
Illustrated by Juan Gimenez
The history of the ultimate warriors continues. The cyborg Metabaron, Steelhead, shakes the galaxy with a reign of violence and murder. But it is his pursuit of love that might doom the Metabarons' bloodline.

 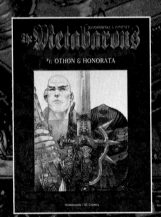 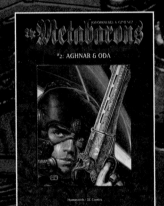 

MEGALEX BOOK 1: THE ANOMALY
Illustrated by Fred Beltran
A clone, only known as the Anomaly, is rescued from certain destruction by the beautiful Adama. With the forces of nature on their side, the two fight to end the stranglehold Megalex has on the planet.

TECHNOPRIESTS BOOK 1: INITIATION
TECHNOPRIESTS BOOK 2: REBELLION
Illustrated by Zoran Janjetov & Fred Beltran
The Technopriest Guild controls the entire galaxy through its technology and mind numbing entertainment. Albino, bastard son of a space pirate, has only one goal-to take over the Guild and destroy it from within.

BOUNCER: RAISING CAIN
Illustrated by François Boucq
A Western tale of a washed-up, one-armed gunslinger and his nephew's quest for vengeance. A complete story.

SON OF THE GUN #1: SINNER
SON OF THE GUN #2: SAINT
Illustrated by Georges Bess
A no-holds-barred tale of a modern day gunslinger's rise to glory and descent through the darkest places in the human soul. A complete story in two volumes.